RT FOR ART'S SAKE
& LITERARY LIFE

HOW POLITICS
AND MARKETS
HELPED SHAPE
THE IDEOLOGY
& CULTURE OF
AESTHETICISM
1790–1990

GENE H. BELL-VILLADA

UNIVERSITY OF NEBRASKA PRESS

LINCOLN & LONDON

Earlier versions of portions of this
work were published in Gene H. Bell-Villada,
"The Idea of Art for Art's Sake," *Science &*
Society 50, no. 4 (winter 1986–87, and Gene H. Bell-
Villada, "A World of Shiny Surfaces,"
The Nation 220, no. 21, The Nation Company, L.P.,
© 1975. © 1996 by the University of Nebraska
Press. All rights reserved. Manufactured in the
United States of America.
First Bison Books printing: 1998
Most recent printing indicated by last digit below:
10 9 8 7 6 5 4 3 2 1
Library of Congress Cataloging-in-Publication Data
Bell-Villada, Gene H., 1941-
Art for art's sake and literary life: how politics
and markets helped shape the ideology and culture
of aestheticism, 1790-1990 / Gene H. Bell-Villada
p. cm. – (Stages)
Includes bibiographical references and index
ISBN 0-8032-1260-7 (cl.: alkaline paper)
ISBN 0-8032-6143-8 (pa.: alkaline paper)
1. Art for art's sake (Movement) 2. Aestheticism
(Literature) I. Title II. Series: Stages (Series)
BH301.A7B45 1996 700'.9–dc20
95-31648 CIP

ad ursam

CONTENTS

Acknowledgments, ix

Introduction
The Idea, the Phrase, the Problem, 1

Chapter 1
The Enlightenment Origins and the Theory of the Mental Faculties, 13

Chapter 2
The New Economy, Poetry Displaced, and the Birth of the Doctrine, 35

Chapter 3
The Diffusion of the Doctrine 1: England, 57

Chapter 4
The Diffusion of the Doctrine 11: Poe (U.S.), *Modernismo* (Latin America), 97

Chapter 5
The Modernist Internationale and the Market, 125

Chapter 6
The Diffusion of the Doctrine 111: Literary Modernism and After, 161

Chapter 7
The Changing Politics of Art for Art's Sake, 203

Conclusion
The Enduring Dilemma, the Academy, the Media, 267

Notes, 293

Bibliography, 307

Index, 329

ACKNOWLEDGMENTS

To the National Endowment for the Humanities, for a 1979 grant that made possible much of the basic research for this study, and also defrayed transportation costs for access to scholarly sources in Mexico and France.

To Julia Prewitt Brown, Sara Castro-Klarén, Chinweizu, Ronald Christ, Linda Danielson, Tom Engelhardt, Antonio Giménez, Paul Holdengräber, Robert Jackall, Katherine Singer Kovács (in memoriam 1946–89), Ilse Hempel Lifschutz, George Pistorius, Arturo Ramos, Eugenio Suárez-Galbán, Jasminka Udovicki, Patricia Wilcox, Susan Woodward, and an anonymous reader for the University of Nebraska Press, whose observations and encouragement at various points in the development of this project made me feel that it was worth pursuing.

To Françoise Pérus in Mexico City, whose ideas, interest, and hospitality helped confirm for me the potential value of the direction of my researches.

To Erica Harth and Michael McKeon, of the Division on Sociological Approaches to Literature (Modern Language Association), to George Katsiaficas of the Wentworth Institute of Technology, and to the Williams College Faculty Lecture Series, for granting me the opportunity to air some of these ideas in public.

To Robert J. Temple, M.D., from whom I first learned, as an undergraduate, about T. S. Eliot's social and political views and their importance to his poetic oeuvre.

To Trudi Abel, Kerry Batchelder, Kanani Bell, Charles Hatten, Tamar Heller, Robert Jackall, Steven Kovács, Jorge Pedraza, and Sandi Clark Watson, for passing on to me various sorts of helpful information relevant to this work.

To Annette Rubinstein and the editors of *Science & Society*, for accepting and publishing, in 1987, parts of this work in essay form.

To Williams College, for a generous policy on leaves, which allowed for two different sabbaticals with much free time to read and write, and also for the periodic support made available via the College's Division I research-funding program.

Acknowledgments

To Audrey, for reading chapters and otherwise lending a helping hand.

To Sharon Ihnen, for a thorough, expert, and sensitive job of copyediting.

To all these individuals and institutions, I offer my sincerest thanks. Any errors, omissions, misjudgments, arguable emphases, instances of awkwardness, and other sorts of gaffes are entirely of my own making.

Albuquerque, New Mexico, 1993

Art for Art's Sake and Literary Life

INTR?DUCTI?N

The Idea, the Phrase, the Problem

In the Far East what is called the "esthetic emotion" still retains a religious dimension, even among intellectuals. — Mircea Eliade, *The Sacred and the Profane*

Art for Art's Sake. The phrase today sounds slightly quaint. It inevitably suggests Oscar Wilde and the epigrams he gave common currency in his preface to *The Picture of Dorian Gray*. To our English and American ears, the aestheticist ideal is most aptly summed up in such provocative Wildean notions as "There is no such thing as a moral or an immoral book. Books are well written, or badly written, that is all"; or that antimoralistic assertion, "No artist has ethical sympathies. . . . Vice and virtue are materials for art"; or Wilde's most ironic and perverse of reflections, "All art is quite useless."

To associate Art for Art's Sake so exclusively with Oscar Wilde, however, is to blind ourselves to the wider spread of aestheticist doctrines, both past and present. The idea neither begins nor ends with Wilde, whose aphorisms are actually a distillation and indeed a simplification of some arguments learned from his high Oxford mentors, John Ruskin and Walter Pater, while his general vision is an outlook consciously akin to that of French Romantic and Symbolist poets such as Gautier and Baudelaire. Baudelaire for his part had learned a few lessons from Poe, who had misread Coleridge, whereas Gautier early on had set forth a much-simplified if memorable version of a theory taught by some Parisian professors, notably Victor Cousin.

Meanwhile, Cousin's lectures take their initial cue from the weighty treatises of a remote, recondite thinker named Immanuel Kant; and Kant's magisterial aesthetic arguments in the *Critique of Judgment*, in turn, stem ultimately from the rapt intuitionism of the Third Earl of Shaftesbury. (The Kantian Idealist traditions, conversely, were to become influential in the critical endeavors of Coleridge and

Pater.) Across Enlightenment and bourgeois Europe, as we see in this study, there is a long history that precedes Oscar Wilde's witty, irreverent, and specifically anti-Victorian brand of aestheticism.

By the same token, our reflex attribution of the aestheticist creed to Oscar Wilde and the British 1890s only obscures the extent to which, between 1945 and the mid-1980s, Art for Art's Sake in various guises was the preponderant literary orientation on the North American campus and still exerts a strong influence today. Starting with the New Criticism and its academic systematization in such textbook classics as Cleanth Brooks and Robert Penn Warren's *Understanding Poetry* (1940) and René Wellek and Austin Warren's *Theory of Literature* (1949), followed thereafter by Northrop Frye's grand and sweeping vision of literature as an all-sufficient body shaped solely from within and never from without,[1] and on to the more linguistically based speculations about the nonreferentiality of all texts (historical and legal texts included),[2] the sharp disjunction between aesthetic experiences and most other human concerns has been regarded as fundamental, axiomatic, the very point of departure for any literary theory that seeks a serious hearing and intellectual respectability.

Doubtless the distinguished scholars to whom I have just alluded (as well as their epigones) would take exception to my placing them in the same company with Oscar Wilde. But it is not my aim at this point to examine Western literary theory in our dizzy fin de siècle decades, nor to discriminate among its multifarious and confused debates. What I intend, first, is to acknowledge the existence of a thorny, problematical, enduring, sometimes complex, and still-unresolved way of thinking about literature. And in the chapters that follow, I hope to chart the broad historical contours and also to account for the emergence and persistence of that particular way of thinking, to suggest who has needed the doctrine, and when, and why.

To this expository end I shall be employing, more or less interchangeably, such terms as "aestheticism" (with a small "a"), "pure poetry," "pure art," "Art for Art's Sake," "formalism" (when discussing critics), and a phrase of my own, "aesthetic separatism." And inevitably there are the French collocations, *l'art pour l'art* and *poésie pure,* which have a certain appropriateness, given that the doctrine made its first appearance as a battle cry in Paris, home of most vanguard movements and cultural slogans.

What is this thing called Art for Art's Sake, particularly in literature? As customarily understood, it is the idea that verse and fiction are without any moral, social, cognitive, or other extraliterary purposes. The sole objective of a work of literature is to be beautiful, well structured, and well written. We "learn" absolutely nothing about life or about values from literature. Questions of "content" therefore have no legitimacy or relevance in writing, reading, studying, and judging literary products. The art of literature, moreover, evolves on its own grounds exclusively; it neither reflects nor is affected by the social, historical, or biographical circumstances of its creation. Literature is one thing (such as combinations of words, images, text; a system of signs, a self-contained artifact, a pure fiction), and the real world another.

Though some nuances or qualifying statements are surely missing from this abstract, it conveys, I believe, the essential core of the doctrine. Still, what is lacking in my summary is a certain matter of time and place. Art for Art's Sake, after all, is an ideology; and like all ideologies it has a definable setting and a history. It is, to begin with, a specifically Western notion, generated on European soil by European writers, and then culturally diffused to such Occidental outposts as the United States and the Creole sectors of Latin America. From my own meager knowledge I gather that the idea of an aesthetic realm, totally separate from life, has no immediate roots in nonindustrial, "primitive" cultures or even in the more "developed" nations of the Near East and Asia, where the arts remain closely bound up with religion or with other, larger, indigenous spiritual traditions and practices. Aestheticism, in sum, is a theory with no major, vital resonances or academic standing outside Western (and Westernized) societies.

And then there is aestheticism's historical life span, which as I write is less than three centuries old. Indeed, aesthetic separatism, a more focused and partisan version of the doctrine, has been with us for 180 years at most; the notion was basically inconceivable to the Western mind before the early nineteenth century and sparked much resistance and hostility when it initially came into public view

3

around 1830. Even today, ideas of "pure art" are first heard about in the classroom (at least in the United States); outside a segment of educated elite circles, such notions are largely unacknowledged or unrecognized in our time.

Nevertheless, within these historical and demographic limits, aestheticism has gone through many incarnations from its Enlightenment origins to the academic sects of our day. (Readers well versed in literary theory, incidentally, have probably taken note of the terminological shifts in my summary, changes that in fact were meant to evoke the transformations of the doctrine over history.) Yet, though the ideas of Shaftesbury and Kant differ radically from the shape those arguments later assumed in Gautier, in the New Critics, or in deconstruction, these authors all belong to the aestheticist tradition.

In this regard a couple of analogies should provide helpful parallels. Few will deny that the four Gospels, St. Paul, St. Augustine, Thomism, John Calvin, Martin Luther, Pope John Paul II, liberation theology, the Spanish Inquisition, and the American televangelist ministers all form part of the history of Christianity, however vast and sometimes bloody the host of differences among them. Similarly, the history of economic liberalism comprises such classic, innovative, broad-ranging thinkers as John Locke, Adam Smith, and John Stuart Mill, but also in recent years the more specialized, scholastic apologetics of Milton Friedman and Robert Nozick, the seductively romantic visions of publicist-novelist Ayn Rand, and the technocratic "Chicago Boys" who served the Pinochet dictatorship in Chile. Art for Art's Sake exhibits as varied a roster as do these two traditions, though inevitably somewhat more esoteric and of shorter duration. It is the intent of this volume to flesh out and lend a more exact profile to that roster, which includes, among others, Schiller, Poe, Pater, Nabokov, the Tennessee Fugitives, and the Belgian expatriate Paul de Man.

Aestheticism poses an unending dilemma. Its very ideals make us ambivalent and uneasy. On one hand, from the work of practicing artists as well as from our own intuitive responses, we know that strictly aesthetical issues do exist. Whether in mounting a multimillion-dollar Hollywood film or crafting a six-line love lyric, there are times when a particular word or voice might be chosen simply because "it sounds good" or "it scans"; there truly are such things as artistic decisions that have virtually nothing to do with market pressures or moral and political demands.

Likewise, in the reception of art, most of us find Gothic cathedrals beautiful, regardless of what we think about the late-medieval popes. We're inevitably delighted by a rose garden, even if a mischievous man may have one in his backyard. *Parsifal* can move us, though we know full well that a German nationalist, crackpot mystic, and unredeemed anti-Semite composed it. We respond to these phenomena with no motive save the gratuitous, intense, playful satisfaction they provide us; and we seek to share such emotions with loved ones and other receptive individuals in our lives.

In addition, we most probably believe that certain sociopolitical attempts to negate the purely aesthetic response have been wrongheaded at best, that the limiting of reading lists and of approved artistic repertories only succeeded in impoverishing the hearts and minds of Cromwell's English citizens or Mao's Chinese. In the USSR from the 1930s until just a few years before its demise, the works of Joyce and Stravinsky were denounced as "formalist," adjudged *ars non grata,* and harshly banned—an exclusionary doctrine deemed acceptable by very few serious artists or art lovers in the East or West.

On the other hand, there are those who feel ill at ease with the moral and social indifferentism of *l'art pour l'art,* with, for example, the view that finding a rare and beautiful butterfly is of greater importance than saving a wounded man in distress. "No artist has ethical sympathies," says Wilde, and the aphorism presumably applies to his ideal public as well. Aesthetic separatism, though, by its very nature is as unable as it is unwilling to confront a genuine dilemma: how to deal with a compelling and beautifully crafted work of art that happens also to convey an overtly racist or militarist or otherwise pernicious message—certain poems by Ezra Pound and films by Leni Riefenstahl being classic instances. The standard aestheticist reply, of course, is to overrule these objections as irrelevant, to deem them matters of mere "content" and to focus its sights solely on the form, technique, and style.

Such Olympian inhumanity can shade further into an amoral nihilism and indeed on occasions has fused much too readily with fascism (see chapter 7). To recall that astute distinction first drawn by Walter Benjamin: whereas communists politicize art, fascists aestheticize politics.³ The latter approach has its locus classicus in Benito Mussolini's own son, who, when commenting on his air raids in the Italian-Ethiopian war, praised *the beauty* of the detonating bombs and compared them to blooming flowers.

For a chillingly prophetic example of absolute aestheticism and its fascist potential, I quote from *Confessions of a Young Man,* a memoir by George Moore, who, presumably under the spell of Nietzsche, dismisses those contemptible pleas for pity and justice with a cadenza that we can only hope is tongue-in-cheek.

> Injustice we worship; all that lifts us out of the miseries of life is the sublime fruit of injustice. . . . Man would not be man but for injustice. Hail, therefore, to the thrice glorious virtue injustice! What care I that some millions of wretched Israelites died under Pharaoh's lash. . . ? It was well that they died that I might have the pyramids to look on, or to fill a musing hour with wonderment. Is there one amongst us who would exchange them for the lives of the ignominious slaves that died. . . ? Nay, more, the knowledge that that was done—that millions of Israelites died in torments—is an added pleasure which I could not afford to spare. Oh, for the silence of marble courts.⁴

Moore's aesthetic visions were to come true again under the Third Reich; and—who knows?—perhaps some delighted spectators today look on "with wonderment" at some Teutonic monuments from those years.

The foregoing discussion, let it be said, aims not to detract from the pure-aesthetic view of art in order to uphold the social or moral conceptions thereof. Citing the perverse lyric transports of George Moore and of Mussolini *fils* serves merely to illustrate the lunatic extremes to which absolute Art for Art's Sake can be pushed—the incidental and sorry lot, alas, of almost every ideology, its own rightful features notwithstanding. Such excesses do belong, however, to the 180-year history of aestheticist thinking, just as Ayn Rand (who also had a thing about big buildings) belongs to the history of market doctrines, Jerry Falwell to the history of Christian faith, and Bruce Barton to both.

Meanwhile, the continuing intellectual hegemony and very real attractions of *l'art pour l'art* can give rise to some categorical assertions and passionate misunderstandings on the part of otherwise intelligent individuals. In his time, the most vocal exponent and practitioner of the aestheticist creed in the United States was Vladimir Nabokov. Ever the virtuoso stylist and master juggler, Nabokov loathed the slightest hint of any "social" conception of literature and, on this basis, sublimely dismissed as trash several hundred books and authors—a list comprising alleged nullities on the order of Balzac, Conrad, Mann, Camus, and Faulkner. Even Picasso's *Guernica*, being a protest painting, is ruled ipso facto unworthy as art by Nabokov.[5]

Ideologues of Nabokov's persuasion, however, seldom address the time-bound and culture-bound nature of their views. That such judgments are post-Enlightenment and specifically Western is a fact that would probably not cross their minds and would certainly not much matter to them. Inasmuch as those broad contexts exist and form so potent and determining a reality, my aim is to trace the growth of aestheticism as it arises as part of the Enlightenment project; then crystallizes as a set phrase and call to arms in 1830s France; is diffused in various ways in England, the United States, and Latin America during the nineteenth century; becomes part of the international Modernist enterprise; and, after 1945, more or less triumphs in the North American academy. Along the way, especially in chapter 7, I shall be noting the surprisingly wide and varied range of political-ideological company that *l'art pour l'art* has managed to keep in the course of its existence.

I should nonetheless remark that this volume is not, strictly speaking, a history of Art for Art's Sake as an idea. "Literary Life," says the title, and in the ensuing narrative I hope to tell how certain writers have *lived* the aesthetical idea, and perhaps suggest what sorts of needs the doctrine has met for them. Similarly, the nouns "Politics" and "Markets" in my subtitle indicate that larger political and economic conditions were prompting literary authors to formulate their aesthetic theory, and moreover that those forces played a role in shaping the theories. The authors' own political and economic life histories, in turn, would be shaped in some degree by their aesthetic ideas.

Finally, I cannot too emphatically stress the adjective "literary." This book will focus on aestheticism as it has been adopted, developed, and used by writers—and almost exclusively writers. To include visual and musical artists would simply have made for too lengthy a book; it is not my wish to produce one of those thick tomes that a few dutiful researchers occasionally consult but no one ever reads. Hence I must regretfully omit such key figures as Whistler and the Pre-Raphaelites in painting, or Hanslick and Stravinsky in music. The sole exceptions to my self-imposed boundary are John Ruskin (an art critic, yet very much a part of the history of literature), as well as the bird's-eye view of the art market and of Modernist painters and composers in chapter 5.

As it is, this volume cuts across several disciplines and covers a great deal of ground. In so panoramic an exposition, errors of fact or of emphasis are inevitable, and specialists will undoubtedly take note of them and call them to my attention. I welcome such corrections. Nevertheless, I do believe that the narrative to follow is fundamentally accurate, valid, and true in its essential larger outlines, even if modifiable and revisable in some of its lesser details. I also should say that, in spite of the considerable amounts of theoretical and historical material gathered here, I make no claim to being either a high theorist or a credentialed historian. I approach this matter simply as a published writer of fiction and satire, of general-interest literary criticism and cultural-political polemic, who, ever since his first love of music and literature during early adolescence, has felt alternately intrigued and troubled by the question of *l'art pour l'art,* and who in addition has always entertained more than a casual interest in the problematical, ongoing issue of the artist in society. In this regard, these pages meet a personal need as well.

Among the basic questions that have led me to research and write this study are: Why does Art for Art's Sake exist at all? What is it about Western culture in these past two or three centuries that has prompted this way of thinking? None of the answers thus far presented are, to my mind, fully satisfactory. The routine textbook or handbook accounts can sometimes verge on the tautological: *l'art pour l'art* sprang to life in the steady march of man's ideas simply because it did, and no one really knows why.[6] On the other hand, in some versions the theory is universalized and allotted quasi-perpetual status. Albert Guérard, in a book in fact entitled *Art for Art's Sake* (1936), states flatly that the tradition "is an eternal tendency, suppressed most of the time, but ready to reassert itself whenever certain checks are removed." He goes so far as to speculate that, up to the end of classical antiquity, "Art for Art's Sake may have been practiced," even if "it never was openly confessed."[7] Despite Guérard's impressive erudition, the case he goes on to make over some 300 pages is vague and less than convincing.

Albert Cassagne's *La théorie de l'art pour l'art en France* (1906) — a pioneering work that is still consulted — explains the emergence of the doctrine as a reaction against the narrow "utilitarianism," "materialism," and "lack of elevation" of nineteenth-century bourgeois life. An analogous line of reasoning is to be found in *L'idée de l'art pour l'art dans la littérature anglaise* (1931) by Louise Rosenblatt, who also singles out the stifling moralism of Victorian England as a dominant force against which Britain's aesthetes were more or less in revolt.[8] These arguments, now established wisdom, are by no means invalid. Their successor-idea in recent times is the general notion, common among liberal humanists, that aestheticism is a symptom of "the alienation of the artist" from bourgeois society or even from mankind at large.

Still, there is a serious degree of simplification here. Many quite reputable authors, after all, have enjoyed fairly harmonious and even prosperous relations with their bourgeois environments. One never thinks of, say, Dickens or Trollope or Hugo or Balzac as an "alienated artist," and it goes without saying that (except for a brief, early phase in Hugo) these novelists did not turn to *l'art pour l'art* when reflecting on their trade. Hypotheses about "reactions against" materialism and the like are thus incomplete insofar as they do not help explain why not all writers have chosen the aestheticist path.

Such arguments, it bears mention, suffer from the shortcomings of almost any theory that accounts for new cultural developments in strict terms of a reaction against the past or present. The result is a mechanist view, founded on analogies from physics (the pendulum of history; action and reaction), and also a subtler tautology, or rather a truism — to wit, certain authors do what has been done before, and certain authors don't. The more complex truth is that writers work with whatever material they have at their disposal—some of it new resources and some their own, some of it already available either within their traditions or from abroad—and then write what they need to write. The element of "revolt" can come later and at times is even an after-the-fact construction.

The ideas of Kant, we see in chapters 1 and 2, played a seminal and decisive role in the growth of *l'art pour l'art* notions during the period of French Romanticism. John Wilcox, in his thoughtful and still-provocative essay (to which portions of this book are much indebted), attributes the rise of the French rubric to a "misreading of Kantian aesthetic theory, a fantastically careless and incompetent misreading at that."[9] Wilcox's is a history-of-ideas sort of approach that charts the dissemination of the concept from its German philosophical origins, through its underground status in Restoration France, and on to its use as a banner in the Parisian culture wars. His insights and rigor notwithstanding, Wilcox studies the process in isolation, without demonstrating exactly how Kant was being misread or suggesting what ideological or "political" ends Kantian philosophy may have been serving for French writers at the time. Similarly, Rose Francis Egan's rather neglected survey of the English and German genesis of Art for Art's Sake performs the indispensable task of exhuming and exhibiting the philosophical sources, yet stops short of saying much about what those sources suffered in the course of their diffusion.[10]

Finally, there is the tortured history of Russian aesthetics and what was to become the unhappy Soviet version thereof. Plekhanov in *Art and Society* (1912)—part scholarly study, part political pamphlet, and surprisingly fresh and readable still—asserts, in italics, *"The belief in art for art's sake arises wherever the artist is at odds with his social environment."* Though lively with ideas and fact, Plekhanov's analysis, once again, fails to determine why some writers are indeed "at odds with their social environment" and why some are not.

Plekhanov further notes with zealous irony the serious contradiction shown by those authors who rail against "the bourgeoisie," yet side squarely with bourgeoisie against proletariat in their own writings—a class allegiance Plekhanov attributes to the Nietzschean cult of a pitiless, superhuman energy "beyond good and evil."[11] Actually, though, what Nietzsche and many aesthetes championed was not bourgeois hegemony, but, rather, a return to aristocratic, *feudal* rule—a complex subject examined in depth in chapter 7.

Here and there in *Art and Society* Plekhanov makes passing references to the "decadent bourgeoisie," a notion that owes more to Spengler, Max Nordau, and "other petty-bourgeois cultural pessimists" than to Marxist theory, as Maynard Solomon notes.[12] The idea nevertheless was to grow into a major concept in official Stalinist aesthetics and among formulaic Marxist followers abroad, in the phenomenon now known as Zhdanovism, after Andrei Zhdanov (1896–1948), the Soviet cultural bureaucrat.

In the Zhdanovist interpretation, Art for Art's Sake, along with the avant-garde and Modernism, is the product of a "decadent bourgeoisie" and therefore lacking in any social or aesthetic value—a simplistic view that blithely ignores the historical record. The most schematic outline of the European arts since 1830 shows that aestheticism and its divers offshoots have always been present in bourgeois culture, whether the latter be new and ascendant or slightly older and "decadent." By the same logic, moreover, one could dismiss, for example, Diderot and the Encyclopedists as mere symptoms of a "decadent aristocracy" and likewise dispatch any other author who writes at the end of an era. So monolithic and singularist a conception of human societies has fortunately since been discredited, in part by the investigations of structuralist Marxists like Louis Althusser.

The conventional explanations for the rise of Art for Art's Sake, then, are either too broad to take in its many nuances and complexities or too narrow to account for the large fact of its continued existence. Hence my undertaking the writing of this book; I believe that there are concrete social, economic, political, and cultural reasons for the emergence, growth, diffusion, and triumph of *l'art pour l'art* over the past two centuries. In the chapters to come, I will be attempting something like an integrated history of that ever-changing causal matrix as well as of the developing general doctrine, its associated politics, and the successive spokesmen who have adapted the idea (and themselves) to the conditions of their respective times and places.

Before pinpointing the crystallization of *l'art pour l'art* as such, however, we need to cast a backward glance at the tangled prehistory of the doctrine as it first appears in the Enlightenment. Without a knowledge of the constitutive part it plays in the thought of those years, and of the maximum expression it attains in Kant's *Critique of Judgment* and in Schiller's *Letters on Aesthetic Education,* one cannot begin to comprehend the strange twists and turns that will take us by surprise when Art for Art's Sake at last bursts out as a cause and creed all its own.

CHAPTER I

The Enlightenment Origins and the Theory of the Mental Faculties

The Enlightenment origins? Some readers might balk at the connection of the Enlightenment with Art for Art's Sake. After all, we associate most of the great eighteenth-century thinkers with their commitment to the use of reason and experience, along with their belief in the ultimate political betterment of humankind. Among the era's textual monuments is the French *Encyclopédie*, that weighty compendium of the latest advances in science and thought. Neither reason nor science nor human progress, however, has served as a call to arms for literary aestheticists, many of whom have been, if not antirationalist, then certainly indifferent to the claims of reason. In addition, their purported antididacticism would seemingly negate the Enlightenment ideal of liberation through knowledge. Either that or they would characterize what we learn from poetry as something not to be found even in the best works of reference.

Yet, at the same time, the Enlightenment was the critical project aimed at freeing humanity from received dogmas and tradition. In concrete political terms this often meant opposition to Church control over life and learning—in a word, anticlericalism, even antireligiosity. Gibbon unabashedly blames the Fall of Rome on a Christian faith that had "insinuated" itself into the Roman Empire. And today every student of European history knows of Voltaire's harsh judgment on the Church: "Ecraser l'infame." Indeed, for the first time since antiquity, respectable men of letters during the Enlightenment made no secret of being deists or atheists, as was Hume. The spirit of questioning hence touched on the very ideological supports of the reigning political order. Among the major historical consequences of this long-term secularizing drive, of course, were the American and French Revolutions, both of which separated Church administration from state power. In this regard, then, aestheticism owes a profound debt to the Enlightenment for having liberated all human practices—

including art—from the hand of the Church and, by extension, from any restrictions of a spiritual or confessional kind.

In the profane arts during the eighteenth century, moreover, the official aesthetic of the noble courts was a staunch neoclassicism. Under this dispensation, poets and dramatists composed poetry and plays strictly according to the famous "rules" set up with the blessing of the late seventeenth-century monarchies. Voltaire himself wrote epics and tragedies that adhere to prescribed conventions and "unities"; he adjudged them his major works, and he thought of *Candide* and *Zadig* as trifles. About the time of Voltaire's death in 1778, however, an alternative aesthetic, under which rules are generated not by external authorities but by the individual work or artist, was emerging slowly into view. Art for Art's Sake in this respect has its ultimate roots in certain Enlightenment thinkers' critique of the cultural status quo. In order simply to exist as an autonomous entity, with criteria of its own, literature needed to shake off religious and neoclassical rules and, beyond that, to free itself from both clerical and courtly limitations.

This rejection of existing artistic dogmas is precisely what the eighteenth-century theorists contributed to the ideological foundations of Art for Art's Sake. Without the pioneering reflections of writers beginning with Shaftesbury and culminating in Kant and Schiller, the publicists of aetheticism would have lacked a "mother lode" from which to extract arguments that would reinforce their bid for literary independence. (In the course of dissemination, though, what the Enlightenment thinkers had envisioned for both art and society was radically reversed. The end result is one of those strange surprises in the history of ideas. That, however, is a matter for subsequent chapters.)

No doctrine, one should emphasize, springs forth from nowhere with arguments completely new. Much of the political thought of the founders of the United States, to cite a classic instance, is a practical distillation of the philosophy of John Locke. Ideas of evolution appeared in Tennyson's *In Memoriam* some years before the publication of Darwin's *Origin of Species*. Notions about "superior" men who stand beyond good and evil are voiced by key characters in Dostoyevsky's novels, suggesting that what Nietzsche eventually did was to develop and give artistic shape to certain conceptions being bandied about by the literati of his day. Aestheticism for its part has Enlightenment sources; among its precursors are a wealthy English lord, a staid and proper Prussian academic, and a rebellious German poet and playwright. Though these authors would scarcely have recognized what became of their thinking, each of them made Art for Art's Sake finally possible.

The first acknowledged exponent of a worldview in which the pure aesthetic plays a key role was a tender-minded gentleman and gifted amateur, Anthony Cooper, Third Earl of Shaftesbury (1671-1713). An independent man of letters who truly loved the arts, Shaftesbury found himself at odds with the coldly mechanistic but then-predominant epistemology of Thomas Hobbes and John Locke. At the same time he felt repelled by the Puritans and their narrow, religiously based intolerance for beauty.[1]

Possessed of an intuitive temperament and a glowing, rhapsodic prose style, Shaftesbury was never to present his ideas in systematic, step-by-step fashion. Owing, perhaps, to that same lack of expository rigor, however, Shaftesbury's major work, the *Characteristics of Men, Manners, Opinions, Times, etc.* enjoyed a considerable following throughout the century. The book went through eleven editions between 1711 and 1790 and exerted a formative influence on several European thinkers, including Kant.

Educated mostly by private tutors — among them, ironically, John Locke — and partly shaped by this informal background, Shaftesbury developed a critical intelligence far removed from that of an academic theorist who marshals logic to build an edifice of rational doctrine; rather, he became a "philosopher" in the popular sense — an inspired seeker of harmonious wisdom. And wisdom in Shaftesbury's view is to be gained not by reason — in which he exhibited no great interest — but by a balanced and harmonious personality that can grasp the order and beauty of this world.

The prime means for judging morals and beauty is our faculty of taste; and, in matters both ethical and aesthetical, the Good is intuited by individuals possessing superior taste. Art thence becomes one possible medium through which the harmony of the world is revealed to us and is apprehended by such men. Shaftesbury speculates in his "Miscellaneous Reflections" that "a little better taste . . . in the affair of life itself would . . . mend the manners . . . of some of our noble countrymen" (2:259).[2]

The key word "disinterested," to be highlighted later by Kant, appears in Shaftesbury's discussions of ethics, and the modern ideal of disinterested beauty is also present in his work, particularly in "The Moralists." In that philosophical dialogue, the character Theocles—a kind of devil's advocate—repeatedly suggests to his interlocutor Philocles that in order to enjoy the beauty of a valley or a tree, he would surely aspire to own it, or that in order to celebrate the beauties of an ocean, Philocles would hope to control it as an admiral does. Philocles finds these notions "absurd" and argues that the pleasures of owning and controlling are "very different from that which should naturally follow from the contemplation of the ocean's beauty" (2:127). Shaftesbury thus dramatically presages the idea of "free beauty" to be seen in Kant and his latter-day popularizers.

Nevertheless, it must be emphasized that Shaftesbury does not sever the love of beauty from matters social or moral. Quite to the contrary, in "An Inquiry Concerning Virtue or Merit" he asserts that "the admiration and love of *order, harmony, and proportion* . . . is naturally improving to the temper, advantageous to *social affection,* and highly assistant to *virtue,* which is itself no other than the love of *order and beauty in society*" (1:279; emphasis added). In converse fashion, Shaftesbury frequently judges morals and mores with regard to the aesthetic pleasure they afford. He suggests, for instance, that there is nothing "as fair as friendship" or "so charming as a generous action" (2:36).

Indeed, he sees not only the Good and the Beautiful but also the True—knowledge, in a word—as belonging to the same broad system of human values. In a rhetorical question he envisions the links thus: "Will it not be found . . . that what is beautiful is harmonious and proportionable; what is harmonious and proportionable is true; and what is at once both beautiful and true is, of consequence, agreeable and good?" (2:268–69). Shaftesbury additionally hints at a doctrine unifying aesthetics, ethics, and science when he asserts that "beauty and truth are plainly joined with the notion of utility and convenience" (2:267). Rather than separate beauty from morals and truth, Shaftesbury argues for a complete sensibility in which all three mental faculties are harmoniously and fruitfully integrated.[3]

Shaftesbury's was a restless, wide-ranging intellect, and his philosophy suggests many ramifications. For our own specific purposes, what most matters is that Shaftesbury defines the experience of beauty as something occurring independently of personal desire or practical use; on the other hand, Shaftesbury conceives of aesthetic experience as an essential part of a larger totality encompassing such issues as harmony of character, concern for morals, and the education of men. These may seem contradictory positions today, owing to the rigid dichotomies that govern contemporary aesthetic debate, but the two in fact were to coexist in eighteenth-century aesthetic theory.

Among Shaftesbury's initial followers was an Ulster-born Scotsman named Francis Hutcheson (1694–1746). After reading theology and liberal arts at the University of Glasgow, Hutcheson went on to found a dissenting Presbyterian academy in Dublin, which he headed for ten years. In 1730 he returned to his alma mater, where he lectured in moral philosophy for the remainder of his life. (Among his students was the young Adam Smith.) Though more academic in style and orientation, Hutcheson's aesthetic speculations are infused with Shaftesbury's doctrines. In *An Inquiry into the Original of Our Ideas of Beauty and Virtue* (1725), Hutcheson argues that, when faced with beauty, we respond with a distinctive pleasure, one that emerges not from profit or use but from the perception of formal beauty itself. He finds it evident that "some Objects are *immediately* the occasions of this Pleasure of Beauty . . . and that it is distinct from the *Joy* which arises upon Prospect of *Advantage*. Nay, do we not often see Convenience and Use neglected to obtain Beauty?" (12; emphasis in original).[4]

As Hutcheson explains it, men are endowed with "a *Sense* of Beauty" (emphasis in original) that exists prior to their desire for a beautiful thing. Our aesthetic sense, in Hutcheson's own words, is "antecedent to Prospects even of this advantage [of possession]." What we experience from beautiful objects is "very distinct from our desire of them." In a forcefully argued evaluative differentiation between utility and the aesthetic, Hutcheson asserts, "Had we no such

Sense of Beauty and Harmony, Houses, Gardens, Dress [and] Equipage might have been recommended to us as convenient, fruitful, warm, easy; but never as *beautiful*" (13; emphasis in original). Hutcheson's precise distinction closely parallels that made in Shaftesbury's *Moralists*, wherein Philocles explicitly separates his apprehension of the beauty of a tree or an ocean from any control he may exert over them. Broadly resembling Shaftesbury's moralized aesthetics, much of Hutcheson's treatise consists of finding unity and variety, "Order, Harmony, and Design" in plants, animals, poetry, and even in theorems, scientific laws, and history.

During the Enlightenment, speculation on matters of beauty and taste became a casual pastime as well as a serious philosophical endeavor. In 1747 *The Universal Spectator* remarked on those modish aspects by noting, "Of all our favourite words lately, none has been more in Vogue, nor so long held in Esteem, as that of Taste." Similarly, in 1753 an anonymous writer for *The World* complained that "the poor monosyllable TASTE" was being bandied about by people for whom the word "has evidently meant nothing." [5]

The technical term "aesthetics" was coined in midcentury by the then-influential German thinker Alexander Gottlieb Baumgarten (1714–62), whose Latin treatise *Aesthetica* (1750) was one of many eighteenth-century attempts at founding a systematic theory of the Beautiful. Baumgarten derived his neologism from the Greek *aesthesis,* "perception," in order to emphasize the sensuousness that sets off the experience of beauty from that of logic and cognition. Nonetheless, Baumgarten had "no intention of separating poetry from the source of thought," for "he defines aesthetics . . . as the art of thinking beautifully." [6] In spite of his pioneering outlook, however, Baumgarten's ideas came cloaked and indeed remained stuck in the rationalistic, deductive, Leibnizian style of school philosophy in which he had been trained. [7]

Almost every backward glance at aesthetic theory ritually credits Baumgarten for having first delimited and defined the field of study. Other contemporary works of aesthetics include Edmund Burke's *A Philosophical Enquiry into Our Ideas of the Sublime and the Beautiful* (1757), David Hume's "Of the Standard of Taste" (one of the four *Dissertations,* 1757), Alexander Gerard's *An Essay on Taste* (1759), and the painter Hogarth's *Analysis of Beauty* (1753) in Great Britain; the abbé Dubos's *Critical Reflections on Poetry, Painting, and Music* (1719) and Denis Diderot's article "Beau" in the *Encyclopédie* (1751) in France; and, in Germany, Baumgarten himself and Gotthold Ephraim Lessing's *Laocoön* (1766)—to name only some of the more outstanding titles.

The theoretical focus of these pioneering works varied according to the outlook of each author, whether the psychological sensationism of Burke, the absolute skepticism of Hume, or the residual rationalism of Baumgarten or Diderot. Nevertheless there were shared assumptions. One such predicated a phenomenon of the aesthetical, whereby certain objects and phenomena possess characteristic values having to do with beauty rather than utility, morals, or truth. Another assumption posited a certain part of the human soul, a mental faculty that responds with serene contemplation to objects of art and beauty.

At the same time, these theorists of the beautiful, being thinkers of broad intellect and general culture rather than literary specialists, were also seeking links and relationships, ways in which those matters aesthetical connect and fit with our other mental faculties. As Cassirer points out, "The union of philosophy and literary and aesthetic criticism is evident in all the eminent minds of the [eighteenth] century." The culture of ideas during the Enlightenment presupposed and envisioned "a deep and intrinsically necessary union of the problems" of philosophy and literary and aesthetic criticism. There was a generalized recognition that "the two were interdependent and in agreement in their indirect effects."[8] Yet there was no consensus either on the fundamental nature of that interdependent unity or on the final objective of so much theorizing. The one overall tendency was that of secularization, of grounding science, morals, and art on bases other than established tradition, divine authority, and ancient rules.

It is idle to speculate on what might have become of these scattered insights had they not been fully absorbed and incorporated into the grand synthesis of mind deployed, in distant Koenigsberg, by the Prussian philosopher Immanuel Kant. While the caveat occasionally warns that Kant's achievement in aesthetics consists chiefly in having assimilated and reduced certain ideas already common among eighteenth-century British writers,[9] prior to Kant those "British" theories still seem like loose intuitions, seem lacking in a fully reasoned relationship to a general theory of the mind, which is precisely what Kant sets forth in his three *Critiques*.

The third of these, the *Critique of Judgment*, eventually came to be viewed as *the* sourcebook for Art for Art's Sake, though often by commentators not fully acquainted with Kant's work, which of course can be daunting to any reader. Among the many aspects of Kant's argument that did achieve some general reputation were his discussions of "beauty," "taste," "imagination," and "disinterestedness." Here follows a brief summary of this fraction of Kant's aesthetic thought:

– The experience of beauty has to do neither with gratification (which, as a criterion, is purely empirical and subjective) nor with concepts (which belong to the realm of reason). The mental territory for aesthetical judgments is taste, which stands midway between reason and the understanding.

– A judgment on the beauty of an object goes beyond immediate pleasure and claims the universal assent of all men. Such a judgment is the manifestation of a reflective and disinterested imagination operating freely, that is, "in free conformity to law."

– A judgment of free and independent beauty assumes that there is no concept or purpose to be served by the beautiful object. Free and independent beauty has the quality of "purposiveness without purpose." What we judge is "formal purposiveness," the form of an object that has no ulterior purpose.

– Beautiful objects are produced by a genius, whose distinguishing mark is *"originality,"* an *"audacity"* that goes beyond rules, but who at the same time creates rules in works that are *"exemplary"* (emphasis in Kant).

Specialists in Kant and more seasoned theorists than I may perhaps object that this summary is a simplification. And they are right, inasmuch as the summary here touches on the few select portions of Kant's aesthetic system that came to be known. These portions were singled out, severed from their larger totality, and eventually used for sustaining quasi-partisan ends. My summary also omits any mention of the all-too-familiar idea that beauty serves its own ends rather than those of truth or morals. Although this "aestheticist" notion has been read retrospectively into Kant's arguments, and is even hinted at here and there in the *Critique of Judgment,* Kant cancels out such passing suggestions with numerous counterreasonings that raise precisely the opposite idea: namely, that beauty has important ties with moral concerns and human knowledge, even if it is not subsumed to such concerns.

Kant came of humble origins (his father was a saddler). Once having joined the academic ranks, he was to remain professorial in style and relatively limited in his life experience, never marrying or venturing outside his native Koenigsberg. And yet he possessed too expansive and cosmopolitan a spirit, too strong a concern with European developments to be restricted in his mental horizons or to drudge along timidly as a pure scholiast. As a result Kant's theories never seem worked out exclusively for theory's sake. At the beginning of the *Critique of Pure Reason* he indirectly suggests that casting off dogmatic speculative reason will help further "the interests of humanity" (xl).[10] He does admit that his theory of knowledge cannot "become popular" but feels it is nonetheless a project that ultimately "benefits the masses" (xli). Among the concluding assertions in *Pure Reason,* his first *Critique,* Kant claims that metaphysics has as its "highest aims" nothing less than "the general happiness of mankind" (540).

These are the words of a man speaking not only for pure intellect but also for general culture, not for privileged ideas but for broad principles. Kant gallantly credited the revolutionary Swiss philosophe Jean-Jacques Rousseau with having "set [him] right" and teaching him "to honor men, and [I] would find myself more useless than the humblest laborer if I did not believe that this perspective could bestow worth on all others, and restore the rights of man."[11]

Kant's unflagging interest in the larger outside world had its professional counterpart in his early concern, as teacher, with the full, unified education of his students' minds. In his years as a youthful lecturer in geography, Kant boldly declared that the abstract disciplines should aim at shaping "first the man of *understanding,* then the man of *reason,*" and only last of all "the *learned* man." [12] This totalizing prospect of the younger philosopher must not be lost sight of by today's readers. Although in the *Critique of Judgment* Kant does focus upon the imagination as the specific ground of the aesthetical experience, there is no indication that he intended to radically divorce that imagination from our other faculties, from truth or morality. The Romantic and aestheticist isolation of imagination from other spiritual aptitudes is not to be found in the broad picture of Kant's thought.

Indeed, Kant's ultimate aim was to establish broad reciprocal links between our different mental functions. In the *Critique of Practical Reason,* the second in the series, he speculates grandly on "the expectation of bringing some day into one view *the unity of the entire pure rational faculty* (both theoretical and practical) and of being able to *derive everything from one principle*" (94; emphasis added).[13] This long-range hope underlies the ideas and arguments of all three of his *Critiques.* Within their respective domains, each of these works attempts to go beyond the intellectual limits of the two rival European philosophies of the time — rationalism and empiricism — yet also to synthesize the discoveries of both schools into a higher totality. Hence the *Critique of Pure Reason* aims to supersede the dogmatic metaphysics and Leibnizian rationalism of Christian Wolff as well as the sensory-based doctrine of the British empiricists; the *Critique of Practical Reason* sets out to transcend an abstract rationalism of moral and religious maxims as well as a selfish empiricism grounded solely in personal interest and pleasure; and the *Critique of Judgment* rejects a rationalist aesthetic built on neoclassical rules as well as a hedonistic empiricism that sees beauty merely in terms of individual pleasure and charm.

Kant's struggle to transcend these two opposed factions led him to stake out certain a priori premises, independent both of pure concepts and of personal experience, that could serve as the grounds for establishing knowledge, morality, and beauty. In his first *Critique* the premise was synthetic a priori judgments; in his second *Critique,* the categorical imperative; and in his third *Critique,* the idea of "general validity," never crystallized by Kant into a neat formula or set phrase, but described, for example, as a universal "ground of satisfaction for all men" (46), or as the "possibility of an aesthetical judgment that can . . . be regarded as valid for everyone" (50).[14] The parallel between Kant's well-known categorical imperative ("so act that the maxim of your will could always hold at the same time as a principle establishing universal law" [30]) in the realm of moral judgment, and the "universally valid ground" in that of taste, is both clear and significant.

The place of the imagination in Kant bears brief examination. James Engell, in his study of German and English Romantic ideas of imagination, notes the shifting senses and divers uses Kant assigns to the imaginative faculty. Engell notes as many as thirteen of these, several of which participate in the process whereby our minds gain knowledge.[15] Here and there throughout the *Critique of Pure Reason* Kant demonstrates how the imagination plays a cognitive role. He asserts that knowledge which is "examined, received, and connected" — that higher form which he terms "a synthesis" — comes as a result of "the faculty of imagination, a blind but indispensable function of the soul, without which we would have no knowledge whatsoever" (61).

In the *Critique of Judgment,* conversely, Kant draws analogous links between artistic creation, judgment, and contemplation on the one hand, and cognitive functions and preoccupations on the other. He notes that for the appreciation of "beautiful art in its entire completeness much science is requisite, *e.g.* a knowledge of ancient languages, a learned familiarity with classical authors, history, a knowledge of antiquities, etc." (147). Although strictly aesthetic attributes, Kant observes, do take the place of logical presentation in art, those aesthetic attributes serve also to "enliven the mind" (158), "[to] accompany the logical and stimulate the imagination so that it thinks more by their aid" (159). In brief, aesthetical experience exists alongside our cognitive capacities and moreover enriches them.

Regarding ethics, Kant again echoes Shaftesbury and establishes causal and developmental links between the Beautiful and the Good. Of course, when discoursing on the intrinsic nature of beauty, Kant rules out any narrow or simplistic moral preoccupations: "the feeling for the beautiful . . . is hardly compatible with the moral interest" (141). He does indicate, however, that trained receptivity to beauty can aid the growth of morals, and, conversely, that moral growth can dispose us to beauty. "Taste," he observes, "makes possible the transition . . . from the charm of sense to habitual moral interest" (200). Both the Sublime and the Beautiful "are purposive in reference to the moral feeling." The Beautiful, for instance, "prepares us to love disinterestedly something, even nature itself" (108). And though Kant is sufficiently sagacious to note that "connoisseurs in taste . . . generally are given up to idle, capricious, and mischievous passions," at the same time he can unabashedly state (doubtless under the influence of Rousseau) that "to take an *immediate interest* in the beauty of nature . . . is always a mark of a good soul," and that this interest "indicates a frame of mind favorable to the moral feeling" (141; emphasis in the original). It is no accident that the final full chapter dealing with aesthetics in the third *Critique* bears the title "Beauty as Symbol of Morality."

In his parting aesthetic arguments Kant dwells on the need to create ties between beauty and ethics, and he foresees damage ensuing should those ties not be acknowledged or strengthened. He warns: "If the beautiful arts are not brought into more or less close combination with moral ideas," the spirit can become "dull" and the mind "disconnected with itself and peevish" (170). Envisioning a shared role for art and morals, Kant winds up his section on aesthetic judgments with a bold assertion that "the true propaedeutic for the foundation of taste is the development of moral ideas and the culture of moral feeling," for "it is only when sensibility is brought into agreement with this that genuine taste can assume a definitive invariable form" (202). The wheel comes full circle: beauty can serve as transition to morality, but morality can also serve as foundation for taste. Hence Kant's advocacy of what, in retrospect, resembles *l'art pour l'art* actually had as its broader premises our growth as social and moral beings, the human process of becoming more civilized—of which the love of beauty is only one among essential parts.

No sooner was Kant's aesthetic theory in print than it began exerting a decisive influence among European intellectuals. His most notable disciple was Friedrich Schiller, who took Kant's concluding moral-cum-aesthetic affirmations as basis for his own philosophic treatise, *On the Aesthetic Education of Man in a Series of Letters*. Initially drafted for private circulation in 1793, Schiller's inspired pedagogical project was then expanded for publication by installments in a distinguished small journal, *The Graces*, in 1795. The first edition in book form of the *Letters on Aesthetic Education* (the common short title of the work) appeared in Leipzig in 1801.

Several commentators have since characterized Schiller's brief opus as one of the greatest works of aesthetic theory ever written — an accurate assessment, to my view. The *Letters* may lack the hermetic rigor of Kant, without whose *Critique of Judgment* Schiller's reflections would of course not have been possible. Schiller's volume nevertheless gains in vitality by hinting at and sharing in the charged political atmosphere of the European 1790s. Schiller's aesthetic arguments further glow with the passion of the revolutionary playwright and poet he was; and his speculations show the practical wisdom and common sense of the actively producing artist. The special greatness of the *Letters*, however, lies not only in Schiller's clear and profound grasp of the internal workings of beauty, but also in the way he sets up dynamic ties and dialectical links between aesthetic experience and other domains such as logic, reason, morals, social life, personality development, the civilizing process, and the education of children.

The book originated, modestly and casually, as a series of letters addressed to a Danish prince named Friedrich Christian von Schleswig-Holstein-Augustenburg. A dedicated patron of the arts, Prince Friedrich Christian had once aided Schiller when the poet found himself in dire straits. The nobleman, despite his aristocratic blood, had initially sympathized with the humanitarian goals of the French Revolution. Schiller's letters to the prince reflect the time and its preoccupations, with such locutions as "freedom," "equality," "inalienable rights," and "the actual State which we want to abolish" figuring not as academic abstractions but as the living terms of an urgent debate spawned by events in France. At the same time Schiller's frightened allusions to "crude, lawless impulses" and to "society uncontrolled . . . relapsing into its original elements" (fifth letter; 35)[16] all vividly articulate the increasing repugnance with which many intellectuals had begun to react to the revolutionary dictatorship known as the Reign of Terror.

Considerably more accessible than Kant's *Critiques*, the *Letters on Aesthetic Education* is nonetheless written in an opaque German idealist idiom. Yet, once patient readers settle with and penetrate its prose style, Schiller's powerful and compelling case moves them on, step by step, to his final, eloquent peroration. While the following summary scarcely does justice to the textured richness of this seminal and even visionary work, it can at least provide the basic drift.

- The modern age is one of scientific and political changes for which man is not yet fully prepared. The uses of art are shrinking, yet it must not stand indifferent to our times, because "it is through Beauty that we arrive at Freedom" (second letter, 27) and move "from . . . mere force to the rule of law" (third letter, 30).

- One result of modern advances is that human beings develop only portions of their total capabilities. The result is a rift between mind and senses, intellect and imagination, abstraction and passion, labor and enjoyment, head and heart (sixth letter, 38–42). These warring sides of man's self can be reconciled through the institution of the fine arts.

- Human beings are driven by two contrasting impulses: the *sensuous*, which roots us, determines us in the real world, and the rational and *formal*, which aims at truth, liberty, and justice. The first is concerned with individual *cases*, the second with *laws*. The two need not clash, and *culture* seeks a harmonious balance between them. Our *play* impulse reconciles these forces by combining the physical and moral, by striving for *living shape* and finding it in Beauty (fifteenth letter, 76; emphasis added).

- Beauty harmonizes the soul, leading "sensuous" men to form and thought, "spiritual" men to matter and sense (eighteenth letter, 87). Rather than exclude either perceiving or thinking, beauty combines the two. A child's pure sensuousness can be maintained, as he rises to a free rationality, via a middle disposition, the *aesthetic*. Pure sensuousness can soften us, pure reason harden us; but beauty, our "second creator," helps us master both powers (twenty-first letter, 102). The "transition from the aesthetical . . . to the logical and moral . . . is infinitely easier than the transition from physical . . . to aesthetical" (twenty-third letter, 109).

– "Beauty alone," then, can shape *"social* character," inasmuch as the aesthetic "carries out the will of the whole through the individual." "[T]he Beautiful unites society, because it relates to what is common to [us] all." Sensuous pleasure is personal; scientific pleasure is social; only beauty do we enjoy as members of a human collective. And so, whatever is related to "the Aesthetic State" is the domain of a "free citizen" with "equal rights before the noblest." "The ideal of equality" finds itself fulfilled in the aesthetic (twenty-seventh letter, 138–40).

Letters on Aesthetic Education yields a remarkable blend of aesthetic, political, social, and ethical theory, along with dashes of historical and metaphysical speculation. Although concerned with a totality of problems, however, it never loses sight of its central topic: the nature and the uses of beauty and art. Indeed, Schiller initially argues persuasively for the modern idea of autonomous and all-sufficient art. He considers "self-contradictory" the idea of an "instructive (didactic) or improving (moral) art, for nothing is more at variance with the concept of beauty than that it should have a tendentious effect upon the character" (twenty-second letter, 107). Few Western artists or theorists of art would dispute such a statement today. In the same way, a familiar if judicious formalism is present in Schiller's confident assertion in the same letter that "in a truly beautiful work of art the content should do nothing, the form everything" (106).

Schiller is thus careful to avoid the implication that art and beauty can bring about immediate consequences of any import: "Beauty gives no individual result whatever, either for the intellect or for the will; it realizes no individual purpose, either intellectual or moral; it discovers no individual truth, helps us to perform no individual duty, and is, in a word, equally incapable of establishing the character and clearing the mind" (twenty-first letter, 101).

The key word here is "individual." A work of beauty does not by itself arouse, impel, uncover, bring alive, or otherwise serve as immediate cause for any specific *individual* purpose, truth, or action.

Nor does the work of beauty occasion any such immediate effects on *individual* human beings. Regarding the one-to-one phase of aesthetic experience and communication, Schiller stands in agreement with W. H. Auden's well-known line of verse: "Poetry makes nothing happen."

Nevertheless, on a higher, contextual level, Schiller envisions a second process: by harmonizing the divers faculties of individuals, aesthetic culture also helps "restore freedom" to them, predisposes them to rationality, and leads them toward the rigor of a free moral will. Just as Kant affirms that training in the Beautiful aids in the development of morals, Schiller further concludes that only the appreciation of beauty creates *"a social character."* Schiller argues the apparent paradox that a receptivity to pure, independent, nondidactic beauty is a necessary precondition for the growth of our rational and moral sides. Art for Art's Sake in Schiller's view is a necessary first stage on the road to the equally necessary goals of truth, morality, and social character. One uses art not to teach morals and truth; one uses Art for Art's Sake as a sensuous grounding for morals and truth. In the pioneering case of Schiller, the later formula *l'art pour l'art* must be extended to the bolder and more complex *l'art pour l'art et ensuite pour le vrai, le bien et le social,* or Art for Art's Sake, and then for the sake of the True, the Good, and the Social.

Kant and Schiller, though outstanding early philosophical exponents of an independent beauty, also voice strong disapproval of any modishly facile, self-indulgently anarchical kinds of art. Kant in the *Critique of Judgment* castigates those "many modern educators" who believe that "the best way to produce a free art is to remove it from all constraint and thus change it from work into mere play" (147). An art produced under conditions of "lawless freedom," he notes elsewhere, is "nothing but nonsense" (163). In the same way Schiller, notwithstanding his assurances that form rather than content determines art, still speaks harshly of a pure aestheticism that shuts itself off from all other sorts of knowledge, experience, and values: "Precisely because taste pays heed to form and never to content, it finally gives the soul a dangerous tendency to neglect all reality entirely and to sacrifice truth and morality to an attractive façade" (tenth letter, 57). That perceived "dangerous tendency to neglect all reality" has the force of prophecy today, in view of the studied unreality that, beginning a century or so after Schiller, would characterize much of Modernist art and its later academic offshoots.

Schiller's aesthetic project has retained its freshness and force in our time. The great British art critic and publicist Sir Herbert Read, for example, acknowledged Schiller as precedent for his own ambitious pedagogical book, *Education through Art* (1943). In addition, the liberating quality of Schiller's thought is well demonstrated in a volume that attained cult status in the 1960s, *Eros and Civilization* (1956), by Herbert Marcuse. In that Freudian-Marxist speculative work, the German philosopher, a member of the original Frankfurt School and then an exile from Hitler's Reich, dedicates a full ten pages to examining the *Letters on Aesthetic Education* and praises its author for "basing morality on a sensuous ground" and for seeking "the liberation of sensuousness rather than reason." This leads Marcuse to his final utopian leap, a call for "the abolition of the repressive controls that civilization has imposed on sensuousness."[17] Fifteen years later the American critical theorist Fredric Jameson was to set aside thirty pages of his seminal volume *Marxism and Form* (1971) for a further gloss on the subject of "Marcuse and Schiller."

Written at the height of 1950s U.S. cold war culture and its revived puritanism, *Eros and Civilization* yet anticipated the changes in American mores that took place in the 1960s, when traditional restrictions on premarital sex, friendly cohabitation, and homo-and female eroticism would be challenged and often swept aside. That Marcuse's vision of liberated sensuality would also, in subsequent decades, assume the form of an eroticized consumerism and a cult of impersonal sex does not negate the original ideal he once dared to extrapolate from Schiller. If anything, the latter-day process of anomic sexualization confirms the perverse dynamic signaled by Marcuse in *One-Dimensional Man* and other works: late capitalism's uncanny ability to absorb and market almost all dissenting visions and utopias.

For our current purposes what most matters is that modern, dialectical thinkers such as Marcuse and Jameson single out Schiller's (rather than Kant's) aesthetics for attention, a fact suggestive of the extent to which the eighteenth-century poet-playwright maintains within his ken the vital network that connects formal art with everything from the basic life of the senses to the most rarefied of social ideals. Indeed what sets off the *Letters* from most academic aesthetics is Schiller's insistence that the fine arts are as much a part of our animal-instinctual as of our "spiritual" side — as much a domain of the id as of the superego, as it were. In a field characterized by much cloistered and abstract theorizing, *Letters on Aesthetic Education* stands out for its rootedness in the world of practical and physical experience, in life as well as art.

There is in addition a basic fruitfulness to Schiller's hypotheses, inasmuch as they can be concretely instanced and, in some degree, verified. In real life we actually encounter and observe the phenomenon of art serving as conduit between ordinary sensuousness and higher reason. History knows its share of activists and statesmen, scientists and thinkers who, coming from uncouth or unintellectual circumstances, at a certain moment in their personal growth (usually adolescence) found their souls sparked by the reading, reciting, or hearing of literary classics, and who sensed that they had come upon a new and qualitatively different stage of existence. In like fashion, many a philosopher or other conceptual specialist, before going on to discover personal talents as pure reasoner (Marx, Piaget, and Erik Erikson come to mind), has made passage through a youthful phase of producing music, visual art, or fiction and verse.

From the other end of our physical-to-rational range, by contrast, come those whose faculties of abstraction had been nourished in disproportion to, even at expense of, their sensuous sides, and who at some point found themselves reawakened and "brought back to earth" by the sensuous agency of works of art. A classic instance in this regard is Kant himself, whose perfectly regularized routines were disrupted on the day in 1762 when he first opened Rousseau's *Émile*. So powerful was the immediate impact of the Swiss writer and publicist's novel of education that Kant — legendary even in our time for his daily stroll around Koenigsberg at precisely 6:00 P.M. — actually forgot himself and stayed home that evening in order to plunge ever deeper into Rousseau instead. As noted earlier, Kant would eventually salute Rousseau for having helped him broaden his theoretical scope and shift his emphasis from pure rationality to larger ethical concerns.[18]

A yet more dramatic instance of this kind of aesthetic education is vividly documented by John Stuart Mill in his *Autobiography*. Mill's idiosyncratic upbringing stands as both renowned exemplar and cautionary tale of the enormous learning potential as well as developmental perils posed by the mind of a highly gifted child. Born into an intellectual household and formally unschooled, the young Mill was privately tutored by his father, the writer, historian, and philosopher James Mill. From age three the boy was reading ancient Greek, and by age twelve he had been led through the Greco-Roman classics.

He then took up logic and mathematics and in his thirteenth year began learning political economy (David Ricardo was a family friend). At seventeen the boy was publishing feature articles in newspapers and magazines. All along, however, Mill had no contact with children his own age, took no physical exercise other than long evening walks with his father, and knew little of English poetry, most of which the elder Mill apparently disliked. His aversion to Shakespeare was shared by the precocious and loyal adolescent.

Then, in his twentieth year, during what Mill calls "the melancholy winter of 1826-7" (118), he found himself "in a dull state of nerves" (113) and succumbed to a deep mental and spiritual crisis.[19] Though duly cranking out his articles and reading as much as ever, Mill now felt completely hollow inside, deadened emotionally. For the first time he understood "what I had always before received with incredulity—that the habit of analysis has a tendency to wear away the feelings: as indeed it has, when no other mental habit is cultivated, and the analysing spirit remains without its natural complements and correctives" (116). He realized that his one-sided education "had failed to create . . . feeling in sufficient strength to resist the dissolving influence of analysis, while the whole course of my intellectual cultivation had made precocious and premature analysis the inveterate habit of my mind" (117).

Mill never turned against the advantages provided by his father's rich intellectual, rationalistic training. Instead, "the maintenance of a due balance among the faculties now seemed to me of primary importance. The cultivation of the feelings became one of the cardinal points in my ethical and philosophical creed" (122). Mill's viewpoint and even some of his phraseology here show a striking likeness to those of Schiller. Moreover, the solution Mill was to arrive at is one that the German author would have applauded. Mill started to "find meaning . . . in the importance of poetry and art as instruments of human culture" (122). More specifically, in what Mill calls "an important event" in his life, he began reading the poetry of Wordsworth in 1828.

The unexpected therapeutic results were enduring and profound. "What made Wordsworth's poems a medicine for my state of mind was that they expressed, not mere outward beauty, but states of feeling, and of thought coloured by feeling under the influence of beauty" (125). From Wordsworth, the intensely subjective, sometimes hyperemotional poet, Mill, the hyperrational, intensely analytical young economist and great philosopher-to-be, miraculously gained "a greatly increased interest in the common feelings and common destiny of human beings" (126). Hence, in the pattern formulated by Schiller, the late-adolescent Mill, a young man excessively mental in attitude and hardened by reason, found himself led back to life via beauty and its attendant emotions — only one dramatic proof of the theory argued in *Letters on Aesthetic Education*.

The *Letters* contains enormous untapped potential. Or, as happened with Mill, its theory is from time to time accidentally tested and proved valid in the laboratory of human life, most probably without full awareness of the Schillerian grand vision on the part of the experimenters. A particularly moving instance in this regard is the admirable work done by Kenneth Koch, the American poet who in the 1960s taught grade school children to write verse in the classroom and thereby to respond more knowingly to Shakespeare, Blake, Lorca, and other great poets. Koch's two books giving an account of the experience, with their lovely gatherings of the youngsters' poems, stand as eloquent testimony to the kind of creative pedagogy and "aesthetic education" that are possible when the circumstances, the teachers, and the historical timing are right.

Koch's own summing up of his labors may be viewed in the light of Schiller's project:

> The educational advantages of a creative intellectual activity which children enjoy are clear. Writing poetry makes children feel happy, capable, and creative. It makes them feel more open

to understanding and appreciating what others have written (literature). It even makes them want to know how to spell and say things correctly (grammar). Once Mrs. Magnani's students were excited about words, they were dying to know how to spell them. Learning becomes part of an activity they enjoy — when my fifth graders were writing their Poems Using Spanish Words they were eager to know more words than I had written on the board; one girl left the room to borrow a dictionary. Of all these advantages, the main one is how writing poetry makes children feel: creative; original; responsive; yet in command.[20]

The play impulse, Schiller's idea of "living shape," the recognition of society (by identifying with and learning from what others have written), and an emergent sense of one's own responsibility are "Schillerian" insights implicit in Koch's paragraph. The pupils moreover engage themselves in the creative use and production of language and (as did Mill) become articulate about their own emotions as well.

Similarly, in his closing recollection of a fifth-grade boy's highly expansive free verse, Koch — almost casually — speculates on the transition to rationality that Schiller saw resulting from aesthetic education: "Chip's line about Carmen might be just the thing to show some dreamy eleven-year-old his connection with Blake and with ideas of cosmic transformation and to *get him started feeling, thinking, and writing.*"[21] In all, Schiller's work offers a wealth of conceptual material for developmental psychologists and art therapists, for sociologists of art and teachers of literacy, for socially concerned novelists, poets, and playwrights, for large-scale cultural theorists, psychohistorians, and even social activists, and of course for aestheticians and educationists.

Schiller's theory occupies a special place in the two-hundred-year history of the doctrine of Art for Art's Sake. *Letters on Aesthetic Education* qualifies as the last instance of a major imaginative Western writer defending the unique powers and prerogatives of beauty, not for special interests of pure artistry, however, but because beauty is part of the civilizing process and contributes to the spiritual growth of individuals and the sociopolitical development of the human family. As with Kant, the theory reflects a moment in Europe when the aesthetic ideal still played a role within a long-range, forward-looking intellectual project, when it shared in a grand critique of then-dominant (if decaying) forms of social organization and thought, a time when proponents of that aesthetic ideal were also envisioning a juster society no longer shackled by feudal privilege, Church authority, or neoclassical rules. As the title of Schiller's great book suggests, the aesthetic is not only self-contained and indivisible, but a component of our total education as well.

CHAPTER 2

The New Economy, Poetry Displaced, and the Birth of the Doctrine

The poet was sorcerer and seer before he became "artist." His structures were not abstract art, or art for its own sake. . . . [They] came
into being to serve not *art* but religion in its most basic sense.
— Albert Lord, *The Singer of Tales*

At the time of Schiller's death in 1805, the ideology of aestheticism did
not yet exist anywhere in Europe. A handful of French intellectuals,
however, were first becoming aware of recent German philosophy,
Kant in particular. Revolutionary turmoil and dictatorship notwithstanding, progressive literati remained weary of old-regime Catholicism and neoclassicism and were hence predisposed to consider new
models from elsewhere. The importation of thought and letters from
Germany thus held promising prospects. The reception of Kantianism in France nevertheless provides an object lesson in what happens
when complex ideas are disseminated among a foreign, latter-day
audience. The ensuing gaps, shifts in emphasis, and other alterations
can prove quite unsettling.

Elements of Kant made tentative headway in post-Napoleonic
France via the work of well-placed popularizers and pedagogues.
Meanwhile, around the same time, in print shops and booksellers'
offices an entirely new system of cultural supply and demand was
taking shape. The twin forces of commercialization and industrialization were fast transforming both the larger economy and the daily
textures of French literary life. Among the unintended social forma-
tions spawned by this overall change was the underclass of artists
in Bohemia, *la bohème*, a phenomenon known to us mostly through
Puccini's romantic (if delightful) opera by that name, but in reality
a harsh, brittle milieu of bare survival and dashed hopes. Into this
subculture there soon trickled the few selected fragments of Kant's

aesthetic theory that ultimately provided the rough template for standard aestheticist doctrine.

Throughout the decades of the Napoleonic Empire, the Bourbon Restoration, and the July Monarchy, the original Kantian texts remained largely inaccessible to French readers, even highly cultured ones. A translation into French of the *Critique of Pure Reason* was not published until 1835, and of the *Critique of Judgment,* only as late as 1846. Much of what had previously passed for Kantian ideas was an incomplete (to say the least), third-hand rendition thereof. Hence, in its initial process of diffusion in France, Kant's theory of art was simplified and debased by publicists who lacked the background, language, time, and sheer stamina to take on the *Critique of Judgment,* let alone deal fruitfully with the other two.

As a result, Kant's mature ideas were effectively reduced to a number of set phrases and slogans. His grand synthesis was lost and his global totality ignored—much as we see happen in our own time with the thought of Marx, Freud, or Adam Smith. Distorted and melted down by agile-witted *Parisiens*, the aesthetic theory of Kant was then recast as ideological buckshot for use in partisan disputes — on either side of the literary barricades.[1]

The Gallicization of Kant began, ironically, during Napoleon's dictatorship, when a number of French progressives were living in exile in Germany. Among those émigré figures was Benjamin Constant (1767–1830), known today mostly for his romantic novel *Adolphe.* One of the great liberal, antimonarchist activists in nineteenth-century France, Constant wrote studies of politics and religion as part of his parallel vocation in the life of letters (as well as demonstrating comparable talents for gambling and womanizing). During his German phase Constant managed to rub shoulders with Schiller and Schelling and their select circle of friends, including an Englishman named Henry Crabb Robinson.

Constant kept a remarkable if uneven diary of those years, and in an entry under 1804 he writes, "Had a chat with Robinson, a disciple of Schelling. His study of the aesthetics of Kant has some lively ideas." The sentence fragment that follows is, in Constant's original French, "L'art pour l'art, sans but, car tout but dénature l'art. Mais l'art atteint un but qu'il n'a pas" [Art for art's sake, with no purpose, since any purpose will denature art. But art does attain a purpose which it does not have.].[2] This of course is Kantian aesthetics at its most rudimentary. It is also the first known instance of the collocation *l'art pour l'art,* though presumably not yet as a readymade phrase.

Constant owed his acquaintance with these literati chiefly to that brilliant and legendary baroness of letters, Mme. Anne-Louise-Germaine de Staël, whose lover he was from 1794 to 1811. Staël's graceful and highly readable introduction to the German cultural scene, *De l'Allemagne,* first appeared in 1810 but became truly influential only after the fall of Napoleon in 1814. The lengthy book grew out of her political exile, when she captivated many a German luminary and also irritated a few — Schiller, for example, who closed his doors to her.

Of Kant's philosophy Mme. de Staël seems to have read rather little, and in discussing his work she depends mostly on hearsay. Still, the fact remains that it was Mme. de Staël who first brought the news of Kant, Schiller, and the Schlegels to a French readership largely bored with the "rules" of neoclassicism and in a mood to seek out alternate literary ways. Seeing "with what sterility our literature is threatened," Staël suggests that "foreign combinations may excite new ideas" (1:203).[3] What she finds attractive about "the literary theory of the Germans" is that it does not "[subject] writers to customs nor to tyrannical restrictions" (2:209). In a dig at long-venerated French traditions, Staël thinks it "infinitely better for the literature of a country that its poetical system should be founded upon philosophical notions . . . than upon simple external rules; for these rules are only barriers to prevent children from falling" (2:210).

Among the excited readers of *De l'Allemagne* was an ambitious young philosophy student, Victor Cousin. The biography of Cousin is a notable instance of those successful intellectual careers — Horatio Algerism in belles-lettres, so to speak — that can take shape in a new and still-emergent sociopolitical system. Cousin was born in Paris in 1792 to parents of modest means (his father was a jeweller; his mother took in washing). An accident of childhood altruism changed his life. In 1803 a mild-mannered but gauche schoolboy named Epagomène Viguier (later a professor of Greek) was being roughed up by some bullies, who taunted him for his oversized coat. Cousin, an eleven-year-old street urchin, rushed over and beat up Viguier's tormentors. In gratitude, Epagomène's mother took it upon herself to pay for Cousin's schooling. The erstwhile street tough went on to do brilliantly as a student, winning prize after prize in his examinations.[4]

In his twenty-fifth year Cousin's fortunes were once again boosted by the influence of a well-placed patroness. Smitten by the Baroness de Staël's graceful Baedeker of German high intellect, Cousin showed up one day at her Rue Royale apartments, where he met and chatted with August Schlegel. Soon thereafter an ambitious Victor Cousin headed for Germany with the express aim of encountering that nation's most illustrious minds. There he knocked on doors, met Schleiermacher, Goethe, and even Hegel, and charmed virtually everybody.[5] On his return to his native city, Cousin was accorded a chair of philosophy at the Université de Paris (Sorbonne).

In post-Napoleonic France the philosophical field was in a sorry state, the simplistic egoism and materialism of the eighteenth-century thinker Condillac having been superseded and forgotten, with nothing as yet available to take its place. Stepping into this vacuum, Professor Cousin in his official capacity brought off something of a miracle: he gave a series of lectures based on his minimal reading of Kant—mainly in poor and incomplete Latin translations, deciphered with much clever guesswork on his part.[6] The students, however, adored Victor Cousin the orator and teacher, and he is to this day memorialized by a street bearing his name along the western edge of the Sorbonne.

Cousin's lectures were published in multiple varied editions, the first in 1826, under the lengthy and all-embracing title *Cours de philosophie professée a la faculté des lettres pendant l'année 1818 sur les fondements des idées absolues du vrai, du beau et du bien*. The prose style of the lectures is resoundingly cadenced and eloquent, luminously beautiful. Their content is most charitably described as a grab-bag of received ideas, stock phrases, well-turned commonplaces, and bits and pieces from contemporary German thought. Cousin in fact unashamedly christened his doctrine Eclecticism, while a sympathetic biographer characterizes Cousin's method as "a little like opportunism."[7]

Among those German idealist bits and pieces was a highly simplified look at Kantian aesthetics. Although the eventual severing of the aesthetic from our other mental faculties had not yet been realized, the complex Kantian ties that once connected beauty with morals and truth became, in Cousin's version, tenuous, less visible, and superficially rendered. The lectures show a familiar drift toward compartmentation, including aesthetic separatism, as exemplified in Cousin's oft-quoted flourish, "Il faut de la religion pour la religion, de la morale pour la morale, comme de l'art pour l'art" (Twenty-second lecture, p. 224). Whether the phrase "l'art pour l'art"—ever so slightly highlighted by Cousin, and strategically placed to end a sentence—is specifically invoked as a set formula is not clear in context. A reasonable guess is that Cousin here articulates and lets float what was becoming a shared idea among the more advanced Parisian intellects. Cousin's use of the phrase is thus both effect and cause.

Today we generally associate Art for Art's Sake with conservatism or at best apoliticism. However, the historical picture, as seen in chapter 7, is a great deal more complex. In France, moreover, literary ideas have always tended to be closely bound up with political partisanship. During its early phase the doctrine of *l'art pour l'art* belonged to the broad party of the antimonarchist left. The Restoration of 1814 had brought back not only old-regime nobles and Bourbon kings but also their tired literary dogmas of neoclassicism. Consequently any spokesman for Art for Art's Sake found himself ipso facto in opposition to ruling doctrines—political as well as cultural. Victor Cousin himself, though not of heroic mold, held to a mildly republican and libertarian stance as well as aestheticist views.

With the assassination of the duc de Berry as he left the opera and the subsequent right-wing repression of 1820, Cousin and other like-minded intellectuals, as one might expect, were removed from their university posts. For most of the decade they did free-lance work or taught privately, their dissident ideas forming part of a kind of ideological underground. Cousin himself prepared an edition of Descartes, began a translation of Plato, and worked as a tutor for the Duke of Montebello's son. In 1824 he took his pupil on a tour of Germany, where the Prussian authorities accused him of Jacobinism and espionage. Arrested in Dresden and sent to prison in Berlin, Cousin soon became a cause célèbre to progressives throughout Europe.[8] Widespread protests and expressions of sympathy in the press led to his release, and he returned to France a hero. In compensation Cousin was restored to his teaching post in 1828, one of the first concrete gains by the French liberal faction during that decade.

Meanwhile anti-Bourbon sentiment and agitation were on the rise, and in this climate there slowly emerged an informal alliance uniting militant liberals (who hated the Bourbon crown) with burgeoning Romantics and defiant aestheticists (who hated the retrograde culture of the Bourbon crown). As often happens in France, the men of letters were as much a part of the political struggles as were the crowds of workers demonstrating in the streets. The literary and countercultural part of the conflict reached its climax at the legendary battle of *Hernani* on 25 February 1830. That "Spanish" verse melodrama of Victor Hugo had its much-awaited debut at the august old playhouse of the Comédie Française, where the opposing factions in the audience took their combat positions a full eight hours in advance. Hugo's youthful defenders wore Spanish cloaks and Robespierre-style waistcoats, and poet Théophile Gautier gained instant notoriety with his shoulder-length hair and lobster-colored vest. The moment arrived: at the very sound of the unorthodox metrics of Hugo's opening lines, the neoclassicist-conservative stalwarts tried to hoot the play down, but the playwright's enthusiasts responded by stamping their feet en masse, and in the end the Hugo party carried the day. French Romanticism was officially launched.

Though the ideology of *l'art pour l'art* did not burst into public debate until a year or so later, indirect evidence suggests that it formed part of the submerged anticlassicist ferment that led to the *Hernani* affair. (The studied viciousness of the attacks on aestheticism in the 1830s, for one, would not have been directed at a doctrine that was newborn.) There is, of course, Cousin's use of the phrase, if in passing, in a lecture. In addition none other than Victor Hugo espouses an Art for Art's Sake approach to verse in his book of exotic lyrics *Les Orientales* (1829). Hugo in his preface to that volume frankly asserts (almost anticipating Oscar Wilde), "In poetry there are neither good nor bad subjects, only good and bad poets." In reply to questions raised about the purpose of "this useless book of pure poetry," Hugo defends his right to his own personal whims and the love of sunsets.

Moreover, he gently mocks the old-regime stalwarts and their obsessions with Louis XIV and Boileau.[9]

Being too much the public bard, Hugo never returned to his youthful aestheticism. His own brief involvement with *poésie pure*, however, symbolizes the initial common front between French Romanticists and *l'art pour l'art*, a moment that Gautier in his memoirs would fondly recall as heroic. Once the battle was won, though, the respective agenda of the two camps necessarily diverged, and aestheticism endured as the separatist tradition we know today.

The anticlassicist struggle roused the polemicist in Hugo, who furnished the Romantics their chief manifesto in the preface to his closet play *Cromwell*, where he defends "artistic freedom against the tyranny of systems and rules" and notes an old regime in literature parallel to the old regime in politics.[10] Similarly, in the preface to *Hernani* Hugo asserts, "Romanticism is nothing more than liberalism in literature," and he calls for throwing off "the old poetic forms together with the old social forms."[11] With the liberal revolution of July 1830 and the installation of "Citizen King" Louis Philippe, the political arena too was definitively won for the new social forces.

Soon thereafter, however, Hugo's inspired vision of a literature without rules would prove illusory. In lieu of those shop-worn neoclassical unities, there emerged a whole new set of rules governing such matters as productivity, size, and format—rules dictated by the culture of the literary market. To understand better those recent dictates, we must move away for a while from the entertaining subject of writers' lives and their aesthetic doctrines, and deal with a drier topic: the material and socioeconomic apparatus for the production and distribution of printed texts.

Since 1789, a vast change had been taking place in the institutional literary machinery of Europe. Under the ancien régime, art had existed almost exclusively under the sway of princely patronage. Louis XIV, for example, set up an entire in-house system for the production of art and literature, bringing in teams of Italian painters and sculptors and lodging them around the grand palace in Versailles. The great dramatist Jean Racine was officially the royal historian, and Corneille actually had the title "royal upholsterer."[12] According to Balzac, before the revolution "seven out of twelve writers received considerable pensions paid by foreign sovereigns, by the court, or by the régime."[13] Authorial deference was the norm for crafting of dedications as well as for public performances of art works. Lord Halifax in Augustan England thought nothing of interrupting Pope's formal reading of his translation of the *Iliad* in order to suggest some poetical improvements.[14]

The publishing trade in France before 1800 was by and large a pre-industrial and precapitalist affair. A mere thirty-six printers were allowed to operate under the old Bourbon monarchy.[15] Books were issued in small quantities—a thousand copies maximum—and were disposed of primarily through subscriptions by the wealthy. Four decades of revolutionary turmoil in France, however, were to do away with aristocratic hegemony and its institutionalized patronage of the literary arts. Into the resulting vacuum there moved the economic liberalism of the free market, which rapidly became, and to this day remains, the dominant means for mass-scale reproduction and general distribution of the written language.

The print market gained immeasurable powers through the industrialization of the book trade. In 1798 a Frenchman named Nicolas-Louis Robert devised the first papermaking machine and thus raised the hourly yield by a factor of ten. This invention was then pirated by the British entrepreneurs Gamble and Fourdrinier and in turn was put to work in the 1810s by the Didot family mills in the Somme. Over the next two decades, a paper made from timber was developed, helping to compensate for the scarcity of rags. In 1790 William Nicolson invented the rubber ink roller, and in 1808 Pierre Lorilleux was the first to produce ink industrially.

The actual print process showed dramatic technological advances. Iron rather than wood was adopted as basic material for printing machines, rendering them more resistant to stress. Manual operation gave way to foot-pedals and then to steam, leading to enormous increases in output.[16] The fastest hand press could print 250 sheets per hour at most; by 1834 mechanical presses were printing 3,600 sheets per hour. The most dynamic sector of the French Restoration economy was printed matter, with annual growth rates of 9 percent. In 1814 there were 2,500 commercially listed book titles; in 1826, almost 8,300.[17]

The basic motive for all this activity was economic—namely, to produce as much as could be sold to satisfy the reading demands of the triumphant middle classes, who, though certainly less sophisticated in their literary tastes than the displaced aristocracy, were nonetheless hungry for suitable printed fare. But at the same time, in typical market fashion, technical advances made increases in sales all the more necessary. In his classic history of market society, Karl Polanyi notes that "since elaborate machines are expensive, they do not pay unless large amounts of goods are produced. . . . For the merchant this means that all factors involved must be on sale, that is, they must be available in needed quantities to anybody who is prepared to pay for them. . . . All incomes must derive from the sale of something or other."[18] Such precisely was the dynamic in the newly technified literary market: costly papermaking and print machines could produce in high quantities; selling in high quantities was necessary to pay off those costly machines.

This economic, demographic, and technological conjuncture made for truly spectacular growth in two literary categories: journalism and fiction. The newspaper business as we now know it emerged in the first half of the nineteenth century. Indeed we can pinpoint the exact year in which journalism became one with the marketplace: 1836, when publisher Emile de Girardin halved the subscription price of his newspaper *La Presse,* choosing to stay afloat not by sales to readers, but through advertising revenue. The journalistic enterprise was thus brought into line with the regular flow of industrial goods. Other French newspapers quickly followed suit in order to survive.[19]

Fiction had coexisted with journalism since the pioneering days of Defoe, who excelled in both. After 1830, however, the free market and new technologies supported vastly expanded productivity from wordsmiths. Those writers capable of keeping up with demand were to accumulate hitherto unheard-of fortunes. Balzac spent twelve hours a day at his desk, producing thirty pages per sitting. Alexandre Dumas wrote 100,000 lines a year at 1.5 francs per line.[20] On another level there was the prolific Paul de Kock, who in his *Memoirs* was frank enough to say, "I'm greedy and I admit it."[21] Certain subgenres cropped up, to the benefit of those authors able to satisfy subgenre conventions. From England came the three-volume novel, the "three-

decker." Trollope, who in his *Autobiography* took great pleasure in describing how he produced 250 words every fifteen minutes and had
cranked out *Barchester Towers* during a journey by train, urged all
young novelists to work in the three-volume format.

Another new form was the serial novel, the *roman feuilleton*, which
fused narrative arts with journalistic rhythms. Serial novels began
running side by side with advertisements and articles in Parisian
papers in the 1830s. The *feuilleton* in turn boosted readership. Eugène
Sue got 100,000 francs from *Le Constitutionnel* for *The Wandering
Jew;* as soon as the novel began appearing, circulation leaped from
3,000 to 40,000.[22] Sainte-Beuve scorned such "industrialized literature," while Champfleury celebrated fiction in the press by likening
it to steam power in the factory.[23] However one felt about the phenomenon, it was only mass-produced print that allowed authors to
earn their keep from output alone. Before 1790 there had existed
neither the cheap paper, the printing machines, nor the large market
to make the rapid composing of thick tomes or weekly copy a profitable or even conceivable enterprise.

On the other hand, the place of verse in the new market system was inevitably slight, owing to the intrinsic nature of lyric and
the way in which it is produced. Consider the old question of what
poetry is and also the practical matter of how poets write. In a well-
known essay, Roman Jakobson persuasively argues that poetry is a
species of art in which the dominant emphasis falls neither on the
thing spoken about nor on the speaker nor on the person spoken
to, but on the verbal fabric of the message itself.[24] The "nexus between sound and meaning" may be negligible in a news report and
of varying relevance in a realist novel, but it is the determining factor
in even the simplest of jingles and the briefest of lyrics. The density
and palpability of a poem's linguistic materials is of overwhelming
importance, and within a mere fourteen lines such things as phono-
logical similarities and contrasts, verbal and other parallels, recurrent
rhythmic devices, and nonreferential figures such as metaphor are all
foregrounded and call attention to themselves. It is not just a matter of choice of words but of their relative positioning within the
overall makeup of a poetical page, where the vertical workings are
somewhat analogous to those of an orchestral score, unlike narrative

prose pages, which are horizontal and linear in their mode of opera-tion. To carry the analogy just a bit further: the music of poetry is like Bach's counterpoint, the music of prose like Verdi's melodies.

Owing precisely to the linguistic density of their medium, the majority of poets in history have been slow producers. Virgil report-edly completed a mere three lines a day, and that effusive Welshman Dylan Thomas would feel satisfaction on having crafted two good lines in a day. Since classical times, poets themselves have firmly ad-vised a leisurely and conscientious writing pace. Horace in the first century B.C. told young versifiers that "you will make an excellent im-pression if you use care and subtlety in placing your words and, by the skillful choice of setting, give fresh meaning to a familiar word." He similarly exhorted readers to "have nothing to do with any poem that has not been trimmed into shape by many a day's toil and . . . corrected down to the smallest detail." [25] Eighteen hundred years later the French neoclassicist Boileau would scorn a fast pen as a sign of poor judgment and would suggest polishing every poem some twenty times. [26]

Suddenly, in the nineteenth century, the poets were fundamentally at odds with the new system of literary production and distribution. In retrospect, they are a painful instance of a pattern studied by labor sociologist Harry Braverman, who notes how, throughout the his-tory of industrial capitalism, the pressure to produce more goods for expanding markets, at ever faster speeds, relegates traditional crafts to the margins of society and renders complex skills obsolete. [27] The poets can be seen as the first instance, in the industrial age, of an an-cient art that finds its purposes marginalized by new technologies, a process to be repeated in the cases of painting and photography, the music hall and radio, prose fiction and the visual media.

The careers of the poets themselves provide dramatic illustrations of Braverman's thesis. With the massive changes in literary reproduc-tion and distribution, most poets were selling their verbal skills—though not their poetry—on the industrial literary market. While their personal passions and chief talents may have been in verse, lyric art became a kind of adjunct activity to their breadwinning chores in journalism or related fields. Today we think of Gautier as a poet, but his complete verse occupies only two volumes, while his journalism, if compiled, would probably fill two hundred. Baudelaire in his lifetime was known far more for his literary criticism and his translations of Poe—which also were his chief sources of income—than for his lyrics. In writing poetry he might revise a line dozens of times, spend hours on a single word; his complete poetry takes up some three hundred pages. Even if newspapers had printed all of Baudelaire's poems, at fees comparable to those of Dumas or Balzac, he still wouldn't have received subsistence income. In his essay "Advice to Young Men of Letters" (1846), Baudelaire himself notes that literature consists first of "filling up so many columns" and that a writer "has to sell at all kinds of prices." "Today it is necessary to produce a great deal; hence one must work quickly . . . and make every blow count." [28]

On the other hand, those poets who, like Hugo and Lord Byron, were spontaneous and prolific—"naive" poets, in Schiller's use of the term—commanded success on the market. (Hugo and Byron, it should also be said in passing, articulated in their verse certain myths of the time, a factor that surely helped sales.) If the complete poetical works of Hugo comprise over 150,000 lines of verse, as is said, no wonder then that Gautier, who spent twenty years crafting his elegant little book of poems, the *Emaux et camées,* has the narrator of *Mademoiselle de Maupin* express envy for those poets who "write a hundred lines in succession without crossing out anything or looking at the ceiling." [29]

The poets, then, were fundamentally at odds with the productivity requirements—the supply side, as it were—of the literary market. (Much the same can be said about their relationship to the reading habits of the new society and the distribution side of verse.) Sales of poetry volumes in France peaked in 1827, when there were 537 verse titles to 295 in fiction. Thereafter the novel gained ground even as poetry declined, with average sales of books of poems finally crashing to around 300 per title. A bookseller named Lesur wisely speculated that prose fiction would someday replace verse. [30]

Several explanations based on social history can be offered for these trends. Before the revolution, lyric activity in France was traditionally supported by direct patronage from the nobility. Courtly rituals of reading poetry aloud (familiar to us from Molière's plays) and the routine use of verse in neoclassical tragedies gave a public function and a palpable existence to the genre. Years of accumulated listening time and exposure to the art, necessary if one is to have an ear attuned to its verbal nuances, constituted part of the normal education of aristocratic young ladies and *gentilhommes*. By 1830, however, after decades of class warfare, the landed nobles and other feudal sectors in France were effectively displaced from power, a fact signifying for verse the twofold loss of a trained, knowledgeable audience and also of what had once been their chief source of sustenance.

The newer contexts and ways of reading, in addition, were by their very nature less than hospitable to the preindustrial traits and practices of verse. The victorious French middle classes had not undergone the thorough poetic training and indoctrination into poetry of the old nobility; their reading tastes thus went rather for prose. Moreover the preeminent verbal medium of the bourgeoisie, the newspaper, stressed efficient informational and narrative content over stylistic and linguistic elegance (headlines aside). Virtually all sections of a newspaper—politics, business, *faits divers* (sensationalism), reviews, and fiction—were meant to be read relatively quickly and soon laid aside. A day's or a week's issue was bought for immediate consumption, then discarded when superseded by the next. The larger continuities in this custom were provided by the ongoing stories—the public topics and the serial novels—with which readers felt compelled to keep up day by day or weekly.

In such a setting, a self-contained and "noninformational" piece such as a poem had no relevant function. Indeed the sheer volume of fast-reading prose in a news daily inevitably overshadowed the few lyric specimens, all the more so if their lines happened to be well-crafted and stylistically dense. During my own initial research into the early-nineteenth-century French press, I was constantly struck by the low incidence of new verse even in intellectually prestigious journals like *L'Artiste,* a magazine whose very name proclaimed its commitments. The most casual inspection of the newspapers and periodicals of the time shows poetry already left out, or on the margins.

One of the fastest-growing markets for printed words was the passenger train sector. The W. H. Smith chain of stores in England, still a thriving international concern, started business in the nineteenth century by selling books in railroad stations. Railway compartments in fact were among the latest new spaces for extended reading, though obviously they would not serve as an appropriate venue for reading poems out loud and were generally unsuitable for the special intensity and concentration of the poetical experience. What was good for W. H. Smith and its regular customers was not necessarily good for poetry and poets.

Coleridge in the *Biographia Literaria* registers his own complaints about the modern publishing business and, without making any theoretical inference, establishes a primary condition of poetic style: "first, that not the poem which *we have read,* but that to which we *return* with the greatest pleasure, possesses genuine powers and claims the name of essential poetry." [31] Coleridge is no doubt right: a true poem becomes itself, and does its job best, when someone rereads and has reread it. Obviously a literary market built on fast, silent reading and on periodical obsolescence (the pun is intended) does not encourage rereading anything, least of all poetry.

Hence on virtually all fronts poetry was the odd man out. France of course had its Bohemia, and there were attempts to reach a poetry audience either through direct sales or by reviving old declamatory customs. Some bolder and brasher souls tried peddling their lyric texts in the streets and public squares of Paris, an informal sort of salesmanship that brought them suspicion and harassment from the police. Later in the century a new breed of poets—bad poets, mostly—recited their work in the cabarets then burgeoning around the city's working-class districts.[32] None of these essentially powerless forums could provide a decent regular income to poets, regardless of the individual writer's talents or business skills.

Significantly, for perhaps the first time in history many writers gave shape to the idea of the suffering poet whose gifts are neglected, exploited, ridiculed, or otherwise ill used. Alfred de Vigny presents the image of the lyrist as victim in his tragedy *Chatterton* (1835), a free reconstruction of the plight of the eighteen-year-old English verse prodigy who in 1770 committed suicide. In another instance, Paul Saulnier, in an 1856 essay on contemporary novels, tells of "a rich and successful writer returning to his elegant apartment after an evening of pleasure. There he opens the door to a small alcove to reveal, bent over a table, the poor down and out poet who is the real author of the books."[33] Baudelaire's powerful "L'Albatros" invokes the mighty bird who, when held captive aboard ship by taunting sailors, looks "clumsy and shameful," "comical and ugly" as he drags his great wings. Baudelaire in the final stanza explicitly compares the poet to

> the prince of clouds who
> ... Exiled on the ground amid catcalls,
> Can't walk because his wings get in the way."[34]

The classic portrait of the industrialization and commercialization of book production, the rise of journalism, and the unsalability of verse is to be found neither in an essay nor in a work of history but in Balzac's *Lost Illusions* (1839). A full third of this novel of the literary life deals with a young printer, David Séchard, who realizes that along with industrialism "there will be a demand for cheap clothes and cheap books." He spends most of his time experimenting with ways of producing low-cost paper from vegetables, and he finally makes a breakthrough, only to have some wily entrepreneurs and shysters pilfer the invention as well as his finances. The other, more ostensibly literary hero is Lucien de Rubempré, an ambitious young poet who comes to Paris with dreams of fame and a manuscript of a sonnet cycle that, according to other characters in the novel, is much better than most of the new verse being printed. But he soon finds out that publishers prefer putting out books with titles such as *Bookkeeping in Twenty Lessons* or *Botany for Ladies*, that "books are to publishers what cotton nightcaps are to drapers, goods to be bought cheap and sold dear." A publisher named Dauriat personally informs Lucien that as a one-book poet he is unsalable, that only quantity sells: "Admitted that you're a good poet. Are you prolific? Do you produce sonnets regularly? Will you ever run to ten volumes? Would you be a profitable enterprise? Of course not."[35] Discouraged in his efforts to be published strictly on the merits of his verse, Lucien instead pursues a career in journalism, where he is quickly sucked into the glittering world of fast phrases and easy money, and becomes glib, successful, and corrupt.

It is no accident that almost all authors associated with Art for Art's Sake have been essentially poets—Gautier, Baudelaire, the French

Parnassians and symbolists, the modernistas in Latin America, and, in the United States, Poe and later the Fugitive Agrarians who became the New Critics. The few major novelists who tended toward aestheticism — Flaubert, Joyce, Nabokov — were authors who, out of temperament or choice, produced slowly. Flaubert's fiction, of course, can be read for its social content, but he personally set out to make the novel into a perfect artifact, with prose as polished as any poetry. With this in mind he spent five years of full-time work on his first novel, *Madame Bovary,* sometimes giving a single paragraph a whole week's attention. (As Sartre notes, Flaubert felt that he had the soul of a poet.) [36] Joyce's entire fictional output consists of four books that involved a total and heroic commitment to craft, twenty years in the case of *Finnegans Wake.* Nabokov, who felt utter contempt for the literary marketplace,[37] during his American phase used to write his books on 3-by 5-inch cards, laboring over the composition of every one of its sentences.

Karl Marx, in his posthumous *Theories of Surplus Value,* makes a passing statement, often quoted, that "capitalist production is hostile to certain aspects of intellectual production, such as art and poetry." [38] Although he himself never elaborated on the idea, I have a partial explanation, and its drift by now is probably clear: *l'art pour l'art* was the position adopted by certain authors whose specific mode of discourse and personal rhythms of production conflicted with the demands of the newly industrialized literary market. Though many poets earned their living in the journalistic marketplace, their own lyric products stood well outside informal market rules of output and genre. Painfully aware by the early 1830s of the discrepancy between their highly special talents and the economic needs of an aggressively prosperous new cultural system, they assumed a militantly defensive posture, expressed via ideals that provided solace for their resentment and a sense of superiority in their craft. Their kind of art being objectively marginal to the dominant literary discourses, they subjectively transformed the unmarketability of their poetic gifts into what they saw as an aesthetic, spiritual, even moral asset.

The doctrine itself, as we now know it, emerged in response to ideological pressures. Once the victory over the Bourbon Restoration and official neoclassicism had been secured, the alliance between French Romantics and pure aesthetes began to come apart. A year or so after the 1830 Revolution, those writers staking their claim on *poésie pure* soon found themselves the target of attacks from all political camps: from conservative Catholics who longed for the old regime, from progressive republicans upholding bourgeois virtues, and from the curious mix of technocratic cultism and utopian socialism that was the Saint-Simon movement. As the decade unfolded, the French press took aim at the idea and proponents of *l'art pour l'art* with broadsides that now seem astonishing in their ferocity. The debate continued off and on throughout the century, spreading beyond Paris and reappearing in various guises in the course of the twentieth as well.

Reading through French newspapers and magazines of the early 1830s, one encounters virtually no defenses of, though plenty of polemics against, emergent notions of aestheticism and *l'art pour l'art*. Such disproportionate representation suggests that the idea at this point still existed largely as an underground phenomenon, in the depths of café gossip and street Bohemia, with scant status in the world of respectable opinion. Yet, despite its initial powerlessness and disreputability, the attitude later drew vicious verbal snipes as well as full-scale salvos from the high custodians of French culture.

Catholic-minded critics lamented the lack of any engagement between militant aestheticism and traditional religion, or at least they blamed so mistaken a stance on the sterile secularism of the modern age. Armand Carrel, the editor of the conservative daily *Le National*, thought "a school that cultivates art as an end and not as a means" to be in "error;" he dismissed it as a "deplorable and ridiculous literary craze" and serenely declared that "there has never been a purely artistic literature." [39]

An angrier Alexis de Saint-Cheron, in the handsome and more noncommittal monthly *L'Artiste*, saw in aestheticist doctrine "the sole possible expression, in art, of a society that chooses to live without belief, authority, or purpose. When Man abandons Catholicism he can conceive no other aim than . . . material satisfaction of his senses and appetites. In the same way, when art abandons Catholicism it has nothing to do but contemplate itself in its fantasies, through whatever shape or form, whether beautiful or grotesque, is dreamt up by

its imagination." Owing to the "brutal divorce between inspiration
and technique," Saint-Cheron continues, we see "[m]an kneeling before form, as if before the golden calf"; we see "art outside religious
law." To Saint-Cheron the only great poets are Catholic, and he looks
back longingly at those artists (Palestrina, Bach) who found their inspiration in Jesus Christ.[40]

To the left side of the Catholic polemicists stood what to this day
remains the other France: the secular-minded, anticlerical, antifeudal
inheritors of the civic-republican ideals of 1789, who ranged ideologically from Enlightenment-style freethinkers, to beneficiaries of the
Napoleonic order (as was Victor Hugo), to the early socialists of the
Saint-Simon school.

The latter, with its odd blend of rationality and dreaminess, merits a brief look. Count Henri de Rouvroy de Saint-Simon (1760–1825)
and his posthumous followers had little to say about the distribution
of property, though their doctrine enshrined industry and had a cult
of *les industriels,* meaning those who work, at all levels of production.
Saint-Simon thinking concerned itself rather with a kind of inner
sympathy for fellow human beings, and also with the spiritual and
intellectual power of a society's administrative sectors. The ultimate
objective of Saint-Simon thought was to organize all knowledge and
apply it scientifically.

The movement eventually fizzled out for lack of a broad social
base, but many of its cadres went on to the upper reaches of France's
banking, engineering, and railway industries. Their ethos, it has been
said, survives today among Rotarians, Kiwanis, and other voluntary
associations, which constitute a kind of "right-wing Saint-Simonism."

The Saint-Simon view of the arts had its complexities, elements
that might encourage both "aesthetic" and "social" ideologues. The
Romantics could find comfort in the Saint-Simonian idea that the artist is a being apart from society, that art is a priesthood and the artist
a priest.[41] On the other hand, given its fundamentally social conception of art, Saint-Simon doctrine came to see self-isolation in a world
of beauty as a sign of inferiority and decadence. As Saint-Simon himself puts it, the poet "is no longer the divine singer, placed at the
head of society as man's interpreter to give him laws." The new artists are those "who ceaselessly impress on mankind the progressive

movement which has made man come up from the crudest brutality to the degree of civilization we have attained." For Saint-Simon, "the men who deserve to be called poets are those to whom the secret of social destiny has been revealed only because their love of mankind made it an imperious need for them to discover it." [42]

The rational faith and optimism of Enlightenment France lived on in the Saint-Simonians; the very name of the *Revue Encyclopédique,* which followed the Saint-Simon line, suggests a continuity in its echo of the eighteenth-century encyclopedists. Accordingly, Hippolyte Fortoul in that magazine in 1833 launched an attack on those artists who "have made selfishness a system, sensualism a religion." The theory of *l'art pour l'art,* he observes, has no "avowed and complete code, but circulates incognito in some misleading prefaces." Seeing a genuine threat from what he calls "the Leviathan that we must fight against," Fortoul appeals to the young to resist "the seductions of this prostitute that glides mysteriously amongst us." [43]

An exemplary case is that of the newspaper *Le Globe* (1824–32), founded by a former lycée professor, P. F. Dubois. Remarkable early on for its high level of discourse and its broad cultural interests, *Le Globe* then had a freewheeling, cosmopolitan, nonsectarian outlook summed up by its original subtitle: *Recueil Philosophique, Politique et Littéraire.* In its first incarnation, *Le Globe* does not adhere to any specific line on aesthetics but is open to a variety of views, including positive reports on literature in Germany.

In 1831 the subtitle of *Le Globe* became *Journal de la Doctrine de Saint-Simon,* and in 1832 it changed once again, to *de la Religion Saint-Simonienne.* The contents also show a marked shift: political reporting all but monopolizes its columns, whereas cultural affairs merit scant attention. When any idea concerning literature elicits discussion, it is along the lines of one A. Rousseau in 1832: "God makes the poet for the people." [44] In a case of aesthetic politics making strange bedfellows, Armand Carrel in the conservative *Le National* praises the writers of *Le Globe* for having shed the ideology of *l'art pour l'art* after 1830.[45]

That first shock of the new literary market and its indifference to poetry, combined with the attacks from social-minded polemicists and the demands being placed on the lyric art, prompted Théophile

Gautier to write the still-classic preface to his erotic novel, *Mademoiselle de Maupin* (1836). A product of the overheated climate of aesthetic debate, Gautier's highly ironic—and at times even flippant—essay nonetheless transcends its circumstantial origins and survives today as the first full, mature manifesto for the doctrine of *l'art pour l'art*. Though Gautier may not have been fully cognizant of the fact, the piece builds on and is permeated by the popularized, bastardized brand of Kantianism that had become common currency in literary Paris. "Nothing is truly beautiful unless it is useless; everything useful is ugly. . . . The most useful place in a house is the lavatory" (39).[46]

Moreover, as befits Gautier the poet, his preface fairly bristles with attacks on the book business, the newspaper business, and on industrialism per se. "A novel has two uses," he says, "one material, the other spiritual. . . . The material use [includes] the thousand francs for the author's pocket . . . ; for the publisher it means a fine thoroughbred horse . . . ; for the paper merchant, another factory on another stream, and a means of spoiling a fine site" (37). Despite the gap that yawns between that hypothetical novelist's thousand francs and the lucrative rewards that accrue to the businessmen, Gautier invokes novels because those literary products were at least selling, whereas poetry books were not, as he had recently learned from disappointing experience.

Many of Gautier's poems are attacks on technology. Taking a mocking tone toward the emerging technological environment, Gautier in an eloquent passage remarks with feisty glee that literature does not contribute to material "progress" as do railroads, syringes, and seamless boots. Focusing more specifically on poetry itself, he remarks that metaphors, rhymes, and metonymies have no "utility" for cobblers or cotton makers but are extremely useful for poets. (Had Kant been still alive, he might have remarked that such devices were "purposive" within an art that has no explicit "purpose.") Gautier's most impassioned invective, however, is reserved for the newspapers, regardless of their ideological hue, and he summons up his purplest prose in exhorting King Louis Philippe to shut them down forever. Ironically, Gautier was to spend thirty-six years as a daily drama reviewer, hating every minute of it, feeling deprived of the time to do what he loved best: craft exquisite verses.

Similar sentiments were expressed a few decades later by Mallarmé, whose poetic theme, his obsession really, is the very act of poetry and its problematic status in an indifferent or hostile world. Unlike Gautier or Baudelaire, Mallarmé never worked in journalism and instead established a pattern for many twentieth-century poets by teaching (English at lycée level) for a living. In "Quant au livre," his set of densely wrought essays, he repeatedly singles out the prime culprit for poetry's woes—the publishing apparatus and what he calls sarcastically "the lofty business of letters." He alludes sombrely to the "extraordinary overproduction" of the press, its abject dependence on advertising, and its exclusion of art. He deplores the success of serial novels at the expense of verse and states that poetry "doesn't sell" and moreover "shouldn't be sold." Poetry, he believes, is true "master of the book," and has nothing to do with book ads, book displays, or book salesmen. Somewhere in the wilderness, "away from and ignored by advertisements, the counters collapsing underneath volumes," the poet lives solely through a private pact with beauty.[47] By contrast, in *Notre-Dame de Paris* Hugo calls print nothing less than "the greatest event in History";[48] he envisions the human mind liberated by the press and rejoices that print will kill off Gothic architecture, whereas Gautier in *Mademoiselle de Maupin* laments that "books have killed architecture" much as newspapers have killed books and artillery has killed physical courage (52).

Excluded from the marketplace, poetry found itself banished from its former cultural uses and applications. At various times in the past the craft of verse had enjoyed ties with Renaissance humanism, courtly neoclassicism, Christian devotion, and secular drama; during the eighteenth century it had been a respectable vehicle for intellectual exposition and epical or comical narrative. But in the newly industrialized marketplace poetry saw itself very much abandoned and alone. Shunted into a near-absolute autonomy it had never really wanted, poetry became a pure art of words, paradigmatic, quasi-simultaneous, a medium intensely focused on its rhythms and dictions, its metaphors and phonology, with no major role to play in a literary culture overwhelmingly narrative, mimetic, and linear. The noble ideal of Art for Art's Sake became the consolation prize for those poets who were dissatisfied with prose but couldn't write verse for money. Few were in much of a position to think otherwise.

Meanwhile, as regards beauty, we have come not full circle but half-circle, to a diametrical opposite. Within a generation or two, Kant's and Schiller's grand theories concerning the uses of art had been altered beyond recognition. Where the German thinker and his playwright-disciple had propounded a receptivity to beauty as the necessary first step toward moral growth and civic education, the French poets and their allies claimed beauty not as a first step toward anything at all but as a self-contained, all-sufficient, even solipsistic experience. In reaction to the moral and social expectations of Catholic, liberal, and socialist critics, France's poets generally took the defensive position that moral and social concerns — whether immediate or ultimate — have no relevance whatsoever to their lyric craft. The literary doctrine of *l'art pour l'art,* as it turns out, came to signify precisely the opposite of what its Enlightenment forebears had originally intended.

Kant and Schiller would most likely have been baffled at so total a transformation of their aesthetic thought and projects. They probably would have felt equally bewildered at the range of political-ideological company that *l'art pour l'art* would eventually keep, as discussed in chapter 7.

CHAPTER 3

The Diffusion of the Doctrine 1: England

The triumph of aesthetic separatism in France came as the result of a conjunction of several key factors: the diffusion and distortion of Kantian ideas, the opposition of young writers to Restoration-sponsored neoclassicism, the emergence of the industrial book trade and the daily press, and the subsequent marginalization of poets in the new literary marketplace. Over the next one hundred years assorted doctrines of *poésie pure* became a major strand in the history of French verse, and the concept spread further, to the novel, with certain practitioners of the so-called *nouveau roman* after 1945, notably Robbe-Grillet and Butor. The Frenchman-as-aesthete, as cultivator of beautiful forms, is a well-known stereotype that nonetheless has roots in certain French realities. The set phrase objets d'art comes trailing an aesthetic refinement and ideological baggage that the plain and prosy "art objects" does not.

The question arises, however, as to why Art for Art's Sake first took hold in France rather than in England, where after all the market economy had gotten off to an earlier start and industrial development had advanced much further. Significantly, the British are not generally regarded as a nation of aesthetes—in contrast to the image of the French. The very fact that we associate aestheticism in England largely with Oscar Wilde and the 1890s suggests that Art for Art's Sake never cast deep roots in English literary theory and practice and that the English aesthetes may be something of a special case. In fact, the more influential British literary critics of the last two centuries— Matthew Arnold, T. S. Eliot in his fashion, F. R. Leavis and his wife Q. D. Leavis—have ultimately taken their stand on the moral and spiritual worth of literature, stressing its abiding and enriching ties with traditional values.

Why France, then, and not England as the nation of aesthetes? The question is a vast and complex one; the correspondingly complex answer can be found in the differing political and ideological histories of the two countries. What follows is, of necessity, only a rough and sketchy overview, to be more fully elaborated, one hopes, by trained historians.

In France, the whirlwind that began in 1789 and subsided only with the final defeat of Napoleon in 1814 displaced all kinds of long-established ideas, clearing the way for radically new cultural notions and ruptures in thought. In England, by contrast, the pact between aristocratic and bourgeois forces had endured since 1688, with much blending, blurring, and compromising of respective class values. This English characteristic was to persist well into the nineteenth century: whereas Britain has its Reform Bills, France has her Revolutions of 1830, 1848, and 1871.

The contrasting relationship of liberalism to government and to religion in England and in France claims attention. French liberalism, reflecting its dissident origins in the Enlightenment philosophes and the *Encyclopédie,* was (unlike its English counterpart) ardently anti-clerical. As de Tocqueville points out, the first and final impulse of the revolutionary movement was antireligion. The philosophes and their followers had "attacked the [Catholic] Church with a sort of studious ferocity," and while Christianity had by then lost much of its ancient hold on the Continental European mind, it was in France especially that irreligion would become "an all-prevailing passion, fierce, intoler-ant, and predatory." With the dynamics of revolution unleashed as a fact of life, "men's minds were in a state of utter confusion; they knew neither what to hold on to, nor where to stop."[1] Among the long-range spiritual consequences was that even after Napoleon many educated French people replaced the traditional Catholic faith with a variety of secular ideals. This break with the old thinking, along with a readiness for the new, laid the mental groundwork for the eventual emergence of aestheticist attitudes and a quasireligion of Art.

So firmly had the ideas of the Enlightenment gained ground with broad sectors of French opinion that in April 1814, at the very be-ginning of the Bourbon Restoration, Louis XVIII promised, among other things, representative government and freedom of religion and of the press. Such concessions strongly suggest how far from "abso-lute" were the reinstated monarchy and its political-clerical outlook.

In the 1820s, granted, there was a marked increase in the numbers of men and women joining Catholic orders; education returned to the hands of the clergy; and the coronation of Louis's brother and successor Charles X at Reims Cathedral in 1824 had "all the appartus of . . . religious revival." Despite all this, however, the hidden, underlying truth was that "anticlericalism had driven too deeply into French soil to be easily uprooted." New men of property understandably resented the indemnities to returning émigrés and the renewed clerical influence. Hence, in 1827, as King Charles reviewed the National Guard of Paris, from the crowd there came cries of "Down with the Jesuits!" and "Vive la liberté de la presse." [2] The first French Revolution may have been militarily and politically defeated, but its ways of thinking had nonetheless survived as a force to be reckoned with.

In England the dynamic was precisely the reverse. Whereas the French middle classes, being part of the Third Estate, were de facto allies of the revolutionary process, England's new manufacturers and old-line aristocrats closed ranks with British officialdom's wars against the revolution and Napoleon. Counterrevolutionary policy abroad, meanwhile, had its equivalent at home. Throughout the 1790s habeas corpus was suspended in order to solidify English support for war. Most of the major radical leaders had been either exiled or imprisoned. During that decade and after, editors, journalists, authors, and other English people who dared to defend the French Revolution or simply to dissent from British *contra* policy were tried and often imprisoned. Among them was Kyd Wake, "a Gosport bookbinder, sentenced at the end of 1796 to five years hard labor, and to the pillory, for saying, 'No George, no war.'" Another dissenter, a basketmaker in Somerset, was jailed for having said, "I wish success to the French." [3] Even advocates of liberal reform were branded subversive—for instance, the radical shoemaker Thomas Hardy, whose struggles on behalf of representative government led to his trial for high treason. In the meantime there was an unequal class war. The Frame-Breaking Bill of 1812 made it a capital felony to destroy any industrial apparatus. During that year and in 1813, some three dozen Luddites were executed by hanging in Chester, Manchester, and Yorkshire.

The domestic repression continued well after the British military victory at Waterloo. Public meetings were largely prohibited; trade union activity remained illegal through the mid-1820s; rioters and dissident printers were subjected to legal actions; and radicals lived under frequent surveillance by spies and provocateurs.[4] The repressive wave peaked in what became known as the Peterloo Massacre, when a mass demonstration in St. Peter's Field, Manchester, calling for equal representation, repeal of the Corn Laws, and annual Parliaments, was fired on by yeomanry and hussar troops, killing eleven demonstrators and wounding hundreds.

Among the ideological and cultural results of the English counter-revolution was the strengthening of traditional Christian sentiment and organized religion, to the benefit of both the official High Church and the newer evangelical sects. With regard to the latter, the Napoleonic Wars saw the growth of itinerant lay preacher activity in Britain; the evangelical educators, in turn, perceived their mission as furnishing moral rescue to the children of the poor, rather than teaching them literacy and cognitive skills. At the same time a sect such as Methodism, "with its open chapel doors, did offer to the uprooted and abandoned of the Industrial Revolution some kind of community to replace the older community-patterns which were being displaced." The Methodists in fact enjoyed major recruiting advances in this period. According to the church's claims, Methodist faithful around 1789 numbered 60,000; the figure topped 90,000 in 1795, climbed to 107,000 in 1805 and 154,000 in 1811, and reached 237,000 in 1817.[5]

As is well known, the first generation of English Romantic poets —Wordsworth, Coleridge, and Southey—started out as ardent supporters of the French Revolution. Wordsworth in his travels through France in the 1790s befriended and was strongly influenced by revolutionary sympathizers from the upper class. Although he personally identified with the moderate Girondin forces, neither the execution of Louis XVI nor the later persecution of the Girondins by Jacobin extremists was to alter his essentially positive view of the revolution. Significantly, most of Wordsworth's very best poems, as well as the new poetics set forth in his preface to the *Lyrical Ballads*, date from or originated in his period as rebel and dissident.

Coleridge, for his part, inherited a rebel streak from his clergy-man father, who had once attacked Britain's war against the American colonists. Later, at the crowded and tyrannical Christ's Church Charity School in London, the adolescent Samuel Coleridge witnessed the enthusiasm about the news of the French Revolution when it first reached students there. He got a whiff of official repression at Cambridge University, where he saw a good friend lose his scholarship because of his republican views and a professor fired and brought to trial for his unorthodox opinions and his critique of British war policy in America. Coleridge himself quit the university a month before graduating, refusing to declare adherence to the thirty-nine articles of the Church of England, an oath then formally required to earn a degree. He moved on to London, where he gained some reputation as a radical young poet, and in Bristol he lectured in strenuous opposition to the domestic antisedition laws and the war on France. He frankly styled himself a Jacobin, and his pamphlet entitled *Fire, Famine, and Slaughter* took aim at the economic ill-consequences of the war—activities that led the government to spy on him.

After 1800 the combination of Napoleon's military aggressiveness and war fever in England pushed the first Romantics into the conservative camp. Wordsworth's own growing family responsibilities, along with his rural remoteness from political issues, facilitated his rightward move, and the generous gifts he received from the baronet Sir George Beaumont, along with a much-desired government sinecure, made the full shift all but inevitable. In his subsequent verse and prose Wordsworth wrote in favor of the established Church, the reactionary Congress of Vienna, a French Royalist, and bond slavery. Coleridge in turn laid to rest his earlier religious doubts, wrote articles favoring war with France, and saw the Restoration of the Bourbon monarchs as a step toward liberty.[6]

The second generation of English Romantics, by contrast, carried on the youthful radicalism of their lyric predecessors. Having been too young to share in the revolutionary high fervor of the 1790s, they were also mercifully spared the numbing disillusionment of the ensuing two decades. Domestic counterrevolutionary repression was what Shelley and Keats experienced during their brief lives, and the two were both wise and well-situated enough to understand it as an unprincipled power play. Indeed, they saw their own literary friends and associates (notably Leigh and John Hunt) being hauled into court and receiving fines and prison sentences, which inevitably alerted them to the duplicity of Britain's official claims to be fighting tyranny.

Shelley's entire life combated the British status quo. His aristocratic family could boast radical and atheist antecedents; his own rebelliousness earned him trouble with the authorities at Oxford, who eventually expelled him for writing a pamphlet entitled *The Necessity of Atheism*. In 1812 in Dublin he distributed another pamphlet, protesting British colonial rule, while his fiery speech at a rally there made newspaper headlines. Over the years Shelley was to devour a vast number of books about the French Revolution, both pro and con. Appropriately, themes of revolt and repression dominate all of his longer poems. *The Masque of Anarchy,* a memorial to the Peterloo Massacre dead, calls on their survivors to "rise like lions after slumber" and "shake your chains to earth like dew." Even that anthology favorite "Ode to the West Wind" can be construed not as a nature poem but as a lyric paean to the sweep of revolution.[7] Still, Shelley was no injudicious or uncritical celebrant of the revolutionary cause. He was concerned lest a populace not fully prepared for political responsibilities might abuse its power, a subtheme that colors his poetic theory.

One seldom thinks of Keats in terms of dissidence, yet his own political opinions, and most of his social circle, were of a staunchly radical and oppositionist cast. Beginning in his teens he doubted orthodox Christian doctrine, and in time came to agree with Voltaire's phrase about religion being a "pious fraud." Young Keats's dissenting views worried his friend George Felton Mathew, who thought him "a fault-finder with everything established."[8] Among Keats's early poems are a sonnet to the Polish revolutionary Kosciuszko and another "Written on the Day that Mr. Leigh Hunt Left Prison."

Unlike Shelley, Keats had no prospects of inheriting wealth; once he had abandoned his medical studies, some other source of income had to be located. As happened with Gautier in France, Keats got a start in theater criticism; he was good at it and hoped to continue with it. (One can only speculate as to how Keats would have felt about journalistic routine had he lived a few more decades.) Nevertheless Keats's scribbling plans were mingled with ideological commitments. Shortly after the Peterloo events, he declared in a letter to Charles Brown, "I will write on the liberal side of the question, for whoever will pay me." Later that year he communicated the same designs to C. W. Dilke: "I am determined to spin . . . any thing for sale. Yea I will traffic. Any thing but Mortgage my Brain to Blackwood. . . . I hope sincerely I shall be able to put a Mite of help to the Liberal side of the Question before I die." [9]

Shelley and Keats lived too briefly either to bring their views to full maturity or to find prosperous refuge in conservatism. Their energetic if truncated life stories represent a second wave of Romantic revolt soon to be forgotten in the consolidation of English hegemony during a protracted Victorian Age. Their example would indeed be outlived and eclipsed by a Wordsworth, a Coleridge, and a Southey all safely aligned with Britain's counterrevolutionary project. Formerly rebels, the three elder statesmen, fully reconciled with official England, would help smooth the literary transition to the distinctive cultural values of Victorianism.

Meanwhile the resurgence of Christian doctrine in nineteenth-century England had definite, palpable consequences at every level of literary thought and practice, from poets laureate to the humblest of book reviews. Leading journals of the Victorian era subscribed to the notion that literature should be at the service of morals; the prose style, accordingly, tended toward the preachy. One scholar, upon examining *Poole's Index to Periodical Literature,* notes an astounding number of articles such as "Art and Morality" and "Ethics of Art." As late as 1870, a negative review of Tennyson in *Fraser's Magazine* reflected on the moral utility of literature. The ideal was that of the poet-as-prophet, and the aim was to impose the Victorian-Christian sensibility on letters.[10] Not surprisingly, many of the articles on contemporary French literature dwell on the moral superiority of England. To some extent, France in the nineteenth century fulfilled for English minds a cultural-political function analogous to that provided by the Soviet Union for Americans during the cold war. The Other, the rival nation across the straits, stood as an inverted mirror representing radicalism, atheism, hedonism, and especially loose morals—everything that England supposedly was not.

Hence the dominant British aesthetic that emerged in contradistinction to French values, was what, retrospectively, we might call moralist realism. As William Gaunt remarks, "The discipline of industry had led . . . to the affirmation of moral principle. . . . That art might go contrary to moral principles or leave them out of account seemed utterly outrageous." [11] In this regard the contrasting development of the two great public poets in nineteenth-century England and France is particularly revealing. Whereas Alfred Lord Tennyson speaks in the melting middle-class tones of Victorian piety and celebrates Empire, Victor Hugo's thunderous voice instead carries on the republican enthusiasms of 1789 and, with socialist overtones, sings out for universal brotherhood and the liberation of humanity.

The theory of verse set forth by the English Romantics stops considerably short of any definitive conceptions of Art for Art's Sake. Inasmuch as the lyrists themselves were either openly siding with Britain's counterrevolution or standing opposed to conservative repression, the idea of a literary art splendidly divorced from the facts of social and political life could not yet enter into their poetics. There was also between France and England a key difference in the intellectual level of the major ideologists. Whereas French readers learned of Kantian philosophy via the elegant though facile publicist work of Mme. de Staël and Professor Victor Cousin, the English had in Coleridge a far deeper and more reliable initial exponent of German aesthetics, who (unlike Staël or Cousin) was an accomplished practicing poet too.

Coleridge went to live in Germany in 1797, with the twin objectives of learning the language and seeking some replacement for his erstwhile radical energies. The long process culminated in the *Biographia Literaria*, that critical classic whose knotty yet rich theoretical investigations are those of a genuine thinker, a serious intellect too well acquainted with German philosophy to be making separatist inferences about poetry and art. Coleridge himself has harsh words for those shallow followers of Kant who, "with a very scanty portion of his spirit, had adopted his dynamic ideas only as a more refined species of mechanics."

Coleridge does reject the didactic (in the broadest sense of the word) view of poetry, a premise encapsulated in his well-known formula "the heresy of paraphrase." (He even reproaches Wordsworth for attempting to elevate readers with his verse.) Nevertheless Coleridge is not indifferent to the moral side of poetry, and indeed he stresses the poet's capacity to address the entirety of our inner being. Rather than preach a separate and all-sufficient agenda of beauty, Coleridge instead affirms that the poet "brings the whole soul of man into activity, with the subordination of its faculties to each other, according to their relative worth and dignity. He diffuses a . . . spirit of unity that blends and . . . fuses, each into each, by that synthetic . . . power . . . of imagination." [12] Poetry, then, helps unify our mental faculties, not subdivide them, stimulates their mutual interaction, not their isolation.

Shelley's *A Defence of Poetry* expounds a theory that in certain broad features resembles that of the mature Coleridge. Written in 1821, it did not see print until 1840. The immediate influence behind its publication was Thomas Love Peacock's *The Four Ages of Poetry,* wherein lyric art is proclaimed a kind of atavistic holdover from our barbarous past, a medium of scant use to modern philosophers, statesmen, or scientists, one whose primitive, prerational audience is fated to diminution. Peacock's is obviously a bleak vision for anyone committed to poetry. In the larger context of world history some equally pressing concerns helped motivate the *Defence.* Like Schiller in the 1790s, Shelley was at heart a Girondin who felt intensely preoccupied with two interrelated if contradictory issues: the spiritual bankruptcy of feudal, monarchical, clerical anciens régimes and the potential of the revolutionary mass for irrational, directionless fury. Shelley allots to poetry the long-term role of tempering and unifying these forces. Finally, with the post-Napoleonic peace, a predatory laissez-faire capitalism had been set loose in England, and—as Shelley sees it—a calculating egoism had come to hold sway over men's souls.

The *Defence,* then, is a reply to all these factors combined. Shelley starts out by passionately summing up what is known to all writers and readers of poetry: namely, that poetic language "is vitally metaphorical," and that its words "become through time, signs for portions of classes of thought" (26). (As a casual example note how, among the Anglophone literate, Hamlet's metaphorized reflections on suicide have become *the* reflections on suicide.) In the same vein Shelley observes that poetry "expresses arrangements of language, and especially metrical language" (27) and moreover builds on a "harmonious recurrence of sound"—both factors as "indispensable [as] the words themselves" (29). Rhythm, repetition, and rhyme: these are the essential poetic staples, eloquently singled out by the lyrist Shelley, much as the theorist Roman Jakobson was to do in his more sober, scientific examination of the phenomena almost a century and a half later.[13]

Shelley then goes on to argue that "poetry strengthens the faculty which is the organ of the *moral* nature of man, in the same manner as exercise strengthens a limb" (33; emphasis added).[14] To Shelley, "whatever strengthens and purifies the affections, . . . and adds spirit to sense, is useful" (49). Moreover he attributes a profound social function to poetry. He looks with dismay upon a time in which "the rich have become richer, and the poor have become poorer"; consequently "the vessel of state is driven between the Scylla and Charibdis of anarchy and despotism" (50). So lamentable a situation Shelley blames on "an unmitigated exercise of the calculating faculty." With the overdevelopment of rational egoism Shelley sees "the mechanical arts" growing in disproportion to "the creative faculty," and similarly "the abuse of all [technical] invention" bringing about "the exasperation of the inequality of mankind" (52). Shelley's sombre prophecy has been borne out globally over two centuries of subsequent history.

Poetry is thus all the more desirable in those periods when "an excess of the selfish and calculating principle" leads to "the accumulation of the materials of external life" to a degree that our internal capacities cannot assimilate (53). The poetical faculty serves as an opposition force that "creates new materials of knowledge, and power, and pleasure" and that furthermore "engenders in the mind a desire to reproduce and arrange them according to a certain rhythm and order, which may be called *the beautiful and the good*" (52; emphasis added). Shelley's account of the role and functioning of poetry greatly resembles, as I have suggested, the aesthetic theory of Schiller, who defended art and beauty as necessary components in the total education of the soul during times both of social upheaval and of narrow specialization.

Keats has on occasion been adjudged a precursor to aestheticism, partly on the basis of his famously enigmatic line "Beauty is Truth, Truth Beauty" in the "Ode on a Grecian Urn." Doubtless Keats strongly felt himself a poet rather than a prophet or publicist. In a letter commenting to Shelley about the latter's *Cenci*, Keats suggests, "you might curb your magnanimity and be more of an artist" (16 August 1820). And in a renowned passage, Keats in a letter to J. H. Reynolds (3 February 1818) observes, "We hate poetry that has a palpable design on us—and if we do not agree, seems to put its hand in its breeches pocket. Poetry should be great & unobtrusive, a thing which enters into one's soul, and does not startle it or amaze it with itself but its subject." One can imagine such a speculation drawing nods of approval from Kant; analogous notions crop up in the poetics of Swinburne and Pater, and many a contemporary lyrist would deem Keats's statement unexceptionable. Regarding the role of the aesthetic, Keats in his celebrated letter (to his brothers George and Tom) on "negative capability" further suggests that "with a great poet the sense of Beauty overcomes every other consideration, or rather obliterates all consideration" (27 December 1817).

The larger conceptual context of Keats's theorizing, however, cancels out any suggestion that Keats was moving toward aesthetic separatism. In a letter to Benjamin Bailey (22 November 1817), Keats reflects on "the truth of the Imagination—What the imagination seizes as Beauty must be the truth—whether it existed before or not." Keats here is not intimating that whatever we imagine is also true. Rather, he is positing an intuitive epistemology whereby the imagination can directly apprehend beauty and truth, without the customary intervention of our other mental faculties. Indeed, in the same letter Keats goes on to admit, "I have never been able to perceive how anything can be known to truth by consequitive [*sic*] reasoning."

Keats in that letter yearns en passant, "O for a Life of Sensations rather than of Thoughts!" Nevertheless in a subsequent missive to Reynolds (3 May 1818), Keats celebrates all knowledge as "excellent and calculated towards a great whole." He therefore feels enormously pleased at not having rid himself of his medical books, for he now can see the importance of all knowledge, recognizes that a pure, untutored sensation is not sufficient and indeed can lead us to sink deep and be "blown up"; sensation fused with knowledge, by contrast, enables us to soar. In brief, our nonrational faculties should be connected with reason and truth. Not accidentally, Keats admired Wordsworth's special gift for combining intellect with knowledge of the human heart.

Drawing the same sorts of links, in the "negative capability" letter Keats ventures to explain the "excellence" and "intensity" of art in that it is "capable of making all disagreeables evaporate, from their being in close relationship with Beauty & Truth." Keats could even say in autumn of 1818 that he was "ambitious of doing the world some good," and see his verse as one possible means to this end. Within the full setting of Keats's total thought and the English poetics of his time, then, the somewhat problematical line "Beauty is Truth, Truth Beauty" may best be construed as posing those two entities neither as distinct nor as identical, but as unitary concepts, as partners within a larger whole. From the globalizing perspective of Coleridge, Shelley, and Keats, art and knowledge exist together, not in isolation, are one and indivisible, not separate or disconnected.

The foregoing helps illustrate, however schematically and imperfectly, the argument set forth at the beginning of this chapter: in brief, that, owing to a number of political and cultural factors, the early-nineteenth-century English mind, the mind of the poet included, was neither ready to stake out claims for a separate beauty nor prepared to recognize or even imagine such claims. To put it in the simplest possible terms: while *l'art pour l'art* was a major component of the French Romantic literary revolt, in English Romanticism it was not, and indeed did not yet so much as exist as a plausible notion. The reassertion of preestablished English values resulting from England's counterrevolution had set informal limits on aesthetic debate and precluded any radical departures from existing doctrine. This *mentalité* was to persist throughout the century, and, significantly, the first English writer to make beauty the central focus of his thought— John Ruskin (1819–1900)—would do so in the name of either Christian concerns or secular social ideals, as we shall see shortly.

Ruskin, one of the towering figures instantly associated with Victorian aesthetics, was also an enormously complex and contradictory man. He is one of the great architectural critics and is of course the best-known nineteenth-century art critic in any language, who in his writing succeeded in "mak[ing] art criticism a major prose form."[15] His judgments, which today may seem commonplace, in their time were fairly bold—for example, his recognizing the artistic worth of Turner's canvases or his discoursing at length on the value of Gothic architecture, dismissed before him as dated and grotesque. An important transitional figure, Ruskin produced work that is a synthesis and culmination of mid-Victorian thinking, yet at the same time it is a key precursor of the assorted heresies of the later Victorian aesthetes (of whom the older Ruskin strenuously disapproved, accusing their ideas of a "moral deficiency").[16]

In certain ways Ruskin is to nineteenth-century English aestheticism what the seminal Enlightenment figures were to French *l'art pour l'art*. Like Shaftesbury, the youthful Ruskin was schooled entirely at home, either by his mother, Margaret, or by a local pastor, Reverend Andrews, and indeed he never set foot in an educational institution until matriculating as a university student at Oxford. Like Kant, the thinker Ruskin was concerned with the larger mental unity of our cognitive, moral, and aesthetic faculties rather than with their forceful separation. Like Schiller, the publicist Ruskin formulated his ideas in response to the political climate of his day, and also like Schiller, his art theory comes well-informed by his experience as art practitioner. Ruskin, it should be remembered, was a skilled and observant draftsman of the highest order, one whose works "just miss greatness" and who (according to Kenneth Clark) produced "some of the most beautiful architectural drawings ever executed."[17] So sharp was his eye that a treatise on geomorphology by J. E. Marr cites Ruskin's *Modern Painters* and acknowledges the art critic's mastery of the study of landscape.[18] One may speculate on the potential of Ruskin as artist had he focused his chief energies on the brush and canvas instead of pen and paper.

It has been observed that Ruskin's mind and stance resemble those of the German idealists—of whose work, ironically, he read precious little. Indeed he scarcely knew the history of aesthetics and held in low regard what he termed "the cobwebs of German metaphysics." [19] Ruskin's impassioned thought emerges from more local and idiosyncratic origins. First of these was the King James Bible, which was read in a daily ritual at his childhood home and which the adult Ruskin could still quote at length from memory. Scripture was in turn filtered through the distinctive ethos of Victorian morality — a mode of feeling that Ruskin never abandoned. Its cadences moreover served as model for the exhortative rhythms and prophetic thunder of his prose. When John was a young boy his parents entertained long-term dreams of a bishopric for him, and while the hope did not materialize, a religiously inculcated Ruskin was eventually to displace his Anglo-Christian pietisms into his own personal religion of art, becoming a kind of bishop of art criticism.

Another formative element in Ruskin's thought was his profound sensitivity to visual beauty, a receptivity to which he gave special and permanent expression in his art crusades. This artistic strength, coupled with personal mission, has its converse side in the near-biblical intensity of Ruskin's abhorrence for the ugliness, vulgarity, and noise holding sway in industrial-capitalist England. (It bears reminding that in Ruskin's time many nonliberal thinkers deemed art and beauty incompatible with capitalism and democracy.) As early as his first book, *Modern Painters* (1843), published in his twenty-fourth year, Ruskin hopes "to make the study of art an instrument of gigantic moral power." [20] Dwelling on the possible "violation of truth" in architecture, he finds such a flaw "as truly deserving of reprobation as any other moral delinquency." [21] And, showing his passionate concern for the social environment beyond the aesthetic sphere, Ruskin asserts in an 1859 lecture, "Beautiful art can only be produced by people who have beautiful things about them." [22] By the same token he lets fly at a Great Britain that "educates a mercenary population ready to produce any quantity of bad articles to anybody's order." [23] Ruskin was not one to praise inferior art that was "morally correct."

Ruskin's combined moral and aesthetic imperative is at the same time linked to a profound concern for the fullness, the wholeness of individual human beings. On repeated occasions he speaks out against the division of labor and specifically decries the separation of manual from intellectual work, noting that "it is not, truly speaking, the labor that is divided, but the men: — Divided into mere segments of men — broken into small fragments and crumbs of life; so that all the little piece of intelligence that is left in a man . . . exhausts itself in making the point of a pen or the head of a nail," for "we manufacture everything . . . except men." British industry may "blanch cotton, and strengthen steel, and refine sugar, but to brighten, to strengthen, to refine, or to form a single living spirit, never enters into our estimate of advantages." [24]

Ruskin, as noted, was educated in religion from his infancy — the Bible was his principal toy, as it were. A consequent religious feeling suffuses all of his works, on art as well as society. While his strictly Christian convictions began slackening from the time he reached Oxford, visual art became for him something like a divine beauty, a means of attaining a spiritual relationship with the world. [25]

In Ruskin's day, ideas of evolution were achieving a status of common currency among educated Britons, even before Darwin's scientific account of change in species would become a publishing legend. Other advances in knowledge — in geology, cosmology, and in biblical criticism — had similarly been eating away at the foundations of traditional Christian belief. The skepticism toward religiosity that had characterized the European Enlightenment was thus being revived and replicated in nineteenth-century England. And though these philosophical challenges to the established English pieties did not give rise to any of the harsh anticlericalisms endemic on the Continent, the eroding of the conventional Victorian-Christian creed did make inevitable the growth of alternate ways of thinking, notably socialism in politics and aestheticism in the arts.

John Ruskin specifically rejected Darwin's theories, yet belonged too much to the milieu of educated England not to be affected in great measure by the shift in mentality. In an era of slow decline in the intellectual persuasiveness of religion (a climate of opinion familiar to readers of Tennyson's and Arnold's more brooding verse), Ruskin was the first prominent Englishman to nourish and then preach what we now see as the religion of Art, though not yet of *l'art pour l'art*, strictly speaking. For Ruskin, beauty, morals, and truth belonged together as human concerns, even after he eventually abandoned the doctrinal Christian bases for that position. In time he would merge his aesthetic preoccupations with a socialist outlook (see chapter 7).

The decline of Ruskin's publicist powers, significantly, began with the unforeseen consequence of his indignant 1877 attack on one of Whistler's *Nocturne*s. Happening upon the piece during a visit to the Grosvenor Gallery, Ruskin felt doubly offended, by the painter's imperfect craft and by the high price being asked for the canvas. In what became his most famous phrase, Ruskin in an installment of *Fors Clavigera* heaped scorn on the "ill-educated conceit" of a "coxcomb" who dared to "ask two hundred guineas for flinging a pot of paint in the public's face." The American expatriate thereupon sued Ruskin for libel. Ruskin at first saw the lawsuit as an opportunity to defend his "principles of art economy" and express his disapproval of those new painters for whom art was, in his words, "mere ornament rather than edification." Owing to his tense state, however, Ruskin could not take the stand in court, and Whistler proceeded to win over the jury with his caustic wit and military-style bearing.[26]

That courtroom drama—legendary in the annals of art history—can be interpreted in a variety of ways: prophet vs. gadfly, critic vs. producer, lofty Briton vs. brash American, the yardstick of technical rigor vs. that of free originality, the academic vs. the Bohemian. For our purposes, the trial represents the vestigial traditionalism of a Ruskin confronted by an uncompromising (some might say intransigent) promoter and militant practitioner of Art for Art's Sake at its purest. As we know, Ruskin lost the case, and though he was required by the court to pay Whistler but a farthing in damages (approximately one U.S. penny), he personally never recovered from the ordeal. The outcome of the trial signals the defeat and slow withdrawal of Ruskin's social-minded, "religious" aestheticism, giving way to an aesthetic separatism whose adepts stand much closer to Whistler in their general doctrines (if not in temperament). Shortly thereafter, Ruskin resigned from his Oxford professorship.

Nonetheless Ruskin's peculiar synthesis of religion, society, and art is precisely the basis on which he still reaches modern readers. While his biblical bombast and personal oddities may well pose something of an embarrassment, he remains, along with Coleridge and Dr. Johnson, one of England's greater critics. Indeed, Ruskin's impassioned commitment to visual beauty and to the presumed benefits of art has its attractions in this era of highly technical and professionalized criticism, with its academic insistence on apparatus and method, terminology and protocol. The priesthood of English-speaking art critics now numbers somewhere in the thousands. Ruskin's strengths as well as weaknesses stem from his having been the sole major art cleric of his time and place, one who, moreover, believed firmly in his creed and could practice what he preached.

Walter Pater (1839–94), though in many respects John Ruskin's intellectual successor, also modified and simplified the elder critic's complex and wide-ranging thoughts into a more narrowly focused and summarizable position. Along with Oscar Wilde, Pater is, of course, the figure most commonly associated with late-Victorian aestheticism—though each man in his own way. Where Wilde became Art for Art's Sake's flamboyant publicist and court comedian, Pater served as its scrivening monk and taciturn priest, for whom the fine arts (as he himself says in the later essay "Style") provide "a sort of cloistral refuge from a certain vulgarity in the actual world," and who likewise finds in Milton and Thackeray "the uses of a religious 'retreat.'" [27] Once he arrived at Oxford as a scholarship student, he never left, having found in that late medieval setting a milieu well suited to his friar-like disposition.

Pater first read Ruskin in 1858, at age nineteen; the influence would remain for the rest of his life. However, as Harold Bloom appropriately points out, Pater made every effort to conceal that formative influence, in both thought and style. As a younger faculty colleague of the renowned art critic, Pater disagreed with Ruskin without openly saying so; Ruskin for his part sublimely ignored the younger Oxonian's extreme claims. Though Pater directly alludes to Ruskin only once in writing, and in a private letter at that, the grand old man's presence nonetheless underlies the Pater oeuvre. [28] Pater's long-term response was to create a system distinctly his own. Where a visionary Ruskin stressed the long-term links connecting beauty, morals, and truth, Pater the thinker would subsume all aspects of our lives to criteria of beauty alone. For Pater, aesthetics became ethics. (At one point during Pater's career as tutor, an Oxford undergraduate asked him why one should be good, to which Pater replied, "Because it is so beautiful.")[29] Similarly, in contrast to Ruskin's stentorian, vatic confidence, his talent for *speaking to* as well as defying the world, Pater forged an instrument appropriate to the timid soul he himself was, a prose style exquisite and indirect, languid with chiaroscuros.

A trait common to all the Victorian literary aesthetes is the eccentric personality, to whatever degree this may be cause or effect — or both. Pater well exemplifies the pattern. His father, a physician, died when Walter was but a boy; his sole games as a child were playing at clergyman and organizing mock processions; his Aunt Bessie hoped he would take holy orders. At age thirteen Walter was sent to King's School in Canterbury, England's oldest public school, founded in the seventh century. His favorite activity there was the occasional saint's day church processional, with its spectacle of white-surpliced scholars filing with reserve beneath the Gothic arches. He also wrote scores of poems and essays, many of them dealing with saints and celibacy. Isolated and unpopular, Pater loathed the snowball fights and sports, never learned cricket, and saw his fellow pupils by and large as "a pack of brutal . . . savages." During an attack by some ruffian elements, Pater received a kick in the knee that affected his gait for life. School friends would later recall Pater's simplicity; one referred to him as "the saintly boy."[30]

Pater's religious fervor caused concern among his friends and teachers, who worried lest he go so far as to turn Catholic. By 1858, when he enrolled at Queen's College in Oxford, however, his adolescent faith was in crisis, the result of his having read Charles Kingsley. During his undergraduate years he baited friends with antireligious and antibiblical jibes, alienating some old schoolmates from King's in the process. Still, even though at Oxford he would mingle neither with the religious revivalists of the era nor (it goes without saying) with the devil-may-care wine-and-revels set, Pater's happiest times as a student in fact were those at Queen's College chapel. He explained his attendance at services by saying, "It doesn't matter in the least what is said, as long as it is said beautifully."

Eventually Pater sold off or gave away his religious books (which led to further breaks with intimates) and also burned his juvenilia. Reading Darwin in 1860 further reinforced his doubts. On the other hand he still contemplated taking holy orders, and even said, "What fun it would be to be ordained and not to believe a single word of what you're saying!" Pater at age twenty-one had effectively lost his Christian faith, yet he came close to seeking ordination, whereupon some friends took it upon themselves to write to the bishop of London informing him of Pater's skeptical stance, thus aborting his attempt at playing the cleric as an adult.[31]

Pater's friends had mercifully spared him the life of a country parson, and in 1864 he was appointed a fellow of Brasenose College, rising to Actual Fellow after a year's probation. The bachelor rooms he held there until his death at age fifty-six were uncommonly austere, and his personal library took up just one set of bookshelves. (He most often borrowed.) Oxford was virtually his entire life, yet he proved to be neither a traditional scholar nor a career administrator. Among his regular lifelong duties were giving lectures and meeting every week with tutees, tasks that he performed acceptably at best, for he never even thought of himself as a professional educator. His lectures, delivered with his head bent down and eyes shielded by his hands, were overwrought and unsuited for oral delivery, clearly conceived not for listeners but for private readers. In his tutorials Pater was loyal, if aloof and shy, and his knowledge of Greek and Latin proved to be weak, though his students liked him and his later acolytes worshiped him.

Pater assisted at Brasenose chapel services with zealous regularity, and his deeply solemn, contemplative mien was much noted. By then of course Pater's ties to Christian doctrine were next to nil, but, in a now-familiar pattern, the visual and aural manifestations of spirituality—the apparatus of ceremony—would remain of utmost importance to him. Indeed he never stopped believing in compulsory chapel.

Such was Pater's complex and contradictory personal adjustment to the climate of intellectual skepticism and the undermining of faith by science in his time. A man of essentially religious and even mystical bent, he happened upon a refuge and home for his temperament in the religious forms and residues, and the quasi-monastic corners, of England's oldest university. In the same way, his speculative mind sought salvation in the high abstractions of German philosophy, a discipline that he, unlike Ruskin, came to know fairly well, with key phrases from Hegel, Schiller, and Novalis studding his prose—though Pater was himself not particularly profound or rigorous thinker. As a writer, his solution was to emulate the working methods of Flaubert, who in his eremitic solitude would distill every sentence to perfection, and of whom Pater as student took to translating a page per day. On the other hand it is significant that Pater's private letters are, in Harold Bloom's words, "incredibly dull and non-revelatory." [32]

The mature Pater gave novelized expression to his stance in *Marius the Epicurean* (1885), tellingly subtitled *His Sensations and Ideas.* The narrative shape is itself revealing. *Marius the Epicurean* may well be the only nineteenth-century novel that has scarcely a stitch of dialogue (save for some Socratic set pieces) and that moreover has no love story. Claustrophobic and opaque, it is the entirely apt product of the apolitical and solipsist mind whence it sprang. The historical setting and scant plot serve as a langorous metaphor for Pater's fin-de-siècle pains and sensibilities. The Roman Empire of the second century A.D. is depicted as caught up in an era of religions a-dying, of slow loss of both local and Imperial traditions. Farms and villas are left unattended; the Latin language flounders in decay; and the glories of the past pose mainly a burden, for "that old pagan world . . . had reached its perfection in the things of poetry and art—a perfection which indicated only too surely the eve of decline" (142).[33]

Within this panorama lives the young Marius, "more given to contemplation than to action," whose worldview is a "subjective philosophy with the individual as its standard of all things" (19). What he is best able to appreciate in the older religions is "the picturesque," as befits his "natural Epicureanism" and his quality of "passive spectator of the world around him" (102). Nonetheless, within Marius "a philosophy which taught that nothing was intrinsically great or small, good or evil" conflicts with "the boy-priest" who always wanted "what was perfect of its kind" (285). Although the "Christian superstition" that Marius later sees emerging will strike him as "but one savagery . . . in a cruel and stupid world" (281), he does look with some irony upon "that wonderful spectacle . . . of those who believe" (305).

It is obvious that Marius is something of a projection of the author himself. Like the youthful Marius, Pater in his prime was fully aware of having come of age in a late kind of epoch when all manner of traditional certainties were being edged aside and dissolved by newer philosophies and knowledge and by the simple passage of time itself. The concern over such a climate of thought is present from early on in Pater's career as man of letters. In the second paragraph of his very first essay, "Coleridge" — written in Pater's middle twenties, published in 1865, and later revised for inclusion in *Appreciations* (1889) — the budding writer states, "Modern thought is distinguished . . . by its cultivation of the 'relative' spirit in place of the 'absolute.' " [34] The observation is followed by a lengthy speculation regarding the effects of the advance of science on "the faculty for truth" and "the moral world" — a passage that in many respects reads like a first draft of the thinking Pater would deploy eight years hence in his best-known work of criticism.

That relativistic spirit, both as program and as problem, underlies Pater's *Studies in the History of the Renaissance* (1873; subsequently entitled simply *The Renaissance*), even if its relativist motives are laid bare only in the notorious Conclusion. While the book was and is Pater's most celebrated single volume, the sole portions that still carry much impact are its controversial finale, the opening preface, and a few passages from perhaps three of its nine full chapters.

The curious fame and legend surrounding *The Renaissance* are nonetheless justified, inasmuch as it became *the* sourcebook for England's late-Victorian aesthetes. Whereas Oscar Wilde would agitate for aestheticism with astounding facility and dazzling wit, Pater's *Renaissance* — without which Oscar Wilde would surely have differed as a thinker and writer — unfolds its Art for Art's Sake arguments with the necessary qualifying nuances and academic reticence.

The two best-known aestheticist notions Pater sets forth in *The Renaissance* are his programmatic stress on the subjective responses of the critic and his emphasis on execution and form at the expense of referential content. Regarding critical response, Pater in his preface asserts that "the first step" in looking fruitfully at an art object is "to know one's own impression as it really is." For Pater, the fundamental questions are "What is this song or picture to *me*? . . . Does it give me pleasure? and if so, what sort or degree of pleasure?" On the other hand the relationship of beauty to "truth or experience" is an "unprofitable" matter that, Pater quietly insists, should be "of no interest to [the critic]." In Pater's conception of art criticism, "all works of art . . . [are] powers or forces producing pleasurable sensations" in the observer, and each of those sensations is "of a more or less peculiar or unique kind" (xii–xiii).[35]

Pater is thus the first important critic radically to shift focus away from the arena of actual artists and their handiwork to the private realm of the critic's inner sensations. Pater himself once casually defined his approach as "imaginative criticism." [36] Later generations would brand his criticism merely impressionistic. It goes without saying that one does not read Pater's *Renaissance* in order to inform oneself "scientifically" about the Renaissance — the facts and dates, the day-to-day details, the lives of artists, the broad cultural panorama. One reads *The Renaissance* so as to share its author's sentiments and sensibilities vis-à-vis the Renaissance, his impressions thereof. Pater's knowledge of art history, significantly, is said to have been uneven and sketchy. And notwithstanding his better acquaintance with German philosophy, Pater's theoretical endeavors once again put us at a far remove from the foundational premises of Kant, whose aim was to establish an objective grounding for subjective taste by postulating such a thing as "universal validity" in the individual's aesthetic judgements. Pater's odd temperament and relativistic times made such a Kantian project well-nigh inconceivable to him.

In his chapter on "Giorgione" (added in the second edition of 1877), Pater asserts twice, and further emphasizes the second time around: "*All art constantly aspires toward the condition of music*" (95) — one of his most striking and oft-quoted statements. To Pater's mind what is truly artistic in a poem and painting are "neither [their] descriptive nor meditative" aspects but the rhythm, color, and song. Pater concedes that lyric verse "may find a noble and quite legitimate function in the conveyance of moral or political aspiration, as often in the poetry of Victor Hugo. In such instances it is easy enough to distinguish between the matter and the form." Ultimately, however, Pater insists that the "ideal types of poetry are those in which this distinction is reduced to its *minimum*" (emphasis in original). From such a position there follows Pater's crowning argument, namely, "Art . . . is always striving to be independent of the mere intelligence, to become a matter of pure perception, to get rid of its responsibilities to its subject or material" (96–97).

Today we recognize this as the purist, aestheticist idea, to be picked up on and further elaborated by Oscar Wilde, Vladimir Nabokov, and latter-day academic theoreticians from the New Critics to deconstructionists: the view whereby all propositional content and human reference are deemed irrelevant to a work of art, and only its form and language count. As has been previously seen in the course of this study, however, Pater's formalist ideal hardly sprang self-willed from the creative depths of his tremulous mind, but rather emerged in response to specific cultural conditions of his time, a situation evoked in his famed Conclusion, the outlook and rhetoric of which can still raise hackles today.

The history of that six-page document is itself revealing. When first published in 1873, its praise of sensuous aestheticism above all other activities offended some proper and respectable intellects. Benjamin Jowett, the great classicist and master of Balliol College, was frankly displeased at the Conclusion. The bishop of Oxford attacked Pater in a sermon. And John Wordsworth — grandnephew of the poet, an erstwhile student of Pater, and a cleric at the time — sent the author an indignant letter virtually accusing him of nihilism and glossing the Conclusion thus: "that no fixed principles either of religion or morality can be regarded as certain, that the only thing worth living for is momentary enjoyment and that probably or certainly the soul dissolves at death into elements which are destined never to reunite." [37] Even a sympathetic early biographer felt that Pater's creed "affords no bulwark against the temptation to sink from a pure . . . beauty of description into a grosser indulgence in sensuous delights." [38] Pater suffered more than moral opprobrium. The Conclusion also blocked his career, costing him academic promotions. The university authorities refused to grant him a proctorship (an annual award to one of the colleges, with an attractive salary supplement), even when simple rotation made it Pater's turn; and they greeted with ridicule his application for the post of professor of poetry.

Pater took quiet exception to his detractors and reportedly complained, "I wish they would not call me a hedonist. It gives such a wrong impression to those who do not know Greek." He nonetheless yielded to pressures and, in 1877, excised the offending chapter from the second edition of his book. For a third edition in 1888 he restored the Conclusion, though neutralizing and softening some presumably dangerous or extreme passages. (The passages are examined later.) Ironically, Pater could never go so far as to criticize, let alone defy, the dominant values of Victorian England. One faces the strange paradox of a shy recluse with no reformist or militant zeal, no bold or transgressive ways, who carved out a philosophy that official minds solemnly condemned as subversive and that restless youths would take as a call to rebellion.[39]

The relativism underlying Pater's stance is stated from the concluding chapter's very outset: "To regard all things and principles . . . as inconstant modes or fashions has . . . become the tendency of modern thought" (156). He depicts even our physical lives and personal identities as elusive and fleeting, with no stable or fixed truths to them. All that remains of "the whole scope of observation," then, is "the narrow chamber of the individual mind"; and all of our impressions are similarly "the impression of the individual in his isolation" (157). Faced by this disorienting panorama, Pater avers that the best "success in life" is "to burn always with [a] hard, gemlike flame" of "ecstasy" sparked by "experience itself." If we live our short lives in this fashion, "we shall hardly have time to make theories," and therefore "what we have to do is to be forever curiously testing new opinions and courting new impressions, never acquiescing in a facile orthodoxy of Comte, or of Hegel, or of our own" (158).

The causal relation is clear: given that all other realities have proved fleeting and undependable, Pater celebrates aesthetic and other pleasures for their own sake. Knowledge and thought are too uncertain; a commitment to any idea stands on too shaky a ground; and hence the optimum available solution is a kind of carpe diem of the soul, a search for "aesthetic bliss" (to anticipate Nabokov's phrase). Combining a subtle logic, a process of elimination, and an intuitive leap, Pater arrives at a mental territory wherein aesthetic separatism serves as both the founding principle and the highest good.

Though in his writings Pater never directly questions the validity of religion, in his first published version of the Conclusion he presented religious concerns as simply one among other means to a higher sensuousness. In the revised version of 1888, significantly, he altered those passages in which religion specifically had been relativized and aestheticized. The later edition, for instance, affirms, "The service of philosophy, of speculative culture, toward the human spirit, is to rouse, to startle it to a life of constant and eager observation" (157). The original passage, however, had included "and of religion" after "philosophy" and "culture." In the next paragraph a chastened Pater eventually chose to speculate, "Philosophical theories or ideas, as points of view . . . may help us to gather up what might otherwise pass unregarded by us" (158). In its initial form, by contrast, the statement had begun, "Theories, *religious* or philosophical ideas. . . ." And in the antepenultimate sentence of his book, Pater finally sermonizes, "Great passions may give us this quickened sense of life" (159). Instead of those vague and general "great passions," Pater had first invoked "Political *or religious* enthusiasm" as quickening our sense of life.[40]

Pater was not being, as Harold Bloom claims, "antireligious" or "anti-Christian" in these vintage passages. He offended rather by failing to privilege religion with any special cognitive, moral, or spiritual powers, by systematically subsuming it, along with philosophy and politics, to worldly concerns such as pleasure and beauty. In an England still dominated by a state church with government-supported clergy, a country where (unlike France) an established anticlerical opposition hardly existed, such thinking could only arouse the righteousness of the religious apparatus's functionaries. One can see why Pater—a man with no taste for the rough-and-tumble of polemics—in the end withdrew those thoughts, in what amounted to an informal recantation if not self-censorship. His original assertions nevertheless bring together a cluster of attitudes that formed part of the English culture of ideas of the time and that are still alive today. Those views, and the artful subtlety and guileless originality with which Pater enunciated them, are what gained him disciples among the next generation.

His attraction for disciples was inadvertent, inasmuch as Pater was a man ill suited for the role of guru or grand master. Still, within

English aestheticism he holds a place roughly analogous to that of Victor Cousin in France. (Of course his was a stronger intellect, even though he lacked the Sorbonne professor's charisma.) Pater stands as a curious and quirky figure in literary history, one whose influence somewhat exceeded his own powers. Not a major thinker, he also evinced no great talent for narrative or verse, indeed no artistic gifts to speak of, save for a distinctive prose style fashioned for his purposes. He did no original research, built no grand synthesis, and though essentially bookish, was not even a traditional literary scholar. (His errors in Scripture and in Greek have been noted by critics.) A kind of bellettrist and free essayist in the French vein, he nonetheless would have been completely out of sorts in the jungle of journalism, with its business pressures and demands for constant and varied output.

Pater was more an intense appreciator who made appreciating a way of life—indeed, *Appreciations* is the title of his 1889 book of essays—and who, via a fittingly elaborate style, gave public shape to his solipsistic self. His latter-day heirs are in modern universities like Yale and Johns Hopkins, while his theory of aesthetic experience survives in popularized form. After all, Pater highlighted the private appreciator's taste above any other criterion; and when in our time someone takes in a poem, picture, or musical piece, and says, "I just like it, that's all," he or she is unknowingly replicating in debased form the Pater axiom from the Conclusion to *The Renaissance*. Needless to say, so banal a proposition as "I just like it" carries a myriad of connotations, depending on who says it about what, and when, and to whom (like the word "tonight," which Stanislavsky's actors spoke as practice). The idea nonetheless first receives full expression and legitimacy, for better or for worse, in Pater's writings. And so long as there are no set religious, social, or ethical values on which there is voluntary agreement, such subjectivism may well remain available within the broad repertory of responses to art.

When one thinks of aestheticism among creative writers in England, it is the 1890s and their maximum representative, Oscar Wilde, that automatically come to mind. The full historical picture is both longer and more complex, yet also thinner and more disappointing. As fits the pattern noted here, the most ardent English advocates of Art for Art's Sake were lyrists rather than novelists and dramatists such as Wilde.

The first English lyrist to identify himself publicly with aestheticist doctrine was the somewhat problematical Algernon Charles Swinburne (1837–1909). Two years older than Pater and a political and religious rebel even as a student, he came fairly close to being expelled from Oxford. (Ruskin thought him a "demonian youth.") Swinburne's first book, *Poems and Ballads* (1866), exhibits the expected themes of illicit sensualism and forbidden love. The verses celebrate lustful pleasures, "the raptures and roses of vice." Taking a cue from Baudelaire, they touch on the satanic and sadomasochistic, with figures such as a destructive Venus and a "Dolores, our Lady of Sensual Pain." [41] Not surprisingly, the book aroused the wrath of the reviewers, who accused the author of perversity and immorality. Ruskin, to his credit, defended Swinburne against his detractors, whereas *Punch* (from then on a persistent enemy of the English aesthetes) referred to the poet as "Swineborne."

Edward Moxon, the publisher of *Poems and Ballads,* got cold feet and withdrew the volume, which was soon picked up by John Camden Hotten, who also commissioned from the author a pamphlet defending himself against the critical furies. Swinburne's defense, *Notes on Poems and Reviews* (1866), scoffs at "prudery" and dismisses as a criterion "whether this book or that can be read by her mother to a young girl." He for his part advocates a literature that will be "large, liberal, sincere" and further insists on the principles of "free speech and fair play." He writes verse, he says, "to please myself." For Swinburne, "adult art" has "its purity . . . not that of the cloister or the harem; . . . all things are good in its sight." [42]

If in this polemical essay Swinburne trumpeted the rights of artists to deal with any materials they choose, in his 1868 study *William Blake,* which singles out the visionary poet as a predecessor, he makes the case for an art separate from moral or other preoccupations. Indeed he states as his fundamental principle, "Art for art's sake first of all, and afterward we may suppose all the rest shall be added to her."

He says in no uncertain terms that "[art] will help in nothing, of her own knowledge or freewill: upon terms of service you will get worse than nothing out of her. Handmaid of religion, exponent of duty, servant of fact, pioneer of morality, she cannot in any way become." Anticipating one of Pater's key arguments, he assures that poets like Dante, Shelley, or Hugo — whose ideological concerns clearly mark their verse — "are no real exceptions," inasmuch as "the work done may be . . . of supreme value to art; but not the moral implied." [43]

Swinburne was an enthusiastic disciple of the contemporary French poets, from whose lives and practices he obviously gleaned such now-familiar concepts. As early as *Notes on Poems and Reviews* he yearns for the day when England will have "a school of poetry . . . as France has now." [44] He even wrote an elegiac ode on the death of Baudelaire, "Ave Atque Vale." The powerful example posed by French verse for certain segments of English literature has been the subject of entire books. What bears brief mention here is the relative meagerness of the concrete literary results. Of the Victorian poets thus influenced, the best by far is Swinburne, who, despite his enormous gifts as verse technician, scarcely comes close to the poetic heights reached by Baudelaire, Verlaine, Rimbaud, Mallarmé, or even Gautier (who, it should be said, also wrote some fine novelistic romances). Swinburne is one of those instances of a virtuoso writer whose art remains less than mature. A first-rate versifier, he lacks insight or vision commensurate with his craft. His long life story is that of a boy prodigy who never grew up. He can dazzle readers, and in his day he could outrage them, but he seldom moves or disturbs us.

The same applies, writ large, to the later poets — Lionel Johnson, Ernest Dowson, and the like — who were directly associated with British aestheticism. Their languid, sensitive voices plumb no depths and remain ever a pallid imitation of the French lyrists who ultimately inspired them. As Graham Hough notes, they are "small beer compared with their French counterparts, . . . translators and adapters of ideas not their own." [45] Not a single one of the verse works of English aestheticism (again, Wilde excepted) has attained the status of representative text or anthology piece. As the Victorian era further recedes from memory, even Swinburne appears more a brilliant curiosity than a writer of enduring substance.

The multifaceted Oscar Wilde (1854–1900) also wrote lyrics, adjudged by one eminent scholar "the best verse that the Aesthetes could produce." [46] Wilde's poetry actually enjoyed good sales; his 1881 volume *Poems* quickly went through five editions, a triumph attributable less to the artistic strengths of its contents than to the fame and notoriety enjoyed by Wilde even in his mid-twenties. The verse certainly shows skill, though less than does Swinburne's, but it lacks anything like a distinctive voice. The better of Wilde's early poems—such as "Requiescat"—have a songful sweetness to them, but are on the whole of an oddly conventional cast, what with their "golden sun" imagery and "thee" and "thou" diction. They scarcely suggest the exuberant wit for which his prose works (and his own personality) are so celebrated. Wilde wrote little verse thereafter until his later years, and appropriately his one poem to rise above such conventionalisms is "The Ballad of Reading Gaol," composed in the aftermath of his prison years and thus bearing the mark of a sobering wisdom gained from that experience.

Few authors elicit as much posthumous controversy as does Wilde. No doubt the cloud still surrounding his reputation has a lot to do with the vast contradictions characterizing his life history. Almost no literary figure has known the combination of world fame enjoyed early on by Wilde, followed by so tragic and complete a reversal of fortunes as he sustained in 1895, when he lost his lawsuit against the Marquess of Queensberry on criminal libel charges (a major "media event" of the day). Wilde suffered two years in prison; then bankruptcy, disgrace and ostracism on his release; finally exile and a piteous death in a Parisian hotel room.

The greatest contradiction for our purposes, however, is in Wilde's role as chief spokesman for pure art among the British. It is a supreme paradox that Wilde's own temperament and career scarcely typify aestheticism. Wilde's phenomenal wit, extroverted social skills, ability to write fast, and enormous success in the commercial theater [47] are in solid contradiction to the Flaubertian image of introverted sainthood, of abstention from worldly enticements, of slow struggle to shape the perfect work of art. There is in Wilde's outrageous pronouncements an unmistakable self-irony, a smiling flippancy inconceivable in a Gautier or Mallarmé. One is as much aware of Wilde the advocate presenting his case as of Wilde the mischief-maker tweaking the nose of Victorian respectability. Though a brilliant—perhaps the most brilliant—publicist for Art for Art's Sake, a practitioner he was not.

The aesthetic and the religious were both among Wilde's preoccupations from his student years until his death. At Trinity College in Dublin, his preferred author was Swinburne, whose lonely struggle against establishment foes Wilde likened to that of Euripides. He also read the Pre-Raphaelites—their books were just beginning to appear—and had some involvement with aesthetic issues in the college Philosophical Society. At the same time, a competing Catholic current ran through much of his life. Wilde's parents, who were Protestant, had had their infant child duly christened in their religion. His mother, Jane, also flirted with the Roman faith, however, and had Oscar privately anointed a Catholic in his fourth or fifth year, though little was apparently made of this "rebaptism" thereafter in the family. During his Trinity days Wilde became friendly with Catholic priests, to his father's concern, and was quite moved by the writings of Cardinal John Henry Newman. Over the next few years Wilde repeatedly considered converting to Catholicism, as had Newman; and in 1878, despondent at having contracted syphilis from a prostitute, he pursued serious talks with an important London priest about joining the Catholic ranks. A date was set. As the story has it, Wilde failed to show up on the appointed day and sent a box of lilies instead.

Some years hence, when asked about his religion, Wilde reportedly said, "I don't think I have any. I am an Irish Protestant." He would nonetheless claim that "for the aesthetic mind," "Catholicism was more attractive than Protestantism," as Ellmann notes. Wilde's yearning for a religious faith comes through in his sonnet "Hélas!", wherein he asks if there was once a time when, faced with "life's dissonances," he might have

> struck one clear chord to reach the ears of God:
> Is that time dead? . . .
> And must I lose a soul's inheritance?

Much later, during his dying days, Wilde at last yielded to those earlier religious longings. Just three weeks before his death he remarked to a *Daily Chronicle* reporter, "Much of my moral obliquity is due to the fact that my father would not allow me to become a Catholic. The artistic side of the Church and the fragrance of its teaching would have cured me of my degeneracies. I intend to be received before long." And indeed on his deathbed in France, semiconscious, with the help of his male lover, Robert Ross, Wilde was admitted into the Catholic fold by an Irish priest named Cuthbert Dunne.[48]

Following two years at Trinity, a restless young Wilde transferred to Magdalen College, Oxford. In that new intellectual haven he sought special guidance from the two individuals he most desired to meet, Ruskin and Pater. During his first semester, in 1874, he faithfully attended the fifty-five-year-old Slade Professor's lectures on Florentine art at the University Museum. Wilde greatly admired the renowned critic's eloquence and wisdom, and even participated in one of the grand *maître*'s organized work projects, rising uncharacteristically early to aid in the construction of an attractive country road, bordered with flowers, in nearby Ferry Hinksey. Later on the two were to become friends, and after leaving the university Wilde wrote Ruskin, "The dearest memories of my Oxford are my walks and talks with you," and praised what there was "of prophet, of priest, and of poet" in Ruskin.[49]

But it was Pater who would exert the strongest influence on the mind of Wilde, whose nonfictional works are thoroughly infused with the thought and spirit (if not the style) of the reclusive Brasenose College tutor. In his first months at Oxford, Wilde read the premier edition of *Studies in the History of the Renaissance,* which had been published only the year before. The effect on Wilde was immediate and lasting. "My golden book," he would often call it; and much of its Conclusion he could cite from memory. Writing from the pain and gloom of his prison years in *De Profundis,* Wilde evokes Pater's *Renaissance* as "that book which has had such a strange influence over my life." [50]

The influence seems to have been personal as well. In July 1877 Wilde published a review of the recently inaugurated Grosvenor Gallery of Art and sent the piece to Pater. In reply, the Oxford don invited the Irish student to visit him in his rooms following the summer holidays. At their first meeting that October, the master reportedly asked the disciple, "Why do you always write poetry? Why do you not write prose? Prose is so much more difficult." Wilde in fact largely followed the suggested path after his first book, *Poems,* was published four years hence. The two remained friendly thereafter, though it is said that in private Pater did not like Wilde so much as admire him. He took exception to "the strange vulgarity which Mr. Wilde mistakes for charm."[51] Wilde was openly enthusiastic about "Sir Walter," as he sometimes called him, and praised Pater in "The Critic as Artist" as "the most perfect master of English prose now creating amongst us," though by then he expressed the caveat that Pater's style may "lack the true rhythmical life of words and the fine freedom and richness of effect that such rhythmical life produces" (53).[52] Pater, in turn, came to regard Wilde's prose as too much resembling speech.

Wilde's publicist works are to a large extent spectacularly brilliant popularizations of, and elaborations on, Pater's thinking—with his own stylistic difference. What in Pater was weighty, humorless, and solemn, in Wilde becomes light, bright, and witty. Where Pater was sacerdotal, Wilde spoke in jest. The disquieting doctrines contained within Pater's lengthy and opaque sentences spontaneously stream forth in Wilde's oral cascades and mellifluous bons mots. And whereas Pater hid and labored as an anchorite in the shadows of old Oxford, Wilde would shine and sparkle amid fashionable, worldly London's smart salons.

Wilde's chief doctrinal texts on aestheticism all date from the remarkably fertile three-year period 1889–91. The aphorisms that now preface *The Picture of Dorian Gray* first appeared independently as "Dogmas for Use of the Aged" in the *Forthnightly Review.* Wilde's preface to *Dorian Gray* is the equivalent in English letters of Gautier's preface to *Mademoiselle de Maupin.* Indeed, when Anglophone readers know anything at all about ideas of Art for Art's Sake, it is usually via this two-page text. There is good reason, for the preface is one of Wilde's wittiest and most provocative expository moments, consisting of a set of lapidary yet bald assertions, their verbal virtuosity compensating for the complete lack of either nuance or argumentation—just as one would expect from what is after all a literary manifesto. The preface is high-wire intellectual juggling at its most self-assured and masterful, however one may feel about the larger truth of its contents.

Wilde's longer writings of this kind are in dialogue form, a deployment of his witty thoughts that is more sustained than a univocal presentation. "The Decay of Lying" (1889) antecedes and is actually more original than his *Dorian Gray* preface, the latter being not so much a breakthrough text as a dazzling summation of aestheticist commonplaces. "The Decay" takes matters a great deal further, and its speculations live on over a century hence. On one hand we recognize a traditional and self-evident notion when Cyril, a kind of straight man in the piece, states, "Art expresses the temper of its age, the spirit of the time, the moral and social conditions that surround it." Sharply disagreeing, Vivian, who is Wilde's mouthpiece, counters, "Certainly not! Art never expresses anything but itself!" (80).[53] So seemingly outrageous a conception of what the arts do has since become familiar enough via deconstruction and other brands of postmodern theorizing. (In this regard, Jonathan Freedman remarks on "the ease with which British aestheticism may be incorporated into the deconstructive canon.")[54] Similarly, Vivian insists that art "has an independent life, just as Thought has, and develops precisely on its own lines" (86), a basic and even axiomatic principle of Western literary thought since 1950, enunciated almost verbatim in the academic classics of Wellek and Warren and of Northrop Frye.

This aesthetic separatism is pushed to yet greater lengths throughout "Decay," wherein Wilde postulates fancies so self-contained and extreme as to be irrefutable (a bit like Bishop Berkeley's arguments about the nonexistence of matter). Among the best known is Vivian's apodictic assertion, "[I]t is none the less true that Life imitates art far more than Art imitates life" (74). Hence it is Turgenev's *Fathers and Sons* that invented the nihilist movement in Russia, it is Balzac's novels that created the nineteenth century's urban jungle, and it is Corot's canvases that generated those open-air fogs and shadows — rather than the other way around. "A great artist invents a type, and Life tries to copy it, to reproduce it in a popular form, like an enterprising publisher" (74). Despite the comical extravagance of the claim, Wilde evokes a complex, twofold process here: artistic representations of a subject can become more familiar and vivid than are the living examples thereof (as we have come to know in an era of Hollywood and of mass electronic media), and may in turn help us better to conceive of the real-life cases; certain individuals or groups tend to find models for conduct in such representations (one might recall the alienated, existential sectors of U.S. life in the 1950s, shaped in part by Camus and Sartre; or the strident U.S. nationalism of the 1980s, "learned" in great measure from Rambo fantasies).

The relativism and transience of all truths shimmeringly noted by Pater in his Conclusion to *The Renaissance* become Wilde's cause for celebration in "The Decay." His mouthpiece Vivian cheerfully looks forward to that day when "Facts will be regarded as discreditable, Truth will be found mourning over her fetters, and Romance, with her temper of wonder, will return to the land" (85). The condition that an introverted Pater had somewhat grimly acknowledged as a fact of modern life becomes the basis for a future utopia to the extroverted sophist Wilde. What we must do to achieve that happy state is to "revive this old art of Lying" (84). Rather than telling the truth, then, "The final revelation is that Lying, the telling of beautiful untrue things, is the proper aim of Art" (87).

Similar assumptions, couched in the same comically extremist terms, inform Wilde's "The Critic as Artist" (1891), even as he foregrounds other aspects. Whereas "Decay" focused on artistic creation and speculated on the problematical relationship to Truth, "Critic as Artist" emphasizes the reception side of art and also declares the complete irrelevance of the Beautiful to the Good and the True. Aesthetic separatism is explicit and total. "The sphere of art and the sphere of Ethics are absolutely distinct and separate. When they are confused, Chaos has come once again" (89). Recalling Enlightenment thinking, Wilde's spokesman Gilbert affirms that "there is in us a beauty-sense," but then, as befits the nineteenth-century pattern, he goes on to proclaim this faculty "separate from other senses and above them, separate from the reason and of nobler import" (90).

The sense of beauty, it bears emphasizing, is here placed *above* the rest of our mental capacities. A few pages hence Wilde's mouthpiece Gilbert elaborates further and makes the ultimate leap, announcing, in fact, "Aesthetics are higher than ethics. They belong to a more spiritual sphere. To discern the beauty of a thing is the finest point to which we can arrive. Even a colour-sense is more important, in the development of the individual, than a sense of right and wrong" (98). Shaftesbury, Kant, and Schiller saw our sense of beauty as the necessary stepping-stone to a sense of morals; the French poets separated the two spheres, yet still saw the moral imperative as an equal, lateral adversary to contend with in literature; Ruskin sermonized on beauty as a fundamental component within his larger moral and then social projects; and Pater transformed the aesthetic into a kind of normative concern and substitute ethic. Wilde is probably the first literary theorist in any language to go as far as to make aesthetics supersede ethics, to claim that beauty matters more than morals.

Pater in his Conclusion to *The Renaissance* had pronounced as his first critical principle, "What does this song or picture . . . mean to *me?*" (xii). As the title of Wilde's philosophic dialogue immediately suggests, "The Critic as Artist" dramatizes Pater's special stress on art appreciators—professional ones in this case. As spokesman Gilbert flatly says, "The highest kind [of criticism] treats the work simply as a starting point for a new creation" (70). Critical writing of this sort promises to be "more creative than creation, as it has least reference to any standard external to itself, and is, in fact, its own reason for existing" (67). Such a free and independent higher criticism is, in the last analysis, nothing less than "the record of one's soul" (98). Wilde's is no doubt the first explicit enunciation of a doctrine of criticism for criticism's sake, to become a highly touted alternate subgenre among French and American academics such as Roland Barthes, Geoffrey Hartman, and Stanley Fish some four score years later.

Among the advantages of a purely creative criticism is that "it is never trammelled by shackles of verisimilitude" nor by "ignoble considerations of probability" (67). Even the literary text is an illusion: "In point of fact there is no such thing as Shakespeare's Hamlet. . . . There are as many Hamlets as there are melancholics" (76). More broadly, there are no foundational truths that the Wildean critic need adhere to. The relativistic ethos that served as point of departure for Pater, then as springboard for Wilde's aesthetic in "Decay of Lying" becomes generalized in "Critic as Artist" as a theory of knowledge that recognizes little more than the random victories in the historical record; Wilde's prose reads like a virtual gloss to the opening lines of Pater's Conclusion. Says Wilde, "To know the truth one must imagine myriads of falsehoods. For what is Truth? In matters of religion, it is simply the opinion that has survived. In matters of science, it is the ultimate sensation. In matters of art, it is one's last mood" (87). And in matters of value, Wilde's is a world now distant from that confidently chauvinistic mid-Victorian moralism with which this chapter started.

Even from the dark night of his prison years, when one might expect a chastened Wilde to have acknowledged some harsher truths or to have sought comfort in more transcendent ones, he could write in *De Profundis* that "the false and the true are merely forms of intellectual existence" (151). At the same time he is keeping his distance from religious belief. "Religion does not help me. The faith that others give to what is unseen, I give to what one can touch, and look at. . . . When I think about religion at all, I feel as if I would like to found an order for those who *cannot* believe: the Confraternity of the Truthless one might call it." Wilde nonetheless concedes the aesthetic and emotional worth of religion and its social comforts, indeed speculates, "Everything to be true must become a religion. And agnosticism should have its ritual no less than faith" (154). The long-standing idea that the late-nineteenth-century writers created a substitute "religion of art" is a platitude so common that we tend to lose sight of its basis in historical reality. Ruskin, Pater, and Wilde, all of them lapsed believers, serve to exemplify this conventionally agreed-upon truth.

Freedman considers Wilde's critical prose "his greatest achievement, and perhaps the only body of work produced by the aesthetic movement that can be called an unequivocal success." These publicist writings, Freedman observes, bring together most successfully Wilde's "subversive inclinations and his literary performance." [55] Nevertheless, it is as a novelist, dramatist, and sometime poet that Wilde is today remembered. Indeed, he is almost the only *imaginative* writer in British aestheticism whose best work still holds up and remains fresh. Among the reasons for his literary survival is that as an author he was, no doubt, smarter and more gifted than most of the others. In addition, there was his outsider status, for Wilde came from colonial Ireland rather than native English stock, and while not having made much of his political opinions, he was republican, nationalist, and anti-Tory—all of which furnished a fresh outlook on Britain's reigning pieties and rules of righteousness. Moreover he often traveled to France, consciously emulated French authors, wrote *Salomé* in French, and died in France, where he is buried. Although at Oxford Wilde made a point of shedding his Irish accent, later, when government authorities banned the London premier of *Salomé* in 1882, he threatened in an interview with the *Pall Mall Budget* to depart Britain and take up French citizenship. He further asserted, "I am not English. I am Irish, which is quite another thing."[56]

It thus took a writer of non-English roots to give Art for Art's Sake high visibility among the English. At any rate the witty intelligence of Wilde's publicist essays raises them well beyond the status of period pieces into classic statements of *l'art pour l'art* doctrine; his *Dorian Gray* depicts a certain aestheticist sensibility and lifestyle with expert vividness and irony (albeit less thoroughly and probingly than did its French model, Huysman's *A Rebours*); and *The Importance of Being Earnest* probably equals Wilde's oral repartee in its sheer originality and brilliance.

The assaults on Wilde himself proliferated, as caricatures rather than intellectual positions. (The anti-Wildeans perhaps knew deep in their hearts that they could not match their prey's debating skills.) Among the cast of characters in the novel *Second Thoughts* (1880) by Rhoda Broughton is a "long pale poet" named Francis Chaloner, "flaccid-limbed," with long hair on his "botticelli head." Wilde's cult of lilies and his knee breeches were the regular butt of hostile jokes; Broughton's book, appropriately, makes mention of "a great white lily standing in a large blue vase" in Chaloner's rooms. *Punch* magazine had a field day with England's aesthetes, and its cartoonist George du Maurier lampooned Wilde almost weekly in the early 1880s, focusing, as others did, on the hair, the lily, and the Frenchness of a figure varyingly called Oscuro Wildegoose, Drawit Milde, and Ossian Wilderness.

The theater was an apt venue for grotesque lampoons of Wilde. F. C. Burnand, editor of *Punch*, wrote *The Colonel* (1881), a play featuring an aesthete named Lambert Stryke, who was rendered unmistakably as Wilde in stage productions at the time. The best-known such dramatic spoof, however, is Gilbert and Sullivan's *Patience,* in which the librettist draws mooning poet Reginald Bunthorne, who styles himself

> a soulful-eyed young man
> An ultra-poetical, super-aesthetical,
> Out-of-the-way young man.

In private, however, Bunthorne admits,

> Then let me own
> I'm an aesthetic sham
> This air severe
> Is but a mere veneer.

He plays the poet, apparently, because the women love it and fall all over him, and in an aria he offers this sage advice:

> If you're anxious for to shine in the high aesthetic
> line as a man of culture rare,
> You must get up all the germs of the transcendental
> terms, and plant them everywhere.
> You must lie upon the daisies and discourse on novel
> phrases of your complicated state of mind.
> The meaning doesn't matter if it's only idle chatter of
> a transcendental kind.
> . . . .
> Though the Philistines may jostle, you will rank as an
> apostle in the high aesthetic band,
> If you walk down Piccadilly with a poppy or a lily in
> your medieval hand.[57]

W. S. Gilbert's portrait of the aesthete-as-charlatan is virtually the only one of the English establishment's sallies against the ways and mores of Art for Art's Sake to remain in print today. Its survival is certainly deserved, inasmuch as Gilbert's lines show the characteristic wit and skill of their versifier, though Wilde's writing, one must grant, is much funnier and moreover has the special virtue of being completely without malice or snobbery. Of course, Wilde's public posturing made for an easy target, and to this day a kind of reflex ridicule of his personal lifestyle beclouds his genuine achievement as artist and publicist.

Modern readers habitually link Wilde's life and doctrines to Victorianism's fin de siècle, and not incorrectly so. The emergence of Art for Art's Sake and the counterattacks against it both ran their course in an era when challenges to British hegemony had been undermining the foundations of that island empire's high chauvinism and moralism. The rise of German power, marked by Bismarck's 1871 victory over France, effectively put an end to the Pax Britannica in Europe. The economic slump beginning in the late 1870s could nourish only skepticism about the once-triumphant set of values that had spiritually reinforced Victorian capitalism. The late-century scramble for empire, paradoxically, laid bare the fundamental insecurity of a system that was unable to stay ahead of its competitors if it lacked easy access to overseas markets and materials.

The attacks on Oscar Wilde and the forcible takeover of Africa and Asia, then, are but two aspects of the same historical moment. Britain's inexorable intrigues against weak adversaries would, at long last, lead the nation's youth joyously marching on to the Great War and its grisly trenches, after which the illusions both of aesthetes and anti-aesthetes, as well as the smug delusions of empire, would begin to assume their faded air and period quality. Fin de siècle can signify not only "century's end" but also "world's end."

The English establishment won its wars against pure art and against German might—the former with ease, the latter at enormous cost (and with some help from colonial petrol and Russian and U.S. troops). More broadly, the twin good fortunes of geographical isolation and a smoothly functioning political consensus spared Britain the radical divisions and shifts in thinking that were sprouting on the Continent. Over the past three centuries, accordingly, a distinctive, traditional *mentalité* has endured in British literary thought and practice, despite successive challenges from Marxists, absurdists, working-class novelists, or European theory.

Pablo Neruda in his delightful "Oda a la crítica" [Ode to criticism] has some jolly good fun satirizing the divers critical sects who do all kinds of complicated stuff with a useful five-line poem he has crafted—everything, that is, save find enjoyment or sustenance in its words. Both Marxists and monarchists are shown getting comically caught up in their fancy schemes and rhetoric, while—Neruda continues—"otros eran ingleses / sencillamente ingleses" [others were English / simply English].[58]

Neruda's witty, insightful couplet cleverly points out a specific cultural formation: the "simply English" literary mind that dates back at least to Addison and Steele, nonpartisan in tone, commonsensical in style—reflecting its coffee-house origins—which remains a force in lofty venues like the great universities, the prestigious weeklies, and the middlebrow fiction trade. The doctrine of aesthetic separatism could make little headway among the English because other traditions in their civil society were too well entrenched for so marginal, so "foreign" a phenomenon as *l'art pour l'art* to evolve into a threat. The English lyrists who tried *poésie pure* were laboring in the wrong country.

CHAPTER 4

The Diffusion of the Doctrine II: Poe (U.S.),
Modernismo *(Latin America)*

Three thousand miles west of Europe, in a bourgeois new republic not yet known for inspiring great artistic passions, there emerged an original and idiosyncratic author who, some decades before the initial hints of Art for Art's Sake were sprouting in British letters, would develop very much on his own what we now recognize as an aestheticist doctrine.

The "first new nation" of which this eccentric poet was a denizen had been settled by white religious enthusiasts whose suspicion of or indifference toward beauty remains notorious. Later there followed the English merchants, whose commercial priorities largely overshadowed the bulk of human affairs. John Locke, the philosopher most influential in the merchants' thinking, had reflected much on government, on religious toleration, and on the empirical growth of knowledge—and had had almost nothing to say concerning art, poetry, or the beautiful. Moreover, Locke's highly denotative and instrumental view of language, his scant interest in the imagination and intuition, and his low regard for men of letters all suggest a certain dry indifference to matters literary on his part. Though the European Enlightenment may have given birth to Anglo America (as Henry Steele Commager has observed), the aesthetic preoccupations that had figured as an important branch of the Enlightenment intellectual enterprise were not part of the transatlantic trade in ideas.

The literature of this incipient democracy showed several strands, none of them as yet mature. On one hand some work tended to the didactic and moralistic or to genteel imitation of literary models from the Anglophone mother country. On the other hand there were the patriotic-minded and nationalist critics, who might praise a poem or novel, however poor or mediocre, if it simply bore the byline of a fellow citizen. Meanwhile, in the southern portions of that aggressive, self-confident land, the dominant literature was an idyllic celebration, with neofeudal overtones, of the reigning gulag of African American slavery.[1] Such an ideological situation is today familiar to us from the world revolutionary upsurge that started in the 1910s and continued on into the proliferating new nations of the later twentieth century. What has been forgotten is that a rough, young, revolutionary United States at one time also experienced a comparable process of polemic in the battlefield of culture.

Edgar Allan Poe (1809–49), born when the United States was but a generation old, stood resolutely aloof from all the literary camps, heaping equal scorn on Anglophile "reactionaries" and on revolutionary "nationalists." As early as his late teens Poe ridiculed those American readers who "cringed to foreign opinion," but he also derides the alternate practice of "liking a stupid book the better, because, sure enough, its stupidity is American."[2] He further elaborates the pattern in his essay "American Critics and Criticism" (1842): "Time was when we imported our critical decisions from the mother country. For many years we enacted a perfect farce of subservience to the *dicta* of Great Britain. At last a revulsion of feeling, with self-disgust, necessarily ensued. Urged by these, we plunged into the opposite extreme. In throwing *totally* off that 'authority' . . . we even surpassed, and by much, our original folly. But the watchword now was, 'A national literature!'—as if any literature could be stage for the literary *histrio*" (108).[3] Neither, Poe felt, need the content of literature be strictly local. In an 1845 defense of his own poetry, he asserts, the notion "that an American should confine himself to American themes, or even prefer them, is rather a political than a literary idea."[4]

It must be remembered that during Poe's lifetime U.S. writing was still a minimal presence on the world literary scene. Even granting the undeniable cultural ferment up north in New England (the ethos of which Poe, as a self-styled southern squire, at any rate despised), the author died some years before Hawthorne's and Melville's major work began appearing in the 1850s. Poe's enormous originality within his extreme isolation, then, is all the more astounding. Though there is precedent for his short stories in the traditions of English Gothic and of German fantasy,[5] his unique talents seem to spring from nowhere, with no homegrown roots for the kinds of narrative and verse he was inventing. He serves as a prime specimen of the freak genius who sometimes flares up here and there, whose imaginative talents stand completely beyond the existing conventions of his society.

A major early biographer of Poe, Joseph Wood Krutch, sees his subject as essentially alien to American literary traditions.[6] Similarly, Vernon Parrington, in his encyclopedic survey, dedicates to Poe a scant if admiring three pages, wherein Poe is granted pioneer status as "an aesthete and a craftsman, the first American critic to be concerned with beauty alone," and indeed the first true artist in U.S. cultural history, one whose ideals nevertheless "ran counter to every major interest of the New England Renaissance."[7] The nature and the causes of Poe's obstinate alienation were of course complex, and entire books have been written—Krutch's being but one instance—in an attempt to account for the Poe "problem."

No classic U.S. author today arouses as much debate as Poe still does. Doubtless his strange life gets in the way of his literary reputation. On one hand it seems certain that Poe suffered from some kind of mental imbalance, even psychotic disorder. Both the causes and the symptoms thereof can be explored in terms of his early orphaning, his sour relations with an uncomprehending stepfather, endless money problems, the bizarre cult of "pure" womanhood along with an apparent impotence, his alcoholism, his fancying himself a southern aristocrat (while lacking any basis for such a notion), his necrophiliac side, his delusions of grandeur, his claims to an erudition that was actually rather slight, and his tendency to quarrel bitterly with most of those in the literary world. On the other hand there are the visionary artist whose inventions include the detective story, the verbal virtuoso whose undeniable power to work a mood can still seize first-time readers almost two centuries later, and the all-around writer whose legacy in the history of letters is incalculable.

These two sides mutually conflict in any latter-day assessment of Poe, yet are ultimately of a piece. The trap of chronic alienation is precisely what nourished Poe's capacity for literary fantasy, his talent for unreal landscape and the pure imaginary. Although some critics once emphasized and dismissed the "provincialism" of Poe, his fiction and verse strike us if anything for their cosmopolitan settings

and lack of provincial roots. At the same time his psychological af-
flictions (along with a relatively early death) prevented Poe's artistry
from evolving further. Poe is one of those curious cases of formidable
literary genius hamstrung by faulty judgment and arrested personal
growth, limitations that finally take their toll on his art.

The place of Poe in American culture, and the enormous admiration his work commands abroad, are issues that will be debated as
long as U.S. literature remains a topic of discussion. The field is considerably clearer in two areas more pertinent to this history: Poe as a
professional man of letters and Poe as critical theorist.

Throughout his adult years Poe made his living exclusively as an
editor—oftentimes as editor in chief—at periodicals and magazines.
Aside from the occasional fee he received for individual written
pieces (forty dollars for "The Bells," thirty for "The Poetic Principle"),
literary journalism was the sole paid work Poe ever knew. In this
respect he rather typifies the new breed of journalistic professional
we saw emerging in the Parisian 1830s. Poe's lot was in fact comparatively fortunate: his was neither the precarious free-lancing life of a
Baudelaire nor the daily reviewing drudgery of a Gautier. Not only
did he often take in a regular salary, he also gained a fair amount of
authority and power within the literary machinery (when he was not
quarreling with everybody in sight). His personal oddities notwithstanding, Poe for his upkeep went the typical nineteenth-century
litterateur's route as hired hand for the expanding periodical press
sector.

Unlike Baudelaire and Gautier, Poe did not hate the profession
of journalistic scribe and actually enjoyed considerable reputation as
a "fearless" man of letters. In this situation he flourished, becoming
in his day the preeminent literary critic on these shores, as well as
the first American to exhibit an analytical technique rather than the
vague and celebratory approach that had been the U.S. norm prior to
him. Nevertheless Poe was at heart a lyrist whose broader gifts were
in the employ of a literary market wherein poetry played a minor
role, and whose only novel, the *Narrative of Arthur Gordon Pym,* he
composed primarily in order to make money, a proposition he knew
was less than feasible with short fiction or verse. Not accidentally,
Poe was also the first American writer to formulate what we now rec-

ognize as a scattered series of genuinely new theoretical reflections that belong to the *l'art pour l'art* doctrine. These poetic speculations inevitably form part of Poe's literary practice.

Poe's doctrines developed according to a pattern already noted in France and England, whereby a wide-ranging and unitary philosophy, concerned with the total functioning of the human soul, in the process of dissemination becomes misinterpreted, divided up, and simplified. For all his intelligence and his originality, Poe repeated the pattern. Much of his poetic theory derives directly from Coleridge, on whom the American lavished his most high-flown superlatives. In his essay "Wordsworth and Coleridge," Poe invokes the *Biographia Literaria* and ardently remarks, "Of Coleridge I cannot but speak with reverence. His towering intellect! his gigantic power!" (75). Coleridge's thought, as seen in chapter 3, staunchly retains the German idealist view that our mental faculties constitute a totality and that the poetic imagination, by blending and fusing those faculties, helps strengthen the unity of our soul.

Poe, in turn, proceeds to take the step that Cousin and Gautier took in France and that Pater and Wilde would in England. In his justly remembered lecture-essay "The Poetic Principle" (1849), Poe subdivides the mind into "Pure Intellect, Taste, and Moral Sense," a schema by now familiar enough from Kant and Schiller. As did the Germans and their English follower Coleridge, Poe places "[t]aste in the middle, because it is just this position which, in the mind, it occupies" (38–39). Poe grants some overlap between the three faculties, but unlike his more philosophically inclined predecessors, he pronounces these respective functions distinct and separate: "Just as the Intellect concerns itself with Truth, so Taste informs us of the Beautiful, while the Moral Sense is regardful of Duty" (39).

Given this outlook, it is only fitting that in his earlier essay "The Philosophy of Composition" (1846), Poe asserts that "Beauty is the sole legitimate province of the poem" (23), and more, that Truth and Passion "are absolutely antagonistic to that Beauty which . . . is the excitement, or pleasurable elevation, of the soul" (24). In sum, beauty is the sole concern in lyric art. These doctrines are reaffirmed and more fully elaborated in "The Poetic Principle," in which Poe, a Wildean aesthete *avant la lettre,* argues that what precisely is indispensable to lyric song is also what has "nothing whatever to do" with truth. In this connection, Poe takes yet further his mentor Coleridge's well-known idea, "the heresy of paraphrase," and targets what he sees as an ever greater fallacy, "the heresy of the Didactic" and its assumption "that the ultimate object of all Poetry is Truth." For Poe, nothing matters except "the poem written solely for the poem's sake" (37–38).

Such, then, is Poe's own reformulation and thinking-through of the doctrine of pure Art for Art's Sake—including an early germ of the very phrase itself. In his "Poetic Principle," Poe, as would Pater, singles out music as the essential model for aesthetic experience: "It is in Music, perhaps, that the soul most nearly attains the great end for which . . . it struggles—the creation of supernal beauty" (40).

When seen through the lenses of early French and later English aestheticism, Poe's theory strikes us as familiar enough (if somewhat rough in its expression). It furnishes a glimpse into a mind pursuing certain investigations independently of other thinkers but arriving at comparable conclusions. Poe's most outrageous speculation in "The Poetic Principle," however, has no next of kin in the annals of lyric art or doctrine; I refer to his oft-quoted dogma "I hold that a long poem does not exist. I maintain that the phrase, 'a long poem,' is simply a flat contradiction in terms" (33). For Poe, an epic poem such as the *Iliad* is actually "a series of lyrics"; even if the poet's epic intent is a given, "I can only say that the work is based on an imperfect sense of art" (34).

Both the thought itself and the apodictic certainty with which Poe asserts it can still amuse or confound readers today. So doctrinaire a statement seems to exemplify Poe's wrongheadedness, his tendency to present his wildly subjective fantasies as though they were axiomatic truths. It also necessarily flies in the face of what was then recent evidence from (among others) the English Romantics, all of whom had composed some very effective and beautiful long poems.

Within the context of Poe's life and times, however, his summary dismissal of the rubric and entity "long poem" can be seen as a prophetic insight from a visionary mind. By the early nineteenth century, epic poetry as a creative practice was all but dead in contemporary European and American letters; in the same way, expository verse as a didactic tool was by then largely a relic among the Western literate;

and verse narrative, it goes without saying, led a precarious life on the sidelines of a literary market in which the traditional story-telling role was being preempted by the prose novel. When Poe claims that "a long poem does not exist," he speaks as an editor for whom, in the light of the emergent book and periodical business of his day, long poems might just as well not exist, given their scant salability.

Unlike most of his Romantic predecessors in England, Poe was closely involved with the administrative and distributive end of the new means of literary production, and hence knew from inside the direction and priorities of the cultural machinery that paid for his labor and his scribbling. (In an 1842 letter to a friend, Poe writes that "the higher order of poetry . . . always will be, in this country, unsaleable.")[8] When Poe declares in "The Poetic Principle" that "the Quarterlies as *yet* . . . have not *insisted* on our estimating Lamartine by the public foot" (35), he indirectly conveys the unstated broader principles of a publishing trade hungry for its raw materials—constant prose output, regular copy—but needing minimal verse. He asserts, moreover, that "the epic mania— . . . the idea that, to merit in poetry, prolixity is indispensable—has, for some years past, been gradually dying out of the public mind" (37), an incontestable statement of social and historical fact. "It is at least clear that no very long poem will ever be popular again" (34), he predicts, a prophecy that has been preponderantly borne out, the rare exceptions being poems such as Browning's *The Ring and the Book* or, more recently, Derek Walcott's *Omeros.*

Thus, when Poe claims viability for the short lyric exclusively, he is creating a virtue out of necessity and, from a doctrinal standpoint, making the best of the situation for practicing poets and editors after 1800. Poe's most farfetched poetic notion is also in some perverse way his most farsighted.

From a historical point of view, Poe's position in U.S. writing can be seen as roughly analogous to that of Gautier in France: he was the first imaginative writer to make a case for pure poetry and *l'art pour l'art* on his native ground. Gautier and Poe, essentially poetical spirits and verse craftsmen who came of age in the newborn literary markets of their respective nations, then proceeded to stake out an Art for Art's Sake doctrine in defense of their threatened poetic interests. The differences in cultural life between France and the United States, on the other hand, were as day to night. While Gautier had the advantage of a mature literary society to which he could feel he belonged, and a rich national history to which he could look back and then romanticize in his fiction, Poe had neither. There was as yet little in the way of past or present high cultural treasure within the Anglo-Saxon sectors of his youthfully rude and puritanical land, and his self-conception as southern gentleman was a delusion as pitiable as it was fruitless. Had Poe been Parisian, he would conceivably have found a niche and even a few admirers in the artistically intense if amorphous Bohemia there.

Perhaps not surprisingly, it was the French symbolist poets who adopted the American as a confrère, finding supporting material for their own doctrines in Poe's theories of poetic mood and in his suggestive lyric cadences. Baudelaire, Mallarmé, and Valéry all welcomed Poe as a kindred spirit—a transnational tie that still elicits controversy in Anglophone letters.

Modernismo is not Modernism, at least not in the sense in which the English word is customarily employed. *Modernismo* in fact is an entity scarcely known beyond the confines of the Spanish-speaking world, where among literary circles it grew into the dominant sensibility and style between 1885 and 1920. Almost any Hispanic verse of any note written during those three or so decades bears the identifiable *modernista* mark. The movement dramatically altered the ways in which the slightest line of Spanish lyric was to be conceived and composed, and hence is a major episode in the uneven, at times painful, history of Hispanic letters.

The only *modernista* figure recognizable to the non-Hispanics is of course José Martí (1853–95), whose verses later served as lyrics for the mid-twentieth-century "folk" song "Guantanamera." Actually Martí is far better known to non-Hispanics for his constant, selfless struggles on behalf of Cuban independence from Spain—struggles that culminated in his death on the island battlefield—than for his amazing literary fecundity. And though Martí is indeed one of the most memorable lyrists in the language, there were at least a dozen *modernistas* who, in his time and in the ensuing generation, succeeded in forging a worthy and enduring lyric art of their own.

Martí is something of an anomaly within the larger *modernista* groundswell, inasmuch as he quietly yet firmly rejected the doctrine of *el arte por el arte* that characterized the movement faithful. Martí believed, rather, in the practical value of the arts, in their ability to awaken people's best emotions, even in their potential to improve society and help shape citizenship.[9]

Modernismo is many things at once. From a literary history point of view, it is the remarkable burst in poetic innovation that spread across the Ibero-American world—from the Caribbean and Meso-America to the Southern Cone capitals—and that in so doing overcame some two hundred years of dreary stagnation in Spanish-language verse. During its century and a half of decadence, Imperial Spain's poetical culture had settled into a stale academicism of tired baroque formulas and neoclassical clichés. Most Romantic poetry in nineteenth-century Spain had in turn demonstrated an excess of that other Iberian disease—bombast—and was itself but a pale imitation of its French and English models.

Meanwhile, during the first five decades of the new Latin American republics, literature was as much in its infancy as it had been in the new Anglo-American nation to the north. Not surprisingly, local Romantic verse and prose showed the same raw, immature energies that had characterized Spain's flaccid, secondhand version. Ironically, the two best specimens of postindependence verse in Ibero-America are cast in thoroughly traditional molds: the solidly neoclassical ode to a great military battle, "La victoria de Junín. Canto a Bolívar" (1825), by the Ecuadorian José Joaquín Olmedo (1780–1847), and "A la agricultura de la zona tórrida" (1826), written in a Renaissance verse form, the *silva,* by the great Venezuelan-Chilean humanist and teacher Andrés Bello (1781–1865). Though they are fine poems, they also prove the limits of a literature that cloaks new material content in older verse forms.

Like Poe in his respective circumstances, a young poet coming of age in the new Latin America had virtually no homegrown Hispanic models to turn to for inspiration and growth. At the same time (but unlike Poe in this case) the young Latin American poets lacked in

Mother Spain a figure who might correspond to Coleridge in originality and stature, the notable exception being Gustavo Adolfo Bécquer (1836–70), whose understated delicacy Martí's verse recalls in many ways.

From a more technical standpoint, the *modernista* movement considerably expanded poetry's verbal means and resources, which the prolonged Spanish cultural sleep had vastly reduced. The *modernistas* also broadened the linguistic materials constituting their art. They invented new verse meters; or they imported them from foreign tongues; or they revived long-forgotten medieval Iberian meters. Although no match for Walt Whitman and his leap into free verse, they mixed varieties of line lengths in bold and unprecedented ways. New or revived rhyme schemes, monorhyme included, were part of the experiments. The *modernistas* widened the poetic lexicon, bringing in locutions from science or from other languages, sometimes employing long, euphonious words with "l" 's in them (such as "libélula," "hipsipila"), chiefly for their sensuousness and sonority. The leading figure of the movement, Nicaragua's Rubén Darío (1867–1916), stands out particularly for his virtuosity in juggling an amazing assortment of poetic forms, as well as for adapting them to his purposes. In its expansion of the artisanal workshop, *modernismo* invites comparison to the creation and diffusion of new verse forms across Europe during the Renaissance.

By the same token, *modernismo* broadened the array of subject matter and settings considered worthy of lyric verse. Going beyond a stylized Greco-Roman antiquity, or a neoclassicized present, or the ersatz Byronism that had been the unfortunate lot of poetry in Spanish, the *modernistas* freely set their stanzas in exotic Asian latitudes or in elegant Bourbon-rococo France, in medieval Norse country or in wholly imaginary lands. Their art fittingly came studded with verbal representations of beautiful things: diamonds, rubies, jade; enamels, goldsmithies; rich palaces with peacocks, water lilies, and swans.[10] Or their verse called attention to what is most dramatic and vivid about the landscape or the past history of South America. Or, taking their cue from Baudelaire, they evoked the tensions and textures peculiar to contemporary urban life, and, the obverse side of the coin, they touched on those hauntingly modern, post-Darwinian problems of rootlessness and boredom, of loneliness and lost faith. In the end, in one of those surprising historic reversals, the *modernistas* would in turn come to influence poetry written in Spain itself.

Modernismo represents the arrival and implanting of the theory of Art for Art's Sake in Latin American literary life. Virtually all *modernista* adepts, Martí excepted, consciously advocated a "pure" verse in which beauty was the sole relevant factor, to the exclusion of all moral, civic, or social content. (The practice, as seen here later, was somewhat less consistent.) Darío himself, in his famous long poem that begins "Yo soy aquél . . ." (roughly translatable as "I am the one who . . ."), mingles autobiographical confession with aesthetic manifesto, extolling the cult of beauty in terms identical to those of religion. Many of the recognizable stock phrases and ideas of *l'art pour l'art* are to be found writ large in this poem. Early on, Darío remarks, "La torre de marfil tentó mi anhelo" [The ivory tower tempted my dreams] (5:863).[11] "El arte puro" [pure art] is likened to none other than Jesus Christ preaching, in the scriptural Latin, "Ego sum lux et veritas et vita" (5:864) (which is paralleled, in English, in the Gospel of John: "I am the Way, the Truth, and the Light"). The poem concludes with an evocation of "la caravana" traveling "hacia Belén" (the caravan traveling toward Bethlehem), presumably the caravan of the Magi, journeying to pay homage to the new aestheticist religion.

Poe, as stated here, appears to have arrived at his rudimentary Art for Art's Sake position on his own, through his misreadings of Coleridge combined with the special dynamics of his personal isolation. The *modernistas,* in contrast, wrote after 1880, a time when the phrase as well as the idea *l'art pour l'art* had become commonplace in France and elsewhere. In the absence of viable artistic models either in their mother tongue or in the mother country, many Latin Americans indeed turned to *la belle France* for their poetic "schooling," and with a most pronounced zeal. Darío in his autobiography vividly reminisces about what the city of Paris had signified to him, both as symbol and as place:

> From the time I was a little boy, I dreamed of Paris, to the point where, in my prayers, I would implore God not to let me die without knowing Paris. Paris for me was like a paradise where one could breathe the essence of happiness on Earth. It was the

city of Art, Beauty, and Glory; and above all it was the capital of Love, the Kingdom of Reverie. And I was going to get to know Paris and fulfill my life's highest yearning. And when at Saint-Lazare station I set foot on Parisian soil, I felt as if I'd touched sacred ground." (1:102)

The most obvious and immediate lyric model for Darío and his fellow *modernistas* was the group of poets associated with the Parnassian movement. So called after their magazine *Le Parnasse*, the Parnassians were known for their impersonality, their cult of formal perfection, and their aristocratic refinements, with such images as those of courtly young *dames* and haughty swans. Darío himself was to include a sonnet in praise of the arch-Parnassian lyrist Leconte de Lisle in the second edition (1890) of his verse and prose collection *Azul. . .*, as well as an adulatory essay in his critical collection *Los raros* [1896; The eccentrics].

Various sources have been adduced for the title of Darío's first significant book, *Azul . . .* (1888), all of them French: Hugo's aphorism "L'art c'est l'azur"; the Parisian journal *Revue Bleue;* Catulle Mendès's 1888 collection of stories, *Les oiseaux bleus;* and Mallarmé's sombre poem "L'Azur," which dwells on the sheer difficulty of creating verse and ends with the outcry "Je suis hanté. L'Azur! L'Azur! L'Azur! L'Azur!" Though no single source can definitively be pinpointed, the broader fact is that French literature was permeating *modernista* practice to an enormous extent, furnishing imagery, vocabulary, titles, and a grand artistic ethos for its Latin American followers.

The innovative *modernistas* also learned from the French poets' language itself. Darío in his *Historia de mis libros* notes how, after Spain's wasteland of "eternal Spanish Golden Age clichés and its indecisive modern poetry," he happened upon "a literary gold mine" in his French lyric counterparts, and found out how to "[apply] their way of adjectivizing, certain syntactic devices, and their verbal aristocratism, to Castilian" (1:196). He claims to have known by memory the *Diccionario de galicismos* of Barat and freely admits to having slipped in the "opportune Gallicism" as a stylistic device in his work wherever useful and appropriate.

From the Parnassian poets, Darío and his coreligionists learned about pictorial qualities and visual beauty, whereas from the great symbolist Paul Verlaine they picked up on the elegant rococo imagery of the *Fêtes galantes* (1869), a work that is an almost overwhelming presence in Darío's ironic vignette of Versailles, "Era un aire suave" [It was a gentle aria]. The roving young Nicaraguan in fact met Verlaine in Paris, and there is a touching memoir of Darío's experience of the legendary lyrist in an essay collected in *Los raros* (2:292–99).

Equally important, Verlaine helped sensitize the inner ear of *modernista* writers to the musicality and melody of verse, as urged in the famous dictum with which his "Art Poétique" begins, "De la musique avant toute chose" [Music above all].[12] The place of music in the culture of English aestheticism, noted in our discussion of Walter Pater, is particularly foregrounded in those *modernista* poems that bear musical titles and thereby draw attention to certain specifically musical features of poetical composition — repetition of sounds, recurrent rhythms, theme-and-variations technique, aural sensuousness. These are precisely the qualities of Darío's anthology piece "Sonatina," with its steady $\frac{6}{8}$, berceuse-like lilt and artful cross-rhythms (5:774–75). Most expressive of all is the second "Nocturno" of Colombian poet José Asunción Silva (1865–96), one of the most celebrated lyrics in Spanish: a stunning tour de force of verbal symmetries, structured phonics, and vocalic song, all masterfully organized into two subtly differentiated movements, as it were.[13]

Such is the accepted wisdom, and in this regard I do not claim to offer much that is new.[14] Literate Hispanics and other readers conversant with traditions of Spanish verse will rightly recognize the foregoing summary, intended for nonspecialists, as the common currency of standard reference books and histories. On the other hand, what is still in the process of being untangled is the set of conditions that prompted the *modernista* ethos and within which its poetic practitioners labored. Many of the key factors that were at work in France, Britain, and the United States are equally applicable to the Latin American situation, though, inevitably, with certain Latin-specific differences. One of these now-familiar factors was the crisis of Christian religious belief in the face of natural science triumphant.

In Darío's poem "Yo soy aquél," we noted the celebration of art and beauty in intense, concretely religious terms. By the same token, in the preface to *El canto errante,* Darío casually describes himself as "this Jansenist flesh for bonfires" who is battling poetic mediocrity in "the name of an instrument that comes from the Greek" (5:948). Like Ruskin, Pater, and Wilde in England, the Nicaraguan lyrist found his orthodox Christian faith undermined by the advance of science and secularism, and he too worked out a substitute creed in the realm of the aesthetic. As happens with many a Latin American liberal, Darío in his youth went through a brief anticlerical phase and questioned the Church dogma of original and actual sin as well as its hidebound suppression of the erotic.

Later Darío's antireligious stance would evolve into the peculiarly modern anxiety at the lack of adequate spiritual foundations: "I am overcome with grief when, examining my beliefs in depth, I have not found my faith to be solid and grounded." Contemplating in his mind's eye a vast and eternal universe in which planet Earth will eventually disappear, he concedes, "In the end, all is nothing, fame included." [15] This existential angst in fact serves as the subject of one of Darío's most frequently anthologized poems, "Lo fatal" [The inevitable], in which he dwells darkly on the tragedy of conscious, sentient life, with its fearsome uncertainties about our past origins, its present terrors, and its opaque, unknowable future.

Darío himself went through a number of philosophical phases, flirting here with the visionary republicanism of a Victor Hugo, there with esoteric cults like Orpheism or Pythagoreanism. Other *modernistas,* in turn, sought solace in spiritualism, Rosicrucianism, or Swedenborgianism as their own replacements for a Catholic belief system that was in epistemological retreat.[16] On the other hand, in a more theoretical, more objective, and even more optimistic vein, Darío in the essay "Dilucidaciones" in *El canto errante* could make some now-familiar claims for poetry as a medium that offers knowledge differing from, yet overlapping with, both science and religion: "The poet has a direct and introspective vision of life and a higher vision that goes beyond what is subject to the laws of general knowledge. Religion and philosophy meet up with art on such boundaries, for in both there is also an artistic ambiance" (5:955–56). At the same time, as has been the case with many a sensible art theorist from Kant onward, Darío in his *Historia de mis libros* feels compelled to remind certain eager youths, for whom mere talent coupled with an individual aesthetic would seem to suffice, that learning and good taste are also important factors in the making of excellent verse (1:205–6).

In addition to the idea of poetry as a substitute faith, the other traditional explanation for the rise of *modernismo* is one briefly examined, along general lines, in my introductory chapter: namely, the artists' reaction against bourgeois mediocrity and the philistine materialism of their times. This oppositional stance is amply present in the publicist writings of the *modernistas* themselves, and Darío, again, articulates the position memorably. In his foreword to *Prosas profanas* (1896), he takes aim at "the absolute lack of high-mindedness among the educated people of our continent, wherein there reigns the universal figure characterized by Rémy de Gourmont as *Celui qui ne comprend pas*" (5:761). The twenty-nine-year-old poet deplores among the talented "a complete ignorance of the very Art they devote themselves to," and he frankly admits, "I detest the life and times in which it was my lot to be born" (5:763). Similarly, in the preface to *Cantos de vida y esperanza* (1905), the poet reaffirms his "respect for the aristocracy of intellect" along with his "abhorrence for mediocrity, for intellectual mongrelism and aesthetic flatness [*chatura*]" (5:859).

A Darío short story, "El rey burgués" (roughly, The middle-class king), spells out this attitude in "allegorical" and not uncertain terms. The story portrays a bourgeois king living in palatial splendor, where he keeps painters and sculptors at his disposal along with fencing masters, rhetoricians, and barbers. One day a "strange sort of man" shows up before the king's throne: a poet. He is hungry, so the king says to him, "Speak and you shall eat." The poet hence delivers a long and eloquent oration on his vast range of experiences, differentiating the august and multifaceted nature of true art from "cold marble trappings" and "gilt pictures," and complaining about the cobblers who criticize his prosody and the professor of pharmacy who checks his punctuation. The king interrupts the poet and calls on his counselors, who recommend that the poet be given a music box to be played regularly in the garden. The advice is implemented; the poet faithfully follows orders. Life goes on, and the day after a festive winter's evening in the palace, the poet is found lying dead out in the snow, "a bitter smile on his lips, and his hand still clutching at the [music box] crank" (5:632).

A more forthright and familiar sort of protest can be found in a novel by José Asunción Silva, *De sobremesa* [After-dinner conversation], in which the gathered friends of one José Fernández, author of two books of verse who has since turned silent, are urging the man to return to his art. Fernández is portrayed as a polymath: he translates English poetry, has been an army officer, knows geology, and is a piano virtuoso and a scholar of Greek and Inca statuary. A cosmopolite, he smokes Havana cigars and sips Danzig liqueurs, and his living-room decor includes Russian furnishings and a copy of a Rembrandt. He is, in a word, a kind of *Übermensch* figure who, when his admiring friends deplore his isolation from "real life," counters by disdaining the latter as a "bourgeois life without grounds for passion or curiosity."

The character Fernández—clearly a projection of Silva himself— is particularly dismissive toward "the public." He notes, " 'Poet,' perhaps, is the label under which I was classified. For the public, one has to *be* something. The common herd gives names to things in order to say them, and attaches labels to individuals in order to classify them." This, needless to say, is fatal to the poet: "The trouble is, I do not want to *say* but rather to suggest, and for suggestion to be produced it is necessary that the reader be an artist." Without artistry in a reader, the results will be nil. Fernández draws a contrastive analogy between knocking on a tabletop and playing Liszt's "Mephisto" on the keyboard of a Steinway: the reading public by and large resembles not a piano but that insentient table. And although he squarely opposes the conservative reaction in his country (presumably Colombia), Fernández nevertheless laments the modern loss of "the sublime" and bemoans the passing of a "blind faith" that had once "offered within its shady lap a pillow on which the world-weary could lay their head to rest."[17]

In another instance, Silva himself in a letter deplores what he saw as the numb indifference of Colombia's salesmen and army generals toward "an intellectual and artistic universe of anything that is not immediately visible [*por delante*]."[18] Farther south, similar accounts in Chile noted with regret that the denizens of that Andean nation regarded poets merely as crazy vagabonds. Such statements varyingly express their authors' isolation and "alienation" from the new bourgeois-materialist current of their time and countries. The view, generally echoed or at least reported in the usual surveys and histories, is founded on legitimately shared experiences and is by no means false.

Nevertheless the socioeconomic textures surrounding the *modernistas'* disaffection with their societies was a great deal more nuanced and complex than their heartfelt complaints would suggest. While Rubén Darío himself came from a modest background, he was the exception. Most other *modernistas* sprang from that very bourgeoisie whose narrow materialism they decried; perhaps not accidentally, their own rich families had suffered serious financial reverses. When Silva's father died in 1887, the son took over the family business until the bankruptcy proceedings of 1892–93 (which also happened to be the period of his most inspired work); thereafter he earned his living in a novelties shop.

Similarly, the parents of Cuban poet-to-be Julián del Casal (1863–93) quit their sugar mill in the face of large-scale competition, while those of Leopoldo Lugones (1874–1938)—who in time emerged as Argentina's great lyrist—abandoned their old family hacienda. The Uruguayan poet Julio Herrera y Reissig (1875–1910) hailed from old criollo (that is, white settler) background, but when his family went into decline he worked as a civil servant and wine merchant. The *modernistas,* in sum, were as much their respective economic elite's social losers as they were its anguished literary marginals.

Latin America, of course, has seldom figured as more than a minor player in the arena of world events (other than as a target of foreign powers). As a result, the troubled history of the region is probably less familiar to most readers of these pages than is the Euro-Atlantic North's two-hundred-year record of growth and triumph. For the sake of those readers, a quick look at the broad contours of that other, "southern" past is now in order.

Following the bloodletting of the wars of independence from Spain (1810–21), the new Latin American republics experienced protracted civil conflicts in which liberal and conservative factions of the ruling oligarchies fought desperately to impose their ways on their societies. (The process is famously depicted in chapters 6 through 9 of García Márquez's novel *One Hundred Years of Solitude.*) Both nonetheless were factions within a landed oligarchy that had roots going back to Spanish invasion, conquest, and colonialism. Independence had brought no real changes in the system of ownership, and indeed throughout the nineteenth century the wealthy elites expanded their landholdings and thus became even wealthier. In the worst of cases, liberal victory degenerated into prolonged military dictatorship, as in the case of Gen. Porfirio Díaz, who ruled Mexico with an iron hand, off and on, from 1875 to 1911.

Even in the best of cases, however, there was virtually no instance of a Latin American nation undergoing serious economic development and diversification. The liberal oligarchies instead made a conscious decision to open their economies to foreign (generally English and French) investment and trade, while remaining content to apply religiously the Ricardian doctrine of "comparative advantage" to their countries and hew to their long-standing role as exporters of primary materials. The inevitable result was not a native, yet varied, liberal capitalism but a neocolonial order in which the ultimate hegemony shifted from a tired Madrid to the expanding metropolises of London and Paris. The Latin American economic elites thus traded not in gold and silver with feudal Spain but rather shipped their industrial ores and agroexports off to liberal England and France, even as they received in return a bewildering array of consumer goods from French and English factories.

The cultural forms engendered by this skewed, dependent brand of market economy have a distinct quality that sets them apart from their models elsewhere. As befits a continental civilization dominated by huge landowners, there failed to arise anything like the U.S. mystique of the yeoman farmer, the Jeffersonian vision of hardy agricultural smallholders, or the cult of the peasant that has been invoked by both left and right in Europe. Meanwhile, in the lack of legitimately native liberal traditions that could counteract oligarchical power, the spiritual and intellectual vacuum was filled by the Catholic church, which thoroughly supported the established social order.

Even the liberal-democratic ideal in the abstract failed to enter substantially into nineteenth-century Latin American discourse. Domingo Faustino Sarmiento (1811–88), author of the nonfictional classic *Facundo*, and arguably the greatest Latin American liberal of his time has in his writings precious little to say about freedom and democracy and more than enough exhortations about the need to "civilize" Argentina, first by liquidating the "barbarian" elements—the Indians and gauchos—and then refashioning the country into another England or France.

Similarly, the positivist doctrine that triumphed in official Latin American circles in the later nineteenth century, which had *científico* ideologues that were in fact quite close to the Mexican dictatorship of Porfirio Díaz, picked up on the arid rationalism and developmental schemes of Comtean theory, yet took in none of the Frenchman's worries about "the disease of individualism" nor his dreams of a "religion of humanity."[19] Latin American liberal notables were much more intent on catching up with Anglo-French Europe than with fulfilling any broader social ideal. As has frequently been pointed out, the *positivistas'* motto was not Liberty, Equality, Fraternity but Order and Progress.[20] The legacy was not a good one: large-scale control of foreign capital over the local economy and a virtually negligible intellectual inheritance. As Octavio Paz has said, "Positivism gave us nothing."[21]

This, then, was the social, economic, and cultural world inhabited by the *modernistas.* As active men of letters they were as much products of that world as its malcontents, accepting of some aspects and displeased with others. The *modernista* configuration shows a profile roughly analogous to that of the region's liberals and positivists. To draw on a type of contrast employed in chapter 3, the first century of independent Latin America produced no great lyrist with a grand humanitarian vision comparable to that of Walt Whitman or Victor Hugo. Save for Martí—who in his struggle against Spanish colonialism in Cuba is a special case—no *modernista* is known for holding and expressing strongly democratic or egalitarian views. Rubén Darío, in the preface to *Prosas profanas* even directs a mocking phrase at "democrat Walt Whitman," though the barb may have been motivated as much by anti-Yankeeism as by antidemocratism. It has also been remarked that Darío's "Frenchified" imagery derives more from Second Empire dictatorship than from Third Republic liberalism.[22]

Owing to their Europhile orientation, the oligarchies that set the tone in Latin America built their social habitats largely from overseas imports: English beers and furniture, French waltzes, German textiles, European coaches, and the like. That list might also include literary products on the international market, part of the elegantly lettered and developed subculture to which many educated Latins—notably in the more prosperous Southern Cone countries—wished to belong. Not a few upper-bourgeois Chilean homes subscribed to the *Revue des Deux Mondes,* while the Santiago newspaper *La Epoca* in turn printed articles by leading foreign journalists.[23]

This legacy has persisted to our time. Claude Lévi-Strauss in *Triste Tropiques* remarks with amazement at the degree to which, in the 1930s, his students in Brazil were up on the latest European intellectual fashions, though superficially;[24] and a magazine such as the Mexican Octavio Paz's prestigious monthly *Vuelta* depends to a great degree on translations from European or U.S. authors. To this day the more educated elements among the Latin American elites can exhibit an impressive knowledge of Western high culture, along with a surprising ignorance of or even contempt for their own countries' homegrown artifacts.

In this unevenly developed civilization, where the literacy rate was woefully low (Argentina aside), a book was a costly investment that few could afford. In the 1890s Rubén Darío, in the earlier stages of his career as an author, actually depended on patronage from rich friends. The printing bill for *Los raros* was paid by Angel de Estrada, while the production costs for *Prosas profanas* were picked up by Carlos Vega Belgrano.[25] The precocious adolescent Darío started out not as a believer in *poésie pure,* but as a maker of traditional civic verse in praise of a rich lady or a local hero.[26] Darío himself admits in "El poeta a las Musas," published when he was just eighteen,

> I long for the crown that Fame
>   gives to the priests of the beautiful
>   and I run in search of the divine laurel
>   that is ever green with Apollo's splendor.
>   (5:399–400; translation mine)

In these lines filled with classical allusion, Darío imagines himself in the quasi-ancient role of priestly singer for an ancient mythology.

"Todo acabó" (It is all gone), the final stanza laments; for he now sees instead "the rays of Olympian Jupiter / enslaved by Franklin and

Edison." The mature Darío labored under the full assumption that the bardic world is vanished, lost in the past. Yet the bardic impulse remained under a new guise: his famous "Marcha triunfal," a dazzlingly virtuosic paean of praise to conquering troops on return from military victory, is in fact an ode to no triumph in particular and no specific nation. Set vividly in a time and place before the existence of firearms, in which warfare is still waged with swords, "Marcha triunfal" is the poetic celebration of martial glory, written in an era when the poets have actually lost their function as public celebrants.

The only way in which a *modernista* poet like Darío could earn a regular living as a writer was to toil as a paid employee within the new, expanding enterprise of journalism. In *Historia de mis libros* he states, "And if the lack of a basic fortune obliged me to do journalistic work, I could dedicate my leisure wanderings to the exercise of pure art and mental creation" (1:206). At age nineteen, Darío left the backwater of Managua, Nicaragua, and headed south to the greater wealth of Santiago de Chile, a fairly cosmopolitan urban center where, it has been remarked, he soon got to know the editorial boards of the newspapers before he was even acquainted with the city's streets.[27] The young wordsmith put out his pen for hire and started at the bottom, writing copy for sensationalist news items and eventually working his way up to the prestige of articles graced with his byline.

Darío remained a journalist all his life, an able and productive (if not very profound) one, whether residing in Santiago or, later, in Buenos Aires, Madrid, or Paris. Moreover, he always took pride in his journalistic craft and thus expressed some concern over the threat posed to artful and thoughtful journalism by the rising U.S.-style breed of the dry, factual "reporter," a type that Darío, Martí, and other *modernistas*-as-journalists strived hard not to be. Darío observed with some dismay that "the Yankees, . . . owing to their mercantilism and the premium that they put on time, have given precedence to dispatches over editorials; have established the reign of information over thought [*doctrina*]."[28] Though Darío did journalism first and foremost for a living, he nonetheless regarded his profession and its traditional ideals seriously.

At the same time, as was the case with Gautier and other French counterparts, Darío—who used to compose verse at his office desk

—perceived a conflict between lyric creativity and the daily drudge of work. Still only in his nineteenth year, Darío lamented in Chile's *El Mercurio* that "almost all [poets] remain silent; almost all have forgotten the friendly commerce of the Graces." He alludes somberly to poets buried amid mathematics papers, business duties, or parliamentary bustle, and he particularly sympathizes with those lost souls who "in prosaic offices count numbers instead of hemistychs." In 1907, forty years old, he refers with praise to the dignity that has been acquired by staff writers in the Argentine daily press, yet laments what he deems the corresponding lack of organization in the sphere of "exclusively literary production of books or magazines." [29]

In addition, Darío notes, the new patrons of letters are the newspapers and the moneyed investors. "Before," he observes, *those* [presumably the aristocrats] were owners, masters. Today, a publisher, a government minister, a millionaire leases [writers]." Darío remarks with bitter irony, "And what are the majority of readers? An editor in this respect has . . . the right to pass over the work of a thinker—and let's not even pronounce those suspicious words 'poet,' 'artist'—for the benefit of a wholesale factory's mental merchandise." [30]

The situation of the *modernistas* is by now a familiar one, analogous in its general contours to that of the poets in France or of Poe in the U.S. They were essentially lyrists whose primary art lacked salability in the new era of journalistic prose. Both Darío and Casal remark that demand determines everything, that writers are under constant pressure from their editors to yield product. The writer, as they see it, is no free creator but rather a salaried scribe or, even worse—to use today's terminology—a piece-worker.

Of course the *modernistas'* poetry, much as elsewhere at the time, was "free" only in that it had negligible sales value. Like most French lyrists, the *modernistas* were accused of residing in an ivory tower, but, as Angel Rama points out, the ivory tower was in truth a defensive measure for those whose poetry could not be compensated. Silva himself writes in a letter, "If you only knew what a horrible prison the Ivory Tower is, when voluntary seclusion becomes a jail cell." Meanwhile the *modernista* poets-as-journalists worked hard in their coverage of a broad range of subjects, even as they needed to write fast, with little time for the pursuit of in-depth study, knowledge, or commentary.[31]

Nevertheless, the poets themselves admitted that writing for hire had its benefits. Casal, for instance, notes that churning out copy for the daily press imparts "a certain suppleness" to his pen. Rama, moreover, has observed that some of the traits we associate with *modernismo* are also those of journalism: "the search for the unusual, the brusque juxtaposition of unlike elements, the constant innovation, the bold choice of subjects, the range of nuances, the interpenetration of differing disciplines, the unyielding, desperate eagerness for originality." These are characteristics "that belong to the new [literary] market, and, simultaneously, are ways of penetrating and controlling it."[32] The relationship between the *modernista* poets and their journalistic tasks, then, was not just another version of Carlyle's cash nexus but a deeper intellectual and artistic symbiosis.

The Latin American *modernistas* were undergoing the experiences of lyric poets elsewhere in a triumphant liberal-capitalist order, wrestling as they were with an irreconcilable split between their fundamentally poetic selves and their journalistic or other bourgeois professions. Unlike Poe, however, they did have the benefit of each other's spiritual support and company, and could therefore feel themselves part of a continent-wide movement; and of course they had in the French Parnassians and symbolists a model for conscious emulation. As a result their isolation was by no means as complete or as tragic as had been that of their lone counterpart in the Anglo north. At the same time, however, their larger struggle was very Latin American in its search for an identity that might take them beyond their given historical traditions. Positivists and *modernistas* both, after all, were repudiating what they saw as a bankrupt Iberian heritage and were seeking instead to "French-ify" their respective spheres of influence, the former through socioeconomic organization, the latter via poetic technique. Not accidentally, the elegant French-style buildings and boulevards that occupy prominent places in Buenos Aires and Mexico City—the Teatro Colón in the former, the Palacio de Bellas Artes in the latter—date from precisely this same period.

Although Darío would have no truck with free market ideology, his need to go beyond the poetic wasteland of old Spain is of a piece

with the liberal free-marketeers' project of updating and modernizing their respective lands by repudiating Castilian statism and feudalism — to their view a necessary first step toward realizing for Hispanic
America the nineteenth-century dream of progress. It is perhaps only
an apparent irony that the poetry of the *modernistas* is among the few
of the Europeanizing texts from that era still potent enough to reach
Latin American readers today.

The Uruguayan journalist and essayist José Enrique Rodó (1871–1917)
is yet less known outside Latin America than are the *modernista* poets.
His *Ariel* (1900), however, enjoys a quasi-proverbial status among
Latin Americans, even among those who have never read it. Structured as a valedictory speech given by a wise old Prospero (from *The
Tempest*) to his graduating disciples, *Ariel* is a paean to delicate inner
spirituality and a call to reject Caliban's sensual baseness and emulate
Ariel's higher nobility. What Rodó's Prospero eloquently advocates is
the full cultivation of the whole human being, whose range of qualities includes "idealism and order in life; noble inspiration in thought;
selflessness in morality; good taste in art; heroism in action; delicacy
in customs" (98).[33]

Ariel is particularly famous for its lengthy final look at the United
States, weighing the Anglo-American sociocultural project in the balance and finding it shortsighted, incomplete, and ultimately empty.
Though many of Rodó's strictures about the United States retain
their validity a century hence, *Ariel* is not at heart an anti-American
tract. The United States and its ways of living serve rather as a negative counterexample to Rodó's vision of the ideal future for Latin
America.

Rodó himself was a fairly multifaceted person and a man of action
who, among other things, served five terms as a member of his country's Chamber of Deputies and was also director of the National
Library. At the same time he shared with his lyric contemporaries a
commitment to beauty, saying, "I too am a *modernista*. I belong to
the grand response that lends character and significance to the evolution of thought at this century's end."[34] Indeed Rodó's place in the
history of Art for Art's Sake in Spanish America roughly corresponds
to that occupied by Kant and Schiller in continental Europe; or, per-

haps more accurately, his *Ariel* is a South American equivalent of the intellectual reprises Coleridge and Ruskin had already launched in the English-speaking world.

As did those thinkers, Rodó seeks to delineate a broad, substantial, rigorous theoretical basis for the cult of the Beautiful. He envisions for beauty a spiritual and psychological context and a network of moral relations strikingly similar to those set forth by his renowned predecessors, particularly Schiller. The chief difference in Rodó's case is that his holistic, large-scale speculations came not *before* the Latin American aestheticist movement but actually arrived at a time when the idea of *el arte por el arte* was already in full swing among Spanish American literati, was in fact at its peak of cultural influence. Chronology aside, however, Rodó's general thinking about the subject manifests the same basic differences from the views of his poetic brethren that divided Kant from Gautier, Ruskin from Wilde, Coleridge from Poe.

At the very core of Rodó's speculations is Prospero's urging on his disciples a "profound awareness of the fundamental unity of our natures," an issue that "must take precedence over the predilections that bind each of us to our different ways of life" (41). As does Matthew Arnold in *Culture and Anarchy* (a book that *Ariel* closely resembles), Rodó takes his ideal from the ancient Greeks and their "concept of the life based on the total harmony of all human faculties." Rodó through Prospero takes his stand against personal and professional specialization, against "the manner in which the mind is diminished by continual commerce with a single mode of activity" (43).

If Rodó's philosophical outlook and ethical project seem strongly reminiscent of Schiller's, the similarity is by no means unintentional. Much of *Ariel* explicitly takes as point of departure the premises and proposals formulated in the *Letters on Aesthetic Education*. Rodó acknowledges the influence early on when his Prospero reflects, "Of all the elements of education that ennoble life, none is more worthy of universal intent than art, because as Schiller has ably illustrated, nothing is more conducive to a culture that is *broad* and complete, in the sense of stimulating all the soul's faculties" (49).

Subliminally interwoven through much of *Ariel* are the German author's argument for nurturing a sense of beauty in individuals as a necessary first step toward inculcating in them a sense of justice, and the importance he attributed to this process in the full development of all human beings. The Uruguayan disciple of Schiller confidently states that "an educated sense of the beautiful is the most effective collaborator in a delicate sensitivity for justice" (50). Or, as Rodó's speaker reflects early on in his text, "[A] higher morality would dictate a culture of aesthetics simply in the best interests of society" (44), not merely as a matter of personal taste. Or, in a passage that echoes the very crux of Schiller's aesthetic education project, "There is no doubt in my mind that he who has learned to distinguish the delicate from the vulgar, the ugly from the beautiful, has made half the journey toward distinguishing good from evil" (51).

Rodó concedes, "Good may be done without the external appearance of beauty. Charity may achieve sublime effects through vulgar, distasteful and coarse means. But charity given with delicacy and good taste is not only more beautiful, it is finer." The author's Prospero goes so far as to admit, "I have always believed that he who demands that good and truth be expressed with sternness and severity is a treacherous friend to good and truth" (50). He nonetheless concedes, "I do not suggest that taste is the most direct path to good. I do suggest that it is a parallel way and will keep the traveler's eyes on the desired path" (51). Although the author recognizes that good taste can be "occasionally joined to absence of sentiment or morality," he holds that this is so "because it was cultivated in isolation and exclusivity, thus annulling the effect of moral perfectibility exerted in a cultural order that allows no beauty of mind to develop independently of others" (53).

On the other hand our divers senses of justice, beauty, and truth will be inseparable "if . . . the soul has been harmoniously stimulated" (53). Prospero advises his graduating class that, if they wish "to popularize respect for the beautiful," the first order of business should be that of "illustrating the possibility of harmonious accord among all legitimate human activities." Future educators "will find [such a goal] an easier task than to convert the multitude directly to a love of beauty for beauty's sake [la hermosura por ella misma]" (56).

For Rodó, then, the value of beauty resides not in its pure, formal qualities in splendid isolation from all else. On the contrary, it has value precisely because it can help shape complete selves in which the triple human senses of truth, justice, and beauty—or, in philosophic terms, cognition, ethics, and aesthetics—are fully conjoined. However, as happened in other countries, this totalizing vision was not truly understood, let alone shared, by Rodó's lyric confreres. The *modernista* poets lacked the Uruguayan essayist's philosophical background and wider preoccupations. For them, the question of poetic beauty was very much an isolated, special-interest concern, as they waged a lonely battle for existence within a market economy.

Though Rodó's ideas of spirituality have trickled down into Latin American popular consciousness, his Schillerian theories have not. His latter-day admirers hailed him as an exponent of Latin soul values (*Arielismo,* as the quality is sometimes called), and his intellectual or ideological detractors generally dismiss him as a hopeless dreamer with little practical sense of how society works. In his time, the poets with whom he felt some kinship simply went their own way, doing what they knew how to do best, which was to arrange words into beautiful verse forms, regardless of the product's use or sellability. In the annals of Art for Art's Sake doctrines, it is by now a familiar story.

CHAPTER 5

The Modernist Internationale and the Market

"Modernism" is the encompassing term whereby Anglophone critics now denote a long list of "-isms," as well as a constellation of original geniuses, who, from Dublin to Petersburg, Oslo to Rome, burgeoned across Europe from approximately 1860 to 1930. In its strictly aesthetic acceptation, however, "Modernism" began achieving common currency only sometime in the 1950s. Previously, "Modernism" had been a theological term, designating certain nineteenth-century efforts to reinterpret Church faith and dogma in the light of the new social, behavioral, and historical sciences; the movement was condemned by the Vatican in 1907.

While the chief American dictionaries today include the artistic one as their most recent of definitions for our "M" word, the major encyclopedias—the *Americana,* the *Britannica,* and most notably the first two editions of the *Princeton Encyclopedia of Poetry and Poetics*—do not even provide a separate entry for "Modernism." Such reticence suggests that, among generalists and critics both, consensus may be lacking as to what "Modernism" is and is not. Alternately, it may be that the word simply presents a semantic field too vast to be adequately summed up within the column inches of a reference book.

At any rate, until not too long ago cultural commentators routinely alluded to the authors, painters, and composers of that era under the general rubric of "avant-garde" or "vanguard" or, less frequently, "experimental." Meanwhile literary critics were characterizing novelists as disparate as Joyce, Proust, and Kafka as symbolist writers. Not accidentally, American undergraduates in literature courses in the 1930s picked up an analytical vocabulary of "symbolism," and many a scholarly volume with origins in those years bears some variant of the word "symbol" in its title. Later, during the 1950s, informal popular speech—especially speech by young practitioners and sympathizers—would formulaically describe Modernist musical pieces or paintings as "far out" or "way out," and friendly listeners understood what was meant.

For now at least, "Modernism" has become an omnibus word embracing phenomena as diverse as imagism and vorticism in England, dadaism in Switzerland and France, futurism in Italy and Russia, symbolism throughout Europe, and naturalism everywhere, as well as French surrealism, German expressionism, the more poetic symbolical plays of Ibsen and Strindberg, the epic theater of Brecht, and idiosyncratic figures such as Yeats and Kafka. In visual art, "Modernism" takes in the Impressionists and their subsequent offshoots (Cézanne, Gauguin, van Gogh), as well as the cubists, the Fauves, German sects such as the Bridge and the Blue Rider groups, abstractionists of every sort, and some of the same literary "-isms" listed here. In music, the term can include the Impressionists Debussy and Ravel, the folk-based creations of Stravinsky and Bartók, Viennese atonality, the unclassifiable inventions of Varèse, and even the neoclassicism of Hindemith and the later Stravinsky and their U.S. imitators.

In the face of so broad a panorama, "Modernism" is at best a bit of highly simplifying shorthand, a retrospective sign evoking an entire process of development and decay. Terms like "avant-garde" and "experimental" belong to a time when the artistic movements either were still alive and productive or remained a vivid memory and strong inspiration to casual followers and devotees. The military French word "avant-garde" suggests street revolts and scruffy manifestos; sectarian strife and a taste for scandal; establishment catcalls and official high dudgeon; Bohemia, buffoonery, and cafés. "Modernism," by contrast, is the lofty logos of institutionalization, a noun more suitable for learned shop talk and grand theory, for academic conferences, graduate school course listings, and thick quarterlies with many long footnotes in them.

The relevant question here is: How much does Modernism belong to the history of Art for Art's Sake? How much is it a part of the aestheticist ethos and creed? These questions are addressed in the next chapter, but first it is more fruitful to focus on the larger fact of Modernism itself and what it is.

The most obvious and well-known feature of Modernism is its fore-grounding of the medium of a work of art, its heightening of form, style, and technique over "content," even at the expense of viewer accessibility. In a classic passage, Ortega y Gasset in *The Dehumanization of Art* (1925) draws the analogy of a garden seen through a window. Simultaneously gazing at the garden and looking at the pane of glass, he says, are "incompatible operations"; and in modern art it is the windowpane not the garden that is most emphasized.[1] (The Latin word *medium* signifies the middle, that which stands between.)

This focus on the medium itself may well result in the ostensible subject matter—the view outside—being rendered remote from or opaque to the unseasoned observer. Ortega of course was a conservative elitist, hostile both to the democratic masses and to realist art; the "dehumanization" in his title is actually meant as a good thing, which he proceeds to defend. (If most people don't like the "windowpane" of modern art, so much the better.) Whatever one may feel about this "political" issue, the striking and inescapable fact is that, during the Modernist period, the formal medium of all the traditional arts evolved to an unprecedented pitch of complexity in degree and in kind, with existent techniques being further elaborated and brand-new techniques being created.

In lyric poetry there is the extreme concentration of language (unexplained juxtapositions, convoluted syntax, avoidance of connectives, and unidentified allusion), along with verbal play, free verse, the pursuit of vivid imagery and metaphor for their own sakes, frequent absence of punctuation, typographical experimentation, and general obscurity of diction.

In prose fiction there is a move from a set, univocal, narrative *forme fixe* to shifting, often "unreliable" narrators, and from a strictly external depiction of character to one that brings in the play of inward, subjective states, represented via such devices as interior monologue and stream of consciousness.

In the larger, organizational aspects of narrative there is what Joseph Frank calls "the spatialization of form," whereby "attention is fixed on the interplay of relationships within the immobilized time-area." Joyce's *Ulysses*, for instance, is composed of "a vast number of references and cross-references that relate to each other independently of the time-sequence of the narrative." The result is "a continuum in which distinctions between past and present are wiped out."[2] As any reader of Joyce, Faulkner, Woolf, or Dos Passos knows, in these authors' works a nineteenth-century European conception of linearity, of an inexorable forward march of time, is largely replaced by a striving for simultaneity in which different times are presented as coexisting entities on the page and in which temporal continuity is subordinated to thematic or structural sorts of considerations. The age-old storytelling conventions of a diachronic realism are henceforth challenged by the highly artful and self-conscious patterns of a synchronic Modernism.

In all literary genres, including drama, traditional mimesis is often put quietly aside in favor of a more obscurely figurative kind of action, made up of highly private and personal symbols — allegory without a key, as it were. (Such is the case with most of Kafka and the later Yeats and Strindberg.) By the same token, individual character development takes on a diminished role within the Modernistic work's total symbolic network of shapes and signifiers. Finally, for many novelists the words themselves occupy center stage; in the hands of the later James as well as in Joyce, Woolf, and Faulkner, narrative prose aspires to the condition of poetry; and the original Flaubertian ideal of a novel in which no phrase is uncrafted or superfluous, and all words are artistically interconnected and justifiable, reaches an especially high level of fruition.

In painting, after the brief moment of realism spearheaded by Constable, Géricault, and Courbet there followed the famous optical experiments with the juxtaposing of patches of light and shade by the Impressionists, succeeded by the minute *pointillisme* of Seurat; the lavish application of color fields onto flat canvas surfaces by Gauguin, van Gogh, the Fauves, and Matisse; the active rendering of geometric shapes, first by Cézanne and later by Picasso and Braque; the invention of collage by the latter two;[3] the hyperrealist technique implemented, paradoxically, by the oneirically inclined surrealists; and the outright leap of abstractionism, with its almost musical emphasis on autonomous formal and chromatic values, by Kandinsky or Malevich or Mondrian.

In sculpture there are the totally stylized figures by Giacometti and Brancusi, wherein what most matters is not their nominal subjects but the respective artist's spare, essential visions of the shape of a human or a bird. (In a telling episode, an early version of Brancusi's *Bird in Space* became the focus of a scandal in 1926, when U.S. Customs officials refused to allow its entry as a work of art. There were charges of attempting to introduce clandestinely an industrial part into the United States. Litigation dragged on for two years, until the courts ruled in favor of the artist.)

In the case of music, owing to its essential nonreferentiality, the Modernist trait of foregrounding of the medium is more readily described and accounted for in strictly technical terms. The elusive chromaticism of a mature Wagner is taken to further extremes by Mahler and Debussy; and the atonal project of Schoenberg, Berg, and Webern, however drastic, can in turn be interpreted as a final and logical step in the process of the breakup of tonality. Two-century-old rules and practices of harmony are likewise abandoned in what becomes a routine use of unresolved chordal dissonance, even in the work of basically tonal composers such as Stravinsky and Ravel. (Stravinsky observes in his Norton Lectures that "dissonance has emancipated itself. It is no longer tied to its former function. Having become an entity in itself, it frequently happens that dissonance neither prepares nor anticipates anything.")[4] Similarly, the metric and rhythmic store available to musicians is considerably enlarged in the complex cross-rhythms and shifting time signatures adopted by Bartók and Stravinsky.

The vast expansion and refinement of orchestral resources serve as a neatly concrete illustration of ever-evolving Modernist technique. During the period a number of new instruments were being patented and then put to symphonic use — for example the Wagner tuba (devised by the composer himself for his *Ring* operas), the contrabassoon (1870), and the celesta (1886). Meanwhile the number of personnel in the orchestra underwent major growth in the second half of the nineteenth century, from the woodwind pairs and maximum three-horn format of Beethoven's time to the four-winds-each and eight horns in Mahler, and, in percussion, from one lone tympanist and an occasional cymbal or triangle supplement in midcentury to a full battery of five or six players in the younger Stravinsky's great ballets. Unusual, newer instruments are allotted key solos — the saxophone in Ravel's *Boléro* and in his orchestration of Moussorgsky's *Pictures at an Exhibition*, the alto flute in Stravinsky's *Rite of Spring* and in Ravel's *Daphnis and Chloe*. Both of these Modernist composers are justly renowned for the dazzling lushness and spread of their orchestral palette, a spectrum of sound inconceivable only a few decades earlier.

This exponential growth in literary, visual, and musical technique, and the resultant intensification and "thickening" of each respective medium, is too all-pervasive in all Modernist art to be explained solely as an aesthetic phenomenon. To some readers the larger source may be obvious, but it bears stating: Modernist technique has its origins in the implacable, hitherto unprecedented growth of product technique that characterizes the encompassing industrial-capitalist society.

In our time we take the immeasurable results for granted, but the Modernist years saw the developing, patenting, and, in varying degrees, commercializing of most of the inventions that serve as the everyday basis for contemporary society: the internal combustion engine (1859), dynamite (1866), the typewriter (1868), the telephone (1877), the phonograph (1877), the filament lamp (1880), the machine gun (1882), the electric streetcar (ca. 1883), rayon (1884), linotype (1886), the bicycle (1886), the pneumatic tire (second version, 1887), instant photography (1888), the automobile (1890), the movie camera (ca. 1896), radio (1896), the airplane (1903), and the helicopter (1907) — to choose only the more salient examples.

These unending waves of technical advancement could only infuse bourgeois society — including its literary and artistic sectors — with that urgent desire, so familiar in our time, to be up-to-date. The word "modern," it should be remarked, started carrying positive connotations and thus overlapping with ideas of progress only during the second half of the nineteenth century,[5] when moreover "progress" more often than not signified technical — rather than social or moral or political — progress. The French sociologist Gabriel Tarde (1843–1904) in fact closely equated progress with technical invention, and the notion persisted in the General Electric slogan from the 1960s, "Progress is our most important product." An essay by Baudelaire, aptly titled "Exposition Universelle, 1855," evokes this way of thinking with special irony: "Ask any Frenchman who reads *his* daily paper in a café what he understands by progress, and he will answer that it is steam, electricity, and gas lighting, miracles unknown to the Romans, and that these discoveries clearly testify to our superiority over the ancients."

In their "classic" phase, then, the Modernists replicate in their own practices that bourgeois ethos of relentless technical innovation and constant upgrading of the material status quo. One of the subheadings in the Baudelaire essay reads, "On the Modern Idea of Progress as Applied to the Fine Arts," and in the same essay he also notes, with irony, "If this year an artist produces a work showing more skill and imaginative power than he showed the year before, it is certain that he has made progress." [6]

Of course, as is only to be expected, the response of artists to the prospect of unending technification varied widely. Creative castes in the more developed industrial-capitalist nations tended on the whole to accept the situation as inevitable while also deploring the concomitant official boosterism, as seen here in the case of Baudelaire. (The Soviets, it should be noted, are not the only ones to have glorified their new machines and foundries.) Some artists were not above incorporating key signs of the reality into their work—for example, the extraordinary pictures of railway stations, or the suburban landscapes with chimney stacks looming in the distance, of the Impressionists; the pieces of product wrappings or of industrial wallpaper in cubist collage; Albertine on the telephone in Proust; or the incipient romance of the motorcar captured by Joyce in his short story "After the Race." The American composer George Antheil even included airplane propellers in his *Ballet mécanique* (1926).

On the other hand certain inspired visionaries from less-developed countries—such as the futurists in Italy and the Soviet Union, or Diego Rivera in Mexico—notoriously celebrated technology and what for them was its exotic aura, its almost miraculous potential for the forward march of mankind. It is perhaps significant that the Italian-born Apollinaire—who famously apotheosizes the machine and the Eiffel Tower in his poem "Zone"—was himself illegitimate and as an immigrant in France first bore his Polish mother's surname, Kostrowitzky, before taking up the classically resonant pseudonym by which he is remembered.

At the same time, as is well known, in their own realms the Modernist artists found themselves directly competing with the relentless technification and speedup of the means of representation. The *locus classicus* in this regard is the evolution and spread of photography — particularly instant photography — which confronted painters with the need to seek new and updated methods of pictorial imitation, to reinvent painting, as it were. In the earlier twentieth century the rise of motion pictures as a prime storytelling medium initiated an analogous situation for the novelists, who of necessity would broaden and transform their narrative technique but also go on to integrate some aspects of the cinema into their own prose fiction (as in the "Newsreel" and "Camera Eye" sections of Dos Passos's *U.S.A.* trilogy). The process continues to this day, for example, in the emergence of musical synthesizers, a boon to orchestral composers and arrangers but also a serious challenge to the job prospects of live instrumental performers. Industrial capitalism, by its very nature, is constantly generating new ways of seeing, of reading and writing, and of listening.

The period of high Modernism was also a time of rapid development in the natural, social, and behavioral sciences. Earlier in the nineteenth century, certain key findings in historical geology, evolutionary biology, and biblical criticism had permanently eroded the foundations of Christian belief among Europe's secular intelligentsia, as discussed in chapter 3. The growth in those disciplines, along with the expansion in knowledge of the human past through such fields as archaeology and comparative philology, had implicitly laid bare the provisional and contingent character of all mankind's endeavors and of society itself. Among the intellectual responses was the relativism, either resigned or cheerful, of the more prominent figures in the English aestheticist movement.

Those vast, diachronic insights, with what in some cases were time frames in hundreds of millions of years, were complemented by a plunge into microphenomena that, while current and quotidian, were equally inaccessible to ordinary observation. The germ theory of Koch, the rise of genetics, and the discovery of such elusive natural forces as X-rays and radioactivity helped further dramatize the extent to which the realm we perceive with our five senses is but a small fraction of our experience. These advances suggested that everyday "truth" is an immensely deeper, nonpalpable reality. At the same time, owing to the decline of religion, some transcendent, spiritual principle beyond the natural-scientific and materialist seemed at the time even less than likely. The outlook, in its broadest outlines, was congruent with the general ethos of artistic Modernism.

Similarly, conceptual developments such as Planck's quantum mechanics, Einstein's special theory of relativity, and Saussure's synchronic linguistics, besides qualifying as major intellectual triumphs in their own right, were also the maximum expressions of a way of thinking that laid stress on unstable, relational wholes rather than on permanent, aggregate conditions of fact. By the same token, sociology gained rigor and visibility—via the investigations of Émile Durkheim and Max Weber—with its focus on society as a dynamic ensemble of relations rather than as merely a sum total of individuals. In all, these theoretical pursuits add up to a way of thinking analogous to the creative practice of so-called spatial form, noted by Joseph Frank as the essential artistic basis of Modernist poetry and fiction.

Finally, it was during these years that the psychological investigations of Richard von Krafft-Ebing (1840–1902), Havelock Ellis (1859–1939), and of course Sigmund Freud (1856–1939) were bringing to the fore the subtle role played by hidden sexual drives in many an aspect of human life once thought of as innocent. Though Joyce had his own reservations concerning psychoanalytic theory, the sexual content of a work like *Ulysses*, completed in 1921, would not have been possible in a novel written some two or three decades earlier. Deeper, more active, more systematic insight into the workings of human sexuality was simply not available to a younger Joyce or to any other European author of an earlier generation. The unsettling sexual knowledge that it succeeds in crystallizing makes *Ulysses* a book very much of its moment in history.

During the era of high Modernism, of course, the divergence between the cultures of art and of science had already begun. Yet artists could not help being affected by the expanding horizons of scientific knowledge, especially by the long-range implications for the relativizing of humankind as well as by the possibilities for artistic development and representation. Not accidentally, it was around this very time that the subgenre of science fiction came into being with the still-popular narratives by liberal progressivists such as Jules Verne (1828–1905) and, later, H. G. Wells (1866–1946). On the other hand, authors such as Yeats or Eliot sought refuge in religion precisely because of the growth of science and on account of their own hostility to its intimidating presence and consequences.

The scientific ethos, in addition, profoundly influenced the Modernists themselves. As early as March 1857, Flaubert in a letter to Mlle. Leroyer de Chantepie says, "Art must rise above personal emotions. . . . It is time to endow it with pitiless method, with the exactness of the physical sciences." [7] Flaubert is known as the first author to enounce an ideal of aesthetic detachment that has since become commonplace: namely, that art must neither preach morals nor express biases but rather represent the truth as objectively and dispassionately as possible. Émile Zola later on builds upon this notion and makes it into a concrete program in his volume of essays *The Experimental Novel* (1880). Taking his cue directly from physiologist Claude Bernard's *Introduction à l'étude de la médecine expérimentale*, Zola starts from the premise that scientific method "should also lead to the knowledge of the passionate and intellectual life," and affirms quite baldly that "the novelist is equally an observer and an experimentalist." [8] Art for Knowledge's, not Art's, Sake, then — and indeed current ideas of heredity found their way into Zola's novels and Ibsen's earlier plays. Though naturalism does not strictly belong within the Modernist camp, it shares in several of the Modernists' key assumptions and, as noted in the next chapter, derives partly from Flaubert's idea of fiction.

The Impressionists are of course a classic instance of an artistic movement that began, in part, with a scientific agenda, that of experimenting with light and color so as to be true to the optics of everyday perception. The *pointilliste* Seurat was to take the Impressionist program even further, striving as he did to "dissect light down to its minutest particles, and to construct an objective grammar of seeing." [9] Seurat's work as a painter was in turn decisively influenced by his reading in studies of color analysis and visual apprehension, in particular by Michel Eugène Chevreul's book *The Law of Simultaneous Color Contrast* (1839).

In our time, "content" in art has come to be devalued by advanced critics as an irrelevant concern, the hobgoblin of naive, pre-Modernist minds who refuse to realize that the "content" of a book or painting is simply the pretext (or the pre-text) upon which a free creative fabulator exercises his or her high formal prowess. Many of the Modernists themselves, however, consciously sought to widen the subject matter and material range of their art, all in the interests of expanding the horizons of truth.

In her now famous essay "Mr. Bennett and Mrs. Brown," Virginia Woolf takes to task the traditional realists Wells, Galsworthy, and the eponymous Arnold Bennett for having dwelled exclusively on the outer details of a hypothetical Mrs. Brown (a sixtyish lady whom Woolf reports having glimpsed in her train compartment), for limiting themselves, say, to the gloves she wears or the house she lives in. These authors, Woolf contends, will look with care at the upholstery in her carriage "but never at her, never at life, never at human nature."[10]

Woolf's solution is propounded in another essay, fittingly entitled "The Novel of Consciousness." In contrast to the "materialists" Bennett and others, Woolf singles out for high praise the "spiritual" Mr. Joyce because "he is concerned at all costs to reveal the flickerings of that innermost flame . . . which flashes its messages through the brain." More generally, any modern novelist, says Woolf, needs "the courage to say that what interests him is no longer 'this' but 'that'" And for the moderns, "'that,' the point of interest, lies very likely in the dark places of psychology."[11]

What Woolf is talking about, of course, is the meticulous exploration of subjectivity via interior monologue or stream of consciousness, as the device came to be known in English. Although novice and even seasoned readers today can still find themselves either bemused or bedazzled by the technique, its specific purpose (as Woolf's essay suggests) is to enlarge the experiential and epistemological scope of the novel by portraying a character's existence in its full range of manifestations—visible and nonvisible, outward and inward. From this point of view, then, stream of consciousness amounts to a qualitative as well as quantitative broadening rather than a simple repudiation of realism. The street life and daily routines of Dublin are every bit as much a part of *Ulysses* as are the secret mental workings of its three main characters.

Those "dark places of psychology" evoked by Woolf in her essay also include, as it turns out, some of the less glamorous aspects of human life. To my knowledge, Joyce's *Ulysses* is the first serious work of modern fiction to include such scenes as a man defecating on a toilet or masturbating on the beach. Woolf herself notes that "the reading of *Ulysses* suggest[s] how much of life is excluded in traditional fiction," and that "there are not only other aspects of life, but more important ones into the bargain." At the same time, her experimental spirit notwithstanding, Woolf still chides Joyce's work for its alleged indecency, thereby revealing the extent to which her upper-middle-class Victorian upbringing remained with her and her compatriots as well.

Joyce of course set out quite consciously to integrate those bodily functions into the texture of *Ulysses*. As he said to his friend the painter Frank Budgen, "Among other things, my book is the epic of the human body. . . . In my book, the body lives in and moves through space and is the home of the full human personality." [12] Or, in Richard Ellmann's words, "For [Joyce], the mind was profoundly physical, containing all the organs of the body. An art which failed to suggest that its characters were capable of defecating, urinating, masturbating, copulating, menstruating, was for Joyce a falsification." [13]

Today the Modernist classics are read in college courses and routinely stocked in stores and libraries. We tend to forget, however, that their contents were at one time deemed a threat to respectable society and elicited condemnation and direct censorship. The landmark precursors to this struggle between Modernism and the custodians of the status quo are Flaubert's *Madame Bovary* and Baudelaire's *Les fleurs du mal*, both of which stood trial in 1857 on grounds of immorality. The newspaper publication of three texts from Joyce's *Dubliners* shocked their Irish readers, and the full manuscript languished for ten years because of book publishers' uneasiness about what they perceived as Joyce's overly harsh portrayal of Irish life. *Ulysses,* as is well known, was banned in the United States until 1934 and could not be widely purchased in the United Kingdom until 1936 (nor in Canada until 1946). The U.S. prohibitions on Lawrence's *Lady Chatterley's Lover* and on Henry Miller's *Tropic of Cancer*—not lifted until the 1960s—show that what was initially objectionable about such works was not their innovative form but their explicit content. Faulkner, though never actually banned in the United States, was not greatly esteemed in his own country until his 1949 Nobel Prize, before which he had largely been dismissed as a hick pornographer conveying a negative and grotesque view of American ways.

For some Modernists, on the other hand, the "content" of a work is indeed a mere pretext, the evocative means to a truer, more authentic artistic end. In her provocatively titled essay "The Novel Démeublé" (1922), Willa Cather notes, "Whatever is felt upon the page without being specifically named there—that, one might say, is created. It is the inexplicable presence of the thing not named, of the overtone, . . . the verbal mood, . . . the emotional aura . . . that gives high quality to the novel or the drama" (41–42).[14] And though she praises Balzac's portrayals of greed and avarice, she finds fault with the "material surroundings upon which he expended such labor and pains . . . the eye glides over them" (38–39; ellipses in the original).

For Cather, "If the novel is an imaginative art, it cannot be at the same time a vivid and brilliant form of journalism. Out of the teeming . . . present it must select the eternal material of art" (40). Significantly, in her advocacy of "suggestion rather than . . . enumeration," Cather occasionally draws analogies from other arts. For instance, in her 1931 essay "My First Novels," she observes, "Too much detail . . . destroys in a book a very satisfying element analogous to what painters call 'composition'" (97). Even as a youthful literary journalist, Cather dwelled at length on those tangled questions of craft, intellect, sentiment, and knowledge in writing, and the complex interrelationship among them.[15] Her prime influence, it is worth noting, was French authors, Flaubert in particular. And in this regard, her final exhortation (in "The Novel Démeublé") that we "throw all the furniture out of the window" and "leave the room as bare as the stage of a Greek theatre" (42–43) can be seen as a less extreme version of Flaubert's dream, expressed in a letter in 1852, of "a book dependent on nothing external, [with] no subject."[16]

Yet one more aspect of the content of Modernism bears discussion: its expanding of the frontiers of language. T. S. Eliot breathed new life into English verse by his crafting of a colloquial, everyday idiom and inclusion of plebian voices, while Pound in his light parody of "Sumer is icumen in" makes use of "goddamn" as a rhythmic refrain. Again, the major pioneer in this regard is Joyce's *Ulysses*, probably the first artistic novel in which four-letter words appear in print—on the lips, quite appropriately, of the aggressively drunken Private Carr, a soldier with the British occupation army. (The episode occurs in the hallucinatory "Circe" chapter, in which there is also a prostitute called "Cunty Kate.") Just as French painters could invite official wrath by some of their portrayals of Parisian courtesans, so could an Irish literary artist provoke censure with his artful deployment of once-taboo words like "piss" and "fucking."

The chief venue of Modernism was the newly commercialized, industrializing, rapidly growing city. Modernism's milieu, spirit, and public are essentially urban, as were its centers of production and distribution. Sources of support that had been available under hegemonic feudalism or modified monarchy were comparatively diminished or even negligible in scale. Though much of Europe outside England and France remained preliberal in its social structure, the very transformative impact of capitalist urbanization across the Continent would inevitably overshadow the direct power and role of onetime patrons (noble, royal, ecclesiastical, and academic) in encouraging, commissioning, and consuming art works. Arno Mayer makes the powerful argument that, throughout the nineteenth century, many ancien régime elements continued to hold sway in all of Europe; nonetheless, he additionally notes that not only the old elites but also the new bourgeoisies tended on the whole to cling steadfastly to traditional, conservative, "classical" tastes in art.[17]

Paradoxically, then, while much of the Modernist avant-garde could find nourishment and raisons d'être only in a life of urbanism, most cultural authorities in the metropolitan power structure remained closed or hostile or at best indifferent to their efforts. Like the lyric poets in industrial capitalism's earlier phase, in a hit-or-miss fashion the Modernist experimenters were creating for a largely alien and unsympathetic contemporary public. This paradox, with its attendant ironies and anxieties, was to shape the artists' lives and outlook in ways that are still only imperfectly understood today.

Even before the Baron de Haussmann started altering the face of Paris, Baudelaire was capturing the qualities we now associate with city life, "the transitory, the fugitive, the contingent" atmosphere, which to him also constituted one-half of art itself. Like many authors and painters who followed in his wake, Baudelaire (in his essay "On the Heroism of Modern Life") expressed fascination with "the spectacle of fashionable life and of thousands of stray souls—criminals, kept women—who drift about in the underground of a great city," elements to which "we need only open our eyes to become aware of our heroism." But he is equally inspired by "the black suit and the frock coat," those distinctive sartorial and social facts that "possess not only their political beauty, which is the expression of universal equality, but also their poetic beauty, which is the expression of the public soul."[18]

As Baudelaire further elaborates, "Parisian life is rich in poetic and marvelous subjects. The marvelous envelops and permeates us, like the atmosphere itself; but we do not see it."[19] The fast pace of the modern city, with its relentless bustle of every class of people and its perpetual whirlwind of manmade perceptions and representations, is the raw material as well as the site of a Modernism that, in Malcolm Bradbury's words, "pluralizes, and surrealizes."[20]

The transformation of Paris itself during the Second Empire (1851–70) of Louis Napoleon fashioned an entirely new physical environment to which the city's creative artists necessarily responded. During those years the Baron Georges Haussmann, the prefect of Paris, tore down countless medieval Parisian quarters and replaced them with the system of boulevards that is among the modern hallmarks of that city. Among his best-known projects were the Rue de Rivoli, the Bois de Boulogne, the Boulevard St. Michel, the Opéra, the radial roads leading to the outer suburbs, and the vast Les Halles food market (the latter replaced only in the late 1970s by the Pompidou arts center and by a yet vaster Forum Les Halles, a shiny, multilevel shopping mall).

The human and cultural consequences went beyond a mere matter of urban design. To begin with, that secret labyrinth of narrow little streets and byways, immortalized by Hugo in *Les Misérables,* and ideally suited for workers' uprisings and combat barricades, was gone—to the distinct military benefit of the French ruling classes. They were replaced by expansive boulevards lined with small shops and restaurants and cafés, and the hundreds of thousands of individuals promenading themselves along those then-new spaces—all of it making for "a uniquely enticing spectacle, a visual and sensual feast." In addition key improvements in paving—the hard, smooth surface of macadam—allowed for a tripling or quadrupling of rolling street traffic.

This highly successful Parisian pattern was repeated, as Marshall Berman points out, "in every corner of the world, from Santiago to Saigon." [21] Hand-in-hand with this purely material growth came the complex and elusive legibility of the new urban system. T. J. Clark observes that, after Haussmann, the modern city becomes "a free field of signs and exhibits, a marketable mass of images," a bewildering spectacle with "the crush of signs, the exchange of signals in a special overcrowded space." [22]

This pullulating panorama was further enhanced by the rise of the department stores. Partly encouraged by the growth of public transportation, these emporia first made their appearance in Paris in the 1860s and were later imitated by American entrepreneurs in New York. In a pattern analogous to those of other urban innovations, already mentioned, the mammoth retail centers such as Au Bon Marché and La Samaritaine helped "put an end to the *privacy* of consumption," to cite T. J. Clark once again; "they took the commodity out of the *quartier* and made its purchase a matter more or less of impersonal skill." [23]

Finally, there was the Eiffel Tower. Commissioned in 1889 to mark the centennial of the French Revolution and built with record speed, it soon became a travel poster cliché. At 990 feet, it stood for four decades as the world's tallest manmade structure, to be surpassed by New York City's Chrysler Building only in 1930. With its assemblage of twelve thousand metal parts and its miracle of zero construction worker casualties, it starkly symbolized the triumph of engineering technique and modern science. And in addition, most important for our purposes, with its Otis elevators the tower offered its visitors a literally new perspective on the city—from on high, a view formerly the preserve of a few intrepid balloonists. In every way, then, the experience of European urbanism during the Modernist era was being metamorphosed in ways not remotely conceivable at mid-nineteenth century.

All this of course is the Paris that is famously, distinctively evoked by the Impressionists' shimmering canvases, the city that will later be "quoted" and hinted at in the snippets of newsprint, packaging, and department store wallpaper arranged by the cubists into collage. But there are also the more intimate anguishes, the sordid hidden corners of urban life, deftly, tragicomically anatomized by Baudelaire in his verse and prose, and consciously picked up on six decades hence by Eliot for the dark, mean London we glimpse in *The Waste Land* and his shorter poems. The city is the seductively dangerous human jungle of Zola's fiction, yet can likewise be rendered as that teeming, infinitely varied totality, implicitly celebrated by novelists as different as Joyce and Biely and Proust.

An urbanized capitalism, well served by a developed system of ships and railways, made possible yet another key feature of Modernism: its international character, a cosmopolitan Bohemia whose autonomous existence by and large supersedes the place of noble and ecclesiastical courts, which in their heyday had recruited artistic personnel from all over Europe. In the Modernist era, there occurred the phenomenon of U.S. painters and literati in London; Spanish painters, Irish novelists, and Rumanian sculptors in Paris; Russian artists and Slavic writers in Berlin; and a pan-European gathering of luminaries in Zurich—all of whom had been drawn to those venues not in response to an invitation from a prelate or a prince, but because, quite simply, that was where the artistic action was. Let us recall, as an instance, the words with which Joyce signs off his *Ulysses:* "Trieste-Zurich-Paris, 1914-21." Many are the stories we know of someone or other fleeing his provincial surroundings and taking off for Paris just "to write" or "to paint," or at least dreaming thereof. Paris, of course, has its very real aura as a city of "Art"; the business fact of cultural impresarios figures much less as part of the alluring legend, and at any rate the work of the writers was aimed at and often published in their own homelands.

"Modernism" conjures up a distinct sensibility, or rather an aggregate of moods and attitudes loosely constituting a sensibility. Some of these traits include: a blasé tolerance ("cool," in current jargon); a jaded hypersensitivity, touched with coldness; cultural refinement mingled with personal toughness; a mordant, passive-aggressive distrust of conventional mores and of official hierarchies and truths; a secularized irreligiosity at the same time desirous of some transcendent truth; a serious frivolity (and vice versa); extreme subjectivism to the point of alienation; some measure of general and diffuse resentment or hostility; margination from the market economy while in search of more genuine and authentic means of expression; awareness of and perhaps direct involvement with pointless hedonism (drugs, liquor, sex); and an overwrought, intense, anxious boredom, as captured in such formulas as *Weltschmerz, tedium vitae,* and *mal du siècle.*

Malcolm Bradbury sums up the environment of Modernism as one of "personal consciousness, flickering impressions." Irving Howe quotes Thomas Mann's illuminating phrase "sympathy for the abyss"; and Howe for his part emphasizes that "subjectivity becomes the typical condition of the modernist outlook," with differing stages ranging from an "inflated self" on through "the world's body" and finally debouching in an "emptying of the self," a process that "keeps approaching . . . the limits of solipsism."[24]

The culture of Modernism generated a type all its own: the *flâneur,* the semiprofessional idler who spends much of his leisure time strolling along the boulevards, taking in and steeping himself within the scene, and making out of his combined roving and observing an entire way of life. As seems appropriate enough, the man most often cited as the great *flâneur* in the new Paris is Baudelaire.[25] Indeed, Baudelaire stands as the consummate pioneer of a Modernistic breed, the author who most fully embodies the outlook and sensibility under examination here — a fact fittingly recognized early on in

an essay by yet another great literary Modernist, the symbolist poet
Paul Verlaine:

> The profound originality of Charles Baudelaire is, to my mind,
> his powerful presentation of the essential modern man . . . , the
> physical man of today, as he has been made by the refinements
> of an excessive civilization: modern man, with his sharpened,
> vibrant senses, his painfully subtle mind, his intellect steeped in
> tobacco, his blood burned by alcohol. . . . The future historian
> of our age should study *Les fleurs du mal* with pious attention. It
> is the quintessence, the extreme concentration, of a whole ele-
> ment of this century.[26]

In France particularly the Modernist project assumed a distinctive
tone of defiance and belligerence, as suggested by the phrase most
often associated with Baudelaire: "épater le bourgeois." As Roger
Shattuck observes, French Modernism evolved "a 'tradition' of het-
erodoxy and opposition which defied civilized values in the name of
individual consciousness," and its adherents "developed a systematic
technique of scandal in order to keep their ideas before the public."[27]

Because of the French "tradition of revolt" that included conse-
crated dates such as 1789, 1830, and 1848, and because of the legendary literary precedent in the "battle of *Hernani*," it was only natural
that Modernist artists and publicists would consider themselves the
latest in a living continuity. Moreover, given the attacks from conservative circles and the respectable press, the avant-garde and its
assorted friends could legitimately feel as if they were involved in a
veritable struggle against the forces of the established cultural order.
The cubists, to take just one example, were assailed as *métèques* (the
French equivalent of the British xenophobic epithet "wogs"), and the
fact of Picasso's being a mere Spaniard was initially made much of.
Critic Louis Vauxcelles, in dismissing the 1912 exposition in the *Salon
d'Automne* and in the *Indépendants,* could deploy his crudest French
chauvinism and racism in branding it the work of "Moldo-Wallachi-
ans, Munichers, Slavs, and Guatemalans." Apollinaire, part Polish
and part Italian, was even arrested in 1911 under suspicion of having
stolen the Mona Lisa.[28] The famously hostile riot sparked by the 1913
premiere of Stravinsky's *Rite of Spring* is but one dramatic skirmish in

an ongoing brushfire war between the French guardians of the artistic canon and the culture of the avant-garde between 1880 and 1914.

A philosophical point also bears brief mention. The urban experience and the Modernist mind serve as the combined breeding grounds for a distinctive epistemology, a multiperspectival outlook whereby no version of a given reality can be construed as the final and definitive one. In the face of so many and such rapid material changes in the cityscape and in daily life, together with a weakened Christian faith and the absence of an overall unifying eschatology, the emergence of such a view was inevitable.

The conception, as is to be expected, is most readily manifested in the visual arts. Monet's many paintings of one angle of the facade of Rouen Cathedral, and Cézanne's of Mount Sainte Victoire, convey the unstated implication that there is no ultimate single way of representing what those solid, secure places "really look like." Changing conditions of light and of weather make instead for possibilities that are potentially infinite. (This should not of course be equated with limitless relativism of the late-twentieth-century type; Monet does after all retain the building's fundamental outline and features, even as he shows that its front wall can always, as it were, be seen in a new light.) From there it takes only an extra imaginative leap to represent persons and things from several simultaneous viewpoints, both visually and verbally.

The relation between artistic Modernism and the bourgeois market society in which the phenomenon sprouted is a most elusive, complex, and contradictory issue. One of the chief sources of complication is the frank hostility that not a few Modernist practitioners felt toward the liberal socioeconomic order in which they lived or, in numerous cases, barely survived. Many of them eventually found their preferred mental space in reactionary right politics (Eliot, Pound, Lewis, the Agrarians). Others, especially after 1918, were to make varying commitments to the revolutionary left (the surrealists, certain expressionists, Brecht, Neruda, Vallejo). Some sought escape and solace in religion, whether of the established and orthodox or of the occult and mystical kind. In both its style and its outlook, Modernist creation from Baudelaire onward, existing as it did on society's margins, has tended loosely to constitute and operate as what Lionel Trilling dubbed the "adversary culture."

Their actual practice as working artists, however, was a more complicated matter. When one considers the Modernists' endless struggle for renewal in form, style, and content, their uncompromisingly free and independent search for new structures as well as materials (for new signifiers as well as signifieds, in current parlance), one sees a dynamic surprisingly analogous to the individualistic and libertarian side of bourgeois life. I have in mind the liberal-capitalist ethos of following one's personal impulses and desires, of pushing beyond existing frontiers and constantly starting anew, a way of life that celebrants of capitalism from Schumpeter on have extolled as the system's capacity for "creative destruction."

Matthew Arnold neatly sums up that personal ethos, which he anatomizes and deplores in an entire chapter of *Culture and Anarchy,* as the English obsession with "Doing As One Likes." For an equivalent phrase from another classically bourgeois sister-nation, one might cite that everyday American set formula "You can do (or say) whatever you want." Hence, while one side of Modernism was at odds with the bourgeois "order" (in both senses of the word), another side was at the same time responding in full to certain of its key ideals. The aesthetic utopia of total artistic freedom has the same logic and configuration as the market utopia of total business freedom, generated by nineteenth-century capitalism and by its survivals and revivals in the late twentieth. The Modernists were certainly "doing as they liked" and "saying what they wanted." What they liked and wanted, though, was in great measure conditioned by a bourgeois society that on principle placed high value on purely personal enterprise and on across-the-board technical innovation, exploration, and experimentation. It was no fault of the artists if "what they wanted" was a crafted kind of artifact not at that time possessing sufficient exchange value to furnish most of them an adequate livelihood.

Ezra Pound captures in a nutshell the experimenting ethos of Modernism in his famous exhortation, "Make It New." Both the experimental and the libertarian side of the movement come through clearly when Virginia Woolf asserts, with high hopes and enthusiasm, that "any method is right, every method is right, that expresses what we wish to express, if we are writers." [29] The same general idea, cloaked in a more sober prose, can be found in the academic summation by Bradbury and McFarlane: "Modernism is less a style than a search for a style in a highly individualistic sense; and indeed the style of one work is no guarantee for the next." [30] Similar descriptions could be applied to an unfettered industrial capitalism that was also "making it new," inventing or redesigning products under the principle that "any, every method is right" if it helps expand the market of an investor-producer, who is fully aware that a current "style" of product "is no guarantee for [a] next" one that could very well supersede the crop of the moment, yet that might itself someday suffer the same fate . . . and so on.

The Modernist idea of expressing what one wishes to express through constantly new forms, moreover, can be seen within an enriched legacy of Romantic ideals of authentic self-expression through more spontaneous and "natural" means. Still, there were telling differences. Romanticism in England and France had been spiritually allied with the revolutionary project of overthrowing a feudal, monarchical, and ecclesiastical past. Its corresponding rejection of the courtly neoclassical aesthetic was hence all but total, and the French events of 1789 and 1830 furnished concrete validation of such a literary project. By contrast the relentless expansion, in the later nineteenth century, of bourgeois market society on so many fronts—urban, colonial, technological, scientific, not to mention the strictly economic—inexorably foreclosed any imagined possibilities for radical social transformation. Among the ideological results (studied in chapter 7) was that a sizable number of Modernist artists, particularly in the wake of disillusionment caused by the failed revolutions of 1848, took to idealizing a distant past when criticizing the present.

The Modernists' approach to established traditions likewise corresponds to their political situation. Bohemianism and its postures of revolt notwithstanding, few serious Modernists saw themselves as challenging the entire past, and many in fact were sincerely surprised and puzzled at the public hostility generated by their work. Their conception was rather one of building upon and reinterpreting former artistic achievements. Flaubert's aim was to improve upon

146

Balzac, whom he nonetheless admired. Kafka's models were not his avant-garde contemporaries but the great nineteenth-century realists like Tolstoy. Apollinaire in his poem "La jolie rousse" stresses his double commitment to "l'Ordre et l'Aventure," and Eliot of course grounded his entire poetic theory and practice on a dialectical interplay between "tradition and the individual talent" in a seminal essay by that name.[31] And there is Joyce's *Ulysses,* a kind of encyclopedic compendium of the literary past, not its negation.

Similarly, Cézanne set out to lend greater formal solidity to the Impressionists' techniques of representation; and the cubists in turn adopted Cézanne as one of their chief precursors and models. The atonal avant-gardists Schoenberg, Berg, and Webern saw themselves not as supplanters but as continuers of the Viennese heritage of Mozart and Beethoven. Much of the strength and originality of Stravinsky and Bartók derives from their having tapped into the resources of Eastern European folk music. The Russian's greatest compositions are in that most tradition-based of art forms—the ballet—and the Hungarian's in classic genres such as the sonata, the fugue, and the string quartet.[32] For every Alfred Jarry or Antonin Artaud who cried rebellion and declared war on the past ("No More Masterpieces!" Artaud's chapter title truculently cries in *The Theatre and Its Double*), there were countless practitioners working at their craft with a view to making something that would enrich those traditions.

The more concretely mundane relationship of Modernist producers to the everyday workings of the market is a yet more complex and contradictory problem and, precisely for that reason, has been studied much less than, say, the political economy of Romantic and Victorian fiction. The fundamental reality, however, was that the creative artists were living in a capitalist society; and the simple fact that their best wares were oftentimes not "salable," or at least not immediately profitable, inevitably generated spiritual malaise and inner discord. Among the persistent themes of the work of Thomas Mann— himself no agonized Modernist and indeed a highly successful realist author—is that of the uneasy coexistence between the artist and bourgeois society, and the countless, convoluted ways in which the two can ultimately clash.

Similarly, Willa Cather, who was also able to make a living mostly from her writing, in her essays has harsh words for commercial fiction. In "The Novel Démeublé" she notes that a "novel manufactured to entertain great multitudes of people must be considered exactly like a cheap soap or a cheap perfume." For such mass market products, "fine quality is a distinct disadvantage" (36). And in another essay—pointedly titled "The Art of Fiction"—she formulates her choice in the starkest possible terms: "Writing ought either to be the manufacture of stories for which there is a market demand—a business as safe and commendable as making soap . . . —or it should be an art, which is always a search for something for which there is no market demand, something new and untried, where the values are intrinsic and have nothing to do with standardized values" (103). Even those more traditional, less experimental artists who earned their keep from fiction, then, have been aware of the problematical relationship between market values and artistic worth.

The panorama nevertheless must not be reduced to the Hollywood depiction of chronically suffering artists, misunderstood and driven mad by the crude philistines—even if that was sometimes truly the case. A revealing instance in this regard is that of the painters, in particular the Impressionists.

During the early nineteenth century the material bases of painting went through some sweeping technical innovations, comparable to those we saw earlier in paper and printing for literature. The invention of lithography in 1796 engendered new kinds of creative specialists and also helped expand the growing bourgeois taste for landscape. Tin tubes for paint were invented in the 1830s and marketed by English firms in the next decade. Preparation of paint was thus no longer the time-consuming chore it had been for centuries; moreover, newer ready-made colors now appeared. In addition, prefabricated canvases became available in 1841, saving the painter yet another purely preliminary step. These product inventions made painting more accessible to the amateur, and similarly made possible the growth in the numbers of professional artistic aspirants in a new, bourgeois France, who, while often undergoing real poverty, could think of themselves as working toward possible middle-class success.

As happened in the print sector, middle-class expansion meant a growing market and at times a speculative fever in decorative paintings for bourgeois walls, especially during the reign of Louis Napoleon (78).[33] Though there were fewer commissions from government sources (as White and White remark), more sales of individual art works were being transacted. The concomitant surge in the size of the painter population demanded a new training and distribution system as an alternative to the near-monopoly once held by the École des Beaux-Arts (the rigorously classical place of instruction for student artists) and by the official Académie de Peinture et Sculpture (the ultimate governing body for artistic salons, prizes, and teaching appointments).

To meet the specific needs of art students who had failed the École's entrance examination and couldn't afford private instruction, some independent, inexpensive, so-called free art schools came into being, such as the Académie Suisse and the Académie Julien. (Courbet and Gauguin, for instance, were both products of these free academies.) Yet another consequence of such changes, this time in the realm of taste, was that large-scale historical canvases, long considered the noblest and most worthy form of art in the annual official salon, were being superseded in market demand by genre pictures and landscapes, items more appropriate to the aesthetic and space requirements of the bourgeois home.

More important for our purposes was what researchers White and White describe as the rise of "the dealer-critic system," which began to make serious inroads on the venerable institution of the academic salon. Since the eighteenth century these Parisian salons, the biggest and most important seasonal art event in all of France, had by their own rules shown a limited number of canvases per painter per year — most often, only a single such canvas, for the focus was on the painting, not on the painter. There was no limit, however, on the number of *artists* to be considered in the exhibition, a fact that carried consequences.

Under the ancien régime, the highest number of paintings so presented had been four hundred. By the 1850s the accepted items numbered in the thousands, and the net result at the Palais d'Industrie was picture upon picture covering the walls from the ceilings on down.

Given both the visual plethora and the human crowds (as many as ten thousand paying visitors per day), a painting easily became lost amid the sheer noise and confusion. And though a salon medal meant a generous cash prize and possible future commissions for a lucky winner, the preferential treatment given to historical works constituted a major obstacle to, say, landscape or still life artists.

In the new system, made possible by the press and the growing art market, critics openly became the publicists or theorists not of a painting but of a painter or a group of painters. Similarly, dealers took on the role of representatives of a painter's entire ongoing oeuvre in the marketplace, buying and reselling their canvases accordingly. The exemplary case in this regard is Durand-Ruel, who "in his first daring coup bought up almost the entire production of several Barbizon painters" (99), which he then went on to retail to collectors at a profit.

Eventually Durand-Ruel was to become the prime dealer for the Impressionists, who in turn came to depend on him for their incomes, much as had been the case with artists under old-regime patronage. Of course the Impressionists, as is legendary, were more or less locked out of the official French system of taste and distribution, and they endured barbs from a hostile public and the more ignorant critics along the way. Nevertheless, they did not consider themselves rebels; indeed, they had undergone "correct" academic training, and desired if not success then at least a decent middle-class living, as might any other French professional. Their own economic biographies, however, strongly suggest that, except for those who managed to lead long lives or who possessed business skills, neither stability nor success was easily achievable by serious innovative painters.

The case of Manet is particularly illustrative. The "father" of the Impressionist movement was fortunate enough to be endowed with a private income that helped see him through the many lean years. Manet's first painting was completed in 1855; his first sale occurred sixteen years later, in 1871. During the thirteen remaining years of his life, "51 of [Manet's] total production of 286 finished oil paintings were sold" (132). Still, despite his being able to sell only 18 percent of his output within his lifetime, Manet earned a respectable income during his final decade. At public auctions held shortly after his death in 1883, however, a full 67 of Manet's paintings were bought, more than he had sold as a living artist, and the total receipts from that single event (89,700 francs) were larger than had been Manet's entire previous income as painter (130–33).

Other Impressionists fared differently at one extreme or another. Pissarro, having married young, had six children to support in 1884, and it was all he could do to make ends meet. For an oil painting he charged 900 francs but, there being a bigger and more reliable market for pastels (150 francs) and painted fans (100 francs), he duly cranked out many of the latter, smaller items. Monet, by contrast, was a shrewd businessman and a wily soul, who often lived on credit, thought nothing of falling far behind on his monthly house rents, and actually dared to turn down offers from dealers if he found the price too low (134–40).

Eventually it was American bourgeois wealth that raised the stakes for the Impressionists. At one point Durand-Ruel bought twenty-three of Manet's oils directly from the painter's studio, paying a total of 35,000 francs. "These . . . paintings were eventually sold for well over 800,000 francs, mostly to various American collectors and museums" (126). In an equally dramatic instance, Monet on his own, for each of his Rouen Cathedral canvases, was fetching sums of 15,000 francs from U.S. buyers.

These new-rich Yankees—overseas foreigners with neither ideological nor other vested interests in old Europe's hallowed traditions —served as the next phase in the world marketing of the Impressionists, who, if they lived long enough, might finally see some income rewarding their long labors. Likewise the cubists, who at first certainly paid their dues in the rigors and deprivation of *la bohème*, were to be greatly helped by enlightened dealers like Kahnweiler and by the expatriate Americans Gertrude Stein and Leo Stein, who served Picasso and Braque as indispensable "angels" on the art market.

On the other hand Gauguin and van Gogh worked in unspeakable poverty, and as is well known the Dutchman sold exactly one painting in his entire life. Had he survived to a ripe old age instead of committing suicide at age thirty-seven, however, it is conceivable that van Gogh would have known some modest success. Whatever the case, the empirical researches by White and White provide ample illustration that "the long period between debut and acceptance by the buying public meant . . . that a painter was burdened with family responsibilities long before he attained a stable income" (140). And this assumes that some form of public acceptance would come at all.

In literature the situation was perhaps generally bleaker. What was earlier deplored by Gautier in his preface to *Mademoiselle de Maupin* becomes dark and sinister in Europe's Modernist phase. Lyric poets in particular faced total isolation, being unable to ally themselves with any of the current national or public mythologies, and in response they inclined toward occult traditions and obscure, profoundly private kinds of language. As Richard Sheppard observes, "[M]odern poetry is permeated by a sense of homelessness" caused by a total "disjunction between social discourse and literary discourse," itself the result of the clash with or rebuff by "the antipathetic institutions of the rising industrial city." [34] The lyrists felt rootless, cut off and "out of it" as the process unleashed earlier in the century by the shift to the industrial-literary market became even more all-pervasive, and thus all the more inimical to their art.

In prose narrative the traditional or conventional realists could still do well within the fiction market, though difficulties of either format or content could crop up—for example, George Gissing's inability to adapt to the move away from three-decker novels (a situation deftly captured by him in his *New Grub Street*), or Hardy's having to endure reviewers' accusations of supposed immorality in his *Jude the Obscure*. On the other hand it was almost expected that those Modernistic spirits who chose to pursue a more symbolist, introverted, poetic sort of novel would find less than hospitable market conditions— as was initially the case with Joyce's *Portrait of the Artist* or Proust's *Swann's Way*. By contrast the stage, being a branch of the performing arts, could provide an established venue for the more evocative and experimental work of playwrights like Strindberg and Maeterlinck. (An unsuccessful and unprofitable theater production can always be canceled and dismounted, hardly the case with a printed novel.)

Few composers were blessed with the entrepreneurial skills or sheer megalomania of Wagner, who had an entire opera house built at Bayreuth solely for the mounting of his mammoth works. Because of the intrinsic peculiarities of musical art, however, some creators were able to survive as conductors (Mahler, Webern), or as instrumental performers of their own products (Stravinsky, Ravel), or even as conservatory teachers (Bartók). Strictly as a maker of new pieces, however, virtually none could have earned his keep, at least not during his initial decades as an artist. It should nevertheless be noted that, throughout musical history, most composers have also functioned as all-around musicians fully engaged in the performative, pedagogical, and even organizational aspects of their trade. (An exception was Schumann, whose hand injury caused him to give up the piano and turn to music journalism instead.) In the case of the Modernist composers, their engagement in the everyday practice of music making was simply part of the job, was in itself enriching, and — unlike the activities available to the poet-critics or the painters — could serve as a medium with which to promote their own compositions.

The unstinting, not to say obsessive, way in which a Mallarmé or van Gogh, a Schoenberg or Joyce, could, at enormous personal and economic cost, dedicate themselves to their art stands as one of the more eloquent refutations to those crude and narrow ideologists of free market society, who glorify greed as the highest human virtue and claim that people will work their best only when prodded by financial gain. Indeed, a counterclaim might be that these artists attained such creative heights largely in spite of, or even by laboring against, the fabled laws of the market. While they had artistic freedom, they paid a serious price in their daily well-being (as well as that of their families) for such freedom. This paradox, this complex irony is one of the most daunting to all sociologists of art, be they of the left, right, or center.

The workings of the market society affected the creative life of Modernism in ways that even now elude our full understanding. In considering the total picture of the various "-isms," the analogies most commonly employed are military, political-cultural, and religious. After a brief look at these three differing analogies, I should like to propose an economic one as well.

The military analogy takes seriously the martial denotations of the French word *avant-garde,* signifying simply vanguard, defined by *Webster's New World Dictionary* as "the part of an army which goes ahead of the main body." In its metaphorical, aesthetic sense, the term was first applied by French journalists in the mid-nineteenth century.[35] In this view, "-isms" are like shock troops, the front lines of the arts, making battle and conquering ground for the forces of the authentically new that are following not too far behind.

In the political-cultural view, "-isms" are a vanguard comparable to those of militant labor or of party activists or of urban guerrillas, all of whom struggle for a more just and equitable social order, one that will accept their respective demands, acknowledge their truth. With the partial victories of an "-ism"—comparable in turn to those of successfully unionized workers or of an elected political party—its allies and followers earn something of a rightful place in society. This in fact is what has happened in many avant-garde instances, and the combative character of provocateurs like Jarry or Marinetti or Pound lends credence to the analogy.

The actual ideological tenor of vanguard Modernisms nonetheless varies enormously from case to case. In backward parts of Europe such as colonial Ireland or Czarist Russia, Modernists and avant-gardists could see their art within the broad context of a battle against local authoritarian power, the ultimate aim being both political and cultural emancipation. By contrast, in those European nations where bourgeois hegemony had largely triumphed (England, France), the Modernist revolt against market civilization tended rather to a vague and amorphous dislike of "the bourgeoisie" for reasons spiritual, not economic, for that undefined bourgeoisie's hostility to their art and its prosaic and narrow ways, and generally not for its labor exploitation or overseas expansion. Not until after World War I, particularly the crisis of the 1930s, did some elements of the avant-garde turn explicitly to the left and to socialism.

The religious analogy interprets the multifarious "-isms" as a series of confessional sects, devotional splinter groups all in their own way believing in, practicing, and laboring for the religion of Art, with its high priests (Mallarmé, Eliot, Breton); its apostles (Pound); its crusaders (Apollinaire); its martyrs (van Gogh); its monks (Flaubert, Proust) and lapsed saints (Rimbaud); its lay workers (Joyce), parable makers (Kafka), and holy sinners (Verlaine); and a small elect comprising those faithful few whose souls are sufficiently advanced to understand, share in, and lend homage to the given spiritual message of a sect's chosen medium. In this view, the vanguard "-isms" can be likened to the plethora of Eastern mystery cults that at one time challenged the legitimacy of Imperial Rome, or to the competing Christian sects that fought it out among themselves prior to the consolidation of papal power.

There is much about all these analogies that makes sense; their explanatory uses are obvious. Still, they remain just that—analogies. Their imperfections derive from their each highlighting only one side of a complex situation that was historically unique: a pan-European artistic movement whose major artists generally received for their art little economic, social, or moral support, either from establishment or from opposition sources; who consequently felt more or less left out of the societies to which they otherwise belonged; whose aesthetic commitments were nevertheless extreme, quasi-religious, and occasionally even pathological in character; and yet who by and large have been proved right insofar as their creations have solidly outlived the more conventionally formulaic, commercial, or academic art products of their time. Given a phenomenon so broad and elusive as Modernism, any analogy that focuses on only one aspect will remain ipso facto incomplete and wanting.

There remains an analogy that, as far as I know, has not yet been applied to Modernism (as I attempt here): the economic. This may seem questionable, given the antimarket orientation of quite a few Modernist practitioners. Such a view is no more outrageous, however, than applying religious analogies to groups that included atheists, or the political analogy to artists who often were apolitical.

From the economic angle, the many "-isms" (whether closely knit associations or loose aggregates of individuals) can be seen as a typically wide and varied assortment of enterprises, as undertakings in the broadest sense of the word, not only in the strictly business denotation but also in the light of *Webster's*: "a bold, *difficult, dangerous, or important* undertaking" (emphasis added). In this regard, one can survey the Modernist roster and identify its entrepreneurs (Stravinsky, the Woolfs); its impresarios (Pound, Diaghilev); its journalistic scribes (Apollinaire); its silent laborers (Henri Rousseau, Juan Gris); its tinker-craftsmen (Joyce); its inspired inventors without business skills (van Gogh); its flamboyant publicists (Tzara, Duchamp); its cooperativist ventures (the Bauhaus); and its salaried functionaries, be they reluctant (Mallarmé) or ambitious (Eliot)—much as one will find within the ranks of the larger market economy itself.

The literary press in the period of high Modernism furnishes a revealing panorama. That era saw the birth and growth of an entire subculture of "little" magazines, some of them now legendary. In the English-speaking world alone there were *Poetry, transatlantic review, Broom, The Egoist, The Criterion,* and *The Dial,* to cite but a famous handful. Short-lived though most of them were, these publishing enterprises nevertheless printed a substantial number of the key Modernist poets, critics, and fiction writers [36]—the most celebrated instance being the serialization of Joyce's *Ulysses* in *The Little Review.* Some authors, on the other hand, still found a niche in journalism, like Apollinaire, who until 1914 was regularly handing in art criticism copy, three times a week, to newspapers.[37] Others might launch their own book publishing ventures, as did Virginia and Leonard Woolf with Hogarth Press.[38] T. S. Eliot, being more career-conscious and more desirous of British respectability, became a senior editor at Faber and Faber. In the visual arts the Bauhaus School gave teaching employment to some of the leading Central European figures in the arts and crafts until it was shut down by the Nazi regime in 1933.

The ephemeral nature of most Modernist enterprises and the singular lack of financial success among many of its individual practitioners would seem to give the lie to the economic analogy. The history of capitalism, however, is also generously strewn with the corpses of failed businesses that made good products, but that either died without a trace or were bought out by larger firms, which recommercialized their ideas and stock. Their downfall was owing to some mixture of more aggressive (or less scrupulous) competitors, inadequate marketing skills on the part of owners, obstacles from big business or other vested powers, lack of capital funding, unexpected changes in fashion, and plain old bad luck.

But there is more. For every Edison or Marconi of official bourgeois myth who excelled both as inventors and as businessmen, there must have been hundreds or thousands of tinkering geniuses whose crucial contributions to technology brought them only modest gains or renown, if any.[39] A telling example is Christopher Sholes, inventor of the typewriter, who, unable to come up with adequate capital to mass produce his brainchild, finally sold all the rights to his device to Remington Rand, the arms factory, for twelve thousand dollars. Similarly, Elias Howe, of Spencer, Massachusetts, patented the sewing machine in 1846, but in the end was bested by Isaac Singer, who went on to perfect and then market the apparatus usually associated with his family name. Even the fabled Wright Brothers had to endure endless stonewalling from the U.S. Army, which refused to believe in their airborne contraption; though the Wrights finally secured deals from contractors in Europe, eventually they too were surpassed by other European competitors.

These cases, it should be said, are among the more salient and more readily documentable ones in the business sector. The lesser-known instances, on the other hand, must be legion. The same pattern can be seen among artists. Stravinsky recalls the occasion when, at the French border crossing, a gendarme "asked me what my profession was. I told him quite naturally that I was an inventor of music." When the gendarme asked Stravinsky why his passport listed him as a composer, the Russian replied that "the expression 'inventor of music' seemed to fit my profession more exactly" than the term listed on his travel document.[40] Most other Modernist "inventors" in the arts, however, were living, creating, barely surviving, and occasionally succeeding much as the technological inventors were. The range of life histories and fates within the two groups is, I venture to speculate, in many ways roughly comparable.

Speaking for some other theorists, Renato Poggioli has made the observation that "avant-garde art can exist only in the type of society that is liberal-democratic from the political point of view, bourgeois-capitalistic from the socioeconomic point of view."[41] This formulation, while potentially fruitful, must be carefully qualified and revised, its conditions narrowed to those of a liberalizing capitalism, yet also expanded to include those of a libertarian-permissive socialism. After all, Wilhelmine Germany, Hapsburg Vienna, and Czarist Russia (where the avant-garde certainly existed) were a far cry from being liberal-democratic societies, indeed were still, in principle, absolute monarchies.

Nevertheless, the presence of a sizable, emerging liberal-market ("bourgeois-capitalistic") sector in such nations allowed for some expanded rights of assembly, of enterprise, and of institutional autonomy that enabled the committed avant-garde to organize themselves and launch their publications, exhibits, and performances. By the same token, the relatively relaxed economic and political atmosphere of the Soviet 1920s, brought about by New Economic Policy reforms, made possible one of the most remarkable periods of Modernist art production, comparable in richness to that of Weimar Germany, as Stephen Cohen eloquently notes.[42]

On the other hand, under the most extreme dictatorships, be they capitalist (Nazi Germany, Fascist Italy, the Latin American barracks states) or communist (the USSR after 1930), virtually no avant-garde activity is allowed. The ban arises not out of any phobia of formal experimentalism as such, but rather because the avant-gardists' stubborn rage for aesthetic autonomy resists the will to total hegemony of the regime; or because the contents and ethos of Modernist art and its sometime erotics might conjure up alternative visions to the official high pieties and puritanism; or (not least of all) because avant-gardists themselves tend toward personal or political nonconformity and are on occasion ethnically or even sexually suspect.

Even in this regard, however, history and its complexities can surprise us. In the wake of the thaw of the late 1950s, the Stalinist successor governments of Central Europe began to tolerate avant-garde music, abstract painting, and experimental drama, if only because the subtle and opaque artistry of those products posed no immediate threat to state interests and might in fact generate international prestige (as in the case of Jerzy Grotowski's lab theater or Andrzei Wajda's films). In my travels through Eastern Europe in 1969, I attended concerts of very up-to-date music in Krakow, saw Alain Resnais's *Last Year at Marienbad* announced on the marquee of a Rumanian small-town movie house, and caught sight of books by Joyce, Borges, Albee, and Cortázar in the stores or in readers' hands. By contrast, within the USSR itself the official system of artistic taste remained starkly, almost monolithically socialist-realist and antiformalist, not least among the more educated, sophisticated residents whom I chanced to meet and engage in conversation.

and the Market

The economic parallel explored here is of course simply another analogy. But it is no more imperfect, I think, than the military, political, and religious analogies regularly employed in characterizing the Modernist avant-garde. The deeper problem is that Modernism has all these elements at once, shows traits from all these divers realms. After all, any society—not only a nation-state but an autonomous body such as a college, a church, or a fraternity, as well as quasi-opposition groups such as a labor union, an artistic counterculture, or a street gang—is itself a complex of political, religious, military, *and* economic factors. A future historian who is better grounded theoretically than this writer, will, I hope, be able to present a unified account of Modernism that deals with it both as product of bourgeois-liberal capitalism and as its spiritual opponent, both as participant (whether marginal or successful) in the market system and as its occasional tragic victim.

CHAPTER 6

The Diffusion of the Doctrine III: Literary Modernism and After

Is literary Modernism a chapter in the history of Art for Art's Sake? On one level, Modernism is indeed the expansion of aestheticist doctrine from lyric poetry to almost all artistic media. On the other hand, an honest answer to the question must be a cautious "Yes, but. . . ." Both the affirmative and the reservation require extensive comment, for the intellectual relationship between the literary vanguard and the aestheticist ethos is unstable and complex. Many Modernist authors believed, after all, that their innovative techniques served to convey larger, less tangible truths. To cite Picasso's famous aphorism, "Art is not the truth. Art is a lie that makes us realize truth." [1]

T. S. Eliot is an exemplary case in the way that his stance as a critic could waver back and forth, sometimes within the same volume. In his introduction to the first edition (1920) of *The Sacred Wood*, Eliot chides Matthew Arnold for his social commitments, for yielding to "the temptation . . . to put literature into the corner until he cleaned up the whole country first." [2] This implicitly aestheticist line is put into bold relief in Eliot's preface to the second edition (1928), in which he asserts that poetry must be considered "primarily as poetry and not [as] another thing."

By this time, however, Eliot had been baptized and confirmed in the Church of England, and his seemingly purist conception of lyric is qualified by his new interest in "the relation of poetry to the spiritual and social life of its time and of other times." Poetry, he further notes, "certainly has something to do with morals, and with religion, and even with politics perhaps, though we cannot say what." [3] Later, in "Religion and Literature" (1935), Eliot declares with the full zeal of a convert that literary criticism should have "a definite ethical and theological standpoint. . . . In ages like our own . . . it is the more necessary for Christian readers to scrutinize their reading . . . with explicit ethical and theological standards. The 'greatness' of literature cannot be determined solely by literary standards." In the same piece, he goes so far as to declare that those readers who enjoy older, established books of religion or history or philosophy "solely because of their literary merit are essentially parasites." [4]

Yet in 1956, a Nobel laureate and a world-renowned public figure, Eliot is so bold as to confess to his enormous stadium audience at the University of Minnesota (in "The Frontiers of Criticism") that certain lines by Shakespeare or Shelley still give him, quite simply, "as keen a thrill as they did fifty years ago." [5] Eliot the Modernist could be both an aesthete and an anti-aesthete, depending on the circumstances of the moment.

Modernism could not have existed without the aestheticist legacy. To put it in concrete terms: Eliot is not possible without the French symbolists and Baudelaire, who in turn are not possible without Gautier; and Joyce for his part is not possible without Flaubert. The relation is aptly summed up by German theorist Peter Bürger, whose use of the plural noun "avant-gardists" can, for our purposes, be construed as by and large synonymous with "Modernists:"

> The avant-gardists . . . adopted an essential element of Aestheticism. Aestheticism had made the distance from the praxis of life the content of [its] works. The praxis of life to which Aestheticism refers and which it negates is the means-ends rationality of [everyday bourgeois life]. Now, it is not the aim of the avant-gardists to integrate into *this* [everyday bourgeois] praxis. On the contrary, they assent to the Aestheticists' rejection of the world and its means-ends rationality. What distinguishes them from [the Aesthetes] is the attempt to organize a new life praxis from a basis in art. In this respect also, *Aestheticism turns out to have been the necessary precondition of the avant-gardist intent.* [6]

To further elaborate on Bürger's observation, the avant-gardists sought not only a separate art and beauty, but, in the process, a separate way of life, too, a counterculture with rules of its own. They rejected liberal-market society first on aesthetic grounds but subsequently on other grounds as well. This complex and shifting ethos can be seen in both the work and the theoretical reflections of three towering figures in the history of Modernism: Baudelaire, Flaubert, and Joyce.

Any examination of modernity and Modernism in art and culture must begin with Baudelaire, arguably the pioneering figure in the tradition. The "content" of Baudelaire's poetry, as noted previously, is that of the urban sensibility, with all its intense nervousness and speed, its moral confusions and loneliness. His diction, also, is modern; before Baudelaire, much of nineteenth-century French verse seems either too sentimental or too exquisite. Though not an innovator in the forms, metrics, or scansion of French verse, he can be credited with having brought to a high level of elaboration the genre of the prose poem (an apt medium for a poet-journalist). His critical writings exhibit those very same uneasy ties with aestheticism, coupled with a longing for a more transcendent reality, remarked on in the previous chapter.

In his earlier prose especially, the French author presents a complex aestheticism more reminiscent of Schiller's theories insofar as it connects issues of beauty with those of morals and truth. His article "Pierre Dupont" (1851) explicitly states, "By excluding morality and often even passion, the puerile utopia of the school of *l'art pour l'art* was inevitably sterile. It was flagrantly contrary to the spirit of humanity" (51–52).[7] And the endless polemic about art vs. utility, or beauty vs. morals, is trenchantly addressed in Baudelaire's 1851 essay "The Respectable [*honnête*] Drama and the Novel," in which he laments the hardened, simplistic, either-or nature assumed by the debate: "A great conflict is taking place, and for want of philosophical wisdom, everyone seizes half the banner for himself, maintaining that the other half has no value" (67).

Not surprisingly, in his 1852 article "The Pagan School," Baudelaire has harsh words for an aestheticizing formalism that excludes from its concerns any interest in the Good or the True. The passage ends with remarks on "the whole man" and on specialization that both Schiller and Shelley would have enthusiastically seconded: *Immoderate love of form leads to monstrous and unknown disorders. Absorbed by the fierce passion for the beautiful, the amusing, the pretty, the picturesque[,] . . . notions of the just and true will disappear. The frenzied passion for art is a canker which devours all else; and since complete* lack of the just and true in art is equivalent to lack of art, *the whole man shrinks;* the excessive *specialization* of one faculty ends in nothingness" (77; emphasis added). Baudelaire in this essay even asserts the need for literature to "walk hand in hand with science and philosophy," lest it become "homicidal and suicidal" (77).

Much of this earlier work grows out of Baudelaire's vague spiritual alignment with the socialist left and his support of the Revolution of 1848, the high hopes of which would be terminally dashed by Louis Napoleon's 1852 coup d'état. Baudelaire's subsequent disillusionment (shared by his literary generation), coupled with his intimate involvement with the writings of Edgar Allan Poe (whom he both translated and wrote about) were factors that eventually led him toward a somewhat more "aesthetical" literary stance.

Baudelaire's 1857 article "New Notes on Poe" makes assertions that seem taken directly from the American writer's lecture-essay "The Poetic Principle." The close resemblance can be seen in Baudelaire's new policy of strict separation of beauty from truth and morals, and in his affirming—in a diction remarkably similar to that of Poe—that "poetry does not have Truth as its object, it has only itself. . . . Truth has nothing to do with songs" (132). In addition, he airs serious reservations about Hugo's verse, on the basis of Poe's own doctrine of "the heresy of the *didactic,*" rendered by Baudelaire as "l'enseignement" (the teaching of a lesson) (135).

Even in the 1857 article, however, Baudelaire manages to retain some of the quasi-Schillerian faith in beauty and its positive effects on the human disposition. In the same essay he grants that poetry can "ennoble manners" and "raise man above the level of vulgar interests" (131). And in his 1861 article on Auguste Barbier, he concedes, "Beauty is something so powerful that it can only ennoble souls." Yet immediately thereafter he states an argument, familiar to us since Kant, that "beauty is absolute" and says that "if you as a poet wish to impose a moral goal on yourself in advance, you will diminish your poetic power" (250).

When in his later works he comes closer to a position of *poésie pure,* Baudelaire correspondingly adjudges the situation for poets and writers in a bourgeois society to be virtually impossible. In the essay on Poe he observes, "It will always be difficult to exercise, both nobly

and fruitfully, the profession of a man of letters, without being ex-
posed to defamation, to the slander of the impotent, to the envy
of the rich, . . . to the vengeance of bourgeois mediocrity." For the
French author, Poe's difficulties stemmed concretely from his living
in bourgeois America, a country where "what is difficult in a limited
monarchy or in an ordinary republic becomes almost impossible."
The land of what he scorns as Benjamin Franklin's "counting-house
morality" is, to Baudelaire, "an environment . . . hardly made for
poets" (125, 126).

Baudelaire's shifting critical reflections neatly demonstrate Modernism's contradictory impulses, its conflicting desires for a pure aestheticism on one hand and for an art that encompasses truth and
morals on the other. In like fashion, the poet vents his moral and aesthetic disaffection with bourgeois society and all that it represents yet
can still suggest a longing for artistic recognition and comprehension
from at least some of his fellow citizens.

Similar contradictions can be seen in the private letters of Flaubert,
whose extensive correspondence served also as a vessel into which
the novelist vented many ideas since become classic statements in
the twin histories of both Modernism and Art for Art's Sake.

Flaubert's outlook and stance overlap in great measure with Baudelaire's. Unlike the poet, however, Flaubert had the benefit of an inherited income that spared him the uncertainties of writing for hire
in the marketplace. (His own thrifty habits and modest needs obviously helped too.) This financial advantage allowed Flaubert the luxury of taking refuge in his house at Croisset, writing and rewriting
in self-enforced isolation anywhere from eight to ten hours a night,
spending an entire week on a single page or (on one occasion) on a
transitional passage of as little as three lines. His mother and his niece,
who shared the household, were his sole steady human contacts.

Flaubert in this way of life represents a more familiar side of aestheticism and Modernism: the flight from bourgeois society, with
minimal professional or political ties thereto (artistic ones excepted),
all in order to fashion the perfect work of art. Shunning the kind of
rapid writing and regularized output that had characterized the fiction market during the initial half of the century, Flaubert expressed
to his mistress, Louise Colet, a particular fear of becoming "another

Paul de Kock" or "a kind of Chateaubriandized Balzac" (September 1851).[8]

Flaubert's choice of an aesthetic eremetism was motivated in no small measure by a deep and chronic discontent with life and himself both. As early as his twenty-fourth year he said to his old friend Alfred Le Poittevin, "The only way not to be unhappy is to shut yourself up in Art and count all the rest as nothing" (13 May 1845). Twelve years later he reasserted and elaborated on the idea to his fan and pen pal, Mlle. Leroyer de Chantepie, "Life is such a hideous business that the only method of bearing is to avoid it. And one does it by living in Art."[9]

Throughout his correspondence, Flaubert spells "Art" with a capital "A." Fittingly, he oftentimes speaks of art in vividly religious terms, as when he complains to Louise Colet that women "do not understand the religion of beauty" (8 August 1846). In September 1852 he tells her that he finds himself "turning toward a kind of aesthetic mysticism"; that same year, writing again to his mistress, he likens his dedication to beauty to that of "self-denial [before] the Jewish God [who] wallows in sacrifice."[10] Complaining to her in 1853 about a society that, "like Manchester's, spends its life making pins" and itself in turn makes "human machines," Flaubert eloquently declares, "We must love one another *in Art,* as the mystics love one another *in God.*"[11]

Flaubert's dedication to pure form and beauty shows the same kinds of contradictions seen in Baudelaire and in the subsequent history of Modernism. The twenty-five-year-old lover of Louise Colet tells her that "what I love above all else is form, provided it be beautiful, and *nothing beyond it.* . . . The only things that exist for me in the world are beautiful verse, well-turned, harmonious, singing sentences, beautiful sunsets, moonlight" (6 or 7 August 1846; emphasis added). From this point of view he engages in one of his most famous speculations: "what I should like to write is a book about nothing, a book dependent on nothing external, which would be held together by the strength of its style, a book which would have no . . . subject, . . . if such a thing is possible" (16 January 1852). And of course for one side of Flaubert, style is everything, a goal that requires "atrocious labor, fanatical and unremitting stubbornness" (14–15 August

1846). The only point of such a quest, he writes Louise on 22 April 1854, is to "sing merely for the sake of singing." Or as Sartre puts it, "One writes *in order to write*. . . . Language, cut off from meaning, has fallen back on itself and is posed for its own sake."[12]

Yet there is another side to Flaubert's aestheticism, a complementary one that not only strives for a separate beauty but that aims also at truth. (The previous chapter cited his hopes for a literature that would be as exact as the sciences.) Indeed, in the same letter to Mlle. Leroyer de Chantepie (18 March 1857), he invokes "that indefinable Beauty . . . representing . . . the splendor of Truth." Writing to her later that year he similarly describes himself as engaged in "the ceaseless quest for Truth presented by Beauty."[13] Or as the older Flaubert writes to his friend George Sand (20 December 1875), "I have always endeavored to penetrate into the essence of things and to emphasize the most general truths."

When the novelist invokes "Truth" it is not meant as empty, high-sounding rhetoric. Flaubert's fierce labors as researcher are almost as legendary as his unsparing efforts as prose stylist. When preparing for each of his major novels, he did massive background reading—a full one hundred books in the case of *Salammbô*. And in order to get right "some six or seven lines" recounting an ill-fated gamble in securities by Frédéric in *Sentimental Education*, Flaubert in late 1866 or early 1867 sent Ernest Feydeau (a writer who also played the stock market) a letter inquiring about the details of finding a broker, winning a bit, and then losing the whole lot. (Flaubert even noted that he wanted information about Bourse dealings specifically for the summer of 1847.)[14]

Still, Flaubert the novelist never wishes to dissociate truth from beauty. They must, on the contrary, be fully conjoined and fused. In a letter to Turgenev (14 December 1876), Flaubert strongly criticizes Zola for "becoming something of a précieuse in reverse" in adhering too narrowly to his "Principles" and in imagining that he has "discovered 'Naturalism.' " What is especially objectionable about Zola, Flaubert continues, is that, "as for poetry and style, the two elements that are natural, he never mentions them."

In Flaubert's own work, by contrast, the two seemingly distinct realms of beauty and truth, form and fact, style and substance, are fully harmonized into a single, indivisible whole. Soon thereafter, unfortunately, Flaubert's twin legacy would be split among various parties (as Vargas Llosa points out), with naturalists from Zola on famously depicting sordid actions while scanting form and style, and "aestheticists" in turn (from James to Robbe-Grillet) narrowing the art of the novel to formal and stylistic questions while often disregarding all else.[15]

Perhaps because of Flaubert's objective, "scientific" approach to novel writing, the issue of the links between morals and aesthetics plays a lesser role in his reflections. Here too, however, a certain wavering between stances can be noted. One the one hand, in a letter to Louise Colet (2 January 1854), he makes the kind of aesthetic observation originating in Kant, seen here in Baudelaire, and commonplace enough in our times: "How true it is that concern with morality makes every work of the imagination false and stupid!" Or, as a Kantian might put it, an art with a moral purpose dilutes its aesthetic strengths.

Nevertheless, when writing to his lover on 21–22 August 1853, Flaubert unwittingly taps into the Schiller current (whereby art provides a first step toward ethical development), saying that "contact with greatness" can help create better and more moral citizens. "I believe that is the direction in which to look for the moral effect of art. Its intrinsic sublimity, like nature's, will lead to a higher morality; by virtue of its very superiority it will serve a useful purpose."[16] In the last year of his life he conveys to Maupassant a related notion, though in terms so vague that, without some sense of its philosophical background, it may seem merely simplistic: "A thing that is Beautiful is moral; there it is, and there's no more to say."[17] By itself the statement could be construed in half a dozen ways; within the larger context of Flaubert's vision, one can reasonably infer that he is speaking here not for aesthetic separatism, but for a unity between ethics and aesthetics.

Within this broader setting, Flaubert, in the same letter in which he daydreams of a novel without a subject, asserts that "there are no noble or ignoble subjects; from the standpoint of pure Art one might establish the axiom that there is no such thing as subject, style in itself being an absolute manner of seeing things" (16 January 1852). There are perhaps two strands here, one simple and one complex. The simple strand is given memorable shape a generation thereafter in Wilde's preface to *Dorian Gray*, where the Irish wit flatly states, "There is no such thing as a moral or immoral book. . . . Virtue and vice are materials for art." The more complex strand is one we more or less take for granted today, namely that what most counts in a work of art is not so much its manifest content as its formal, technical, and stylistic treatment thereof.

Flaubert is a "peak" figure who, at the same time that he perfects narrative realism, also demonstrates the potential for a more aesthetically achieved and perfect, even poetic, brand of narrative. For him the choice of a single transition word in a novel can be of an urgency equal to that of the book's overall subject. His exacting standards of truth and style, his combined insistence on "scientific" accuracy as well as on formal beauty, together mark the beginnings of the Modernist tradition in fiction. And his towering heir in the "English" novel, of course, is the Dubliner James Joyce, who takes these Flaubertian ideals to their highest possible realization.

When one thinks of narrative Modernism in the English-speaking world, the name first conjured up is that of Joyce. More than a novel, *Ulysses* is a larger-than-life phenomenon that, in time, has come to be regarded as the maximum instance of a whole new way of conceiving of and "doing" literature. In addition, Joyce the person exhibits many of the Modernist traits we saw in chapter 5—not the least of them being his inveterate bohemianism. His brother Stanislaus, in a memoir of the author, remarks that James "believed in individual freedom more thoroughly than any man I have ever known."[18] And his temperament and life history indeed both speak for that libertarian impulse we have observed previously as a constitutive element in the Modernist ethos.

The irony is that Joyce's art emerges not from what we now recognize as bourgeois modernity but from a colonial Ireland that was still basically premodern—largely agricultural in its economy and politically dominated by a Counter-Reformation Church in league with the imperial monarchy. Joyce's most fundamental literary struggle was thus neither with bourgeois individualism nor with the vagaries of the market, but against the twin pillars of British viceregal authority and a retrograde, oppressive Church, the latter of which, since the Act of Union of 1800, had officially collaborated with British power. Joyce hence grew up in circumstances ideologically more akin to those of Europe before 1789 than of France after 1830. His writing and its general tenor both come out of that local set of conditions.

Ever since the Soviets officially condemned Joyce as a "formalist" in 1934, his image as a pure aesthete standing remote from ordinary life has persisted in our time. And the bad press would appear confirmed by the hundreds and perhaps thousands of formalist critics at American universities who deal with the Irish author along precisely those lines. Of course it cannot be denied that, far more than does the work of any other novelist, Joyce's two longer books exhibit such classic aestheticist traits as avoidance of didacticism, foregrounding of style and form, and intricacy in design—all of which lend credence to the widespread notion of Joyce as an aloof précieux for whom verbal and structural ingenuities are of greater import than is human "content."

The idea of Joyce-as-aesthete is further bolstered by some of his own private statements as to his aims. Probably the most famous of these is his riposte in 1936 to his brother Stanislaus: "For God's sake, don't talk politics! The only thing that interests me is style." [19] In a more strictly descriptive and thus all the more revealing instance, when Joyce's friend Frank Budgen praised a certain (unnamed) living writer, Joyce asked, "Tell me something of it in his own words." When Budgen said he could not, Joyce then remonstrated: " 'But why can't you? When you remember a scene or a sonnet of Shakespeare you can tell me about it in the words that conveyed it to you. Why can't you do it in this case? . . . When you talk painting, . . . you don't talk about the object represented but about the painting. It is the material that conveys the image of jug, loaf of bread, or whatever it is, that interests you. And quite rightly, I should say, because that is where the beauty of the artists' thought and handiwork become one.' " [20]

Clearly, then, for Joyce the specific words of a novel matter every bit as much as (or even more than) does its primary scaffold of plot and character, the equivalents to that jug or loaf of bread in a painting. The special attention and high priority that Joyce allots to prose style grow, however, not out of mere indifference to basic, vital truths on his part, but rather reflect something quite the opposite, as I hope to demonstrate in the pages that follow.

Joyce's outlook and his life, along with the broader context of his literary development, add up to a reality too far-flung and complex to be summed up either by facile Soviet labels of "formalism" or by the specialized, rococo preoccupations of U.S. campuses. (The Irish author's sympathy for anarchist theoreticians and his self-concept as socialist, for instance, present a series of ideological issues addressed in the next chapter.) More pertinent to our concerns of the moment, Joyce's incessant striving for perfect form itself had an ampler field of operation, one that had more in common with the wide intellectual range explored by Baudelaire and Flaubert than with the "aestheticist" project's solipsistic quest for an isolated beauty. In some measure Joyce's vision and life's work are a continuation of the Enlightenment tradition that sought not aesthetic separatism but an experience of the Beautiful that unifies and connects with other fundamental aspects of our mind and soul.

Joyce's output as literary critic, however meager, clearly illustrates the complexity of his thought. His very first major critical statement, "Drama and Life" (a paper that he presented as an eighteen-year-old student at University College, Dublin), with its more than suggestive title, exhibits early on Joyce's aim of encompassing reality in its full range of manifestations. Of course, at the time when the essay was written (1900), much of aesthetic doctrine in Europe had fractured into diverse sects, each one claiming, respectively, that art should serve either morals or religion or society or simply art itself. The still-adolescent Joyce, by contrast, passionately desired to transcend every sort of narrow aesthetical reductiveness.

Joyce takes issue on one hand with "the votaries of the antique school [who say] that the drama should . . . instruct, elevate, and amuse." To Joyce this is "yet another gyve [shackle] that the jailers have bestowed." The young man does not deny "that drama may . . . fulfill any or all of these functions, but I deny that it is essential that it should fulfill them. Art, elevated into the high sphere of religion, generally loses its true soul in stagnant quietism" (43).[21] Even in his youth, then, Joyce rejected—on the basis of principles that have their ancestry in Kant—the uses of art as an ethical or religious force.

Nonetheless Joyce has even harsher words for the aesthetic separatists. In his very next paragraph the young author pointedly asserts, "A yet more insidious claim is the claim for beauty," which, Joyce feels, can often become "an anemic spirituality," and for that reason, "to pin drama to dealing with it [that is, with beauty exclusively] would be hazardous." With gentle scorn our eighteen-year-old rejects the ideal of pure beauty as the "swerga [the heaven of Gods in Hindu literature] of the aesthete" and states confidently that "truth has a more ascertainable and more real dominion. Art is true to itself when it deals with the truth" (44). For a precocious Joyce, then, beauty and truth are not mutually exclusive concerns, but rather belong together in a genuine art.

Joyce further challenges the views of critic Beerbohm Tree, who felt that art should "give us light," should "not point to our relationship with monkeys but rather remind us of our affinity with the angels," and in sum should evoke the eternal ideals and conditions of mankind. In refutation, Joyce the youthful student notes in passing that "those eternal conditions are not the conditions of modern communities" (44) — his shorthand way of pronouncing secular, bourgeois modernity a setting less than appropriate for the traditions and high concerns Tree invokes.

Summing up, Joyce observes: "Art is marred by such mistaken insistence on its religious, its moral, its beautiful, its idealizing tendencies." For Joyce, the supreme mistake is to tie art to any one single trait and thereby fail to respect its full range of preoccupations and relations. *Everything* about art is what ultimately matters, not least of all its representations of "life," which "we must accept as we see it before our eyes." Young Joyce evokes with wonder "the great human comedy in which each has share" (45), a Balzacian turn of phrase that is presumably not casual.

Joyce as a student author feels himself embattled against a variety of forces, though as yet without the sobered desperation of a mature Flaubert or Baudelaire. On repeated occasions he states his admiration for and identification with Giordano Bruno (1548–1600), the Italian philosopher who defied the Catholic authorities, broke with scholastic thought, and was finally imprisoned and burned at the stake for his tenacity of intellect. Similarly, the "Philistine chorus" and "smug commercialism" (44) of modern times — those familiar targets — earn verbal barbs from young Joyce. As early as his late teens he disdained George Moore (the most famous Irish novelist at the time) for the kind of commercially successful naturalism the elder author represented, with a new volume duly provided every two or three years. At the same time, though Joyce was passionately opposed to British colonialism's control over Ireland, he strongly objected to the narrow turn that cultural nationalism was taking, and in this regard he publicly applauded Yeats's play *The Countess Cathleen,* refusing to close ranks with his fellow students who were vociferously protesting the stage production of the work.

Feeling alone on so many fronts, Joyce understandably starts out his essay "The Day of Rabblement" (1901) by expressing his special affinity with Bruno. (Because Bruno was from the town of Nola, his name is cleverly Celticized by the nineteen-year-old Joyce as "the Nolan.") Purporting to cite the Italian thinker, Joyce asserts, "No man, said the Nolan, can be a lover of the true or the good unless he abhors the multitude; and the artist, though he may employ the crowd, is very careful to isolate himself" (69). Elaborating further on, he states, "If an artist courts the favor of the multitude, he cannot escape the contagion of its fetishism and deliberate self-deception, and if he joins in a popular movement he does so at his own risk" (71). Joyce, it should be remarked, is not rejecting an art that has genuinely popular roots or sincere political motives. What he objects to here is the facile marketeering or sloganeering that casts truth and artistic standards to the winds and calculatedly, shamelessly deals in large numbers, pandering to what today we might call the lowest common denominator of mass audiences.

Lacking mature models for emulation at home, young Joyce turned instead to Ibsen, whose independence and artistic integrity he frankly venerated and whose dramatic art he was to imitate a bit too closely in his own play *Exiles.* Perhaps not accidentally, Ibsen also had been writing in a country that, like Ireland, was going through a long process of separation and emancipation from a more powerful and populous eastern neighbor.

Young Joyce's independence of mind did not go unchallenged by the spiritual authorities in Ireland. When Father William Delaney, president of University College, read the manuscript of "Drama and Life" prior to its presentation, he requested certain textual changes, for the churchman and administrator was not pleased with what he saw as Joyce's slighting of the ethical content of art. It was only because the rebellious youth adamantly stood his ground that the full, unedited text of the paper was finally retained and publicly read.

"The Day of the Rabblement" fared less well. When Joyce submitted the polemic to *St. Stephen's,* a student magazine, religious officials within the university blocked publication, in part because the essay referred to a banned book, D'Annunzio's *Il Fuoca.* Joyce's sole recourse this time was to have the piece printed at his own expense in pamphlet form, with a press run of eighty-five copies. Even as a novice author, then, Joyce would get a taste of the power of Church censorship in his native land.

Most of Joyce's critical writings are book reviews done for the general press in Dublin. Had he so desired, he could in all probability have built a career as literary journalist and salaried man of letters (à la Gabriel Conroy in "The Dead"). He soon rejected the role, for he did not wish to find himself caught up in the routine and regularized grind of scribbling for hire. Joyce's entire existence as a mature writer, then, is that of the pure artist who pursues writing for its own sake; his first novel is in part a quasi-apologia for that life choice. Not having Flaubert's luck of a private income, however, he survived mainly via assorted teaching jobs at a number of Berlitz language schools all over Europe (as well as many loans), living with his wife and two children mostly on the edge of poverty.

In the title *A Portrait of the Artist as a Young Man,* the noun "portrait" is somewhat inaccurate, as it suggests a fixed and frozen quality, which is not at all the case: rather, *A Portrait* tells the story of the growth of an intelligent, sensitive Irish boy who, in late adolescence, evolves into an irreversible awareness of being a literary artist. Through a carefully chosen series of *portraits* over the space of five chapters, it narrates the development of its protagonist, Stephen Dedalus, from infancy until college life, as well as the corresponding sets of battles with which his surrounding society confronts him. The book thus qualifies as an example of the bildungsroman subgenre first crystallized in Goethe's *Wilhelm Meister.*

At the same time *A Portrait* provides a highly subjective though dependable look at turn-of-the-century Irish religiosity in the lived contexts of family, church, school, and university. It is, in addition, a prime instance of the poetic novel, given its carefully wrought prose and its indirect use of unreliable narrators (a device that was carried to full fruition in *Ulysses*). Last but not least, the book articulates an aesthetic theory that parallels the final moment in the story of Stephen's coming-of-age, and that has a place within the history of the Modernist idea.

On the last page of the novel's regular third-person narrative, Stephen makes to Cranly his oft-quoted avowal never to serve "that in which I no longer believe whether it call itself my home, my fatherland or my church: and I will try to express myself in some mode of life or art as freely as I can and as wholly as I can" (247).[22] This deservedly famous passage is of course a declaration of independence by the artist, a classically libertarian aestheticist and Modernist assertion of complete autonomy, of freedom from any domestic (social), political, or religious demands on art. The statement is strategically placed: it appears just one page before the novel finally shifts its narrative point of view to that of Stephen himself, who is depicted thereafter in the first person exclusively, via his personal diary. What has been leading up to that culminating moment?

Set in an arch-Catholic country, *A Portrait* tells of Stephen's eventual break with his country's Catholic faith. Appropriately, the novel is filled with religious material of every sort, whether lengthy and discursive or casual and routine. As a schoolboy at Clongowes school, Stephen reflects for most of a paragraph on the nature of God. Later, in the famous Christmas dinner scene back home, he is called upon to say grace before the meal, and, more important, we are witnesses to his aunt Dante's dogged and moralistic defense of the Church (and of its abandonment of Parnell) in the most unyielding of terms: "If we are a priest-ridden nation we ought to be proud of it" (38), she insists. Much of *A Portrait* in fact goes on to dramatize some of the concrete and more ugly consequences of living in a "priest-ridden" land.

Both priests and lay teachers at Clongowes and Belvedere schools are portrayed as tyrannical, intolerant, and sometimes vicious. We see Stephen being unjustly pandybatted for not having his eyeglasses in class even though they have been broken. ("It was unfair and cruel" [51].) Later on Mr. Tate, the English teacher, publicly accuses Stephen, "This fellow has heresy in his essay" (79).

Nevertheless the boy duly internalizes Catholic doctrine; he belongs to the sodality of the Virgin Mary, and, like many a good Catholic pupil, writes the initials of the Jesuit motto ("A.M.D.G.") at the top of every page. He feels terrible guilt about his sexual desires and for a while seriously leans toward the prospect of taking holy orders. The hair-raising sermon by Father Arnall in chapter 3, on the horrors of eternal damnation in hell, has a powerful effect on first-time readers of *Portrait*, and more so, we assume, on the book's protagonist. Chapter 4 starts out with Stephen's personal religious rituals, with every day of the week listed in terms of its respective devotionals. The overly dutiful young man mortifies his senses and sensuality, and goes so far as to contemplate joining the cloister.

Nonetheless the adolescent Stephen feels uneasy with "the grave and ordered and passionless life that awaited him" (160), and he ponders the difficulties of being "The Reverend Stephen Dedalus, S.J." (162). What makes him suddenly shift course is the extended revelation that, toward the end of chapter 4, seizes him as he stands at the edge of the River Liffey. First, he sees three schoolmates of his, bathing in the water in their "medley of wet nakedness," awakening Stephen to "the mystery of his own body" (168) and, by calling his full name in friendly banter, making him aware of the artistic "freedom and power in his soul" (170).

Stephen then wades into the river and is smitten by the sight of a delicate young girl who "stood before him in midstream, alone and still, gazing out to sea." In a long paragraph that reads much like a prose poem, the girl is described in sensuous, highly figurative, but also magical terms. Stephen gazes at her until "his cheeks were aflame; his body was aglow." And in a conversion experience not unlike that of Saul on the road to Damascus, Stephen responds to that image with a joyful and climactic inspiration "to err, to fall, to triumph, to recreate life out of life!" (171–72).

Following that episode, everything strictly religious in *A Portrait* takes on a questionable, even negative cast. As a university student in chapter 5, Stephen worries that the "monkish learning" he had acquired in school "was held no higher by the age he lived in than the subtle and curious jargons of heraldry and falconry" (180). In a word, Catholicism may well be a totally spent, feudal doctrine in these modern times. One of his student acquaintances, the peasant athlete and ardent nationalist Mat Davin, looks upon Roman Catholicism with "the attitude of a dullwitted loyal serf" (181). (The medieval, feudal word "serf" has a clear significance.) The dean of studies, a joyless Englishman, is dried up by pietistic religion and lacking in any "light and beauty" (185). A quarter of the way into the lengthy chapter 5, Stephen in his thoughts disparagingly characterizes Ireland's churches as "the scullery maid of christendom" (220).

Our third chapter remarked how the high priests of English aestheticism — Ruskin, Pater, and Wilde — started out as religious believers, lost their faith along the way, and then found a substitute religion in art. Pater, as did Stephen, even gave some thought to being ordained before finally working out his aesthetical salvation. Joyce's *Portrait* traces that very process of development. Accordingly, the book is steeped in religious culture and religious sentiments. There are numerous casual references to Catholic thinkers and Jesuit theologians (Pascal, Gonzaga, Juan de Talavera), several of them from the distant, reactionary orbit of Counter-Reformation Spain. In addition Father Arnall's fire-and-brimstone sermons, one critic has observed, are structured like Dante's *Divine Comedy,* while the religious retreat in chapter 3 is based on St. Ignatius Loyola's *Spiritual Exercises.*[23]

When Stephen undergoes his mystic revelation (a kind of aesthetic theophany, as it were) by the river, the diction is pointedly religious and secular both: " —*Heavenly God!,* cried Stephen's soul, in an outburst of *profane joy*" (171; emphasis added). Later on, Stephen compared himself to a monk or to a "priest of eternal imagination." Moreover, Stephen's oft-quoted phrase summing up his three weapons as artist — "silence, exile, and cunning" — rather suggests the rhythms of holy vows.[24] As Stephen's friend Cranly tells him, "It is a curious thing, how your mind is supersaturated with the religion in which you say you disbelieve" (230). The very name "Stephen," as often mentioned, is that of the first Christian saint; hence Stephen Dedalus is a kind of first Irish saint of the aesthetic, and also a potential artificer as evoked by his ancient Greek surname.

In this regard, the narrative practice devised by Joyce himself— the "epiphany," whereby one finds "a sudden spiritual manifestation" in some given, trivial episode of everyday life—carries strongly religious overtones. The author took the term, of course, from the appearing of the infant Jesus (and by extension the presence of God) before the three Magi in Bethlehem, an event commemorated as a major holiday in Catholic countries on 6 January. The notion, discussed by Dedalus in *Ulysses* and in Joyce's early manuscript *Stephen Hero*, is masterfully applied in the stories in *Dubliners*, and in climactic episodes such as that of Stephen's vision by the River Liffey. Created by a man who had actually rejected his national religion, the idea of a literary "epiphany" provides a means of finding quasi-religious significance in the secular and the quotidian.

For schoolboy Stephen, politics is something remote and shadowy that he cannot as yet understand. Part of the power of the Christmas dinner scene is precisely that the quarrel is seen and heard through the bewildered and objective eyes of a child. There are ironies: for all her conventional religiosity, Dante is even more passionately anti-British than the others. Stephen can recall the occasion during which she thwacked a man with her umbrella because he, an Irishman, was so unpatriotic as to take off his hat at the sound of "God Save the Queen." Whatever their individual differences, the entire Dedalus family, as one, favors independence for Ireland.

Irish politics resurfaces as a major issue only in the final, university chapter of *A Portrait*. The book in this regard comes full circle, with those questions of colonialism and independence placed strategically in its outer portions, first during Stephen's childhood, later when he is entering adulthood. The subtly illuminating episode, in which the dried-up dean of studies and a nonplussed Stephen argue politely about the appropriateness of the Irish word "tundish" over the English "funnel," provides a masterful look at everyday colonialism cropping up at the most seemingly trivial levels. The "courtesy" with which the dean considers the "tundish" is characterized as ringing "a little false" (188), and the event briefly arouses in the mind of budding writer Stephen a kind of linguistic inferiority complex: "The language in which we are speaking is his before it is mine. . . . His language, so familiar and so foreign, will always be for me an acquired speech" (189). And the incident will further stick in Stephen's craw. Part of the entry for 13 April in the concluding diary reads, "Damn the dean of studies and his funnel!" (251).

On the other hand, the individual nationalist students do not come off as credible alternatives. The peasant Mat Davin vents his simplistic anti-English feelings as if by "password," and his narrow provincialism is suggested by the fact that the one thing he seems to know about the world beyond England is the existence of a French foreign legion. Stephen Dedalus, conversely, is not esteemed by his classmates, who resent his independent mind. Davin in particular accuses Dedalus of being "a born sneerer," and asks him, "Are you Irish at all?" (202). When Davin insists that "a man's country comes first. You can be a poet or mystic after," Stephen responds with "cold violence" that "Ireland is the old sow that eats her farrow" (203).

Though Stephen, like the rest of his kin, opposes British control over Ireland, his loyalty rests rather with a larger, more cosmopolitan and universalist truth, embodied perhaps in a modern, secular Europe. It is no doubt significant that, immediately before his double epiphany on the banks of the River Liffey, Stephen has been contemplating the dappled seaborne clouds and reflecting, "The Europe they had come from lay out there beyond the Irish Sea, Europe of strange tongues . . . and of entrenched and marshalled races" (167). (This is the Europe, of course, where Joyce himself would go into life-long exile, fleeing the multiple constraints of his native land. His custom of indicating dialogue via dashes instead of by quotation marks would become his formal way of identifying his work as European rather than "English.") Hence while Stephen struggles to shake off the bonds of church and colony, he also refuses to bend his artistry to exclusivist and nationalist concerns.

As part of Stephen's gradual coming-of-age as an artist, we see him formulating an appropriate system of literary tastes and in the end developing a consistent aesthetic doctrine of his own. These poetic discriminations become cause for conflict, "political" issues as it were. Significantly, young Stephen's preferred authors are all "subversive writers" (78), the acknowledged symbols of Romantic revolt. In chapter 2 of *Portrait,* a trio of students that includes "Boland . . . the dunce and Nash the idler of the class" physically confronts him one night on a road. When Heron, the leader of the group, aggressively asserts that the greatest poet is Lord Tennyson, Stephen dismisses this icon of Victorianism as "only a rhymester," and instead proposes "Byron, of course" for the high title. From the threesome there come claims that Byron "was a heretic and immoral too" as well as "a bad man"; Stephen counters hotly, "I don't care what he was." In retaliation the three challengers rough him up quite badly until he wriggles free, after which they run off "laughing and jeering at him" (80–82).

Toward the end of that same chapter, as Stephen sits in a pub with his inept father and the latter's drinking cronies, he finds solace in Shelley's verses, "Art thou pale for weariness / Of climbing heaven and gazing on the earth. . . ?" which he repeats to himself so as to forget his own melancholy. Later, near the beginning of chapter 4, he overhears an unidentified priest lightly damning Victor Hugo and saying that the Frenchman was a much better writer in his earlier phase as Catholic than in his subsequent republican and antichurch years, a passing incident that sparks strange memories of Clongowes in Stephen's mind. I have noted previously aestheticism's continuities with Romantic ideals of self-expression and revolt, and *A Portrait* neatly demonstrates that vital link.

Among the intellectual high points in *A Portrait*'s crucial last chapter is the episode during which a garrulous Stephen, out on a casual stroll for a smoke with Lynch, sets forth to his captive friend his own aesthetic theory. Though Stephen describes his ideas as an attempt to update St. Thomas's version of Aristotle, there is more than that to them, as we shall soon see. The key paragraph of his exposition:

"The tragic emotion is static. Or rather the dramatic emotion is. The feelings excited by improper art are kinetic, desire or loathing. Desire urges us to possess, to go to something. . . . These are kinetic emotions. The arts which excite them, pornographical or didactic, are therefore improper arts. The esthetic emotion (I use the general term) is therefore static. The mind is arrested and raised above desire and loathing" (205).

It should be noted first that for Dedalus in this passage, "static" is a positive term and "kinetic" a pejorative one, whereas current connotations of such words tend to the precise opposite. More important for our purposes, one can discern here a legacy with roots in the earliest Enlightenment stages of aestheticist doctrine. (Perhaps not accidentally, the episode functions as a sort of philosophical dialogue in the tradition of Berkeley and Hume.) Stephen's rejection of both "pornographic" and "didactic" arts is in direct line with Kant's methodical relegation of the "practical" or "dependent" to a lesser role in the experience of the Beautiful.

Moreover, Stephen's characterization of the highest aesthetic emotion as a static arrest that stands above desire and loathing has as its original progenitor the Earl of Shaftesbury, who upheld a contemplative approach to beauty that transcends such worldly concerns as ownership and control (the "kinetic" aspect, which Dedalus also repudiates). Though the words differ, the aesthetic theory unfolded by Joyce's Stephen is congruent in its basic outlines with those of the eighteenth-century thinkers who first formulated the conditions of the aesthetic.

The element that sustains this high aesthetic stasis, Dedalus asserts, is "the rhythm of beauty," by which he means the "formal esthetic relation of part to part in any esthetic whole or of an esthetic whole to its part or parts" (206), and so on. By "rhythm" Stephen here is invoking what we usually denote with words like "form" and "structure"; an omnibus term, it comprises everything from broad matters of organization to the minutiae of style. Given what we now know of Joyce's total conception of his novelistic art, it is no surprise that he should have his artist-as-young-man make form so crucial an aspect of his theory.

Nevertheless—an essential point—Stephen decidedly does not separate beauty from truth, but on the contrary insists a few pages hence that "the true and the beautiful are kin. Truth is beheld by the intellect which is appeased by the most satisfying relations of the intelligible; beauty is beheld by the imagination which is appeased by the most satisfying relations of the sensible" (208). Dedalus here posits not a split between truth and beauty, but an elective affinity, an analogous relation, a "kinship," to build on his own word. He envisions them as two realms that, while apprehended by correspondingly distinct faculties, are nevertheless conjoined by the human mind. Though the many subtleties and side issues further explored (somewhat long-windedly) by Joyce's protagonist cannot be summed up within this brief space, it should be manifestly clear that young Stephen is by no means advocating a pure formalism, but rather is allying form with truthfulness.

The total of Joyce's trajectory as an author constitutes a kind of history-in-little of literary Modernism. The stories in *Dubliners* bring to a luminous intensity the poeticized realism of Flaubert, with both poetry and realism equally heightened: a rigorous and unsparing accuracy, mingled with the sacral-yet-secular aura of the epiphanies, all of it achieved via Joyce's carefully elaborated prose style. They mark the beginnings of the twentieth-century short story as we now know it. Joyce's play *Exiles,* in turn, picks up on the symbolist tendencies in the later Ibsen.

A Portrait of the Artist represents the next, "aestheticist" stage of a still young and developing Modernism, one that seeks a higher and contemplative "static" beauty existing free from the demands of morals, religion, or politics—not in pure isolation, however, but with ties to a larger and more encompassing truth. The following phase is that of *Ulysses*—a "total" book that vastly expands the truth ranges (mental, sexual, physiological) of prose fiction and that also multiplies exponentially the technical resources of narrative, inserts itself parodically into the world of ancient myth, and subjects chronological sequence to a simultaneous "spatialization of form." Finally, in *Finnegans Wake,* with its cyclical shape, self-referentialism, and endless verbal play, Joyce anticipates the open form, the linguistic preoccupations, and the ideas of narrativity that obsess much of post-Modern literature, as exemplified in novelists like Queneau and particularly Nabokov (whose overwrought *Ada* is in direct line with the genre created by the *Wake*).

In the three major Modernists Baudelaire, Flaubert, and Joyce, the relationship between the sensibility, theory, and practice of literary Modernism on one hand, and the ideals and ideology of Art for Art's Sake on the other, is a profoundly unstable one, with no final views or definitive positions from them on the matter. Depending on the respective moment in their life histories, the reigning cultural and political configurations, their own specific adversaries at the time, and even the particular mood when making a statement, these writers could either sound almost like stereotypically pure aesthetes or—in the Enlightenment spirit of Kant and Schiller—could invoke a broad totality in which nonliterary factors such as morals and truth play an equally important part in the experience of beauty.

This very uncertainty in their "aestheticism" effectively suggests that reducing Modernist authors to the status of pure aesthetes is a simplistic, summary judgment, even a caricature. Such a view took hold on a grand scale in the 1930s, when the Stalinist left, including its greatest thinker, György Lukács, began harshly dismissing the entire Modernist movement as "formalist" and "decadent bourgeois," rejecting its work and experimentation on grounds of "inwardness" and "subjectivism."

In response, the spiritual right (under the ultimate sway of T. S. Eliot and the Agrarians-New Critics) took to defending high Modernism and thence all of literature as, precisely, a separate formal domain, with the cold war liberals in time politely dismissing the broad spheres of history and society as less-than-relevant, "extraliterary" sorts of concerns. The existence of independent critical voices— Trotskyites, social democrats, or free-floating progressives such as Kenneth Burke, Eric Bentley, and Irving Howe (to cite some random U.S. instances)—could do only so much to challenge this polarization in cultural politics.

Sometime in the second decade of the twentieth century there occurred the beginnings of a change in the institutions of literature that, in its own way, is an event as momentous as was the establishing of an industrialized literary market a hundred years earlier. I am referring to the process whereby literary critics as well as creators started finding regular employment in the North American university system. The pattern was eventually followed up on a lesser scale in Britain and France, and in our time has reached vast proportions.

The shift had many causes. First, for reasons ranging from the federated structure of the United States to the availability of cheap land, the American system of postsecondary education is vastly larger than that of all of Europe. Owing to its comparatively more youthful history, moreover, American higher learning has not been so intimately bound up with the official, historical, hegemonic culture of the past as is the case in the Old World. (In the 1920s some major U.S. colleges and universities were scarcely more than forty years old.) In addition, the greater operational autonomy of the American campus (particularly the private colleges) meant greater ease in the hiring of certain instructors who may have lacked state-certified credentials yet could claim other sorts of qualifications. In special instances, such as Bennington College, one could even replicate Bohemia within a rustic setting.

After 1945, as is well known, the entirety of the U.S. higher education system underwent spectacular growth (a process that has only begun to appear threatened in the 1990s). Among the prime reasons was the G.I. Bill, which for two decades provided 10 million military returnees with unprecedented access to university-level training, leading in turn to expansion in college physical plant—classroom space, dormitories, faculty offices, libraries, laboratories, and the like. In addition, because of the increasingly complex bureaucratization of the American economy–cum–national security state, enormous amounts of federal funding were awarded for scientific and social research at the universities, inasmuch as both private and public sectors were to need numerically and verbally skilled personnel to expand the white-collar ranks of what we now see variously as the "service" or "paper" or "postindustrial" economy.

University growth brought with it the expansion of English departments or of their "Communications" or "Language Arts" equivalents. In the process, virtually all literary critics were to move away from the general-press sector or the bohemian netherworld of "little" magazines and become salaried employees of these educational combines. Owing to the poor training in English given to students in most U.S. high schools, an essential fraction of the task of these new educators was to impart minimum writing skills—in freshman composition and remedial English classes—to their callow trainees and mustered-out servicemen and -women. Through the same dynamic of factors, the study of English itself now experienced major overall growth in its programs, creating a need for instructors in everything from sophomore "survey of lit." courses to the most minutely specialized graduate seminars focusing on one author, say, or even on a single book.

Along with the critics, many a poet and novelist went on to join the academic payrolls, a process that accelerated exponentially after World War II. Some of these artists-turned-professors taught the traditional English literature courses ("Shakespeare," "Victorian Novel"); others shared their creative-writing skills with student writers; and a few scattered souls in the foreign languages combined their grammatical and literary teaching duties with narrative or verse production in their native French or Spanish.

Again, the reasons for the move were multiple (as examined in this book's Conclusion). The general-interest periodicals (*Collier's, Saturday Evening Post*) that had printed short fiction were being killed off by the electronic media and replaced by special-interest magazines, a shift depriving the higher scribblers of regular publishing outlets and editorial employment. Beginning in the 1960s, transnational conglomerates like RCA, ITT, and Gulf & Western were to buy up most trade-book houses. Meanwhile the old bohemian milieus underwent commercialization and gentrification, even as writers' fees for all but the superstars remained generally frozen.

The mass transfer of literati from the hurly-burly of the print market to the predictable security of the campus is, in retrospect, a perfectly understandable phenomenon. Most writers—critics included—frankly prefer drawing a monthly salary to surviving hand-to-mouth in Greenwich Village. Add in the paid vacations and sabbaticals, the health and retirement benefits (virtually unavailable within the United States to anyone who is not a full-time employee)—and the attractions of the academy became simply too great to resist.

Moreover the United States, as a rougher, cruder country than England or France, has always had a correspondingly thinner literary life and a comparatively smaller serious reading public, factors that further compound the day-to-day problems of a "free" writer on these shores. It is not for nothing that, beginning in the late nineteenth century, so many leading U.S. authors—from Henry James to James Baldwin—have opted for permanent expatriation to Europe, where they in fact have thrived as literary artists. After 1960, however, that expatriate culture dwindled to nearly nothing, and the nation's vast academic system has since emerged as an "expatriate" community of its own kind.

A group that exemplifies this shift from market to academy is the movement known as the New Critics, itself a significant force in the development of Art for Art's Sake doctrines in the United States. Prior to World War II the cognomen applied to them was Agrarians, and, in describing their very first phase, historical writing refers to them as the Fugitives. What is seldom mentioned about this sect is that it originally comprised able and excellent poets on the order of John Crowe Ransom, Allen Tate, and Robert Penn Warren (the latter far better known to the broad public for his novel of southern populism, *All the King's Men,* than for his critical labors). The "criticism" part of their story came later.

The *cénacle* got its start at Vanderbilt University in the early 1920s, where Ransom, who had already published a book of verse with Henry Holt, was employed as an assistant professor of English. In that capacity he served as mentor to some bright undergraduates, including Warren and Tate. The group got its initial appellation from *The Fugitive,* a self-published magazine they launched in 1922 and that, until its demise in 1925, gave the budding lyrists their first venue in print. The name of the journal, according to Tate himself some twenty years later, originated in a poem by Sidney Hirsch (another group member). The title helped to convey the notion that — in Tate's words — "a Fugitive was quite simply a Poet: the Wanderer, or even the Wandering Jew, the Outcast, the man who carries the secret wisdom around the world." [25]

The Fugitives were to become ardent spokesmen for the pre-1865 South, its bond slavery included. They praised the defunct system for what they saw as its virtues and also because, in their view, the liberal, industrial, secular, and scientific regime that followed had proved worse in every respect. The position was one they clung to well into the 1940s. Ransom's *God without Thunder* (1930) stands as a particularly weighty instance of their thought. The three-hundred-page book is a sophisticated, nonsectarian defense of fundamentalist religious faith and its practical, economic, and cultural uses. The enemy, accordingly, is science and secularism, or, as Ransom puts it, "Work, Power, Activity, Business, Industry, Production." In contrast to an agrarian, plantation world dominated by old-time religion, "Industrialism . . . seems a miserable fate for any people to suffer; but it is one which we have invited upon ourselves with our worship of the God of Science." [26]

Similarly, Allen Tate in his 1940 essay "The Present Function of Criticism" asserts that "historicism, scientism, biologism . . . [have] created or at any rate [are] the expression of a spiritual disorder." [27] Throughout much of his life, Tate was to work as an articulate publicist not only for the Agrarians' lost cause but for broader cultural questions as well.

Significantly, Tate spent several years as a literary journalist in New York (where he and his wife shared half of a house with Hart Crane). As a result he got a taste of the peculiar anxieties and "freedoms" of the literary market, a milieu he would later comment on with some acerbity. His essay "The Profession of Letters in the South" (1935) laments the fact that "our books are sold on a competitive . . . luxury market; and luxury markets must be competitive." In this regard Tate actually finds common ground with a British leftist critic's analysis: "The overhead in the system is so high that the author gets only 10 to 15 per cent of the gross. It is the smallest return that any producer gets in our whole economic system. . . . One must agree with Mr. Herbert Read . . . that authors under capitalism are a sweated class." [28]

This is a familiar enough battle: we have seen it in Gautier during the French 1830s and the Latin American *modernistas* in the 1890s. Being analogously situated, Ransom and Tate fell in with the tradition and vented their discontent as the poets they felt themselves to be. And though they did not employ the French "b" word, they nonetheless rejected in principle the new bourgeois society, from whose ways they felt cut off and against which—for over a decade beginning in 1929—they ardently polemicized in the name of an idealized feudal utopia of their own.

The quirky nostalgic politics of the Agrarians is a topic for the next chapter. What concerns us for the moment is the Art for Art's Sake stance that was defended and developed by more prominent members of the circle and by its abler followers, in the course of their careers. A landmark item in that history is Ransom's book *The New Criticism* (1941), the title of which was soon universally adopted as shorthand to designate an entire critical movement (as well as a mood and outlook) that swept into the American universities following the war. The volume — actually a collection — contains some dense close-readings of verse, a technique that would emerge as the New Critical mainstay, one that was already becoming formalized via the now-legendary textbook *Understanding Poetry* (1940) by Cleanth Brooks and Robert Penn Warren.

As a matter of principle the Agrarians–New Critics, being poets at heart, were seeking in the medium and the analysis of poetry a deeper vision and a nobler way of life, not to be found in a liberal capitalist system they had made no secret of disliking. Strictly as a pedagogical matter, their new method of poetic explication was an orderly, focused, self-contained procedure ideally suited to the college classrooms in which the New Critical approach would soon be embraced. In the process, explication became institutionalized into a twentieth-century avatar of the older academic practice of reading and translating Greek and Latin texts in class meetings. In the long run, however, both the technique and the accompanying outlook were the beginnings of the study of verse and fiction in isolation from — in the phrase of the time — "extra-literary factors."

The original New Critics and their converts were waging an intellectual war against two fronts, one of them established, the other recent and revolutionary. The first was the historicist method, solidly founded on German philology, that read and studied literary texts from the point of view of sources, biography, nation, or race, yet seldom grappled with the formal side of the art. Having arrived on and triumphed in the U.S. campuses during the latter part of the nineteenth century, historicism effectively was to become the expression of American bourgeois progressivism and as such could arouse scant sympathy from the Ransom circle, given their neofeudal views and aestheticist attitudes. The other enemy of the Agrarians–New Critics was the cultural Marxism that, in response to the general atmosphere of world economic collapse, attained favor among some literati in the 1930s — but that in Tate's eyes simply wished to reduce literature to a branch of sociology.

Still, by the late 1930s, as the Agrarians evolved into the New Critics, they demonstrated a willingness to shed their retrograde antiscientism and adapt certain aspects of the scientific enterprise to their poetical commentaries. A passage from Ransom's 1938 essay

"Criticism, Inc." is almost prophetic in this regard: "Criticism must become more scientific, or precise and systematic, and this means that it must be developed by the collective and sustained effort of learned persons—which means that its proper seat is in the universities." [29]

Ransom's urgings came truer than he could ever have imagined, for in just ten years his New Criticism was triumphing on U.S. campuses. The original Fugitives themselves settled into the liberal establishment, Warren starting out on a decades-long career at Yale, and Ransom and Tate going on to teach at Kenyon College in Ohio, where promising young poets like Robert Lowell would come under their expert literary tutelage.

More broadly, the New Critical school all but imposed itself through the mid-1960s as the reigning method in college English departments, for two immediate "political" reasons. One was the sheer exhaustion of the paradigm of the historicists, who had in great measure run out of historical, biographical, and archival materials for their types of research, and whose outlook and tastes were ill-suited to the study of Modernist fiction and verse. The other reason for the New Critical victory was the purge of the left from academic life—the phenomenon known, less than accurately, as McCarthyism. With old-fashioned historicism a-dying and Marxian methods expelled, the stage was set for the easy expansion of a Fugitive aestheticism that, in its critical garb and minus its Old South roots, became the dominant literary ideology, ironically enough, in a land notorious worldwide for its philistine Babbittry and its hostility to art and the aesthetic.

The solid conquest made by the New Criticism and its aestheticist worldview is classically exemplified in René Wellek and Austin Warren's *Theory of Literature* (1948), a handbook and broad critical survey that became for the expanding graduate schools what *Understanding Poetry* already was for freshman courses. The coauthors draw a clearcut distinction between the purely extrinsic (for instance, psychological, historical, philosophical) and the genuinely intrinsic (formal, stylistic, and the like) study of literature, and they come down repeatedly, in no uncertain terms, in favor of the latter. Their recurrent dichotomy would go on to establish itself as the ideological basis of at least two generations of graduate students in English and modern languages, and would shape the cultural conceptions of any number of educated readers in the process.

What finally ended up as a critical school, however, had actually started out as a literary, quasi-political, vaguely religious sect of a handful of southern poets. Though its initial members tried to maintain a tradition of the "free" man of letters, the academy in due time absorbed them. On the other hand, even some of its acolytes in criticism retained some of the preacademic ethos. None of its founding figures held doctorates, and a talented follower like R. P. Blackmur never attended so much as a day of college. Blackmur himself characterized criticism as "the formal discourse of an amateur" who comments on works "it loves"—a view that few professional, fully certified academic theorists would conceive of today, let alone commit to paper.[30]

Despite the myriad of methodologies that succeeded the New Criticism in the 1970s, its teachings have left their mark on U.S. literary culture. At their best, in the work of a Blackmur or a Brooks, the New Critics illuminate the subtleties and complexities of a poem, and thanks to their labors many an American student learned something about how poetry operates. On the other hand, in the worst and most vulgarized of cases, there are countless professors who have preached that literature has absolutely nothing to do with its external contexts and can thus be fully understood without reference to the circumstances of its creation—and who have thereby aided and abetted in the historical ignorance and social amnesia now rife even among well-educated Americans.

The novelist who best represents the triumph of Art for Art's Sake on U.S. campuses following the war is the émigré Russian Vladimir Nabokov (1899–1977). As with the New Critics, the process whereby he arrived at that unofficial position was long and complex. After growing up as a scion of one of Czarist Russia's richest, most powerful, and long-established clans, the adolescent Vladimir with his immediate family fled the Bolshevik Revolution for Germany in 1918. The sale of some of his mother's jewels in the early 1920s helped finance Nabokov's undergraduate studies in Russian literature at Cambridge University, after which the young man rejoined the fairly large community of Russian expatriates in Berlin.

Living within that feverish and uncertain milieu, Nabokov wrote his ingenious Russian novels and verse at night. In the daytime he survived mostly by giving private lessons in English, French, tennis, prosody, and pugilism. As Nabokov's reputation grew somewhat, his precarious income was modestly supplemented by royalties from German translations of his books and from fees for public readings. Curiously, during his fifteen years in Berlin, Nabokov managed never to learn any German.[31]

With his immigration to the United States in 1940, Nabokov took on his first regularly salaried jobs—a series of teaching and research posts, first at Harvard and Wellesley and finally at Cornell, where from 1948 to 1958 he was an associate professor of English. Thereafter the unexpected world sales of *Lolita* allowed him to retire from academic duties, return to Europe, and write full-time in a hotel in Montreux, Switzerland (a town well known for its summer cultural fare).

Throughout Nabokov's entire life he was the pure artist, standing aloof from all social or political causes (save for anticommunism). His sole commitment being to literary art, he carried on the Flaubertian tradition of making perfect prose, crafting his novels a sentence at a time—on 3 by 5-inch cards during his U.S. phase—and of course fashioning the intricate puns and puzzles that became his trademark. Though balking at any association with Oscar Wilde, Nabokov in an interview once described his own position as roughly akin to that of "Art for Art's Sake," however much he may have disliked the phrase itself.[32] With this choice of intellectual terrain Nabokov was not only repudiating the hated official Soviet line on the arts but was also differentiating himself from a larger Russian legacy—dating from the early nineteenth-century critic Belinsky—of social usefulness in literature, as well as from the broad political expectations of the western European left.

Nabokov in all his relevant public statements insists on the absolute separation of literature from almost everything else—from ideas, society, history, and from what he repeatedly dismisses with high contempt as "human interest."[33] Some of the earlier Nabokov novels actually serve as direct expository vehicles for his aestheticist doctrine. For example *The Gift*, a highly specialized account of sectarian squabbles in Russian and émigré literature, offers a polemic, via

Chernyshevsky, against social art. Similarly, *The Real Life of Sebastian Knight,* through the target furnished by its mediocre hack, Goodman, mocks historically minded critics while implying artistic and even moral superiority for the smirking writer who remains at a lofty remove from collective ills like famine, unemployment, or war—Ayn Rand for the aesthetes, one might say.

Although Nabokov did not write much criticism, his views come through loud (some would say "harsh") and clear in the prefaces he wrote to the English versions of his Russian work, in interviews, and in the *Lectures on Literature* that were compiled posthumously from his teaching years at Cornell. Not surprisingly, Nabokov in his literary analysis mostly shuns matters of intellectual, historical, or social background. Gone are those tentative and contradictory attempts of Flaubert and Joyce and other of the great Modernists, who wrestled with ways of reconciling truth with beauty, or even morals with art. ("Reality," Nabokov often quipped, is a word that always belongs within quotation marks.)

Nabokov hence finds "the sociological side" of Dickens to be "neither interesting nor important," and he discusses *Bleak House* as a purely formal construct, brushing aside key aspects of the time such as the legal system or the Victorian crusades on behalf of children— what Nabokov blithely pooh-poohs as "child labor and all that." [34] And he can deny the worth of biographical and historical data in ways that seem dogmatic and capricious; Nabokov gleefully recalls having given a student "a C-minus, or perhaps a D-plus just for applying to [*Ulysses's*] chapters the titles borrowed from Homer," [35] even though Joyce in conversing about his manuscript-in-progress reportedly used the Homeric titles—which, moreover, were in fact included as headings in *The Little Review's* serialization of the book.

Though Nabokov possessed some reputation as a butterfly researcher, his chief focus apparently was taxonomical, with little regard for larger, relational sorts of investigations. (It is worth noting that, in his lecture on *Madame Bovary,* he dispatches "environment" as "by far the least important" of forces that shape a human being.) [36] His vast powers of observation notwithstanding, Nabokov's sense of the thinking, inferential side of the sciences appears to have been slight, and his scorn for "general ideas" and for "thinkers" is legendary.

Nabokov's stated ideas about Freud—whom he anathematizes
with an obsessiveness bordering on the pathological—seldom go beyond caricatures about sex and Oedipus and are at times garnered
from the feeblest specimens of Freudian lit-crit. Physics is not spared:
in an interview Nabokov actually snipes at what he calls "Einstein's
slick formulae," though the jibe may well be motivated by his dislike
of the German scientist's left-wing views.[37] In his last novel, *Look at
the Harlequins!*, Nabokov adds "Neochomsk" and "the About-Noth-
ing land of philosophic linguistics" to his list of hates.[38]

There is much ridiculing, yet little evidence of reading, in Nabokov's endless potshots. Of course, being the kind of liberalizing aristocrat he was, Nabokov could feel convinced as to the absolute autonomy of his mind, and understandably deny the existence of any
determining forces, be they economic, psychological, or biological.
In the worst of instances, however, Nabokov with his narrow certainties can come off as something of an unusually articulate idiot savant,
a Bobby Fischer of literature, as it were.

Nabokov's competitive dislike of literally hundreds of major authors likewise reflects his principles of pure art and aesthetic separatism. He recoils at any author whose style or structure may lack polish
but through whose imperfections there radiates a raw humanity (Cervantes, Dostoevsky, Céline). "Human interest" being a prime Nabokov pejorative, he naturally disdains van Gogh. He also heaps scorn
on novelists of "ideas"—Mann, Camus, Sartre, and any other writer
who sees fit to depict the role of certain intangible (say "spiritual")
presences in human life. Above all a stylist whose novels exclude the
intellect and keep the lid over stray passion, Nabokov rejects any art
marked by intellect or stray passions.

In addition, through a kind of antisocialist realism, a Zhdanovism
in reverse, Nabokov rules out as ipso facto inferior any art marked
by "social content"—Balzac's descriptions of the French bourgeoisie, Conrad's of imperialism, Faulkner's of the Deep South, even
Picasso's *Guernica*. Among the few figures spared his dustbin are Flaubert, Joyce, and Proust, high Modernists with whose aestheticist side
he readily identifies, even as their struggles to portray larger realities
and be true to life in all of its manifestations mean virtually nothing
to him. Hence, though Nabokov's technical and stylistic apparatus

may make him something of an heir-apparent to the major Modernists, what sets him apart is his narrowed spirit, the cramped perspective from which he sees and writes about life.

Nabokov's full literary career presents a curious general picture. Despite their avid defenders in academe, the Russian books, all since translated, amount to a minor if formally fascinating achievement. (In its sheer dazzle their prose reportedly surpasses Nabokov's own English.) Though showing no major breaks from traditional narrative, they grapple in fresh and striking ways with problems of transition, of coincidence, of moving characters across the chessboard, of "he said–she said." Seldom exceeding two hundred pages, these well-chiseled and amusing artifacts have their share of descriptive beauties and also can be touching—yet are more often cruel, as in the case of *Laughter in the Dark.* The latter volume excepted, they rarely echo any deep strains in the human heart.

Nabokov's English output is more uneven. *Sebastian Knight* and *Bend Sinister,* shallow works with snobbery and sarcasm among their chief sentiments, are saved only by their good prose,[39] and *Pnin* is a college novel a bit more clever than are those of Kingsley Amis, Bernard Malamud, or Randall Jarrell. *Pale Fire,* also set at a campus, is a freak masterpiece. Though much of its 1,001–line poem is prosy and its two protagonists' obsessions shade over into those of Nabokov, it demonstrates how the slightest of material—academic intrigues, scholarly megalomania—can be kindled into art by a seasoned virtuoso performer. Adjectival *Ada,* on the other hand, with its trilingual puns, casual conceits and alliterations, and endless snipes at writing rivals, qualifies as a literary monster. Nabokov's mannered prose, so well suited to the first-person narrators of *Pale Fire* and *Lolita,* here lacks any external moorings and hence falls flat, like emperor's clothes minus the emperor. *Look at the Harlequins!,* Nabokov's swan song, is the ultimate special-interest novel, a chunk of self-indulgent fluff conceived for the master's cheering cultists, Nabokov included.

Lolita is Nabokov's one truly major opus, formally perfect save for the creaky background material. It is read and reread precisely because, for all of Nabokov's indifference to modern life and human interest, it crystallizes a number of current phenomena-the motel odyssey, the mindless and sassy American adolescent, suburbia, and the cultivated psychopath-buffoon. Strictly as a novel *Lolita* fits so well together because Nabokov's obsessions either are missing or are blended with the content. Inasmuch as Humbert Humbert is crazy, the anti-Freudian asides are entirely appropriate to him and hence unobtrusive; his sheltered French-English origins rule out any anti-communist snortings (indeed, the only major émigré moment is the hilarious escapade with the czarist cab driver); and the unliterary nature of the subject precludes any harangues about other authors.

Owing to his verbal genius and originality, Nabokov's legacy is greater and of a different kind than that of the Agrarians-New Critics. *Lolita,* now more than just a female name, exists as a kind of popular myth and evokes the idea of any erotically precocious pubescent girl or oldster-youngster love affair. In *Pale Fire* Nabokov perfects a narrative subgenre previously devised by Borges and makes possible such later works as D. M. Thomas's *The White Hotel* and Ariel Dorfman's *Widows.* His artful prose, finally, serves as a reminder to all writers to keep their sentences free of set phrases and clichés.

At the same time, Nabokov's ingenious artifices were to generate fanciful scripture for an entire army of academic acolytes, little Nabokovs who mimicked his conceits and parroted the man's silliest and most outrageous pronouncements. While the literature departments on U.S. campuses, it should be said, did give the twice-uprooted Nabokov a new lease on life, a sympathetic environment for his talents and turn of mind, and a (to him) exotic setting for some novels, the system nonetheless feeds on itself, and his writings and "thought" would later provide rapt admirers a thick textual world of allusions, puns, and manias for them to annotate and celebrate.

Current critics place Nabokov (along with authors like Beckett and Borges) under the rubric of post-Modernism, an umbrella term that poses as many problems as those we saw in examining the Modernist label. Certainly Nabokov demonstrates some of the techniques and attitudes associated with that ethos: the detached irony, the device of texts within texts (and nothing outside the texts), the focus on language and on metalanguage, the love of wordplay, and the special emphasis on surfaces, on the textured "look" of things.

Living as we are in the post-Modern era itself, however, this is not the moment to define its characteristics and its nature. Only time will tell whether the various post-Modernisms amount to a genuine paradigm shift and cultural breakthrough—or are simply a further continuation of the Modernist project under an academic (and consumerist) guise.[40] What concerns us here, and only briefly, is how much the post-Modern structure of feeling can be placed within the history of Art for Art's Sake, can be seen as congruent with the general outlook and now-familiar thought habits of the aestheticist turn of mind.

The most widely disseminated academic manifestation of the post-Modern literary mood is the set of arguments known as deconstruction, derived in the main from the work of French philosopher Jacques Derrida and considered to be the chief poststructuralist school of thought. The deconstructive movement has had many U.S. subsects; its ideas have made their presence felt in feminism, Marxism, ethnic studies, historiography, anthropology, and law. Nevertheless, many of its American adherents tend to be rather typically mainstream, centrist sorts of liberals who have found in deconstruction a means of beefing up their methodology. It is not for nothing that one prominent deconstructionist, Barbara Johnson, defends the doctrine as "a denial of what both the left and the right hold dear." [41]

In many respects, moreover, deconstruction and its kin qualify as latter-day elaborations of the Western tradition of Art for Art's Sake. The primary focus of the divers structuralist and poststructuralist schools that flourished in France in the 1960s, and in the United States in the 1970s, is not so much on form or style as on the very medium of language itself. Their common point of origin is the linguistic theory of Ferdinand de Saussure (1857–1913), who starts from the premise that language, having no real substance or essence, is rather comprised of totally arbitrary signs, which are held together by an infinite series of differential relations. The English signifier "cat" has as its signified the idea of a cat (and not a particular domestic feline); and what enables the item "cat" so to signify derives not from anything inherent in the item's nature, but from its differing phonologically from other signifiers such as "cap" or "cut" or "sat" or "kit."

From the above there follows the critical leap whereby literature, being a branch of language, is deemed to be little more than a network of arbitrary signifiers. The referentiality of a novel or poem hence becomes of far less importance than are the work's—the text's

—inner relations of difference. Literature, then, *is* language; there is no reality outside of its endless regress of signifiers; there is only the text, a self-reflexive, language-based fiction. More, say certain critics: literature is primarily *about* language, about its problematics as text, and whosoever believes otherwise is a naive reader, akin to those naive realists who think cold temperature is a substance inhering in ice cubes.

The linguistic "spin" given to aestheticism by deconstruction is well exemplified in Paul de Man's 1971 essay "Criticism and Crisis." De Man's initial axiom is "the untruth that we take for granted in the everyday use of language." After all, "our entire social language is an intricate system of rhetorical devices designed to escape from the direct expression of desires that are, in the fullest sense of the term, unnameable, not because they are ethically shameful . . . but because unmediated expression is a philosophical impossibility" (9). Or, to simplify de Man's argument somewhat: language, being basically nonreferential, serves only to mask and conceal, rather than to show and reveal, its alleged referents.

Poems and novels, being made up solely of language, also do this. Literature, however, is the only kind of human discourse that knowingly does this, that consciously eludes what it cannot tell — its very nature, after all, is to be *"fiction."* It becomes the job of critics to show how the "discrepancy between sign and meaning (*signifiant* and *signifié*) prevails in literature" as well.[42] For just as language cannot refer us to society, neither can the literary text — which indeed, being by definition fictional, can have no such intent or purpose. Literary art, then, bears no relation to truth inasmuch as there is no truth to be found outside its signifieds. Or, as Gerald Graff wittily sums up the argument: "[L]iterature . . . becomes once again the great oracle of truth, but now the truth is that there is no truth."[43] There is nothing more than *la langue pour la langue* — the latest academic incarnation of *l'art pour l'art* — if only because *le vrai* does not exist.

Once these assumptions became current in the literary halls of American universities, the stage was set for the restless minds of many a critic to spotlight the deconstructive story as the main event. J. Hillis Miller can thus examine *Sketches by Boz* — a work of reportage — and conclude that Dickens's text is not so much about "an externally existing reality" of Victorian London as about "the imposition of fictitious patterns" and the "uncovering of the fictitiousness of the fictive." [44] Conversely, Rosalind Krauss praises "paraliterary" writings like Derrida's *Glas* or Barthes's *S/Z* precisely because they deal *not* with "love or money or the July Monarchy," but rather with their "own linguistic operations" and "the problematics of reading." [45]

Taking things still further, Geoffrey Hartman sets forth a declaration of independence for academic critics, urging them to fashion an "avant-garde criticism" that exists as an autonomous art form, free of any ties to poems or novels. Stanley Fish's inspired belief is that the critic "brings texts into being and makes them available for analysis and appreciation," and furthermore, that literary criticism is "absolutely essential . . . to the very production" of the literary work." [46]

The earlier New Critics, we have seen, started out as poets and novelists; and Allen Tate, who spent several years in the rough-and-tumble of the literary market, wrote biographies and reviews and also did translations of French verse. The higher-flown theoretical critics, by contrast, are seldom called upon to read new fiction and verse and write reviews thereof; and none qualify as poets or novelists. In their dreams, however, of an autotelic criticism (or of "paraliterature" or "metacommentary"), they unknowingly insert themselves within the tradition, the consoling idea, and the fond hopes that, since Gautier penned his preface to *Mademoiselle de Maupin,* have sustained a century and a half of aestheticism.

From its originally marginal and quasi-adversarial status, Modernism has grown and evolved into our dominant, semiofficial culture, both in the more highbrow sectors and in the mass media. On the campuses, not only the Modernist classics but recent literary texts are routinely taught and intensively studied. This is a far cry from the situation evoked in *Theory of Literature* by Wellek and Warren, who in the late 1940s still felt it necessary to defend the inclusion of modern works on required reading lists.

Meanwhile the highly suggestive techniques of modern verse — fragmentation, parataxis, violation of the rules of syntax, surprise juxtapositions, ambiguity — are now standard fare in the advertising messages that surround us all. Narrative devices like shifting point of view, interior monologue, and nonlinear time are utilized at every level of prose fiction, from the agonizing and artful depictions of Chippewa Indians in Louise Erdrich's novels, to many a fast-food thriller stocked on the revolving bookshelves of the discount stores. By the same token, the explicit sexual content and the four-letter words that, in the writings of Joyce, Lawrence, and Henry Miller, at one time outraged the authorities and sparked courtroom battles legendary in the annals of the law are now utterly commonplace in mass market periodicals, in the movies, and even in some segments of broadcasting.

Just as the sacred texts of Modernism serve as starting points for solemn exegeses or hip, "free" glosses by our post-Modern priesthood, paintings by Impressionists, Fauves, and surrealists (many of whom were despised in their time) are now the stuff of blockbuster exhibits in our monumental museums. The shimmering beauty of the Impressionists is a look emulated by ad illustrators; collage and montage are the very basis of MTV production values; Magritte's floating rocks and bowler hats have been absorbed into the iconography of commercial art; and in 1987, in a swinging, post-Franco Madrid, I saw numerous specimens of wall graffiti done in the manner of Picasso and Miró. In the meantime, original canvases by van Gogh fetch prices in the tens of millions of dollars, the anguished Dutchman thereby enjoying, albeit posthumously, the absolute height of what is considered bourgeois success.

Though the works of Schoenberg and his school remain on the sidelines of mainstream concert programs, atonality more or less triumphed as a style on U.S. campuses in the postwar decades. (The music building at UCLA is Schoenberg Hall, in honor of the composer's days as a teacher there.) Stravinsky's neoclassical disciples fared somewhat better on the performance circuit, and on music department faculties they shared space with the Schoenbergians. Perhaps the most fruitful and enduring transculturation of Euromodernist harmonies and technique was in the jazz field—in bebop and cool, in the pianism of Thelonious Monk and Bill Evans, and in the more innovative songs ("Prelude to a Kiss," "Sophisticated Lady") and later arrangements of Duke Ellington.

The battle for modern music, however, was won on a grand scale elsewhere. Atonality and its jagged chords regularly serve as background to movie and TV suspense sequences; Stravinsky's percussive rhythms can be heard on the soundtracks of crowd scenes and car chases; and the harmonic inventions of Debussy and Ravel, bold in their day, now soothe us in supermarkets and fast elevators. In an ironic echo of Pater, Robert Hughes notes, "As far as today's politics is concerned, most art aspires to the condition of Muzak." [47] For all intents and purposes, Modernism has become firmly entrenched as *the* international style in the educational system and, subsequently, in the culture, communications, and entertainment industries.

Such a development was in many ways inevitable. The "creative people" (as they are called in advertising), who hire out their skills on the mass-culture markets, tend to be well schooled in Modernist ethos and techniques, which they have absorbed via their high-power backgrounds in the liberal arts, fine arts, or performing arts. It is these men and women who provide the indispensable daily "software" for the production schedules of our ever-expanding "media society" (in Fredric Jameson's phrase). Hence, in one of history's ironies, an artistic movement that started out as a passionate bid for authenticity, for something transcending or even in opposition to bourgeois society, through its spiritual offspring now helps furnish the syntax, sounds, and imagery for a global bourgeois market's communications needs.

This of course is hardly the first such surprise in human history. A helpful analogy for our purposes is that of neoclassicism, the high culture, based primarily on Greco-Roman art and letters, that we associate with the monarchies of Western Europe, roughly 1660–1789. By contrast, in an earlier era the rediscovery and teaching of those ancient classics—the humanist project—had started out as a contestatory activity, posing a challenge to the entrenched power and scholasticism of the Vatican and leading ultimately to the Protestant rift.

Following the destructive wars of early seventeenth-century Europe, however, the humanist legacy was to be absorbed and assimilated by the centralizing Bourbon state and by the refashioned English aristocracy. Under this new dispensation the Ancient heritage was to reach its apogee in the conscious (neo)classicism of

Racine in France and Pope in England, with Dr. Johnson providing its great last gasp in late eighteenth-century London. Only with the violent emergence of a revolutionary new bourgeois society between 1789 and 1830, and the concomitant revolt of the Romantics, would Europe's literati put an exhausted neoclassicism firmly behind them.

Similarly, Modernism in the arts, like the aestheticism that was its precondition, started out as a means of spiritually contesting a market society with whose ways the writers and artists felt dissatisfied and embattled. Following the horrific political, economic, and military crises that engulfed the bourgeois powers from 1914 to 1945, artistic Modernism in the postwar order emerged as the most highly prized of styles, eventually assuming a normative role in the elite institutions, and becoming a readily available lexicon (a kind of data base) for the "creative" departments in the media sector.

And so, in its later reincarnation as an academicized, commercialized, "neoclassicized" Modernism, Art for Art's Sake has triumphed. As French absolutism did with the Greco-Roman patrimony, so has postindustrial capitalism done with aestheticism. Few of Modernism's apostles, saints, or martyrs could have foreseen such an outcome, but their works now nourish the high-cultural reaches of a bourgeois society that, in its earlier, rawer stages, gave them grudging support at best. Whether they would feel pleased at what they would see today is anybody's guess.

CHAPTER 7

The Changing Politics of Art for Art's Sake

Let us return once again to Théophile Gautier's preface to *Mademoiselle de Maupin*. The selections cited at some length here have in common a precise and definable historical outlook:

> I prefer to a certain useful pot a Chinese pot which is sprinkled with mandarins and dragons. . . . I should most joyfully renounce my rights as a Frenchman and as a citizen to see an authentic picture by Raphael . . . or Princess Borghese. . . . I should very readily agree . . . to the return of that cannibal, Charles X, if he brought me back a hamper of Tokay . . . from his castle in Bohemia. . . . I prefer the sound of screeching fiddles and tambourines to that of the President's little bell.[1] (39–40)

The basic drift in this passage is a wholesale scorn for the prosaic pettiness of the new bourgeois values ("my rights . . . as a citizen") and bourgeois artifacts ("a useful pot," "the President's little bell"), in favor of the aesthetic attractions of institutions ("Charles X," "Princess Borghese"), artifacts ("Tokay"), and art objects ("Raphael," "a Chinese pot," "fiddles and tambourines") that are *pre*-bourgeois.

Gautier then takes this temporal contrast to vivid and extravagant heights:

> What economist will enlarge our stomach so that it will hold as many beefsteaks as the late Milo of Crotona, who ate an ox? The menu of the Café Anglais . . . seems to me very meagre . . . compared to the menu of Trimalcio's dinner. . . . The little houses on the outskirts of Paris . . . are miserable country cottages if one compares them to the villas of the Roman politicians. (41)

Here, the niggling triviality of bourgeois economists, cafés, and homes is mocked even as antiquity and its hedonistic grandeurs are flamboyantly praised. Similarly, later on in the preface the poplars and the Opéra of contemporary Paris are compared with Egypt's rows of obelisks and with the sheer scale of ancient Roman circuses, and found sadly wanting (45).

Returning to the matter of bourgeois government, Gautier pokes fun at the growth of Parliament, and at the expansion of electoral rights, on the following grounds:

> Don't you think that there are enough errors of French as it is, in Parliament . . . ? I hardly understand the point of shutting up two or three hundred provincials in a wooden shed, with a ceiling painted by M. Fragonard, to make them mess about with . . . countless silly . . . little laws? What does it matter whether it's a sabre, a holy-water sprinkler, or an umbrella that governs you? It's always a stick . . . . It would be much more progressive . . . to break it and send the pieces to the devil. (42)

Poet that he is, Gautier articulates his political thought in the form of images. Hence the "sabre" stands for feudal lords, the "holy-water sprinkler" for the priests, the "umbrella" for the bourgeoisie. And although an anarchistic side of Gautier becomes slightly manifest in his suggestion that *all* those several "sticks" be broken, it is a passing, minor impulse. Far more significant for our purposes, the poet ironically juxtaposes ceiling art by Fragonard (and its implications of rococo beauty and refinement) with what he sees as the bad French and provincial silliness of bourgeois Parliamentary deliberations.

The dominant emotion in these passages is a profound nostalgia for past eras at the expense of the present. The Romance languages have words to denote this attitude: the French *passéisme* (adjective *passéiste*), the Spanish *pasatismo* (adjective *pasatista*). A literal rendering in English would be "past-ism" and "past-ist," though neither the noun nor the adjective comes off; they ring inadequate and ugly, both in speech and on the page. The general idea is more effectively conveyed via a full phrase such as "the cult of a distant, radically different past, more or less idealized."

Gautier's *passéisme* is the first outstanding instance of what would emerge as a major strand in the ideological development of literary aestheticism and Modernism. One finds similar longings, for example, in Flaubert's occasional ruminations about the desirability of government by mandarins; in Leconte de Lisle's highly pictorial ancient and Oriental motifs; in Rubén Darío's fanciful evocations of Versailles; in Eliot's avowed royalism and Anglo-Catholic utopianism; in Pound's self-conception as medieval troubadour and in his yearnings for Renaissance art patrons (which partly motivated his support for Mussolini); in the romanticized antebellum South of the Fugitives-Agrarians-New Critics; and in that completely fantastical entity dreamed up by Yeats and known as "Byzantium."

Save for Eliot (who stood a mere boat trip away from earning his Harvard doctorate in philosophy), none of these authors qualifies as a serious thinker. Their imagery and thought nonetheless start from the premise that modern society is politically suspect and culturally contemptible and that only past eras are attractive and deserving of respect. Behind this sweeping judgment there stands a big truth that they too well and rather painfully intuited: namely, that closely crafted verse had no function in the new bourgeois industrial system by which they were feeling slighted, whereas their lyric art had indeed played some role in the divers anciens régimes that they looked back to and longed for. In assuming this "political" stance, the aesthetes and Modernists effectively became the spiritual allies of nineteenth-and early-twentieth-century conservatives.

Conservative ideology today, of course, is a way of thinking very different from what it was a century and a half ago. In our time, conservatives believe first and foremost in the ideal of an unfettered free market, operating with minimal government controls, and in their rhetoric they tend to favor at least the outward forms of political republicanism, if not full-fledged democratic rule. Naturally, divisions exist, particularly regarding private morality and religious practice. The more old-fashioned conservatives advocate a major role for traditional values and for religion, while secular, rationalistic, "libertarian" conservatives (Ayn Rand being the best known) tend to hold agnostic or atheist views and are indifferent and occasionally hostile to church power. Both factions, however, are allies in their broad convictions about free markets and economic limits on government.

In the nineteenth century it was precisely the reverse. The organic conservatives (as I call them) were essentially feudal, monarchical, and pro-Church in their general beliefs. For them, the enemy was the French Revolution and everything that cataclysm stood for. The most famous instance in this regard is Edmund Burke, whose *Reflexions on the Revolution in France* (1790), written in the heat of the moment, is the pioneering effort, the first of many backward-looking opinions that defend a society based on royal succession, hierarchical class privilege, traditional religion, and a certain amount of healthy irrationalism in human affairs. Burke's ideological offspring were many, such as the most extreme case of the Comte Joseph de Maistre (1754–1821), a bitter enemy of republicanism in any form and an ardent apologist for absolute monarchy and sovereign papal authority.

The fundamental quarrel of the organic conservatives was not with the revolution's blood and violence but rather with its very ideals and ends: liberty, egalitarianism, republican government, and a secular citizenry held together by bonds other than time-honored feudal and ecclesiastical custom. In addition, the organic conservatives tended to advocate subordination for and even intolerance toward religious and racial minorities. Precisely because the revolution had granted equal rights as citizens to France's Jews, counterrevolutionary thinking on the Continent in reaction was to demonstrate a strong anti-Semitic cast. In the course of the nineteenth century, French anti-Semitism grew and reached a kind of climax in Edouard Drumont's best-selling work of "history," *La France Juive* (1886), and in the notorious Dreyfus case that divided French society in the 1890s.

In general it was the leveling process, the trend to equality unleashed by the events of 1789 (and of 1848 and 1871) that the organic conservatives broadly rejected. Mention is due, however, of another brand of conservatism, vividly embodied in the views expressed by the characters Gradgrind and Mr. Bounderby in Dickens's *Hard Times*. This ideology is conservative only insofar as it firmly supports a new status quo—in this case the liberal industrial order that was triumphing in Victorian England. Appropriately, the actual content of such thinking is positivistic (Gradgrind's "facts"), bourgeois (Bounderby's "self-made man" rhetoric), and staunchly oriented to the economic here and now—in contrast to the nostalgic, feudal religiosity typified by organic conservatism. The successors to Gradgrind and Bounderby in our time are Milton Friedman, Robert

Nozick, Newt Gingrich, and other well-known upholders of the libertarian, individualistic, free market creed.

The ideas of the organic conservative thinkers are now largely discredited. Though democratization may have been an issue open to debate 125 years ago, today by contrast democracy is the expectation (even where it is not happening). More pointedly, much of nineteenth-century conservative thought was to serve as intellectual fountainhead for the varieties of twentieth-century fascism. The official ideology of the royalist Action Française, for instance, was a characteristic assemblage of organic conservative attitudes, integrated into the concrete program of an aggressively right-wing political party.

The major European fascist regimes took state power in what already were fairly developed industrial capitalist nations (Spain excepted). Nevertheless their choice of collective imagery and dreams was largely *passéiste* in character.[2] The Action Française—which found a belated role in the collaborationist Vichy rump state—harked back to the era of Bourbon power (like monarchists without a monarch, as it were). The Italian Fascisti looked to a more distant Imperial Rome; indeed the very name of their party is derived from the fasces, the bundle of rods tied around an ax blade, symbolizing the authority of the ancient Roman magistrates. In Spain the Francoist forces conjured up long-lost memories of Spanish Empire and of Catholic crusades against alien heretics. The vision of the German Nazis, inspired in part by Wagner's operas, was one either of the medieval small towns imagined in *Die Meistersinger* or of the Nordic warriors famously mythified in the composer's *Ring* cycle.

Fascist ideology of course was not only antiliberal and antidemocratic but virulently anti-Soviet and anticommunist as well. In this regard it carried on a tradition of the organic conservatives, for whom socialism was merely a further extension of the leveling dynamics they despised. At the same time, however, owing to its anti-Bolshevist stance, European fascism was at first viewed quite favorably by Western capitalism and its professional publicists. Until early 1939, libertarian conservative spokesmen such as Henry Luce (of *Time-Life*) and most of the respectable British press found much to defend in Hitler, Franco, and Mussolini's war against the "Reds." It was only when Nazi Germany seized Czechoslovakia and invaded Poland in

1939 that Tory opinion began to shift away from accommodating Hitler. And needless to say, by the time of the Battle of Britain and the *Luftwaffe* raids on English towns, not many British conservatives — organic or otherwise — were to deem German fascism an attractive political prospect.

Few major Western aesthetes qualify as committed fascists. On the other hand many leading Modernists entertained opinions that overlap uncomfortably with the fascist worldview. At the same time, the unsavory side of certain Modernists' politics should not be construed as the sole and inevitable path taken by Art for Art's Sake movements. As demonstrated in the following pages, the political component of aestheticism and its adepts has varied considerably throughout history, depending on the particular writer's circumstances, his or her battles at the moment, and the broad configuration of the surrounding social forces.

For this purpose we must visit again the original sources in the Enlightenment.

The aesthetic theory of Kant, as seen in chapter 1, was conceived within an intellectual, political, and social landscape radically different from the world that began modifying his thought and then gave rise to aestheticist poetic doctrines in the nineteenth century. Kant's avowed purpose, after all, was to transcend the reigning set of ideas of his time regarding knowledge, morals, and art. The three great *Critiques* set forth a contestatory, reformationist, and even (as he saw it) revolutionary project in the three chief branches of Western philosophy. His accumulated arguments add up to a single broad critique of the established mind of ancien régime Europe.

It is thus quite fitting that Kant's ideas on politics and society, both in his writings and in recorded private conversations, should tend toward a forward-looking Enlightenment progressivism. While not by temperament a man of action, Kant nonetheless held quietly to the antimonarchist, antifeudal, and anticlerical (though not necessarily antireligious) attitudes that were the common property of republican-minded intellects in his time.

Anecdotes by contemporaries testify to the brave independence of Kant's political views. Indeed his reported oral opinions show considerably more bite than do his rather cautious written reflections. In conversation he invoked Lockean arguments (then revolutionary in Central Europe) about the freedom of individuals to pursue happiness as they choose. A memoirist recalls Kant saying, "My whole being shudders when I think of serfdom." On one occasion Kant criticized George III's policy toward the American colonists, and when an English merchant residing in Koenigsberg consequently challenged the philosopher to a duel, Kant replied with arguments so persuasive that the Englishman apologized instead.

As regards the French Revolution, Kant remained a staunch believer in its basic principles, even while criticizing the new regime's excesses and the execution of Louis XVI. As late as 1794, Nicolovius observes that Kant "is still a thorough democrat. He said all the horrors of France were unimportant compared with the chronic evil of despotism from which France had suffered, and the Jacobins were probably right in all they were doing." Similarly, a medical colleague named Metzger reports that Kant defended the revolution with "boldness and fearlessness."[3] It thus should come as no surprise that the philosopher believed in abolishing hereditary titles of nobility and felt that the only just constitution was a republican one.[4]

In his own occasional political texts Kant also speaks up for ascendant liberalism and individual freedom. For instance his 1784 essay "What Is Enlightenment?" champions "every man's vocation for thinking for himself," asserts that "if only freedom is granted, enlightenment is almost sure to follow," and frankly states that a prince should "prescribe nothing . . . in religious matters" but rather leave the individual "free to make use of his reason in matters of conscience."[5]

Kant's thinking on these issues did not go unchallenged. A man once described by Frederick the Great as "a swindling, scheming parson,"[6] J. Christoph Woellner, became minister of education and religion in 1788 and imposed inquisitorial measures, among them a special commission to censor all Prussian printed matter as well as a requirement that all theology students submit to cross-examination regarding their faith. Kant responded with the essay "The End of All Things," in which he alludes obliquely yet angrily to the repression. Any educated Prussian reader at the time would have inferred what is meant when the philosopher writes, "Christianity viewed as an assemblage of voluntarily received maxims of life does not threaten here, while the law does." Christian faith, he notes darkly, might "reach the point where it ceases to be worthy of love (which might well happen if it were armed with dictatorial authority instead of its gentle spirit)." [7] In such a case, Kant suggests, rebellion might become inevitable.

Woellner denounced Kant's religious writings as disloyal to the youth of Prussia and the king. A new essay of Kant's, "On the Struggle of the Good Principle with the Evil for Mastery over Mankind," was banned by theological censors. Rumors ran of proposals to bar him from any literary or publicist activity and even to remove him from his teaching post. Finally, in October of 1794, King Friedrich Wilhelm II himself sent a letter to the philosopher, accusing him of "the distortion and debasing of many . . . basic teachings of Holy Scripture" and exhorting him to desist or face "unpleasant consequences."

Kant never retracted any of his past statements. Feeling his remaining life's work threatened, however, in his personal reply to the king he declares himself "Your Royal Majesty's most faithful subject" and promises to "refrain entirely in the future from all public discussions concerning religion, . . . in teaching and in writing alike." [8]

Aside from his one prudent moment of obeisance before reactionary state power, the whole of Kant's oeuvre forms part of the Enlightenment's struggle for rationality and freedom. Kant's first and final concern is the autonomy of the individual mind—whether the particular faculty under examination be cognition freeing itself from both rationalist and empiricist dogma, ethics both from maxims and from inclination, or our sense of beauty both from rules and from mere pleasure. Within the public arena, moreover, the Kantian project stands as a triple challenge to absolute monarchy, religious orthodoxy, and neoclassical art. It is not that Kant's aesthetics in and of itself could pose a threat to the status quo, but rather that his ideas on aesthetics constitute but one portion of his broad critique of the status quo. The spirit of that critique would continue in the work of his great literary disciple Schiller.

Schiller's temperament and life history could not differ more from those of Kant. The concern with "freedom" that prevails in the *Letters on Aesthetic Education* and in almost all his other writings grows out of some prolonged bitter personal experiences. Schiller in his youth endured unrelenting oppression under Duke Karl Eugen of Würt-temberg, for whom the boy's father was director of gardens. Duke Karl Eugen has been described as "one of the most notoriously . . . tyrannical of the eighteenth-century despots."[9] By way of example: a local pastor had inspired in young Schiller a desire to become a clergy-man, but the child was forced instead into the Karlschule, a boarding school founded by Karl Eugen himself, where all of the duke's offi-cials were required to matriculate their sons.

Schiller spent a miserable eight years at that local institution, with-out so much as a single day's leave and with parental visits kept brief and under surveillance. Still barred from pursuing his theologi-cal bent when he later entered the university, Schiller then took up the study of medicine. Eventually he broke with Karl Eugen and fled Württemberg, but his anger at the Karlschule and its reigning duke never subsided. In reaction to those years of provincial and feudal serfdom, Schiller finally came to see himself as "a citizen of the world who serves no prince."[10]

These experiences were no doubt the primal source for Schiller's numerous works that celebrate the struggle of the oppressed against unworthy tyrants, a theme present in both his historical and dramatic output. In his introduction to *The Revolt in the Netherlands,* a lengthy recounting of the Dutch war of liberation against the Spanish Empire, the author admits to feeling "stirred by a situation in which oppressed humanity struggled for its noblest rights,"[11] while the focus of his his-tory play *The Maid of Orleans* is Joan of Arc's missionary battle against the occupying British.

In fact the recurring clash in Schillerian theater involves humble folk or enlightened upper-class renegades on one side and aristocrats and clergy, feudal and religious intolerance on the other. The de-sired outcome, either as envisioned by protagonists or as implied by events, is a liberal, republican society. The vision as well as its effects could be quite passionate. *The Robbers* (1781) made the twenty-one-year-old playwright famous almost overnight after its scandalous pre-mier, when women fainted in the audience and strangers in tears embraced each other. The play depicts the outlandish adventures of Karl Moor, a rebel against his aristocratic past, whose army of brigands makes war on priests and nobles, stealing their wealth. An ever-recalcitrant Moor refuses to "squeeze my body into stays" while also dreaming that "out of Germany shall spring a Republic."[12]

A Bourgeois Tragedy is the telling subtitle of the melodrama *Intrigue and Love*. That an ancient, noble genre such as tragedy could be qualified as "bourgeois" in itself challenges the prevailing courtly neoclassicism. "Bourgeois" here of course represents a positive alternative to the cynicism and corruption of the aristocrats in the play, whereas Luisa Miller, the modest daughter of a common music master, is portrayed as contrastingly natural and pure in spirit. Similarly, *Wilhelm Tell* gets maximum theatrical excitement out of the legendary struggle between Swiss peasants and their despotic Austrian oppressor. Spokesman Tell attacks the "king and bishop" for their exclusive control of "the land," "the fruits," and "the rivers, sea and salt." When the peasantry rise up in revolt, tyrant Gessler poses the basic question: "Shall emperor or peasant be the master?" In the course of the work, however, the more prescient noblemen realize that their time is passing, and the piece ends with a former apologist for the Austrians saying, "And from this day my serfs my bondmen shall be free."[13]

Classic liberal principles are brought directly to bear in *Don Carlos*, in which the enlightened and courageous Marquis of Posa is depicted as a liberal before his time, "a citizen of ages yet to come." Toward the Spanish royal court he maintains a correct if hostile stance, for "I cannot be / The servant of a prince." When Posa addresses the intolerant King Philip in a lengthy confrontation, he caps his speech with a plea that in many a past stage production elicited applause from its European audiences: "Man is greater / Than you esteem him / . . . Grant us liberty of thought!"[14]

During Schiller's lifetime and after, many Europeans were to perceive the questioning and rebellion in his plays as revolutionary. A high point came on 25 August 1792, when the French Assembly conferred upon Schiller the honorary title of French Citizen, a distinction they simultaneously bestowed upon George Washington, Count Kosciuszko, and Thomas Paine, among others. And in 1795, a scandalized Viennese newspaper characterized Schiller as "the father of the revolutionary spirit."[15] By that time, however, Schiller had recoiled at the execution of Louis XVI and had generally soured on politics; he appears never to have responded to the high honor from a tumultuous France.

In spite of his own private shift, throughout much of the following century Schiller's work would be mined for artistic purposes by European progressives in the arts. This was the case above all in politically backward countries like Germany and Italy, where the hopes of liberal reform were consistently blocked by ongoing feudal systems, reactionary governments, and Church power. There is of course the well-known instance of Beethoven—whose republican views were no secret—using the "Ode to Joy" for the finale of the Ninth Symphony. Schiller's dramas in particular provided an indispensable stimulus to opera librettists. Verdi (who himself served as a symbol of Italian emancipation) based no less than four of his operas—*Don Carlo, Luisa Miller, Giovanna D'Arco,* and *I Mesnadieri* [The robbers]— on Schiller plays.

Schiller's *Letters on Aesthetic Education*, we saw, reflects his changes in political stance. One must nonetheless emphasize that, in spite of his disillusion with the turmoil in France, Schiller did not move to the other extreme of turning *passéiste* or idealizing a feudal past. Though he alludes obliquely to the revolution's "crude, lawless impulses" and "society uncontrolled," he finds yet more repugnant the aristocratic "spectacle of indolence" (fifth letter, p. 35) and the oppression formerly authorized by the Church" (seventh letter, p. 47). His own position is best likened to that of the Girondists, the revolution's moderate faction, who favored overthrowing the monarchy and establishing a republic, but who in turn were opposed by the more radical Jacobins (who crushed them during the Terror of 1793).

Whatever we make of its political nuances and ambivalence, Schiller's aesthetic theory still emerges from the larger Enlightenment project of combating a status quo then dominated by nobles, priests, and neoclassicism. The *Letters* may focus on reshaping the individual rather than on transforming society, but their ultimate aim remains a better social order. There is no hint of reactionary nostalgia anywhere in the book's pages.

Much the same can be observed about the French personalities who were in some way responsible for the early diffusion of Kant's and Schiller's ideas in France and thereby for the subsequent emergence of *l'art pour l'art* (chapter 2). The respective political opinions of Mme. de Staël, Benjamin Constant, and Victor Cousin ranged from the constitutional monarchism of the woman activist to the moderate republicanism of the two male writers. While varyingly opposed to Napoleon, none of them felt much love for the Bourbon Restoration of Louis XVIII; Mme. de Staël in fact insisted that the returning royal power be countervailed with a liberal constitution.[16]

There is also Victor Hugo's brief aestheticist episode with the book of verses the *Orientales* (1829); his entire life history in effect stands for French republican ideals with a strong touch of socialism. Only with the consolidation of King Louis Philippe's liberal regime, and of the literary free market after 1830, would a disenchanted Théophile Gautier give vent to a *passéisme* that carries the seeds of like attitudes in the work of numerous future poets, as we shall see below.

Neither does Ruskin or Wilde, England's two most vocal Art for Art's Sake publicists, exhibit such reactionary nostalgia. Each in his own way was probably much too secure in his respective chosen role—Ruskin as preeminent English art critic and later as Oxford don, Wilde as a highly successful playwright and man-about-town—to yearn for feudal or princely patronage. At the same time both dissented sharply with Victorianism—Ruskin for its narrowness, ugliness, and philistine vulgarity, Wilde for its stiff moralism and all-around smugness. Hence, to them the present was certainly a time to be fought or mocked, but not in the name of an idealized past. Youthful religiosity was something they both eventually put behind them, and though Wilde remained drawn to Catholicism and finally converted on his deathbed, his was more an aesthetic love of ritual beauties than an intellectual receptivity to Church doctrines or power.

While Ruskin for his part found much that was defensible in the enterprise of building medieval cathedrals, his defense was premised not on any belief in Catholicism or feudal organization as such, but on the collective, shared nature of the enterprise. In fact, as his distaste for Victorian capitalism grew, Ruskin came to identify himself as a socialist, and his later works, notably *Fors Clavigera,* combine art criticism with socialist propaganda. In one of the subsections of this work Ruskin actually says of himself, "For indeed I am a Communist of the old school—reddest also of the red." [17]

Ruskin's own ideas in this regard could spark controversy and even shock English readers. In *Unto This Last,* his treatise on political economy, Ruskin takes passionate aim at the theory that human beings are driven solely by greed. He finds the conception of a purely Economic Man as delusional as the notion of an Aesthetic Man who responds only to pure beauty. *Unto This Last* began as a serial in *Cornhill* magazine, edited by Thackeray; yet so angry was the public response that Thackeray informed Ruskin that the fourth installment of this work would be the final one.

Still, despite his socialist leanings, Ruskin's dislike of liberal capitalism has the feel of old-fashioned Toryism to it. He saw salvation not in popular revolt (for which he held scant sympathy) but in the work of strong, superior, aristocratic gentlemen. Ruskin belongs more within the tradition of the feudal socialists attacked by Marx and Engels in *The Communist Manifesto.*[18] Still, the contradictory nature of Ruskin's thought as well as of his position—his preaching to the very people with whose thinking he disagreed—probably helped contribute in some measure to the bouts of insanity that troubled his later years.

Though we seldom think of Oscar Wilde, strictly speaking, as a political writer, his only explicitly political major article bears the striking title "The Soul of Man under Socialism" (1891). Unusually eloquent for Wilde, it was prompted by a talk that George Bernard Shaw gave on socialism at a meeting at Westminster the same year. Liberally sprinkled with memorable samples of Wildean wit, the essay is nonetheless a long paean of praise to the socialist dream— for reasons utterly unlike the usual ones, however. (Wilde never fails to surprise his readers.)

The piece starts by singling out "the chief advantage of . . . socialism," namely that "it would relieve us from that sordid necessity of living for others," which, alas, is the present condition (19).[19] From there Wilde draws an inference that he varyingly restates in the course of the essay: the value of socialism is that "it will lead to Individualism" (20). For Wilde, the pursuit of private property has harmed individualism "by confusing a man with what he possesses"

(25). Hence, "with the abolition of private property, . . . we shall have true, beautiful, healthy Individualism" (26). Such a system, moreover, will reduce the need of artists such as Byron or Shelley to expend their creative genius in the task of mere rebellion.

While much of "The Soul of Man under Socialism" deals with aesthetic issues that seem tangential to its central political reasoning, the underlying implication is that, in a socialist arrangement, artists would be able simply to follow their individual impulses and not have to please either a prince, a pope, or the people. Arising from "no compulsion over man" (49), the arts would then be truly free.

Both ingenious and moving in its arguments, "The Soul of Man under Socialism" remains as fresh today as when it first saw print in the 1890s. Its focus on an inner, individual freedom recalls aspects of Schiller's aesthetic explorations; and its rejection of charity for being a degrading stopgap, its refusal to sentimentalize manual labor, and its vision of a freewheeling brand of socialism are notions that hark back to the ideas of the early Marx. The essay becomes all the more attractive with the collapse of socialist regimes that, in the twentieth century, have unfortunately emerged in nation-states too much weighed down with past authoritarian traditions. "The Soul of Man under Socialism" forcefully represents a libertarian side of aestheticism that we have seen arise at various moments in history. Wilde's origins in a backward, colonial Ireland no doubt had a lot to do with his forward-looking opinions.

Of the English aesthetes, Walter Pater appears to have been genuinely apolitical insofar as no major reflections on governmental or societal issues are to be found in his writings. Pater's extreme timidity probably made any kind of "politics" — whether academic or national — difficult for him, and his willingness to delete the offending passages from subsequent editions of *The Renaissance* bespeaks a desire to avoid conflict at all costs. There were, of course, his personal struggles with Christian doctrine, but they were philosophical and epistemological in nature rather than concerned with priestly privilege; and as we saw in chapter 3, he remained attached to religious ritual even while disbelieving Church creeds.

Swinburne stands as a notable instance in matters ideological. The only lyrist of any importance in the ranks of English aestheticism, he went a route similar to that taken by many other Western European poets. Originally influenced by Hugo and Mazzini (the latter of whom he met in 1867), Swinburne started out as a rebel, a republican, a defender of Italian emancipation, and a reader of the works of the Marquis de Sade. In time, however, Swinburne would be cured of his recalcitrance when literary critic Theodore Watts-Dunton saved him from dissolution. He then spent his last thirty years living sequestered and in a dependent relationship with Watts-Dunton. The quondam enfant terrible became a moralistic and conservative patriot who ardently defended the Boer War, opposed home rule for the Irish, and produced in great quantities though in declining quality.

Swinburne's later years, while pitiful, in many ways exemplify the ideological ground chosen by the lyrists (as well as the poetic novelists) under the bourgeois-industrial system well into the 1940s. Aside from exceptional cases like that of Mallarmé (who flirted with anarchism), serious poets on the whole inclined to *passéiste* imagery and views readily identifiable as reactionary nostalgia. In instances such as Yeats and Eliot this outlook signified a passing, if unconsummated, relationship with fascism, and in Ezra Pound a time of active collaboration as a radio propagandist for the Mussolini regime.

These broad tendencies, I believe, are attributable to a double isolation regularly endured by the lyrists: first, their professional and artistic isolation as poets living on the margins of an industrialized literary market; and second (the result of the first), a general isolation within a bourgeois society from which they felt more or less left out.

As one might expect, their unfavorable poetic circumstances led them to speculate — idly or less so — on other societal arrangements that would benefit and sustain their lyric needs. Inasmuch as words were their sole medium, voluntary migration to a different language milieu was mostly out of the question for them — in contrast to the composers or painters or even novelists, some of whom moved freely from one linguistic geography to another. Meanwhile, the United States was ideologically off bounds, being the very embodiment of a bourgeois social order against which they were doing battle. (Indeed, many U.S. writers, when faced with the opportunity, chose to cross the Atlantic in the other direction.)

The only logical alternative to emerge in the poets' minds, then, was some acknowledged social order in which lyrists and versifiers enjoyed access to and support from the powerful, and in which an artisanal beauty played a definable role. The possibilities might include ways of life that were historically prebourgeois—feudalism or monarchy, the Renaissance, the Middle Ages, or the ancient world.

The nostalgic option is hence understandable, inasmuch as the lyric poets did not fully belong within industrial capitalism's mass-print culture. The nineteenth-century bourgeois dreams of progress —of expanding markets, ever-new technology, and gradual democratization—had little to offer in the way of tangible, significant benefit to the poets' verse commitments, and in fact each step in "progress" only stressed all the more their marginality. Freedom of the press and of speech, while providing safeguards against state prosecution (such as that suffered by Baudelaire for *Les fleurs du mal*), constituted but a negative gain, a freedom *from,* rather than a positive improvement in the day-to-day situation of the lyrists, whose "free" discourse counted for little in the verbal marketplace's aggregate production figures and bottom lines.

The novelists, by contrast, could earn a living and possibly even get rich from periodical serializations and from volume sales (pun intended) of their prose narratives. Even the industrial proletariat had the advantage of collective working conditions that enabled them to fight back as a group, to withhold their laboring skills so as to extract concessions from bourgeois owners. Workers' struggles, however, were a tactic quite remote from the options available to the lyrists, what with their preindustrial craft. (The very idea of poets on strike seems faintly comical.) Moreover, when French workers did take control of the machinery in the Paris Commune of 1871, aesthetes like Gautier, Leconte de Lisle, and Flaubert unabashedly supported the return of the forces of order and the bloody reprisals against some ten thousand Communards that followed.

Similarly, professional crusades such as Dickens's battle against piracy in publishing could make only the slightest difference for new verse, in view of poetry's minimal "exchange value," its infinitesimal home market and even lesser one abroad. The underlying truth was that any legislation, whether in the interests of bourgeois wealth or wage earners' justice, would have made scarcely a dent in the special working conditions of slow-producing poets. Given that no government faction had either the means or the will to advance the interests of poets *as poets,* the isolation of the verse makers thus became political and ideological as well. Feeling marginalized by the reigning class system and its issues, the poets and aesthetes opted instead to "vote with their heads," to form loyalties via their lively imaginations and affective nostalgia, and to cast their inner lot with some past aristocracy of their own mental making.

The situation of the poets prompts analogies with that of other groups who, throughout the history of Western capitalism, have suffered displacement and loss due to broad changes in productive or distributive sectors. One thinks of artisans whose crafts have been rendered economically unviable and obsolete by factory automation—the Luddites, for example.[20] Or one thinks of small shopkeepers who have felt threatened with extinction by the large retailing outfits and who constituted the mass base for the Poujadiste movement in postwar France. The social resentment of these displaced groups is not necessarily progressive and can be nostalgic and reactionary, as indeed was the case with Poujade and his followers.

And then there is the infamous *lumpenproletariat,* the term coined by Karl Marx to characterize the amorphous and disreputable mob that furnished the initial shock troops for Louis Bonaparte's 1851 coup d'état. Marx sums up the demographics of the *lumpen* in a justifiably renowned passage:

> Alongside the decayed *roués* with dubious means of existence and of dubious origin, alongside ruined and adventurous offshoots of the bourgeoisie, were vagabonds, discharged soldiers, discharged jailbirds, escaped galley slaves, swindlers, mountebanks, lazzaroni, pickpockets, tricksters, gamblers, maquereaus [pimps], brothel keepers, porters, *literati,* organ-grinders, ragpickers, knife-grinders, tinkers, beggars—in short, the whole, indefinite, disintegrated mass, thrown hither and thither, which the French call *la bohème.*[21]

The literati here serve as components within Marx's long list of *lumpen.* Though the inclusion is partly for dramatic effect, it bears examination and is subject to debate. Jerrold Seigel, for instance, notes that, at least before 1848, many French literati stood at the left end of the political spectrum.[22] Still, the fact remains that there have been numerous poets and other literary kin whose ideological attitudes and reflexes (seldom are their views sufficiently developed to qualify as thought) put them in the same camp not only with organic conservatives but with *lumpen* elements as well. The poets were thus a kind of spiritual *lumpen*-bourgeoisie, as it were.

In another analogous example, Hannah Arendt describes the initial phases of the Nazi movement: "Hitler's early party, almost exclusively composed of misfits, failures and adventurers, indeed represented the 'armed bohemians' who were only the reverse side of bourgeois society." Arendt in turn takes her cue from an observation by K. Heiden: "From the wreckage of dead classes arises the new class of intellectuals, and at the head march the most ruthless, those with the least to lose, hence the strongest; the armed bohemians, to whom war is home and civil war fatherland."[23]

None of the major poets, of course, were street fighters, let alone "armed bohemians." Yet their individualistic work habits and subjectivism, their confused mixture of resentment at modern life together with a longing for lyric prestige, and their own sense of being losers and feeling "out of it," all predisposed them to side in some measure with the more retrograde and authoritarian elements in their respective societies. Living as they did in a condition of chronic estrangement even as they knew inwardly of their poetic skills and even genius, their response was to translate their literary strengths into a moral superiority that helped place them in the elite ranks, making them either aristocrats *in potentia* or spiritual allies of aristocracies in the past. From there, it was only a small step to believing that, in the neofeudal system they envisioned, it would be they, the poets, who wielded power or who at least would receive the support and esteem of the powerful.

The letters of Flaubert furnish a portrait of his political views almost as thorough as that of his aesthetic theory. Among Flaubert's chief refrains after 1851 is his utter scorn for what he calls "the bourgeoisie," though the term for him denotes not so much a concrete socioeconomic class as "all of mankind including 'the people'" (to

Louise Colet, 22 November 1852). In a letter to George Sand (17 May 1867) he states his famous dictum that "hatred of the Bourgeois is the beginning of virtue," then proceeds directly to widen the semantic field: "But for me the term 'bourgeois' includes the bourgeois in overalls as well as the bourgeois who wears a frock coat."

He goes on, "It is we, and we alone—that is, the educated—who are the People, or more accurately, the tradition of humanity." Flaubert's solution to his anguish and isolation has very precise limits. Being too much the secular scientist, he cannot seek salvation in religion. Hence in mid-1869 he writes to George Sand, "Pure intellectuals have been of greater use to the human race than all the Saint Vincent de Pauls in the world." Indeed he places Catholicism in the same league as socialism: "Neo-Catholicism on the one hand and socialism on the other have brought France to stupidity. Between the Immaculate Conception and free lunches for workmen, everything marches toward ruin" (to George Sand, late September 1868).

What is to be done about this lamentable situation? Conveying to George Sand (29 April 1871) his hatred of the Paris Commune, Flaubert remarks, "The only thing that makes sense is a government of mandarins. . . . Our salvation now lies in a legitimate aristocracy." In 1870 he feels more revolted by the idea of universal suffrage than by doctrines of papal infallibility, and he asserts that the war with Prussia could have been avoided had France been "governed by the mandarins instead of . . . the mob," or better yet "if we had set about instructing the upper classes instead of trying to enlighten the lower." [24]

Flaubert on occasion has something specifically positive to say about the ancien régime: "In the eighteenth century, diplomacy was paramount. 'Cabinet secrets' really existed. Peoples were still sufficiently meek to submit to divisions and unions. That order of things, it seems to me, took its last bow in 1815" (to George Sand, June or July 1869). This backward glance can take the shape of a powerful longing, as in his 1852 letter to Louise Colet: "Why did I not live at least under Louis XIV, with a great wig and stockings without a crease, in the company of M. Descartes? Or in Ronsard's time, or Nero's?" [25] The touch of nostalgia for the higher circles of Rome is further expanded upon when Flaubert remarks to Turgenev (13 November 1872), "My sadness is like that of the Roman patricians of the fourth century. I feel an invincible flood of barbarism arising out of the depths. . . . Never have hatred of all greatness, scorn of Beauty, and execration of literature been so outspoken."

Flaubert's scattered political reflections are by no means rigorous or systematic, but they add up to a consistent outlook that can be safely summed up as follows: an intense dislike of modern society (both its bourgeois and its populist-socialist sectors), a self-conception as belonging to a morally privileged elite, and a yearning for and identification with unspecified mandarinates or with certain ruling classes in France or antiquity. It is a structure of feeling that we have already seen present in Gautier, and that will be varyingly replicated in the works and views of many aestheticists and Modernists after Flaubert.

W. B. Yeats, it is well known, had a personal inclination for aristocrats, an attitude to which he gives expression in both his poetry and his prose. In the *Autobiographies* he regrets the loss of "all the nobility of earth" and sees links between "the long-established life of the well-born" and the life of artists. To him, poets "carry in their heads that form of society aristocracies created now and again at Versailles and Urbino." And he explains Lady Gregory's literary gifts as the result of "semi-feudal Roxborough, her inherited sense of caste, her knowledge of that top of the world where men and women are valued for their manhood and their charm." [26]

Similarly, in his poem "The Curse of Cromwell," Yeats laments the passing of "the tall men and the swordsmen and the horsemen, where are they?" With their loss, "we and all the Muses are things of no account" for "[t]hey have schooling of their own." Nonetheless he sets forth the hope

> That the swordsmen and the ladies can still keep company,
> *Can pay the poet for a verse* and hear the fiddle sound,
> *That I am still their servant* though all be underground.[27]

Yeats's idealized notion of poets carrying past aristocracies in their heads, evoked in the *Autobiographies*, also appears in the poem "The People," which he starts out by regretting his labors amidst "[t]he daily spite of this unmannerly town," wishing that he could have lived "[i]n the green shadow of Ferrara wall" or climbed "the steep street of Urbino / To where the Duchess and her people talked."[28]

Yeats's longing for an aristocratic past assumes its most lasting shape in the two renowned poems about a place he calls Byzantium. By the time he crafts his "Sailing to Byzantium," however, he is framing the situation not so much in political terms as along the more general, traditional lines of a quest for permanence in a world where "the young" and the entirety of creation, "Caught in their sensual music all neglect / Monuments of unaging intellect." In the mythic kingdom of Yeats's making, by contrast, artistic beauty can "keep a drowsy Emperor awake" and the poet himself "will sing / To lords and ladies of Byzantium." Later, in "Byzantium" itself, the poet achieves a high and singular state of being as he is verbally transported to "the Emperor's pavement," where he shares space with "the golden smithies of the Emperor."[29] Yeats's Byzantium thus functions as a kind of substitute heaven, an aesthetic utopia where the refined and godly despots of yore are well served by their retinue of poets.

The mental, mythic role that Byzantium represents in Yeats's speculations is made more explicit in *A Vision*, where, as he imagines it, "All about [Byzantium] is an *antithetical* aristocratic civilization in its completed form, every detail of life hierarchical, . . . great wealth everywhere in few men's hands, all dependent upon a few, up to the Emperor himself who is a God dependent upon a greater God." Yeats avows that, given the choice of "a month of antiquity, . . . I would spend it in Byzantium. . . . I think I could find in some little wineshop some philosophical worker in mosaic who could answer all my questions, . . . for the pride of his delicate skill would make what was an instrument of power to princes and clerics."

Yeats's singling out the artisans of Byzantine mosaic for possible camaraderie is in the tradition of preindustrial longings we have been seeing among nineteenth-century lyrists. What most draws Yeats to that unchanging aristocratic world and its Emperor-as-demigod, however, is his broader assumption that "never before or since in recorded history, religious, aesthetic, and practical life were one." It exemplifies, for him, a society in which the painter, the mosaicist, the goldsmith, and the illuminator of sacred books could work impersonally to give shape to "the vision of a whole people." [30]

The Byzantium of Yeats, it goes without saying, is a highly romanticized if superbly distilled construct, an idealization that stands as a high point in the *passéiste* patterns of aestheticism and its politics. Yeats's stance also had personal sources. His father, the painter John Butler Yeats, was in many ways a classic nineteenth-century rational, liberal progressivist; and in his ensuing oedipal struggles Yeats the son found it necessary to locate some "political" terrain outside his father's thinking—hence the attraction to mysticism and the nostalgia for a feudal past, both of which Yeats *père* would have rejected in principle. Significantly, William Yeats during the 1910s, in a bid to ally himself with the old Irish aristocracy, tried tracing family genealogies with a view to discovering aristocratic antecedents of his own.[31]

In the decades between the wars, pro-fascist attitudes were rather commonplace among the Irish Protestant middle class. Yeats himself was occasionally seen wearing the blue shirts of the Irish Fascists, with whom he became slightly involved. He met their leader General O'Duffy, and even wrote marching songs for the general's men ("What's equality?—Muck in the yard / Historic nations grow / From above to below"). In private conversation, moreover, Yeats customarily and frankly expressed his favoring despotic rule by an educated elite.[32]

Probably no lyric poet has achieved such reigning status in the Anglo-American orbit as did Thomas Stearns Eliot from the 1920s until his death in 1964. Over those decades Eliot evolved into the "pope," the "king" of letters, an authority he was to exercise through his great verse, his Olympian essays and his uneven plays, but also in his capacity as editor of *The Criterion* (a journal with an influence that went well beyond its list of fewer than a thousand subscribers) and finally as a high-ranking officer in the publishing house of Faber and Faber.

Eliot's ideological and personal development presents so enormously complex a picture that any critic must take pains not to reduce it to political or aesthetic formulae. In writing about Eliot one can easily succumb to the extreme danger of either credulous adulation or simplistic debunking. The great poet, the major literary intellect, the scion of an illustrious U.S. family, the committed émigré, the snob and protofascist of the 1920s and 1930s, the man of religion and the inner light in the later years — these are all Eliot and must be taken account of accordingly.

Eliot's poetry is also many things at once, and its artistic greatness stems from its richly complex mixture of vision, intellect, irony, intensity, and technique. Nevertheless the essential theme fundamentally shaping several of his major works, and giving them their motive force, is a thoroughgoing *passéisme* in which glorious, heroic former times are juxtaposed with a sordidly repulsive present. The classic instance of course is *The Waste Land*, the very beginning of which is an all but explicit contrast with the famous opening lines of Chaucer's *Canterbury Tales*, an April now rendered cruel and inhospitable. Part 2 of the poem, "A Game of Chess," unfolds a vicious, highly detailed parody of Enobarbus's wondrous reminiscence of Cleopatra's barge in *Antony and Cleopatra*, here degraded so as to mock the slatternly artificiality of a modern housewife seated in her London boudoir (76-100).[33]

In like fashion part 3, "The Fire Sermon," cites sarcastically the refrain from Spenser's *Prothalamium* ("Sweet Thames, run softly, till I end my song") to depict a river that serves not as the setting for courtly Elizabethan ceremonies but as dumpsite for modern life's debris — the "empty bottles, sandwich papers, . . . cigarette ends" and used condoms ("other testimony of summer nights") (177-79). Significantly, among the few tender and evocative moments in the poem's 434 lines is the initial collage of German voices from the Russian borderlands, one of whom recalls a time of idyllic childhood visits "at the Archduke's," a gracious way of life now presumably threatened by the Marxist turmoil in that region (8-18) — what Eliot, in the notes to part 5, refers to as "the present decay of eastern Europe."[34]

The short poem "Sweeney among the Nightingales," more pointedly, is set in a brothel, where aggressive whores and animalistic clients engage in unsavory power games. The sleazy goings-on are framed by an epigraph (in Greek) from Aeschylus's *Oresteia* citing Agamemnon's cry of pain on being murdered and by an analogous allusion in English in the poem's final stanza, in which the nightingales sing near a powerless Convent of the Sacred Heart. The motley crew of lower-class revelers is too corrupt and insensitive, however, to grasp the import of a sacred heroic past or of the birds that link us with that past.

"Sweeney among the Nightingales" enjoys notoriety for its brief anti-Semitic reference to the person of a Jewish whore, "Rachel née Rabinovitch," portrayed as particularly bestial as she "[t]ears at the grapes with murderous paws" (35). Similarly, in "Gerontion," an elderly narrator in a decayed house remarks about its proprietor, "[T]he jew squats in the windowsill, the owner," whose roguish, drifting history he then passes unflatteringly in review (21). A yet more unpleasant and hostile episode appears in "Burbank with a Baedeker: Bleistein with a Cigar." Both these characters are American tourists in Europe, Burbank from the genteel WASP upper class, Bleistein of more recent Jewish origin. A pitifully innocent Burbank becomes sexual prey to the courtesan Princess Volupine as his "God Hercules" abandons him. Cigar-smoking Bleistein comes off as much more unsympathetic, his posture presented as "A saggy bending of the knees / And elbows, with the palms turned out"—abject as well as money-grubbing. And his rootless identity is summed up in the line "Chicago Semite Viennese" (24).

Bleistein's physique is rendered grotesque: "A lustreless protrusive eye / Stares from the protozoic slime" at a Canaletto canvas that, one assumes, Bleistein lacks the capacity to understand. Further on, the poem makes the sinister collocation, "The rats are underneath the piles. / The jew is underneath the lot." (The latter line may well be a pun, "lot" also signifying "bunch.") Years later, Eliot's poem occasioned an incident when the author was on a business trip to South Africa in the 1950s, staying as a guest in the home of Justice and Sarah Millin. At bedtime, a dutiful Mrs. Millin picked Eliot's collected verse off the shelf, and eventually chanced upon "Burbank . . . Bleistein. . . ." Mrs. Millin, who was Jewish, thereupon went and knocked on Eliot's bedroom door. She asked if the offending lines were his; he acknowledged them, and she requested his immediate departure in the morning.[35]

A yet more vicious anti-Semitic portrait appears in "Dirge," one of the numerous original portions of *The Waste Land* that, following Ezra Pound's wise counsel, Eliot prudently excised. The passage, at first intended for the poem's brief "Death by Water" section, goes as follows:

> Full fathom five your Bleistein lies
> Under the flatfish and the squids.
>   Graves' Disease is a dead jew's eyes.
>   When the crabs have eat the lids![36]

What in "Burbank . . . Bleistein . . ." was only a strong flicker of suggestion here becomes a full and rather disquieting occasion for reveling, more or less, in the fact of a Jewish corpse. Eliot's subsequent reputation as poet and intellect would certainly have been somewhat shakier had he retained this passage in the definitive version of *The Waste Land*.

In his available personal correspondence Eliot makes occasional anti-Semitic remarks of the passing, thoughtless sort that were then commonplace among Gentiles, most of them, though not necessarily all, conservatives, and among privileged and poor alike. For example, in a 1923 letter to the collector John Quinn, the poet yearns for a "Christian publisher" who might replace his "Jew publisher" of the time.[37]

Still, Eliot's routine anti-Semitic prejudices do not him a Hitlerite make. (One can state this without exonerating him.) In the 1920s, after all, German fascism was scarcely more than a marginal blip on the European horizon, and even until the *Kristallnacht* of 1938 there was no way of suspecting the extent and horror of the impending Judeocide. During the initial years of the Hitler regime, moreover, the worst of the Nazi repression was to be borne not by German Jewry but by the Communist and Socialist parties—repression to which few Western conservatives objected and which many indeed lauded.

The anti-Semitic ingredients of Eliot's worldview have a complex personal, historical, and ideological context. Despite his birth and rearing in St. Louis, T. S. Eliot heralded from an old, patrician Yankee family. For two centuries the Eliots had distinguished themselves, not in business but in civic service as lawyers, educators, and—most important—Unitarian ministers. An early ancestor had been a juror at the Salem witch trials, another the pastor of Boston's legendary

Old North Church. Among the poet's closer kin were cousins such as Charles W. Eliot, the president of Harvard University for forty years, and Samuel Eliot Morison, the renowned official historiographer.

T. S. Eliot's grandfather William Greenleaf Eliot, also a pastor, had moved to Missouri to help "civilize" the frontier by building churches and doing good works. In St. Louis he founded what was to become Washington University (he purposely requested that the institution not be named after him), and his efforts drew praise from none less than Emerson. Dr. Eliot died a year before the poet-to-be was born, but the elder's example would cast a long shadow over the family household, even on its mavericks. The poet's father, Henry Ware Eliot, broke with tradition by going into business, becoming president of the Hydraulic-Press Brick Company. When asked why he had shunned the ministry, Henry used to reply cryptically, "Too much pudding choked the dog."[38] His own apostasy was to be taken much further in the trajectory of his youngest son, Tom.

Though Eliot himself scarcely touched on the issue in public, subsequent documentation has revealed the uneasiness he always felt with some aspects of his American identity. In St. Louis he had been raised to feel like a New Englander, and thereby superior to the local, provincial masses. Back East, however, during his year at Milton Academy (1905–06) and thereafter at Harvard, his southern drawl marked the precocious young student as an outsider in the land of his ancestors.

Then there was the matter of his family's Unitarian religion—the tolerant, optimistic, progressivist, quasi-secular creed that generations of Eliots had actively preached and supported. As did the British aesthetes, Eliot lost his faith while an undergraduate—but in a very different way. What eventually replaced his Unitarianism was neither atheism nor socialism nor the cult of beauty, but rather a desire for stern and established order and orthodoxy, a yearning for old dogmas like those of original sin, the incarnation of Christ, the Holy Trinity, and the damnation of sinners.

In a talk given at the Harvard Philosophical Society in 1913 or 1914, Eliot dismisses the ideas of progress and relativism as fallacies; he also finds contemptible any easy attempts at solving human misery on earth.[39] Moreover Eliot in time came to feel that the Protestant

Reformation had led to an impoverishment of European culture, and, by the same token, that the mythology of the Puritans suffered from a "historical thinness." [40] Not surprisingly, then, it was in the old state churches of premodern Europe that the poet would at last find a permanent intellectual refuge and a home. By the late 1910s he had, in spirit, shifted to a position of staunch orthodoxy. The commitment was formalized with Eliot's baptism in the Church of England (the branch of Protestantism that most resembles Roman Catholicism) in 1926.

In addition there is the peculiar relationship of Eliot to the native land from which he chose to expatriate. In a 1928 letter to Herbert Read, Eliot observes that "the U.S.A. up to a hundred years ago was a family extension" and notes that he feels more at home in America as it had been before 1830.[41] He does not elaborate further, but one may recall that the years since that date had seen the rise of Jacksonian democracy, the Civil War, the rise of aggressive robber-baron wealth, and—most important of all—the influx of immigration from backward Ireland, southern Italy, and Eastern Europe. (In 1928, it bears mention, Eliot wrote a preface to Edgar Ansel Mowrer's *This American World*, a book that in part deplores the flood of "immature" immigrants and that also laments the loss of an "aristocratic" tradition in the fall of the South.)[42] All of these developments contributed to Eliot's sense that the United States in which he had grown up was not the country he wanted.

Not that his own family and "tribe" are spared either. As a budding symbolist poet and aspiring European, Eliot was much inclined to put behind him the genteel culture of his cousins and aunts and other associates in old-time Boston circles, a milieu he found stifling, "quite uncivilized" yet also "refined beyond the point of civilization," as he characterizes it in a 1918 essay on Henry James.[43] Ten years later, in a review of *The Education of Henry Adams,* Eliot describes the Boston mind as hobbled with doubt and scepticism—precisely the sort of qualities he was fleeing from in his religious background.[44]

Eliot expresses his detached view of this desiccated elite in some of his mature early verse. "Portrait of a Lady" is a subtly ironic account of a voluble upper-class matron whose recurrent refrain is "I shall sit here, serving tea to friends" (8–11). She goes to hear "the latest Pole" play Chopin and involves herself with music in a superficial way, much like the women, of "Prufrock" fame, who "come and go / Talking of Michelangelo" (4). Seen through the perplexed eyes of a bemused young male guest—presumably modeled after Eliot himself—the "lady" has been associated in identity with Adeline Moffat, a Boston grande dame whom the student-poet was wont to visit.[45] Eliot's shorter spoofs—"The Boston Evening Transcript," "Aunt Helen," "Cousin Nancy" (16–18)—come close to being simple, if clever, satires of local kin or of their friends. In this regard, "The Love Song of J. Alfred Prufrock" can be quite fruitfully imagined as a comically loveless monologue, muttered in nasal tenor by a tired, bloodless Yankee of the sort one can still see, strolling shortly "after the teacups" (6)—his silver fringes balding, his hands folded behind his back—around coastal Marblehead or up Lewisburg Square.

Eliot's unsympathetic view of the new immigrants comes through in the rather disquieting "Sweeney" poems. The recurring character, we may infer, is an Irishman, simply one vivid specimen from among the vulgar, low-class hordes looked down upon by Boston's old Yankees. In "Sweeney among the Nightingales," the best-known and artistically most successful of the three, the eponymous hero is compared to an ape and a giraffe; and he shows his degenerate spirit as he laughs with his arms dangling down and horses about with a cape-clad prostitute.

The same *passéiste* structure we noted early on in "Nightingales" is replicated in "Sweeney Erect," which likewise begins with ancient Greek allusions ("the unstilled Cyclades," "Aeolus above," "Ariadne's hair"), here also invoked at the expense of the "orang-outang" protagonist as he "rises from the sheets in steam." (The immediate setting, the title suggests, is again a brothel, where Sweeney has just engaged in some fast fornication.) The antihero's facial features are described in grotesque terms quite similar to those applied to Bleistein in the "Burbank" piece; and Eliot slips in a reference to Emerson's grand historical vision only to undercut it when sarcastically remarking that the philosopher "had not seen the silhouette of Sweeney" (25–26). Eliot once told Nevill Coghill that he imagined his Sweeney as a former, mildly successful boxer who retires to become a tavernkeeper.[46]

The larger, national setting of these two poems is left vague enough to be either English or American, though the question of place is mostly immaterial here. Eliot's Irish whoremonger serves to represent all that is lowly and base in modern life—on both sides of the Atlantic. He embodies the idea of "mass man" that preoccupied European conservative thought until the late 1930s. In this regard, then, Eliot's anti-Semitism must be construed within a broader context, seen as part of a more generalized dislike of and snobbery toward the upstart lower orders—"the vertical invasion of the barbarians," as Ortega y Gasset, citing Rathenau, puts it [47]—who lack any sense or understanding of the nobility and grandeur of Western culture's past.

That Eliot should articulate this conception in racial terms is, in part, a handy narrative resource (ethnic folk are easily depicted, not to mention caricatured), but it is also, in part, the standard response of conservatives almost anywhere (who ipso facto are negatively disposed toward ethnic upstarts). Nonetheless the broad issue of social class in Eliot's worldview, I believe, overrides these matters strictly ethnic. Eliot could portray as quite colorful the cast of plebeian characters in his unfinished melodrama "Sweeney Agonistes," where the demotic speech rhythms of the Jewish-American tourists Klipstein and Krumpacker are vividly distilled into a compelling songlike verse; the English prostitutes and their foreign visitors, moreover, are not drawn viciously and are even imparted a certain popular charm.

On the other hand, "Lune de miel," one of Eliot's poems in French, is a sharp satirical jibe at a nameless newlywed couple from Terre Haute, Indiana (that is, provincials, and in this case presumably Anglo-Saxon), who go hopping from one European country to another and stay in smelly, flea-bitten hotels. (The twosome, we infer, are lower class). The husband dwells almost exclusively on tips and other expenses, thus sharing in the monetary myopia of Eliot's Jewish merchant characters. Looming over the couple there stands the church of Saint Apollinaire, in Ravenna, a mute reminder of an ancient Byzantium (the reader assumes) that is well beyond the rustic twosome's mental means (29). "Lune de miel" thus plays on the well-known twentieth-century tale of ignorant, boorish Americans, comically oblivious to the subtle grandeurs of an old Europe they blindly rush by. The point of view both in this piece and in "Sweeney Agonistes," however, is that of an upper-class WASP, who condescends to the lesser-born even when portraying them as picturesque.

This, then, is the personal and class setting for Eliot's garden-variety anti-Semitism. But there is an ideological source from Europe as well. In 1910–11, on an allowance from his father, Eliot spent a year in Paris, studying, reading, and writing. To him the city represented many things at once, the first of them being poetry. He actually toyed with the idea of settling there and even wrote some competent French verse. He seems not to have had any sexual encounters (indeed, at age twenty-six Eliot could still claim to be a virgin), but he became aware of the low-life world of pimps and prostitutes via Charles-Louis Philippe's *Bubu de Montparnasse,* a book that probably helped shape his own ditty-like poems about the lower depths. He also got a taste of the glamour and excitement of French intellectual life at the massively attended lectures by Henri Bergson at the Collège de France.

And, most important of all for our purposes, he discovered French monarchist Charles Maurras, whose sociopolitical thought was to influence the poet on through the very last years of his life. Maurras was the leader of what would become the French fascist movement, the Action Française (AF). Founded in the 1890s under the name La Ligue des Patriotes, its initial rallying cry took aim at left-wingers then defending Captain Alfred Dreyfus, a Jew, whose years of imprisonment on Devil's Island had been the result of anti-Semitism in the French army. The general ideology of AF was ardently monarchist, Catholic, nationalist, and anti-Semitic. AF activists lived these views by engaging in assorted provocations, for example, successfully disrupting a play by Henri Bernstein, a Jewish writer. *Action Française,* the official AF newspaper, was founded in 1908 and drew nationwide support from antirepublican and proclerical French readers.[48]

Above all a literary man, Maurras was a lover of Homer and the classics, and his cultural tastes inclined strongly in favor of simplicity, orderliness, and clarity, favoring the eternal and enduring as against what he saw as the confusion and aimlessness of Romanticism and its aftermath. Maurras's ultimate objective, accordingly, was a return to the days of the ancien régime, when power was held by traditional authorities and the Church; in one of his books, *Enquête sur la monarchie,* there are actually suggestions about a coup to restore the French throne.

Irving Babbitt, the conservative humanist who was Eliot's principal mentor at Harvard, had brought Maurras—a kindred spirit—to the attention of his bright young student, but it was during his year in Paris that Eliot truly discovered the French thinker-activist for himself. As a budding lyrist, he admired Maurras's literary talents and his prose, which he praised as "le style d'un maître." [49] What Eliot primarily found in the French right-winger, however, was a solid, intelligent, even artistic validation of his own tentative search for a premodern social order in Europe.

Eliot's vision of a stern, authoritarian Church allied with kings and helping thereby to sustain a healthy, homogeneous provincialism, is a notion he derived directly from Maurras's political thought. Moreover, Eliot's famous self-characterization in his preface to *For Lancelot Andrews* (1928)—"classicist in literature, royalist in politics, and anglo-catholic in religion"—appears most likely to be an elaboration of the terms in which Maurras is summed up ("classique, catholique, monarchique") in the March 1913 issue of *Nouvelle Revue Française,* a magazine Eliot subscribed to at the time. [50]

In December 1926 the Vatican condemned the Action Française as "a school that puts party interests above religion." [51] Although the decision came as a shock to Eliot, he nonetheless dedicated his short book on Dante (1929) to the Frenchman. In 1940, moreover, Maurras embarked on his four-year career of collaboration with the puppet Vichy regime of Marshall Pétain; for his sins Maurras was sentenced to life imprisonment following Allied liberation. Despite all this, Eliot's sense of discipleship never once flagged. Even after Maurras had been politically discredited, Eliot wrote an article in 1948 for the right-wing French newspaper *Aspects de la France* in which he asserts that "for some of us, Maurras represented a kind of Virgil leading us to the doors of the temple," avows that he feels very close to Maurras's "ideas of monarchy and hierarchy," and laments the lack of sympathy for Maurras in England. Eliot in his last years still cleaved to the literary lessons he had learned from the elegant French fascist; his sole regret was that Maurras had gone into political activism rather than sticking to his writing.[52]

The AF reportedly had between twenty thousand and forty thousand followers in the 1920s, a respectable though not impressive set of figures. At the time, fascism in the West had gained state power only in relatively weak countries such as Italy and Spain, where it seemed more an old-fashioned, paternalistic dictatorship than the expansionist, racist, genocidal movement it was to become. Among Western elite circles, of course, the principal fear was of Bolshevism; fascism was regarded as a lesser evil, as a line of defense against the threat of Marxism.

Given the climate of the 1920s, it is not surprising that Eliot, in *The Criterion,* should speak favorably of fascism or, as the magazine's editor, run pieces by authors then seeing fascism in a positive light. For example, in the February 1928 issue, Eliot notes that he finds "wholly admirable" the policy statement published by the British fascists in their house journal; and in July 1929 he says, "I confess to a preference for fascism in practice, which I dare say most of my readers share." [53]

In 1933 Eliot went on a long and exhausting lecture tour of the United States, partly for money, partly to get away from his ailing marriage to Vivien Haigh-Wood. In the three talks he delivered at the University of Virginia in April, the harsher and more unsavory aspects of Eliot's conservative *passéisme* come to the fore, reaching a kind of public climax. The lectures were published under the title *After Strange Gods: A Primer of Modern Heresy* (1934).

Before examining its more troubling passages, I should first state exactly what that text is: a sophisticated, well-argued defense of established traditions and religious orthodoxy in literature; a lofty rejection of individualism and of novelty for its own sake, both in ideas and in art; and a critique of selected literary heretics. Eliot in his brief preface to the book openly despairs of a society "worm-eaten with Liberalism" (13).[54] In the lectures themselves he deplores "economic determinism" as "a god before whom we fall down and worship" (17); he quotes with high disfavor certain liberal theologians who seek to eliminate "the belief in the Scriptures" and also hope to admit "Unitarian infidels as fellow-believers" (22); and he takes issue with a flabby modern tolerance that believes "one man's 'view of life' is as good as another's" (32).

Within this framework, then, Eliot in his third section observes, unexceptionably, "It is impossible to separate the 'poetry' in *Paradise Lost* from the peculiar doctrines that it enshrines"; and he grants only grudgingly that we can "enjoy the poetry and yet be fully aware of the intellectual and moral aberrations of the author" (32–33). Gerard Manley Hopkins, though a Jesuit priest, is deemed too remote from "the struggle . . . against Liberalism" and from the aim of renewing "a vital connexion between the individual and the race" (48). Yeats's vision is merely "a highly sophisticated lower mythology" (46), and D. H. Lawrence is "spiritually sick" (60) because of his hatred for orthodoxy, even if he also condemns "Liberalism, Progress, and Modern Civilisation" (61).

By themselves, these are basically the lucid, articulate opinions of a cultural and religious conservative. There is, however, a more sinister undercurrent to the thinking in *After Strange Gods*. In his opening statements, Eliot praises his (presumably all-white Anglo-Saxon) audience of Virginians for having "at least some recollection of a 'tradition,' such as the influx of foreign populations has almost effaced in some parts of the North" (15). After this subtly derogatory reference to the impoverished European immigrants then altering northeastern ways, Eliot goes on to commend the southern Agrarians' manifesto, *I'll Take My Stand*, their defense of the antebellum South.

Eliot then deplores "the immense pressure toward monotony exerted by industrial expansion"; with this in mind he describes the Civil War, retrospectively, as "the greatest *disaster* in the whole of American history" (16; emphasis added) — his veiled way of implying that the South suffered not only as victim of Northern guns, but as target of the expanding liberal, industrial ethos. Yet Eliot finds consolation in one fact of which he eloquently reminds the white Virginians: "You are farther away from New York; you have been less industrialized and less invaded by foreign races; and you have a more opulent soil" (16). The allusion to New York, of course, serves as U.S. shorthand for the full dynamic of northern manufacture and of Mediterranean and East European immigration that, in the view both of Eliot and of southern conservatives, poses a threat to "tradition."

The passage from *After Strange Gods* that has achieved the greatest notoriety reads as follows: "The population should be homogeneous. . . . What is still more important is unity of religious background; and reasons of race and religion combine to make any large number of free-thinking Jews undesirable" (19–20). Today, in the light of what became the Nazi Judeocide, such a statement is rather chilling. Hitler had already been three months in power at the time of Eliot's lectures; and the poet's speculations are scarcely mitigated when we observe that official Nazi policy thus far had consisted mostly of firing Jews from government positions. The reference to "free-thinking Jews" was nonetheless offensive enough that Eliot's own friend George Boas, a philosophy professor at Johns Hopkins University and also a Jew, in a letter broke relations with Eliot, saying, "I can at least rid you of the company of one."

Though Eliot did not allow *After Strange Gods* to be reprinted, he never disclaimed its contents. In fairness one should note that, some years later, he explained his racial remarks by describing their author as "a very sick man" at the time he had written them. Still, he continued to justify his proscriptive statement, laying stress on the nuanced qualifier "free-thinking" as describing Jews whose outlook, he felt, went beyond even that of the free-thinking Unitarians he had repudiated. As he puts it, "[T]he Jew who is separated from his religious faith is much more deracinated thereby than the descendant of Christians, and it is their deracination that I think dangerous and tending to irresponsibility."[55]

Eliot means, one supposes, that they become "heretics," political radicals for instance. Whatever the case, *After Strange Gods* does represent the poet's nineteenth-century, "Maurrasian" conservatism at its harshest and most unforgiving. No doubt the controversy prompted by its racial statements was a reason for Eliot's subsequently modifying his right-wing views somewhat. Throughout most of the 1930s *The Criterion* concentrates more on ridiculing or chiding antifascists than on actually defending fascism itself. Hence in March 1937, Eliot rebukes the "weakness" of then-leftist poet C. Day Lewis and his ilk, who, alas, feel that "there is nothing . . . to be said for fascism." That year he also denounces an Oxford decision to boycott the bicentennial celebrations of the University of Göttingen.[56] By the same token,

The Criterion around this time says precious little about the worsening dictatorship in Germany or the bloody military revolt against the legally elected republican government of Spain.[57]

At this point it bears remarking that there was little that was odd or idiosyncratic about Eliot's political stance in the 1930s. Indeed, until Germany's total seizure of Czechoslovakia, the British elite and Western conservatives tended by and large to endorse the Nazi regime as a bulwark against Bolshevism. During that period the entire British press (with the notable exception of the *Manchester Guardian*) consistently defended European fascist states while blithely reproaching their English detractors. And though in the official histories the blame for "appeasing" Nazism has been affixed solely on Neville Chamberlain and his personal "cowardice," the unpleasant truth is that Chamberlain at Munich in 1938 had the enthusiastic backing of his Conservative party, and he returned to Great Britain a hero, welcomed by banner headlines and a Parliamentary ovation. (*Time* magazine, in a report gleefully entitled "Kiss the Reds Good-by," slyly noted that most of the French opponents of the Munich pact were "Communists.")[58] Hitler's lightning war on the West, of course, made the fascist option a great deal less attractive to English conservatives, though some Tories still lauded his anticommunism. However, as we know from both legend and history, beginning in 1940 all sectors of the British nation finally rallied and closed ranks to face up to the German menace.[59]

As T. S. Eliot grew into a public and religious figure, his verse took on a corresponding new turn, with "Ash Wednesday" (1930) and its prayer-like cadences eloquently marking his conversion. Eliot's social life thereafter increasingly involved religious people, and he devoted himself eagerly to ecclesiastic types of chores—doing churchwarden duty at St. Stephen's, addressing Anglo-Catholic congresses, and participating visibly in campaigns and marches for the preservation of old church buildings. Clearly, the poet had embarked on a spiritual journey; and in great measure the poem-cycle *Four Quartets* is a lyric record of that inner journey.

Perhaps the most important background item to *Four Quartets* is the fact that, save for the first of them, "Burnt Norton," they were written at the height of British resistance against Germany. By then

Eliot's vision had attained a condition of pure, mystic spirituality, a kind of religiosity stripped of conventional right-wing politics, and the contemplative beauties of the lyric cycle (partly inspired by the late string quartets of Beethoven) serve to deploy and give verbal shape to that mature vision.

Eliot's decision not to seek refuge in America but to stay on in England—in the face of a seemingly imminent German invasion—took some courage, as has been pointed out; and his volunteer work as air raid warden and as fire watcher during the blitz provided a collective experience that enabled him to transcend once and for all his attitude of sheer revulsion at modern life and its lower-class upstarts. The first printing of "East Coker" sold a brisk twelve thousand copies and gave spiritual sustenance to many English readers during the grim uncertainty of the war years. Moreover, as some critics have observed, the references to falling houses in "East Coker," and the litany of meditations on "ash," "dust," and "fire" in "Little Gidding," can be seen as oblique accounts of damage from the air war.[60]

Nevertheless, the association of each poem with a specific place bespeaks Eliot's ongoing conservative quest for hallowed, enduring traditions of the soil. Little Gidding, a remote English village and diminutive medieval church—memorialized in the title of the fourth and greatest *Quartet*—had been the site of a small, seventeenth-century Anglican community whose devout members gave refuge to King Charles I during the English civil war. In reprisal, Cromwell's troops thoroughly ransacked the inside of the church in 1646. Hence Little Gidding, the place, serves here as emblem for an old official Church that survives the depredations of wrong-headed rebels, symbolizes an order that persists in the face of assault by revolutionary changes that Eliot, the past-oriented poet, had never deemed desirable.

Although critical opinion varies widely, *Four Quartets,* I believe, contains poetry as inspired and memorable as anything produced by the earlier Eliot, but conceived and crafted by a very different sort of man. It is the serene high art of a mature soul who, after much inner strife and anguish, has arrived at his individual faith and linked it with a palpable, luminous past, both personal and national, and along the way has shared in the battle for survival of his adopted, ancestral land. The *passéisme* that expresses itself with a truculent disgust and despair in *The Waste Land,* and with a supercilious sarcasm in the "Sweeney" poems, here becomes a kind of secular prayer, a rationalist's mystical evocation of those seemingly small, local spaces that can help transport us to an immediate grasp of the oneness of all nature and human history. Eliot's combined intelligence, experience, vision, and artistry at long last allowed him to transcend the narrow limits of a rococo Toryism, protofascism, and orthodoxy that he had aspired to and then achieved in the 1930s.

Among the acknowledged formal innovators of twentieth-century Modernism, Eliot, paradoxically, was "only superficially a man of his time." His deeper sensibility has much more in common with that of the medieval mystics or the seventeenth-century Puritans, as Lyndall Gordon notes.[61] Yet this émigré nostalgist loomed over Anglo-American literary life and, to some degree, its social outlook as probably no poet had since Dryden or Pope. Significantly, Eliot's teacher Irving Babbitt saw but two possible choices for early-twentieth-century intellectuals: to be either a Bolshevik or a Jesuit. Eliot, after his fashion, took the latter path, and his teachings were revered or at least closely watched by the legions of followers within the groves of U.S. academe.

One direct influence from Eliot, the result of genuine spiritual affinities, was his sway over the Tennessee Agrarians, later to be known as the New Critics. From the very year that *The Waste Land* first ran in *The Dial* magazine, Eliot was to constitute a major lyric and intellectual force within the original Fugitive group. Their ideas about poetry were shaped in great measure by Eliot's verse and theory; and his tone, as essayist, of hard, intelligent irony, is easily discernible in the early prose of Tate and Warren. (Only Ransom maintained reservations about the American expatriate.) Meanwhile, as Eliot's *passéiste* position began to take on clear contours, the influence became ideological as well. In 1927 the imagist poet John Gould Fletcher spent some time in Nashville with the Fugitives, and he reported that the group appeared to be following Eliot in every way, save for their choosing to stay home and remain local, committed as they were to Old South modes of feeling in their work.[62]

Young Tate in particular was an Eliot enthusiast, and the example of the master's conversion to religious orthodoxy led him to prod Ransom into writing *God without Thunder,* an apology for fundamentalism.[63] In *The World's Body,* moreover, Ransom speculates on the kind of world he would like to see: "in manners, aristocratic; in religion, ritualistic; in art, traditional"—a tripartite construction clearly echoing Eliot's renowned self-description as classicist, royalist, and Anglo-Catholic.[64] Throughout the 1930s Eliot and the Fugitives corresponded with each other, the elder writer providing support and criticism for their lyric and other efforts. In *After Strange Gods* he publicly compliments them, singling out for special praise their manifesto *I'll Take My Stand* and encouraging "any further statements by the same group of writers" (15).

Like the prose writings of Eliot himself, *I'll Take My Stand* was to exert an influence—particularly in the South—well out of proportion to its actual sales. The volume gathers essays by twelve southerners, most of them members of the original Fugitive *cénacle,* who have taken it upon themselves to defend the Old South with passion and conviction. The "symposium," as Tate called it, emerged partly in response to the enormously bad national press being generated by the infamous 1925 "monkey trial" of biology teacher John T. Scopes in Dayton, Tennessee. The journalistic attacks on the South by the acerbic pen of H. L. Mencken, among others, sparked a *crise de conscience* among the Fugitives. They thus felt duty-bound to stand up and speak loud and clear for what they considered admirable about the Old South, and, conversely, to spell out in no uncertain terms what they deemed objectionable and distasteful about the modern world.

As befits the poets who constituted its chief voices, what unifies the book, as stated in their "Introduction: A Statement of Principle," is an absolute dislike of industrialism, whether liberal or socialist. (Indeed, one of the projected titles of the volume was *Tracts against Communism.*) The arts, the authors contend, lack "a proper life under industrialism. . . . Neither the creation nor the understanding of works of art is possible in an industrial age" (xliii).[65] Along the way they criticize applied science and single out for attack certain ills that many in our time would find unexceptionable: "overproduction, unemployment, . . . inequality" (xli), and the public of "loyal and steady

consumers" who help "keep the machines running" (xlvi), all characteristic evils of a modern secular economy, in their view.

The cure they propose is a religious and agrarian society—hence
the name by which the group thereafter became known. The term
"Agrarians," however, is incomplete and deceptive. What the Fugitives-
Agrarians are defending in *I'll Take My Stand* is the Euro-American
South *as it was before 1860,* with African bond slavery very much an
essential factor in the full equation. By the same token, all past efforts
by abolitionists and revolutionaries to bring an end to the Cotton
Gulag are pooh-poohed and dismissed by the polemicists from Tennessee.

Ransom in his essay, "Reconstructed but Unregenerate," says that
the slave South was "a kindly society" in which "people were for
the most part in their right places. Slavery was a feature monstrous
enough in theory, but, more often than not, humane in practice." It
is Ransom's thesis "that all were committed to a form of leisure, and
that their labor itself was leisurely" (14).

In a 1929 article published in *The New Republic,* Tate argues that
the condition of the slaves "was not different from that of other laboring classes, except that . . . they were certain of care, often affection-
ate, to their graves." [66] Similarly, in his biography of Stonewall Jackson, Tate asserts that slavery "had become a necessary element in a
stable society" and "only in a society of fixed classes can men be free."
Slavery, Tate believes, provided a "benevolent protection," because
"the Black man, 'free,' would have been exploited." [67] In his book on
John Brown, accordingly, the armed abolitionist is presented by Tate
as a fanatic who called up the slaves to "fall upon their masters and
murder them." [68]

Robert Penn Warren himself wrote an unsympathetic biography
of John Brown. The budding poet-novelist says Brown "could not
understand the philosophy that all must live in an imperfect world"
and work with its imperfect institutions. [69] Warren's own piece in
I'll Take My Stand, "The Briar Patch," starts from the premise that
the Africans were inferior and uneducable; he conjures up unsavory
images of blacks who, during Reconstruction, "got an office out of it
and all smoked cigars in the chair of a legislature" (248)—the kind of
racist stereotypes made notorious by D. W. Griffith's disturbing film

The Birth of a Nation. By Warren's own retrospective admission, the piece was "a defense of segregation," a stance he would subsequently repudiate.[70]

At the same time the Agrarians make positive claims for the South that go beyond questions of race or class and enter into larger questions of civilization. The Old South, in Ransom's view, was more "European" than the rest of North America; it had "founded and defended a culture which was according to the European principle of culture" (3); and it embodied thereby an "un-adulterated Europeanism, with its self-sufficient, backward-looking, intensely provincial communities" (5). Similarly, Tate in his essay "Remarks on the Southern Religion" affirms that "the South could be ignorant of Europe because it *was* Europe." Being rooted in a mature soil, the Old South's way of life, he asserts, "was European where the New England position was self-conscious and colonial" (171). In his 1935 article "The Profession of Letters in the South" (discussed in chapter 6), Tate argues for the region's "greater resemblance to France" in its having, as he sees it, certain religious and social kinds of feeling "that were crushed by the French Revolution."[71]

A further attractive feature of the South, says Tate in *I'll Take My Stand,* is that it was "feudal," albeit "without a feudal religion" (166). It had the benefits of "aristocratic rule," as he likewise contends in "The Profession of Letters in the South"; and though "the planter class was about one-fifth of the population, . . . the majority followed its lead." To Tate, as a practicing poet, what most matters is that "under feudalism the artist was a member of an organic society. The writer's loss of professional standing" is attributable not only to the rise of industrialism but to "the extinction of aristocracy."[72]

Toward the end of the same essay, Tate looks back to the occasion of the premier of Milton's *Comus.* He evokes that event with warm nostalgia: "In . . . the year 1634, a young, finical man, . . . was invited by the Earl of Bridgewater to write a masque for certain revels to be celebrated at Ludlow Castle. The masque was *Comus,* and the revels were in the feudal tradition. The whole celebration was 'at home'; it was a part of the community life, the common people were present, and the poet was a spiritual member of the society gathered there." Had Milton stayed on at Bridgewater's, Tate concedes, it would have been as "a sort of upper servant" of the household, yet "he would have been a member of the social and spiritual community."[73] Thus Tate in 1935, as a self-described member of the "sweated class" of writers under modern, secular, liberal, competitive industrial capitalism, can find in the ancien régime, in both Europe and Anglo-America, a better, richer, and more fulfilling society for artists.

Because of its peculiar history, the South is the only area of the United States to have generated conservative ideologues of a consciously neofeudal and precapitalist persuasion, George Fitzhugh being the most famous nineteenth-century instance. The view of the South as "feudal" may be arguable—the planter classes actually inclined to free trade in their economic thinking—but that is too large an issue to tease out in these pages. Still, though the South lost the Civil War, it went on subsequently to win the counterrevolution against local and federal demands for black citizens' rights; and the dream of the South's "lost cause" could thence perpetuate itself for several generations to come.

As novice writers the Agrarians represent the neofeudal strand in southern intellectual history, and they proclaim it with youthful zeal in *I'll Take My Stand* and elsewhere. As mature men they mostly were to put such sterile notions behind them, and their philosophy now seems as quaint and distant as does that of Eliot. If Eliot's social thought strikes us as overly abstract and speculative, the Agrarian program is simply too much associated with southern regionalism and racism for it to be very palatable.

Today one encounters occasional defenders of Agrarianism who try enlisting Tate and associates as critics of unfettered capitalism or as precursors of environmental consciousness. While such attitudes can certainly be found scattered within their work, their fundamental concern, the unpleasant fact remains, was their justification of plantocracy and of black slavery. The Fugitives-Agrarians were no doubt eloquent and intelligent polemicists, though this did not suffice to make them major thinkers. They were good poets, however, and *that* first of all was the source of their disaffection with modern society—the lot of many poets since 1830, as we have been seeing. The romance of the slave pastorale has generated some able mass entertainments such as *Gone with the Wind* (our nation's cinematic equivalent of *Triumph of the Will*), but it cannot be taken seriously as a social vision.

The *passéiste* nostalgia under examination here can also be traced as a central theme in Latin American *modernismo*. The Nicaraguan poet Rubén Darío is highly representative in this regard. His yearned-for utopia, we saw in chapter 4, is the elegant Versailles of rococo France. In the preface to *Prosas profanas* (1896), Darío likens his verse to "an old Pompadour clavichord" that resounds with gavottes to which merry grandparents once danced. He muses somberly about possible African or indigenous blood in his veins, "despite," he says, his having "the hands of a marquis" (5:762).

Darío makes no secret of detesting the times he lives in, and, in a comparison that echoes Gautier's "political" rhetoric in the preface to *Maupin*, he admits to a preference for the luxuries and beauties of "princesses, monarchs, imperial things" and "the court of Heliogabalus" over any modern president of a republic (5:763). Similarly, in his preface to the *Cantos de vida y esperanza* (1905), Darío states his "respect for the aristocracy of mind, for the nobility of Art" and his abhorrence of "mediocrity" and "intellectual mongrelism" (5:859).

Nevertheless, Darío's specific situation as a Latin American makes for certain crucial differences. On the home front he could not have romanticized the colonial court of the viceroys, inasmuch as it represented an old Spain then largely discredited—by poets as well as others—throughout most of Ibero-American civilization. When expressing nostalgia for New World subjects, Darío feels called upon to observe, "If there is poetry in our America, it is in its old things: in Palenke and Utatlán [sites of Mayan ruins], in the legendary Indian, and in the sensual and subtle Inka; and in the great Moctezuma of the golden throne" (5:763). Darío thus locates in the native Precolumbian empires what stands in for him as a venerably feudal, prebourgeois past. Almost incidentally, he is granting to non-Western peoples a cultural respect that was far from fashionable at the time among Europeanized Latin Americans.

Darío's prime as a poet happens to coincide, however, with the implacable rise of United States economic and military might in the Caribbean. The marines landed in Nicaragua some four times in the 1890s; in 1898, U.S. armed forces intervened massively in Cuba's ongoing war of independence against Spain, thereby consolidating U.S. control over the Greater Antilles; soon thereafter the administration of Theodore Roosevelt fomented the separatist movement that helped splinter off Panama from the nation of Colombia, making way for the now-mythic construction of the Panama Canal. Responding in a general way to this encroaching imperial power, Darío in his preface to the *Cantos de vida y esperanza* (5:860) raises a prophetic specter: "Tomorrow we [Latin Americans] could well be Yankees (and that's most likely)," while elsewhere he asks, of some future time, "Will so many millions of us speak English?"

The situation ultimately prompted Darío's most famous political poem, the impassioned, slightly sarcastic ode "A Roosevelt" [To Roosevelt]. The aggressive U.S. president—horse tamer, tiger killer, and "future invader of a naive Latin America"—is likened to Nimrod, Alexander, and Nebuchadnezzar, and is described as a "professor of Energy." Behind Roosevelt there stands a United States that combines "the cult of Hercules with the cult of Mammon." In opposition, Darío evokes the Indian grandeurs of old—for example those of Netzahualcóyotl (1431–72), the legendary philosopher-king of Texcoco—and speaks generally for a Latin America that "has indigenous blood" and that can claim Moctezuma, Cuauhtémoc, and the Inka among its forebears. At the same time Darío calls on the America of Columbus and Catholicism and ends with the bold assertion that though Roosevelt may have it all, he lacks what the Latin Americans still have: "God!" (5:878–80).

"To Roosevelt" is renowned more for its subject matter than for its uneven lyric accomplishment. Two things are nevertheless notable about it; the first is the fact that Darío wrote the poem at all. Faced, as it were, by Northern invaders, he forgets about pure beauty and registers a political protest. Second, the weapons conjured up by Darío to fend off U.S. power are neither modern strengths nor revolutionary forces, but past indigenous heroes, along with those very traditions of a Hispanism and Catholic religiosity that a younger Darío had spurned as stale and mummified. *Passéiste* nostalgia is in this case deployed—if not very effectively—as a means of resistance against foreign invasion.

Still, that Darío the aesthete could see fit to take on a matter as nonaesthetical as U.S. expansion says a lot about the differences between a dependent Latin America on one hand and an imperial Europe and United States on the other. In this regard it is scarcely surprising that José Martí, who was thoroughly engaged in the struggle against Spanish colonialism in Cuba (and, more discreetly, against a looming threat of U.S. empire), should have developed a poetics and ideology radically divergent from the stance famously typified by his *modernista* brethren. There are no Versailles fantasies in Martí's verse, no aristocratizing notions about the poet being above the common herd—at the same time that there is plenty of sheer joy in the simple beauty of everyday existence. Significantly, Martí in his essays defends indigenous and African art and civilizations—not as a *passéiste*, however, but as a kind of anticolonial nationalist who acknowledges the best in his society's products, and who moreover judges the non-Western peoples' contributions to Latin America as the equal of and in some instances superior to those of Europe.

The mind and art of Martí serve as eloquent proof that a life of struggle for justice has the potential to be spiritually more fulfilling than an angst undeniably brought about by poetic isolation and literary marginality. Martí's twentieth-century inheritors are the many poets who have since fought dictatorship and injustice in Latin America and also in Turkey, in Africa, and in the authoritarian parts of Europe, and for whom writing verse is simply one part of a larger battle for cultural values and for the dignity of the human being.[74]

Unlike Martí, Joyce was not a political activist, yet his ideas and outlook likewise set him apart from the other Anglophone Modernists—particularly Eliot—in whose company he is usually placed. The differences are telling: where Eliot's best-known poetry expresses a fierce disgust with the sexual instincts, the lower orders, and the everyday world, Joyce by contrast celebrates the body's pleasures, the popular classes, and the delights of the quotidian. Yeats once remarked that, save for William Morris, nobody he ever met showed such joy of life as did the Irish novelist.[75]

Of course Joyce in his early fictions and elsewhere casts a decidedly critical glance at Irish Catholicism and at daily life in turn-of-the-century Dublin, showing the suffocating limits of both. His unsparing picture of his country, however, grows out of a very specifically progressive worldview. Joyce, it should be established from the outset, is as far as possible from a nostalgic *passéiste*. His general stance can be roughly summed up as follows: against British (and other) imperialisms, against Church control over Irish life, solidly pronationalist yet also cosmopolitan and against any facile xenophobia, and strongly inclined to anarchist as well as socialist views.

Wilde's essay "The Soul of Man under Socialism" had a powerful impact on the young Joyce, and he at times alluded privately to socialism as "the generous idea." Among the books in Joyce's personal library at Trieste were a good number of socialist publications, including the first 173 Fabian tracts, bound in a single volume. He also owned works by the anarchists Kropotkin, Bakunin, and Proudhon. The Italian socialists, with whom Joyce was friendly, exerted a major influence on his views; he felt a need for socialist consciousness among the workers. Anarchism, on the other hand, was seen by Joyce as a means of liberating the individual.[76]

Certain turns of phrase by Bakunin that mock the Church and its cruelties crop up here and there in *Ulysses*. Moreover we find out in the course of the novel that Bloom in his youth was a Utopian Socialist and annoyed Molly by referring to Jesus Christ as the first socialist. Marx's famous phrase from the *Critique of the Gotha Program* is altered by Bloom thus: "To everyone according to his needs, and to everyone according to his deeds."[77] In the "Circe" episode, a mature Bloom can still think of the free market system as a "hideous hobgoblin produced by a horde of capitalistic lusts upon our prostituted labor."[78] He also favored home rule for Ireland, but at this time sympathizes with the more radical Sinn Fein ("Ourselves Alone") movement, leading Molly to fear for his job at the newspaper.

Not surprisingly, Bloom's casual leftism is in some degree a projection of the opinions of Joyce. During his exile in Trieste, the author gave public lectures and also wrote articles for the Italian press, in which he champions home rule for Ireland; and in a 1907 lecture entitled "Ireland, Island of Saints and Sages," he shows how British imperial policy has destroyed the Irish woollen trade, killed Irish manufactures, and let Irish people simply die in the potato famine (167).[79]

(Joyce, incidentally, did not dislike industrialism per se, but rather the imposition of British industries; indeed he reportedly liked factories.)[80] He pointedly observes that "for so many years the Englishman has done in Ireland only what the Belgian is doing today in the Congo" (166). And in his English-language classes he used to employ as teaching tools such epigrams as "Ireland is a great country," or "The metropolitan government, after centuries of strangling it, has laid it waste," and "The government sowed hunger, syphilis, superstition and alcoholism."[81]

As early as 1906 Joyce was saying that things had reached a point where either Sinn Fein or British imperialism would conquer Ireland. With matters worsening for Ireland in the 1910s, Joyce frankly favored the Sinn Fein program over what he considered the "ineffectual" struggles in Parliament. During the Great War, Joyce experienced all manner of hassles with the British diplomatic authorities in Trieste, who were urging the writer to join in the propaganda effort, pressures that instead led Joyce to cheer the German military offensive by way of reaction.

Needless to say, given the richness and complexity of his aesthetic, Joyce was not one to shape his art to some purely denunciatory agenda. Rather he imbeds his anti-imperialist views within the larger texture of a narrative, by means of subtle ironies and all but invisible techniques. For example, at the climax of the short story "Araby," two men with English accents successfully engage the attention of the young working girl at the fair, flirting with her and thereby further marginalizing the disoriented little boy who is protagonist and narrator.

More tellingly, in the "Wandering Rocks" episode of *Ulysses*, the afternoon cavalcade of the British viceroy and his retinue through Dublin unfolds in what is a deadpan-style parody of journalistic reportage, with its endless array of names that suggests a newspaper's social pages. Each and every mention of the viceroy includes one or other of his high titles—"William Humble, earl of Dudley," "The Right Honourable William Humble," "His Excellency"—so scrupulously as to strike a somewhat pompous note. The viceroy is initially "saluted by obsequious policemen"; and after numerous references to specific Dubliners, many of whom show him due obeisance as he wends his way through town, the chapter ends comically with "the salute of Almidano Artifori's sturdy trousers swallowed by a closing door" (255).[82]

When anti-British opinion appears in *Ulysses*, it is voiced by concrete characters and thus individualized by their respective traits. In the book's opening pages, a voluble Buck Mulligan complains to Stephen about their third housemate, the Englishman Haines: "God, these bloody English. Bursting with money and indigestion. Because he comes from Oxford" (4); alluding obliquely to the empire, Mulligan further asserts, "His old fellow made his tin by selling jalap to Zulus or some bloody swindle or other. . . . And to think of your having to beg from these swine" (7). On the other hand the ignorant and anti-Semitic bile of the pugnacious (if colorful) tavern citizen in the "Cyclops" episode shows the dangers of a revolutionary nationalism that has turned hard-line and xenophobic.

The few English characters in *Ulysses*, it is worth noting, are scarcely sympathetic. Haines, tall and properly Oxonian, sounds a bit complacent when he opines solemnly, "We feel in England that we have treated you [Irish] rather unfairly. It seems history is to blame" (20); and Haines's own insular nationalism glimmers forth in his assertion "I'm a Britisher. . . . I don't want to see my country fall into the hands of the German jews either" (21). Of course, the high point of the British element in *Ulysses* (and indeed the very climax of the book) is the episode in the "Circe" chapter when an aggressive Private Carr verbally abuses and then punches Stephen, allegedly for "say[ing] a word against my fucking king" (595). For ideological emphasis, Lord Tennyson makes a cameo appearance in this scene, wearing a "Union Jack blazer" and citing a famous line from his imperialist poem "The Charge of the Light Brigade."

"I am the servant of two masters, . . . the Imperial British state and the Holy Roman Apostolic Church" (20). Thus remarks Stephen in the opening chapter of *Ulysses*. Joyce, in his own article on "Fenianism" (1907), notes that Ireland "has fulfilled what has hitherto been considered an impossible task—serving both God and Mammon" (190), that is, serving both a spiritual Vatican and a commercial Great Britain. Accordingly, in *A Portrait of the Artist*, the high point in Stephen's coming-of-age conflicts is his quiet confrontation with the dean of studies over the word "tundish." The dean is a high cleric as well as an Englishman; his power and authority over Stephen are thus double.

These ideologically charged passages, it goes without saying, reflect Joyce's view that the twin oppressors of Ireland are Britain and Rome, the latter perhaps constituting an even more dangerous enemy. By first banishing Catholicism, Joyce remarks in "Ireland, Island of Saints and Sages," the British heightened the religion's moral value, making Ireland "the most faithful daughter of the Vatican" (169), a favor not returned by the popes. By the mid-nineteenth century, however, the Church was cooperating with the British government, which had granted the Catholics their institutions in exchange for an oath of loyalty to the Crown. Thereafter the Church denounced revolutionary organizations in order to maintain its privileged status.

Its artistic subject matter aside, *A Portrait* is principally the fictive record of a young Irish intellectual's slow process of freeing himself from the formidable shackles—both external and internalized—of the Roman Catholic faith, a battle Joyce himself was furiously waging. The previous chapter noted the budding writer's own struggles with Church censorship at University College, and the struggle would continue through much of his existence. As he eloquently remarks in a 1904 letter to his wife Nora, "Six years ago I left the Catholic Church, hating it fervently. . . . I made secret war upon it when I was a student. . . . Now I make war upon it by what I write and say and do." [83] By way of replacement, Joyce thought of poets as "repositories of the genuine spiritual life," believing, conversely, that "priests were usurpers," his brother Stanislaus observes.[84] Ironically, much of what Joyce achieved with his gifts of mind he did as a consequence of the rigorous education he had received under the Jesuits; not surprisingly, a Jesuit review once said of Joyce that his was "a great Jesuit-trained intellect that had gone over to the powers of Satan." [85]

Given his origins, his situation, and his battles, the Irish author understandably exhibited not the slightest attraction for the kind of society desired by Eliot and other right-wing Modernists. Having grown up in a theocratic monarchy of the very sort that Eliot longed for, he knew from experience how such a system can stultify art and thought. By the same token, neither could Joyce sympathize with

Yeats's idealization of a Celtic past nor with the nationalist project of reviving the Gaelic language. In both temperament and ideology Joyce had nothing of the nostalgist or *passéiste* about him. And whereas much of Eliot's verse juxtaposes the heroic nobility of ages past with the sordidness and vulgarity of the present, Joyce in his *Ulysses* takes up the ancient heroism of the *Odyssey* only to parody it (as he does with mastery and humor in the "Cyclops" episode particularly). "I am sure," he remarks revealingly in a 1905 letter to his brother, "that the whole structure of heroism is, and always was, a damned lie."[86]

As I suggest in earlier chapters, Joyce in several respects was reliving the Enlightenment struggle against king and clergy, and, in the process, finding in art a more genuine way to spiritual truth. At the same time, though some Irish might deny it, he too is a manifestation of his country's long battle for liberation from British monarchy and empire. He can therefore be seen as the twentieth century's first major anticolonial artist, a writer who broke with the existing paradigms of both metropolitan and traditional aesthetics by fashioning a newer and grander literary art. In his life, writing, and thought, then, Joyce incarnates some of the more crucial issues of the last three centuries—yet another aspect of his greatness as a mind and maker.

World War II and its aftermath brought a major ideological realignment in Europe and the United States. By 1945 the organic conservatism of which Eliot and the Agrarians were leading literary spokesmen was politically and intellectually a spent force, defeated or marginalized by the antifascist Grande Alliance, however temporary, between liberal capitalism and a secular socialism—the very forces long despised by nostalgists and *passéistes*. Conservative thinking thence had to redefine itself.

In Western Europe particularly, conservatism would accommodate itself to the Anglo-American occupation and move toward the quasi-official position of the United States, where the ideology of a "Vital Center," allegedly standing equally opposed to extremes of right and left, was to triumph at most levels. (The idea received its classic exposition in historian Arthur M. Schlesinger's well-known book of that name.) Centrist impulses took hold especially in the former

Axis powers, where the discrediting of fascism forced its lesser adherents to seek a new formula for refuge, respectability, and power. The emerging Christian Democratic parties (the very term at first being something of an oxymoron) served in part as regroupings of old-line religious and organic conservatives, who made their peace with a liberal-democratic ethos against which they had previously fought. Meanwhile thousands of fascist small fry found safe haven in the reactionary atmosphere being assertively established in the United States.

Since the advent of the cold war, conservatism in English has come to mean mostly global anti-Marxism in order to make the world safe for markets and investments, along with an ideological suspicion of state intervention in domestic economies — a revival, essentially, of nineteenth-century liberalism. The European old order — feudal, monarchical, clerical — that Arno Mayer convincingly traces as persisting well into the twentieth century was truly in the past.[87] The 150-year battle waged by organic conservatives against the French Revolution, against secularism and markets, against democratization and equality, had been lost and was finally over.

Accordingly, a Christian conservative like Eliot stressed his religiosity without the former monarchism and class snobbery, even going so far as to speak positively of democracy in his social writings. The modern irritants that had spurred the nostalgic *passéiste* had also made possible the intense poet, however; and without his erstwhile urgency and revulsion, or without the drive for ceaseless inner exploration evoked in *Four Quartets,* his sensibility and artistic impetus were mostly gone. Reconciliation with the present, together with his 1948 Nobel Prize, helped in great measure to finish off what had been creative in Eliot.

The Marxist left posed a more complex and intractable matter. In France and Italy the mass-based leftist parties had gained considerable prestige via their crucial involvement in the antifascist underground. The enormous war casualties and impressive battlefield victories of the USSR in fighting the Nazi juggernaut, moreover, had imparted a reflected glory to the Western resistants. Involving as it did millions of individuals, the culture of the left was simply too large to suppress without a frank reversion to fascist tactics. Hence the best that the occupying U.S. authorities could aim for was to block any Communist parties from inclusion in the postwar French or Italian governments, which the Marshall Plan stipulations indeed succeeded in doing.

In the United States, on the other hand, the left was comparatively small and powerless. Purging its supporters and sympathizers from the education, entertainment, labor, and government sectors was therefore accomplished with relative ease (and rhetoric aplenty) via congressional vehicles—the House Un-American Activities Committee (HUAC), the Senate Internal Security Subcommittee, and the McCarthy hearings—as well as the FBI. The hysterical antileft repression in postwar America, I believe, was a matter not so much of confronting a national Marxist presence (which in any event was slight) as it was of conservative Republicans lashing back at a New Deal (which they thoroughly loathed). They hence targeted the weak link of "Communism," with a view to winning back the political stage. The end result by the early 1950s was a two-party duumvirate, a center-right compromise in which both Republican and Democratic conservatives grudgingly tolerated existing New Deal reforms but also established anti-Marxism as the overriding national and global priority.

The consequences for the intellectual arena were vast. Essentially the culture of the U.S. left was destroyed, and not only that of the Communist Party (membership in which suddenly became retroactively illegal). There were also such instances as the deportation of Charlie Chaplin, the market death of left-leaning dailies like New York's PM, the Hollywood blacklist, the federal prison terms served by writers including Dashiell Hammett and Howard Fast, the professional silencing of any China specialist who argued that Mao's guerrillas had triumphed not by Soviet expansion but by their own efforts, and the general narrowing of the limits of permissible debate.

On many campuses, leftist groups and speakers were routinely banned, including novelist Pearl Buck, historian and editor Carey McWilliams, actor Paul Robeson, literary critics Kenneth Burke and Malcolm Cowley, as well as Quaker pacifists, Keynesian economists, and anyone who risked challenging the prevailing center-right dogmas and two-party line. The universities mostly collaborated with governmental repression; among the few exceptions that resisted McCarthyism were Columbia and Brandeis Universities and Sarah Lawrence and Williams Colleges.[88]

Within this larger situation, the libertarian side of the idea of Art for Art's Sake was revived and drafted to play a part in the cold war formula, to wit: whereas Communism dictates total artistic conformity, under capitalism art is absolutely free, and a writer "can write whatever he wants," as the expression goes. The dichotomy is neatly demonstrated in the question that then-chairman of HUAC, Clyde Doyle of California, addressed to film animator John Hubley on 5 July 1956: "We have evidence from other [artists] who were at one time members of the communist conspiracy. . . . At times artistical interests were directed in order to put across a certain message sponsored by Soviet Communism, rather than art for art's sake. That, of course, is one of the purposes of this question, . . . to see . . . if in your experience, communism . . . succeeded in directing your specialized talents to put across a certain communistic message rather than art for art's sake." Hubley replied, "My work has been my own work, and my own talent, and my own opinions."[89]

The need to differentiate American from Soviet cultural practices was likewise a factor that reinforced the victory of Art for Art's Sake on U.S. campuses. As I suggested earlier, the New Critics (at that point no longer insistent Agrarians) won their place in the ivied cloisters largely by default. Their postwar hegemony in university English departments came about, in great measure, because the exponents of nineteenth-century historicism were dying out and because the left had been banished from the priesthood. The New Criticism, of course, generally rejected in principle any social or historical method in literary analysis; and its founding members still saw much of human history since 1865 as a mistake, though dwelling less on the ideological issue and tempering it somewhat. Their antihistoricist amnesia nonetheless suited the purposes of an emerging center-right ideology that needed to occlude not only conservatives' past preferences for fascism but also a hundred years of conflict-ridden global capitalist expansion (in both liberal and fascist forms). The theory of totalitarianism served the same beclouding function in the social science fields as did aestheticist doctrines in the arts and humanities.

Meanwhile the Agrarians in their new-won respectability moved to the political center, accommodating themselves in some degree to the moderately liberal, secular project of a victorious and powerful United States. Much like Eliot with his high religiosity stripped of its royalism and protofascism, the former Fugitives-Agrarians for their part went on to become the campus representatives of an aestheticism conveniently rid of its quondam complement of nostalgia for the antebellum South.

The Agrarians' adaptation to the new political climate is well exemplified in the post-1945 essays of Tate. Gone from his updated vision are the defense of slavery, the yearning for aristocracy, and the racist drivel, but gone also are his earlier complaints, in "The Profession of Letters in the South," about "the competitive racket" and "self-sweat shop" of the literary market.[90] Whereas a younger Tate would lament the marginalization of poets in modern liberal society and look back longingly at feudal patronage, by contrast in his lecture-essay "To Whom Is the Poet Responsible?" (1950) he all but champions poetic isolation and answers the titular query thus: there is solely the "responsibility to be a poet, to write poems, and not to gad about using the rumor of his verse . . . to appear on platforms and to view with alarm."[91] In this regard Tate finds both the fascist broadcaster Pound and the liberal publicist MacLeish equally mistaken, for, in Tate's new conception, the responsibility of poets is precisely *not* to involve themselves in public matters. Needless to say, the Agrarians had managed to "appear on platforms and to view with alarm" quite visibly when they took their stand against liberalism in the 1920s and 1930s.

Amid the century's horrors, Tate in his 1952 article "The Man of Letters in the Modern World" sees as chief consolation "at least one light which even the black slaves of the old South were permitted to keep burning but which the white slaves of Russia were not: I mean the inalienable right to talk back of which I cite the present discourse as an imperfect example."[92]

Imbedded within Tate's resonant southern rhetoric is the standard argument of cold war ideologues when explaining U.S. military actions abroad: we are fighting for free speech, for the right of protesters here and elsewhere to "talk back," something you cannot do in Communist Russia. (The reconstructed Fugitive appears to imply that black Americans in the Old South did enjoy this right.) Incidentally, Tate read portions of his essay at a Paris exposition sponsored by the Congress for Cultural Freedom—an organization subsequently revealed to be a front for the Central Intelligence Agency (CIA), the latter not known for its efforts on behalf of freedom of speech in the non-Western world. Tate's invoking of the classic Enlightenment issue of free speech nonetheless demonstrates the extent to which he and his Agrarian cohorts had shed their neofeudal *passéisme* and accepted the northern liberal outlook. The South once again had lost the Civil War.

In our previous chapter we examined Nabokov as a maximum instance of postwar aestheticism among U.S. novelists. His personal and family history likewise embodies several key aspects of the changing politics of Art for Art's Sake. The author's father, V. D. Nabokov, was a Russian liberal activist who figured prominently in the local struggles for a constitutional monarchy modeled after that of Great Britain. These labors earned him three months in a czarist prison in 1908; and in 1922, at an émigré political meeting in Berlin, V. D. Nabokov was shot dead by two Russian monarchists, one of whom would later serve as a minor functionary for the Hitler regime. Nabokov *fils* could thus make legitimate claims to a legacy of antimonarchist liberalism, proven by his father's heroism and martyrdom.

As he settled into the life of a *lumpenproletarian* in émigré Berlin, the writer retained this liberal outlook. Organic conservatism, unsurprisingly, held no attraction for a secular Nabokov sublimely indifferent to religious, moral, or eschatological issues. (From his scattered remarks one infers that he was probably an atheist.)[93] At the same time, matters of social and economic justice did not interest Nabokov in the slightest. As a political mind he thus stands midway between the religious royalism of Eliot on the right, and the anarchism, socialism, and anti-imperialism of Joyce on the left. His centrist ideology nevertheless was to remain frozen in time, with no subsequent growth or development of nuances after his flight from Russia—a fact that largely explains his quasi-religious affair with centrist America during the cold war.

In a conversation with Alvin Toffler, Nabokov grants the elementary nature of his political views: "Since my youth . . . my political creed has remained as bleak and changeless as an old gray rock[,] . . . classical to the point of triteness. Freedom of speech, freedom of thought, freedom of art. The social or economic structure of the ideal state is of little concern to me." [94] Such simple, formulaic notions recall in their crude eloquence those of Nabokov's fellow–émigré novelist Ayn Rand. For just as the author of *Atlas Shrugged* is preoccupied solely with the rights of superior architects and entrepreneurs, and the devil take the rest (most of whom are contemptible fools anyway), Nabokov's ideology by the same token involves the right of superior aesthetes to devise aesthetical fictions—and the devil take any nonentities not involved in high phrase making (including the countless contemptible scribblers from Balzac on). Nabokov's *Real Life of Sebastian Knight* in fact shares many similarities in tone and thinking with Ayn Rand's *The Fountainhead* (1943), though his book has a better prose style.

Nabokov would surely have bristled at any comparison with Rand, given his avowed dislike of publicist art. Yet there is far more sociopolitical content to his fiction than he and his cultists would care to admit. Many Nabokov novels are implicit defenses of Russian émigré culture, while conversely the Soviet characters he inserts into *Glory*, *The Defense*, and *Pale Fire* are simple caricatures, the mirror images of capitalists in socialist realism. (Balzac's satirizing French financiers is merely "social," whereas Nabokov's lampooning Soviet tourists is "art.")

Bend Sinister, Nabokov's second-worst novel, is also an anticommunist tract that exhibits no understanding of the dynamics of political conflict and dictatorship. Rather it depicts revolution as the work of spiteful oafs who hate professors. The fanatical "Ekwilists" (that is, "Equalists") who take over a nameless Eastern European state also exemplify the leveling process that is attacked throughout the book, Nabokov thereby looking back to nineteenth-century antidemocratic rhetoric and forward to Senator Barry Goldwater. *Pnin* and *Pale Fire* let fly at anti-McCarthyite opinion, portraying as merely silly the current complaints about passports being revoked;[95] and the idyll of prerevolutionary Zembla in *Pale Fire* closely resembles Nabokov's liberal utopia and idea of America. As Borges once said: those who object to social doctrines in literature secretly mean doctrines different from their own.

During the 1930s many Russian émigrés in Berlin saw Nazism as a possible savior against Bolshevism. Even after June 1941, when the Germans, along with their Hungarian and Rumanian confederates, invaded the USSR, there were important expatriate literati—such as the poet Zenaida Gippius—who hoped for a *Wehrmacht* victory against Moscow. Nabokov himself contributed his small portion to the earlier climate by lumping together murderous French anti-Semites with the 1936 Popular Front (the only broad-based anti-Nazi group at the time) as "idle idiots."[96] Still, Nabokov's eventual opposition to the German fascists was genuine. Owing precisely to his nineteenth-century liberalism, he could hardly have shared in the anti-Semitism of the Nazis, however anti-Bolshevik they were; and his wife of many decades to come, Véra Slonim, was Jewish.

Unlike Eliot's work, Nabokov's makes few attacks on ethnics, save for some potshots at Mexicans and Latinos in *Ada,* and the reference in *Transparent Things* to "certain Far Eastern people, virtually halfwits in many other respects."[97] Rather he directs his centrist barbs at the ideological left, and his upper-class hauteur at any art that smacks of plebeianism. Nabokov's own sense of aristocratic superiority is regularly projected onto the tall, handsome heroes (always Slavic, mostly Cambridge-educated) of his Russian fiction, those blithe and breezy youngbloods for whom everything works out well, in contrast to their subhuman victims, who are frequently characterized in terms of dogs, frogs, and toads. The narrator of *Look at the Harlequins!,* for example, speaks of "a particularly stupid baby sitter," and remarks that "Mrs. Blogovo was a half-witted cripple."[98] Similarly, in *Laughter in the Dark,* the author all but revels in the sadistic pranks that an arch and clever Rex (the royal name is significant) plays on a blinded and pitiful Albinus.

Nabokov's projects and persona contain little in the way of historical and neofeudal longings, in contrast with Gautier, Yeats, Eliot, or the Agrarians. The reason is that Nabokov himself, as a scion of the Russian landed gentry, heralds from that very milieu of feudalism. There was no need for ideological *passéisme,* inasmuch as he sprang

258

from precisely that stock. *Speak, Memory,* that lush memoir of his youth in old Russia, lovingly evokes the family's ancient estates, thick as they once were with coats of arms, formal portraits, and other mementos of five centuries. Feudal nostalgia is thus neither a personal aspiration nor a subjective dream but a concretely lived expression for Nabokov, who puts to work his most meltingly purple prose in order to conjure up a vanished idyll of unlimited wealth and comfort, with five-bathroom houses, fifty servants, trips to Biarritz, and (this in the 1910s) two large motorcars. Nabokov *père* is even recalled as participating in that most aristocratic of rituals—a duel—and winning.

So where other aesthetes and Modernists dream of feudal beauties and lost heroism, all Nabokov need do is glance back at his privileged youth and puissant ancestors. And yet this past, however material and palpable it be, is itself an idealization. Nabokov's memoirs contain virtually no reference to the lives then being led by the less than rich, except for some glowing, quasi-feudal evocations of the many loyal peasants who loved his father. One would not gather from Nabokov's account that nonaristocratic Russians were barely surviving and were being set upon by the Czarist police. But then Nabokov's sole interest (aside from his prose style) lies in the sumptuous joys—country houses, British toothpaste, Pears soap—of his upper-class boyhood; *this* is the life we led before the revolution, he says, presenting it not as an abstract political principle or desideratum but as a personal narrative that, just incidentally, helps discredit that revolution.

At the same time Nabokov argues that feudal inequities were on their way out, on account of his father's and other liberals' struggles for constitutionalism. The novelist even attempts to build a case for old Russia as a nation of long-standing liberal traditions, coming to fruition via Nabokov *père*'s generation but cut short by the Red coup. This, however, is as much a fantasy as anything in Gautier or Yeats. Even a conservative historian such as Richard Pipes forcefully notes the absence in old Russia of anything resembling an independent, forward-looking, technically advanced bourgeoisie,[99] a lack that made impossible the emergence of a genuine native liberalism. As Barrington Moore has persuasively shown, authoritarian feudalism ultimately gives way to democracy only when there is a bourgeoisie large and conscious enough to challenge monarchical rule.[100] After all, the British constitutional system, so dear to Eastern European liberals such as the Nabokovs, took hold in the late seventeenth century only following decades of Stuart decay, Puritan revolution, civil war, and Restoration. No political order comes into being merely because someone wishes it so.

In the end, with Russian feudal privilege as well as liberal struggles irretrievably lost, Nabokov realized his aristocratism via his aesthetic-separatist hauteur and his icily aloof prose style, recreating in his writings the magical kingdom of his youth and the closed subculture of Russian émigré life. And his liberal side he brought to full blossom in cold war America's manorial campuses, where a center-right politics and a dogmatic aestheticism—both much like his—would enjoy an unusual hegemony and stability. These were the means by which Nabokov fulfilled his anti-Bolshevism. What *passéisme* there was in his makeup found satisfaction and inspiration in the U.S. present.

In my previous chapter I viewed deconstruction and other related post-Modern ideas as updated reincarnations of the doctrine of Art for Art's Sake. Matters of course are more complex than that, and the same can be said about the concomitant politics of deconstruction. I must deal initially, however, with the many polemicists of the New Right—notably the late Allan Bloom—who have routinely blamed 1960s radicalism as well as German philosophy (Nietzsche and Heidegger in particular) for the triumphal arrival of deconstruction in American academe, and who also single out deconstruction as a major culprit and prime mover in the relativist climate that prevails on U.S. campuses today.

Too much originating power and motive force, however, were attributed to the Yale Derrideans and their acolytes across the nation. Their way of thought and its peculiar influences constitute more of an elaborate symptom than an effective cause. Actually, the 1970s triumph of deconstruction in U.S. literary studies presents yet one more instance of what happens when European ideas and arts traverse the Atlantic. In France, where both the state and the leftist opposition have been traditionally of a centralizing and authoritarian cast, Derridean notions of "decentering," "dissemination," and "freeplay" pose a kind of counter-Utopia, an ideology of contestation before hierarchic privilege and its claims to transcendental signification.[101]

In the American ideological setting, by contrast, such thinking—if we ignore Derrida's opaque idiom for a moment—has a comfortable, footloose familiarity to it. The U.S. intellectual tradition, after all, comprises such key components as the Lockean tolerance of all faiths, the Millsian doctrine of the "marketplace of ideas," the Jamesian pragmatism that stresses results over principles, Ruth Benedict's cultural relativism, the academic ideology of "perspectivism," the journalistic ideology of "showing all sides," and the conventional, everyday rhetoric about openness, multiplicity, and pluralism.[102]

In our time, moreover, both liberal and conservative segments of U.S. opinion take pride in American society's decentralized ways, while media and faction sectors are noted for their lack of adherence to any set signs of original presences. Given this larger context, Terry Eagleton quite fittingly reflects on deconstructionism in America as follows: "The modest disownment of theory, method, and system; . . . the privileging of plurality and heterogeneity, the recurrent gestures of hesitation and indeterminacy, . . . the distaste for the definitive—it is not difficult to see why such an idiom should become absorbed so quickly within the Anglo-Saxon academies."[103]

Without it having been their intention, then, the American deconstructors have furnished the latest installment in that ongoing U.S. tradition of pluralistic tolerance, of skepticism toward ultimate truths or universal orthodoxy. What happened with Max Weber, psychoanalysis, and existentialism has been the lot of deconstruction: it has been absorbed and domesticated to provide further sustenance to the status quo. Not accidentally, publicists for deconstruction such as Barbara Johnson or Stanley Fish defend the doctrine as "a denial of what both the left and the right hold dear."[104] The Vital Center wins again.

Finally, it might be noted that our frenzied consumer culture fosters an attitude whereby truth and principle matter less than the immediate question "Does it feel good?" As Graff observes, we live in a society "where boredom is more conspicuous than poverty and exploitation, and where authority encourages hedonistic consumption and a flabby, end-of-ideology tolerance."[105] The dizzying relativism of U.S. life thus has Anglo-American roots and is a distinctly American episode. What the deconstructors did was to give European finesse, German weightiness, and Parisian garb to a local formation, much as the with-it designers and "idea people" do in other branches of U.S. marketing and media. To blame Teutonic philosophers and 1960s leftists for fin-de-siècle relativism is to trot out once more the scapegoat of "outside agitators."

The Belgian expatriate Paul de Man (1919–83) during his thirty-five years in the United States achieved a high reputation, not only as a man of great intellect and learning, but also as a pioneer disseminator of Derridean theory from his final post at Yale, where he taught after 1971. He was arguably the most influential American literary critic in the late 1970s and early 1980s, and his untimely death prompted many strongly felt eulogies from friends and colleagues throughout the academic world. Then, late in 1987, the scandal erupted: archival researches in Belgium showed beyond a doubt that the twenty-three-year-old de Man had published anti-Semitic articles in the Nazi collaborationist daily *Le Soir*—a past that he had never since acknowledged in public or private. Indeed, throughout his American period de Man floated various contradictory statements about his activities during the Occupation, including false hints that he had been involved in the Resistance. In addition, some of de Man's personal and business dealings turned out to have been rather questionable in retrospect.[106]

In the light of these disquieting facts, de Man's high-flown speculations about language, literature, and meaning would take on an ironic and even sinister twist. When in his key essay, "Criticism and Crisis," de Man asserts "the impossibility of making the actual expression coincide with what has to be expressed," and when he praises "the distinctive privilege of language to be able to hide meaning behind a misleading sign,"[107] it comes perilously close to sounding like a self-description (de Man hiding "the unspeakable"—to employ a favored deconstructionist word—behind his misleading signs). Similarly, when he argues in so many words that language does not tell the truth—that "sign" and "signified" have no relation[108]—and then further celebrates the art of literature on the precise grounds that it *cannot* tell the truth, one can only reflect on the "signified" of de Man's past and the network of pure "fictions" he subsequently spun off in its wake.

Finally, when, in "Form and Intent in the American New Criticism," de Man affirms that literature "originates in the void that separates intent from reality," and when he goes on to assert that "considerations of the actual and historial experience of writers are a waste of time from a critical viewpoint," [109] one inevitably asks if the primal "intent" and surrounding "reality" of a young de Man and the "actual and historical" collaborator he was, are matters likewise to be dismissed as "a waste of time." (As the ensuing brouhaha dramatically demonstrates, they are not.) The many sincere defenders of de Man no doubt find such a connection debatable — yet it is also unavoidable.

The *affaire* de Man, however, is only symptomatic of a larger intellectual drift we have been noting in American life since the onset of the cold war. Whereas official thinking in an openly dictatorial state resorts regularly to crude falsehood and to sheer denial of hard facts (along with swift repression of dissidents), in a mature liberal democracy the high priests tend rather to fashion opaque discourses that varyingly obfuscate, confuse, rearrange, or simply drown out certain unpleasant realities of past and present. In this regard, Noam Chomsky argues that thought control is actually stronger and more abundant in democratic societies, precisely because the latter are under compulsion to live up to their ideas and rely to the utmost on persuasion before any final recourse to the police.

Hence the theory of "totalitarianism," as I have remarked, served to exclude Nazi Germany from the broad history of capitalism and anticommunism, and also furnished philosophic cover for the many conservatives — organic and libertarian both — who had defended fascism throughout the 1920s and 1930s. Similarly, the postwar New Criticism, with its strictly "formalist" emphases, effectively ruled out from discussion the earlier pro-slavery views of its exponents as well as the snobbism and protofascism of their mentor Eliot. And in its own subtle way, de Man's antireferentialist doctrines helped cast a thick smokescreen over the historical referent of his minor-league anti-Semitism and temporarily exorcise his collaborationist phase.

By this point aestheticism is no longer *passéiste* in outlook. On the contrary, it seeks to hide its own past behind baroque theoretical

263

pyrotechnics and the discourse of timeless synchrony, of a changeless poetical-linguistic present.

As the foregoing survey demonstrates, there has never been anything like a single or final political stance associated with Art for Art's Sake and its Modernist heirs. On the contrary, the ranks of two centuries of aestheticism have seen monarchists and republicans, rebels and reactionaries, socialists and fascists, liberals and conservatives of every stripe. There have been progressivists who called for radical change, centrists who celebrated the status quo, and nostalgists who pined for a status quo ante. What political ideology the differing artistic purists may have happened to espouse has depended primarily on their relation to the constellation of forces prevailing within their respective societies, on that always intricate equilibrium among constitutive elements such as old aristocracy, new bourgeoisie, clergy, state power, external control, and foreign war—and, not least of all, on who (or what) it is that the particular aesthete chooses to single out as adversaries.

Certain patterns nevertheless stand out. When combating the ancien régime system of Crown and Church, Art for Art's Sake has tended to function as part of the antifeudal, pro-republican struggle. Once the liberal free market has displaced feudalism, however, things get more complicated. Victorian capitalism with its Christian revival drove Ruskin and Wilde to an oppositional and generally socialist stance in their time. The lyric poets, by contrast, found themselves so totally alienated from market society that many of them eventually dreamed of a return to some form of the once-hated old regime (England before Cromwell, France before 1789, the U.S. South before 1860), and they imagined feudal, aristocratic roles for themselves. Some aesthetes openly sided with right-wing repression, as did Gautier and Flaubert with the anti-Communard reprisals, and Pound with Italian fascism.

Yet further variants crop up in a colonial or quasi-colonial situation, wherein aestheticism and its "modernizing" literary technique provide a means of counteracting imperial power and of advancing in some measure a national cause. In an analogous dynamics, certain neofeudal nostalgists, sitting resentfully on the margins of liberal-industrial society, shed their fascist tendencies when confronted with a foreign fascist danger. Thereafter, the overwhelming triumph of capitalist democracy in the West, along with official U.S. anti-Marxist policies, would lead not a few conservative aesthetic separatists to adapt to the norms of a hegemonic liberalism. On the other hand many French structuralist investigations of the 1960s, while largely "aestheticist" in their approach, nevertheless functioned on the Marxist left end of the political spectrum.

Like many other literary doctrines, Art for Art's Sake can share in the space and discourse of most any ideology, be it established or emergent, regnant or marginal, official or oppositional. Many new combinations, some of them unforeseeable, are possible in the future.

CØNCLUSIØN

The Enduring Dilemma, the Academy, the Media

"Literary criticism is not your forte, my dear fellow. Don't try it. You should leave that to people who haven't been to a University." — Algernon Moncrieff in Oscar Wilde, *The Importance of Being Earnest,* act 1

Art for Art's Sake, as shown in the course of this narrative, is not simply a single concept of the sort given notoriety by Wilde's wit. It is, rather, a set of ideas, an intellectual and artistic horizon that, over its two-hundred-year history, has constantly shifted its arguments and position, depending both on the larger circumstances in which its adherents happen to be situated and on the specific predispositions of the respective authors. Kant and Schiller had with their aesthetic theories something very different in mind from what Gautier or Poe or the Latin American *modernistas* did with the doctrine, but then Gautier and cohorts were verbal-visual melodists, not abstract, grand-scale thinkers. The Euro-American Modernists for their part picked up on the ideas and practices of *l'art pour l'art* at the same time that they hoped to link literature once again with basic truths and even values; they in turn could not have foreseen the ways in which their works would be construed by the bewildering varieties of aesthetic separatism that became the standard fashion in university life after 1945.

For better or for worse, the ideology of Art for Art's Sake is most probably here to stay in some form or other. After all, many a doctrine has a way of surviving its original raisons d'être and becoming an available legacy thereafter. A century ago it was widely believed that, with the spectacular advance of natural science, religion was all but finished; yet religious thinking and feeling have repeatedly reemerged as major contenders in modern life, scientific triumphs notwithstanding. Even so repugnant a worldview as fascism—supposedly discredited with the defeat of the Axis powers—has managed to resurface in new garb in the 1980s and 1990s. Ideas that have gained power and diffusion in the past are a bit like old big buildings or accumulated fortunes; they are simply there, and their sheer large presence stands at the disposal of future generations.

On the other hand, an idea that remains sufficiently rich and fruitful can be mined with profit even by its adversaries. In our day, non-Marxist and anti-Marxist intellectuals commonly make use of Marxist arguments, as for example when U.S. historians routinely explain the Civil War as an economic battle between Northern industrial and Southern slaveholder class interests, or when neoconservative polemicist Allan Bloom anatomizes rock music as a mere product of big business.[1] "We are all Marxists" today, the Mexican poet Octavio Paz has observed—in the sense that, without our realizing it, many of our own categories about "the future, . . . about the present or about justice, peace and war" are "impregnated with [a] Marxism" that is now "part of our intellectual life-blood and moral sensibility."[2]

And yet by the same token one might say that we have all become aestheticists as well. Certain aspects of the Art for Art's Sake doctrine, we saw earlier, are perfectly unexceptionable, and they now belong to our shared store of ways of thinking about literature. Even a frankly left-wing author like Gabriel García Márquez is fond of noting to his many interviewers that a novel is not a transcription of reality but a wholly new artifact in its own right. With regard to the social question, García Márquez has been known to remark that a good-quality love story is also a valuable contribution to society; and on the controversial subject of literature and revolution he quips, "The writer's duty—his revolutionary duty if you like—is to write well."[3] Form and style—not content—are the criteria here invoked by the great novelist, however much he considers himself a "realist" author.

Meanwhile, so long as the dominant societies on this earth continue to be organized more or less along the lines they have been for the past two centuries, and so long as there are artistic people whose work lacks immediate functions or salability, aestheticism and even aesthetic separatism will persist as a general doctrine suiting the purposes of those who need it. The first "believers" in the cult of pure beauty, we saw in chapters 2 and 4, were the lyric poets, marginalized as they had been by the industrial literary market. Poets, however, are not precisely analogous to tailors or chandlers whose trade has been rendered obsolete by textile mills or electric lighting. In this regard, so long as human beings have natural language — with its rhythmic, phonic, and figurative devices — there will continue to be a poetic function (as any greeting card writer or jingle composer knows), and hence there will still be men and women who find in lyric verse a means of conveying something special about experience, irrespective of whether their craft is salable.

Many poets, of course, can today claim a legitimate niche as literary educators within the university and public school system. That, however, is a comparatively recent historical development, one that could very well be superseded as certain other social forces (privatization of education, cuts in arts budgets, and the like) assert themselves in years to come. Still, the ongoing revival in the United States of, say, arts-and-crafts, organic foods, and improvisatory theater, helps demonstrate that the reign of industrialism is never absolute nor final, that there are always maverick elements who wish to keep certain preindustrial (and at times more authentic) arts alive, for any set of utilitarian, aesthetic, or even spiritual aims and motives.

Whatever the case, Art for Art's Sake remains among the most daunting of aesthetic questions, especially in the areas of reception and criticism. Once broached, it sparks endless discussion, a perversely circular dialectic that spins and spirals about and leads us back essentially to where we started. The problem is not that aestheticism is false or without foundation. On the contrary, its persuasive appeal is that it rests on a truism: namely, that, like any other human endeavor — be it home construction, horticulture, or winter sport — verse and narrative have procedures, techniques, and values of their own. To deny this is either bourgeois philistinism, Stalinist dogma, or priestly excess. That a fetish has been made of those literature-specific concerns by modern professionalism and academic specialization does not in the end invalidate what is fruitful about the theory. Moreover, unlike, say, anti-Semitism or scientific "creationism" — ideologies ultimately not worth taking seriously as thought — aestheticism boasts a long and venerable list of subtle, intelligent, and sometimes enlightened followers, not a few of them major writers themselves.

Aestheticism, however, is at best a partial truth—"partial" in the sense both of "partisan" (or "sectarian") and "incomplete." After all, literature is made by human beings, whose social, historical, cultural, ideological, and sexual backgrounds determine in divers ways the subject and shape of their writing. This too is a truism, yet in the decades from the onset of the cold war until 1990 it had largely been ruled out from discussion, much as, in similar fashion, the content—the "aboutness"—of literary texts was blithely scanted or, worse, deemed nonexistent. As a personal example I have in mind an eminent scholar and former graduate school professor of mine, who was on record as being against all external interpretations of literature and thus bristled at the very mention of words such as "sociology" and "psychoanalysis," and who, accordingly, when teaching Latin American novels chose to ignore their thickly textured political and historical materials—wars, revolutions, dictatorships—and deal with the works as pure formal and stylistic constructs.

For an analogy one might imagine a Japanese professor of U.S. literature at Kyoto University delivering three lectures on Faulkner's *Absalom! Absalom!* and focusing exclusively on its style, structure, and "problematics of representation," with no mention made of such factors as Anglo-Saxon settlement, African American slavery, racism, the secessionist attempt, the Confederate defeat, the cultural significance of New Orleans, why Shreve is Canadian, and what it means for Quentin Compson to be at Yankee Harvard. The Japanese nineteen-year-olds, needless to say, would end up without the slightest notion of what Faulkner was *about*. And so it was for those of us enrolled in the class on Latin American novels in the late 1960s.

Abstracted aestheticism of this sort has persisted through its Fryean-archetypal, structuralist, and—last but not least—deconstructive avatars, sometimes with a muscular acrobatics that juggles literary texts in order cheerfully to pronounce them both "meaning less" and "signifying nothing," and that relies on many clever volumes to demonstrate that this is so. Even an idiosyncratic aesthete like Harold Bloom can find in literature little more than "the experience of an isolate and solipsizing glory," at best "a solitary transport, which we try desperately to communicate to others." [4] These are astounding words from a man whose very job is to teach and communicate a body of knowledge yet for whom all writers and readers, living or dead, add up to three thousand years of solipsism. Fittingly, Bloom himself is a kind of literary Social Darwinist who conceives of poetic history as a battlefield of purely individual strengths, competition, and triumphs.

Our climate of aestheticized nihilism, however, is not an eternal condition but rather a particular moment in history. In another, less jaded era (the 1930s), so sophisticated a critic as Kenneth Burke—in an essay entitled "Literature as Equipment for Living"—could optimistically state that *Madame Bovary* "is the strategic naming of a situation. It singles out a pattern of experience that is sufficiently representative of our social structure . . . for people to 'need a word for it.' " In Burke's view, then, "each work of art is the addition of a word to our informal dictionary." [5]

For more recent theorists, by contrast, the dictionary may well be just another fiction, and Burke most probably under a logocentric delusion. That poetry and fiction might have "referential values" (to use a Gerald Graff phrase),[6] tell us something about love or politics, and possibly even help us see the truth, understand life, or commune with the past—all this was the pre-Derridean preserve of naive readers, those pathetic souls incapable of realizing that the literature they were moved by is not "about" anything other than the trap of its own language.

Such lofty and detached speculation will eventually run up against the reality of our world, most especially when a literary text tells of monstrous realities like slavery, torture, or Nazism (be it for or against). Deconstructive analyses of, say, novels dealing with brutal South American repression actually cropped up in the late 1970s and mid-1980s, and while on the outer fringe of the movement, such readings were inevitable. Alfred MacAdam, for example, pithily observes that García Márquez's *One Hundred Years of Solitude* "places the blame for the perverted status of things on the creation and propagation of fictions which deform reality" [7]—no role here for the banana imperialists, conservative bureaucrats, government troops, and other forces that "deform reality" in Macondo.

In a more extreme example, James Young in PMLA says of the testimonial fiction of Argentine writer Rodolfo Walsh, "Even though these narratives would aspire—and then claim—to document a set of events, all they can actually document is their own coming into being, their own reconstruction of events." Seeing in Rodolfo Walsh's writings only their "rhetorical facticity," their "putative function as *works* of fact," Young further admonishes "the uncritical reader" not to "accept the '*texture*' of truth for truth itself," not to risk "confusing a work in the documentary mode for the document it rhetorically purports to be," for these texts have "whitened from view the shaping hand of their authors' governing mythoi." In sum, Young believes in "calling into question the celebrated documentary claims of this literature." [8]

In a reply in the same PMLA issue, David William Foster gently reminds Young that the official statements of the Argentine military junta were probably much more "creatively fictive" than is Walsh's testimonial work, and also that Walsh himself was "disappeared" by the regime's death squads (and was thus quite literally "whitened from view"). The Argentine generals, of course, also believed in "calling into question the . . . documentary claims of this literature," and Young inadvertently ends up supporting their version.

Critics of course come and go, while good writing remains. There is yet another truism in the cultural fact that mature literary works provide a means to knowledge more vivid and at times more reliable than nonfiction is capable of. Novels like García Márquez's *One Hundred Years of Solitude* or Fuentes's *The Death of Artemio Cruz* appear regularly on reading lists for Latin American history and politics classes in the United States, and Robert Coover's *The Public Burning* is in some instances the only book that literate North Americans will read about the Rosenberg case and the McCarthyite repression. For that matter, the best work of Dreiser, Dos Passos, Fitzgerald, Faulkner, Steinbeck, Doctorow, and Ishmael Reed can convey a great deal more about the day-to-day experience of the American Civil War, the Reconstruction, white prejudice, westward expansion, the rise of new wealth, World War I, labor struggles, the Red scare, and the 1930s Depression than do most purely factual, positivistic books by historians or social scientists.

Not only that, but great works of art (as they were once called) also have been known to serve as powerful sources of consolation, solace, and even wisdom to human beings in times of stress and torment. There are wide-ranging accounts of Latin Americans in jail cells who find moral comfort in reciting the poetry of Pablo Neruda; of idealists under dictatorial regimes who obtain a glimpse of salvation in their nation's or the world's classics; of lonely, alienated souls who gain insight into or even a love of life through key passages in Jane Austen or Shakespeare; or (as seen in chapter 1) of John Stuart Mill being rescued from nervous breakdown by reading Wordsworth; or (in chapter 7) of embattled Londoners during the German blitz feeling roused and encouraged by Eliot's *Four Quartets*. These are experiences too large to qualify as "purely aesthetic" or "textual" affairs, though the aesthetic obviously forms part of them. If such encounters did not exist, occupational fields like art therapy would be without foundation, and Freud—whose work is filled with literary allusion—would have been somewhat less great as a thinker.

Given the sometime prominence of the idea of music in aestheticism's history, I should like to contribute an instance of my own by considering the genre of instrumental, small-ensemble, postwar, "cool" jazz. This is a music meant neither for dancing nor verbalizing but exclusively for listening, and is hence a "pure" art. (For random examples, one might cite Clifford Brown's "Joy Spring," Miles Davis's "Seven Steps to Heaven," or Freddie Hubbard's "Red Clay.") At a performance of a jazz piece the basic elements are the opening chorus (with its thematic line, horn counterpoints, metric shifts, and harmonic sequence); the break just before the improvisatory portions; the technical skills and extemporaneous flights shown by the various soloists; the melodic surprises and eloquence, and the allusions to other works (intertextuality) in their solos; the overall drive and suppleness of their rendition; the final return of the theme, with minor variants; and a coda ranging from a few chords and arpeggios to yet another instrumental episode. These are the constituent elements we listen for in a jazz work, without which it would simply not be what it is. On this level, then, jazz is just music, a self-contained language, and to be responded to as such, without any search for a message.

But there are other aspects. Many jazz lovers of course have little or no knowledge of musical technique, and some listen more for the Dionysiac transport and ecstasies evoked in them by the rhythms and by a fine performance. This we recognize as the ritualistic, "religious" side of us, with which music has often been associated, an emotion partly implied in such familiar phrases as "I just dig it." And there is the social side as well, the fact that jazz is a people's music with plebeian roots, as reflected in the routine use of given names or nicknames—"Miles," "Diz," "the Duke"—when referring to its top artists; that it is the product of a despised social caste, long oppressed by slavery, deprivation, and prejudice; that the art emerges from the complex social and cultural textures of the black urban ghetto; and that, owing to the forced African diaspora, it has musics closely akin to it in Brazil and the Caribbean.

To ignore this range of contexts is, in its own way, not fully to understand jazz as a human phenomenon. Granted, an academic researcher who addressed only the sociology of jazz and applied to it a battery of graphs, statistics, and computer printouts, yet had no feeling for the music itself, would simply not be "getting it," and his sense of the art would obviously be quite partial and incomplete. However, much the same could be said, *mutatis mutandi,* about a purely formalist critic who, utilizing an opaque, hermetic methodology (along with the corresponding tables and graphs) discussed nothing but technique and scanted everything else, from the beauty and vitality of the music to the larger history within which the developers of that technique had lived and grown.

The literary equivalents of these (entirely hypothetical, let me say) jazz theorists can be found on American campuses, though more often within the formalist camp. And it is the extraordinary growth of the higher-education sector in the last forty or so years that has made such fine-grained, elaborate researches possible. Over the last two generations academic literary study has been licensed to take on a life of its own; and its formalisms, largely unchallenged by politics or history (and often in frank denial of same), until quite recently soared to rarefied heights, creating the often precious and involuted subculture that oftentimes predominates in our universities' humanities halls.

The near-universal hegemony enjoyed by Art for Art's Sake ideology in those upper reaches, however, did not necessarily lead to a qualitatively greater understanding of what literature is and does either in its glorious separateness or as living human agency. Rather we have had a vast, bureaucratized literary clerisy, tens of thousands strong and feeding constantly on itself, within which every few years newer, bolder fashions have contrived to outdo existing ones in their chic outrageousness and in their remoteness from real life as well as literature. It brings to mind the future as intuited by Max Weber, who, at the end of *The Protestant Ethic and the Spirit of Capitalism,* speaks in passing of the United States, "where the pursuit of wealth, stripped of its ethical and religious meaning, tends to become associated with purely mundane passions which often actually give it the character of sport." Weber envisions for the "last stage of this cultural development" a world of " 'specialists without spirit, sensualists without heart.' "[9] In this brief, aphoristic, surprisingly prescient passage, Weber foresees the coming of our society of chill hedonism and soulless technocracy, to which our literary-academic mandarinate aptly belongs. (On the other hand, Weber was unable to envision the rise of a New Right that would be religiously pro-capitalist in outlook.)

Alexandrian. Baroque. Rococo. Ivory tower. Fin de siècle. These are the words we sometimes see applied to our broad situation (literary and otherwise) here at the double turn of the millenium and the century. The phrase "ivory tower" in fact was reportedly coined by French critic Sainte-Beuve when characterizing the phenomenon of poetic aestheticism. Randall Jarrell for his part employs the term "Alexandrian" three times in his classic essay "The Age of Criticism," a piece that, in its diagnosis of the increasing domination of literary culture by academic critics, is as fresh and relevant today as when it first appeared in 1952.[10] Such adjectives, more suggestive than they are precise, serve nonetheless to convey the notion of our living in a late, overripe civilization, one in which certain of its enlightened sectors, having turned narrow, inward-looking, and excessively arcane, have lost contact with some of life's fundamental realities.

As literature and other arts in the United States march on their inexorable twin paths of hypercommercialization and academicization, the lure of the adjectives listed proves irresistible. On the commercial path, conglomerate publishing has brought about cutbacks in quality fiction and other less-profitable product lines. Editing in the United States, formerly a profession that allowed free writing time (as it still does abroad), has fallen prey to production quotas, "scientific management" directives, and the infamous bottom-line outlook. The middlebrow readership that used to subscribe to *Look* and *Saturday Review* has fragmented into a lonely crowd of special-interest magazine consumers. Television of course has moved into and preempted much of the narrative function, reducing the role of novel reading and all but killing off the once-thriving short story market. The legendary expatriate community in Europe is a thing of the past, and the *Paris Review* currently comes out of New York City.

Today's expatriates, by contrast, tend to be academic personnel. The American university, with its preprofessional and technical programs, has always been a prime means of social mobility (and status maintenance) for our bright or ambitious youth, but such became even more the case following World War II. Moreover, the campuses have remained, for better or for worse, the one major national setting where literature possesses anything resembling a steady, visible, material existence—in the undergraduate curriculum but also in public lectures, poetry readings, and almost every subsidized journal from prestigious quarterlies such as *Salmagundi* to single-number student magazines. There is also flexible time for writing, and hence, not surprisingly, many poets and novelists want jobs on campus, where most critics are already payrolled.

At the same time the past five decades saw unprecedented growth in the research and graduate school branches of higher learning, which in literature signified a vast expansion in the critical department and a proliferation of schools of criticism, oftentimes at the expense of literature itself. Whereas the onetime "service" functions of the critic—reviewing current verse and fiction, keeping up with new writing, shaping tastes—came to be regarded as quaintly journalistic, outdated, and dull, the methodologies for reading past texts still continue to generate more catechists and to further multiply themselves. Likewise the old-fashioned role of the public critic, who ranged freely over political and social as well as literary topics, eventually succumbed to the profusion of formalist sects that, both in principle and in dead earnest, isolated the art from real-life issues.[11]

The end result is that a literary criticism of, by, and for professors has flourished by the bushels on academic grounds, and that most serious critics and aspiring theorists-in-training tend to read more crit. than lit. Concerns about the divergent "two cultures" of natural science and humanities, first raised by C. P. Snow in the 1950s, now must deal with a second rift, between the highly aestheticized rococo of the literary gallants on one hand, and the positivistic, quantitative baroque of social science technocrats on the other. But there is also the more recent blurring of boundaries, the growing fashion for regarding history, anthropology, or law as if they too were literary genres, irrespective of questions of fact and falsehood. Such is the outcome of the aestheticist and Modernist legacy in an Age of Criticism.

Despite the grandeur of our academic baroque, with its participants in the lower five figures on at least hundreds of U.S. campuses, it is for the most part a strictly local phenomenon, just one more special-interest group jockeying for position within the great American pluralith. The very same period, by contrast, has witnessed the rise of Latin American literature, in which the experimenting ethos of Modernism has combined with a passion to create works that address those urgent historical, political, and existential realities too large for garden-variety aestheticisms to contain or do justice to. The poetry of Neruda, Vallejo, Nicolás Guillén, and Paz, and the narratives of Borges, Rulfo, Carpentier, Cortázar, García Márquez, Puig, Fuentes, Galeano, and the early Vargas Llosa (among others) all carry on the artistic commitment to technical innovation, though not merely "for Art's Sake" but rather for a fuller vision of the truth and of human existence. These authors, thoroughly conversant with the Euro-American literary legacy, have at the same time made it their own, breathing new life into those traditions by adapting them to Latin American experiences and needs. Their work will long outlive the precious emanations of the critical priests who presume to a literary wisdom surpassing that of the poets and mere novelists.

In the late 1980s, literary studies in the United States began experiencing an important new shift in direction and contents—itself part of a larger change in U.S. literary demographics. By then, of course, the diverse post-Modern imports and their American equivalents had been institutionalized and become routine in university classrooms and publishing. Much as had happened with the New Criticism in the 1950s, deconstruction quickly crystallized into what Peter Brooks calls a "kind of textual exegesis, easy to learn and use because American literary studies have long had an exegetical bias."

Indeed, for many bright, with-it humanities majors and graduate students, deconstruction took on the qualities of "a brand of New Criticism in a new and more unconstrained form: a way of reading texts, without much context, in a kind of naked confrontation of reader and verbal art, in a 'democratic' classroom practice where the individual's response—what the individual made of the text— was the starting point for discussion." [12] The discourse in turn was disseminated and sustained by hundreds—even thousands—of scholars whose publications either expatiated on the theory or exercised it with all sorts of writings, canonical and otherwise, literary or not.

In the meantime, however, some of the more restless, broader-ranging minds were feeling constrained by the limits of these formalisms, by the numbing "erasure" of history and politics from U.S. literary thinking since 1945. Applying what they had been learning about the role of textual discourse and the power of representations in human culture, they began producing works that redefine the literary past as well as their own respective disciplines. While no single term can as yet sum up this newer current, one can point to the wide variety of subsects such as New Historicism (or, cultural poetics); cultural studies; "postcolonial," ethnic, and feminist studies; the complex Marxism of Fredric Jameson; and the many combinations of the race-class-gender triad.

Marxist sorts of ideas, in fact, are generally taken for granted by these scholars, though their set of references tends rather toward, say, Foucault, Gramsci, Bakhtin, and the Frankfurt school, whose investigations focus not so much on matters of class politics and economics as on those softer, less strictly quantifiable mediating structures like language, folklore, or ideology, and on more specific institutional practices like medicine or sexual mores. In addition, Benedict Anderson's unclassifiable, even novel account of the intellectual construction of nationhood, *Imagined Communities,* has furnished a way of seeing modern-day nation building as a cultural (and not merely governmental and military) process. "The Imaginary," we are being reminded, is the realm not only of the arts but of every other human pursuit, is indeed a key component of our shared humanity.

Some of these studies have become classics of their kind, notably the work of Edward Said, whose *Orientalism* (1978), a pathbreaking investigation into the higher discourses on the Near East fashioned by Western humanists and "policy scientists," has also succeeded (through its stark, simple title) in giving common currency and a new meaning to a quaint, old-fashioned noun. His more recent *Culture and Imperialism* (1993) offers a veritable encyclopedia of the ways in which the great nineteenth-century European novelists (and composers such as Verdi) overlapped and interacted with the imperial enterprise both in their lives and in their products, yet is also a useful, up-to-date look at those Third World authors who have been "writing back" (by analogy with "talking back") to their colonial ex-masters.

The term "New Historicism" was coined by Stephen Greenblatt to describe his own wide-ranging and in-depth reexaminations of the English Renaissance. Breaking new ground in what has traditionally been a rather staid academic field, Greenblatt situates Shakespeare within the world context of early European expansion and conquest overseas, and he sees in the great plays the "textual traces" of cultural borrowings and exchange from that era. Writing with unusual grace and eloquence, with a poet's flair and an almost novelistic eye for revealing detail, Greenblatt speaks for "those who love literature," particularly the works of "the supremely gifted alumnus of the Stratford grammar school"; yet at the same time he finds in the Shakespearean oeuvre "a sublime confrontation between a total artist and a totalizing society."[13] Greenblatt's professed love and enthusiasms have not spared him hostile and simplistic charges of reductionism from the right; his ideas in fact prompted an attack from columnist George Will, who accuses such scholarship of "draining culture of its dignity." (In yet another incarnation of Art for Art's Sake, Will nobly invokes "the autonomy of culture.")[14]

Following in these newly blazed trails, younger scholars have gone on to rediscover and map out hitherto unstudied regions of human endeavor (whether autonomous or not). Thomas Richards in *The Commodity Culture of Victorian England* brings off a masterful series of readings of the Crystal Palace Catalog, the Jubilee celebrations of Queen Victoria, the cults of empire, the patent medicine industry, and the "seaside girl" icon of consumer product ads (who was in turn re-created as Gerty MacDowell in Joyce's *Ulysses*). Similarly, Rosalind Williams's *Notes on the Underground* conjures up not a Dostoyevskian universe but an earthbound and literal one: the growth of the geological and archaeological sciences; the exhuming of the sphinx and of ancient Troy; the excavations for modern canals, sewers, and telephone lines; and, last but not least, the vivid imaginings of subterranean worlds by novelists as diverse as Jules Verne and E. M. Forster.

The field of Latin American literature particularly has reaped some excellent works of synthesis—not surprisingly, inasmuch as Latin America is a continent where those grand topics of European expansion and empire, postcolonialism and nationalism, and class, race, and patriarchy all jointly intersect. Francine Masiello in *Between Civilization and Barbarism* and Nicolas Shumway in *The Invention of Argentina* expertly turn their telescopes and microscopes on the foundational role played by literary intellectuals, Creole notables, and women writers in shaping the young Argentine republic. And Margarita Zamora's *Reading Columbus* examines the navigational diaries of the eponymous admiral for the rhetorical conventions and mental paradigms of his era, and brings to her analysis an astounding panoply of geographical, nautical, and cartographic knowledge. Impressive amounts of archival research, incidentally, have gone into the making of these volumes—yet one more sign that certain segments of the literary studies profession have put behind them the obsessive aestheticism and purely internal approaches that prevailed during the cold war era.

Indeed, the onset of these and countless kindred books comes almost as a surprise, given the dogmatically formalist, ahistorical focus that, until the 1980s, had characterized U.S. literary thinking, from the southern New Critics on through later importations out of Canada, France, and Germany. The new trends do not fall from nowhere, however; they have a distinctly definable social base and cultural setting. The intellectual revolt of the 1960s eventually cleared the way for prolonged forays into what had at one time been dismissed as merely extrinsic or extraliterary issues. In addition, the expansion of educational opportunities and greater equality for women in the 1960s and after served as a necessary precondition for the flowering of feminist theory—for the spawning of fresh, luminous works such as Gilbert and Gubar's *The Madwoman in the Attic,* and for gender-inflected studies even of male authors, such as Tamar Heller's *Dead Secrets,* in which Wilkie Collins's novels are placed within the generic tradition of "buried writing" that typified the "female Gothic" imagination.

The national and international context was also shifting. The change in immigrant quotas effected under Presidents Kennedy and Johnson, whereby applicants from the Third World were to be considered on an equal basis with those from Europe, as well as the struggles of the various ethnic movements of the 1960s, led to a diversification of the student body and professoriate that is still in process today. With citizens of Asian, Hispanic, or African origin becoming a sizable presence in U.S. life and in our gigantic postsecondary education system, the emergence of other writing voices—Chinese American, Hindu American, African American, U.S.-Latino, and Native American (the last of whom are of course unique in *not* being immigrants)—was all but inevitable. The prolonged war in Indochina, moreover, had imparted something of a Third World consciousness among these groups, while the Latin American boom in narrative helped demonstrate that great literature was possible outside the traditionally white European orbit.

This upsurge in non-European and gendered thinking comprises what has become known as multiculturalism in some instances, identity politics in others. Though prompting the ire of the right, each of these trends has much that is recognizably American about it: the cult of pluralism ("E Pluribus Unum"), but also the rage for individual or group autonomy ("Just let me be!"). Both, moreover, inevitably filled the spiritual vacuum left by the fading of melting-pot myths during the 1960s, and by the retreat and quiescence of the communitarian, New Deal–based, national dream of social justice for all, a grand narrative that, since 1981, has come under ever-increasing assault by a combative and triumphant free market, "libertarian" ideology.

Multiculturalism and identity politics are but the latest installment in a cultural process that has gone hand in hand with U.S. growth and higher education since the nineteenth century. The emergence of a Jewish American middle class after 1945, for example, made possible the rise of Jewish American novelists (Bellow, Malamud, Philip Roth) along with the legitimation of academic studies of the Holocaust during those decades. Concerning education, Gerald Graff tells of the continuing shifts in the humanities curriculum: the Greco-Latin studies that dominated the classical colleges of the early republic, the arrival of the modern languages on the academic scene, the importation of Germanic philology, the accepting of American literature in the classroom (as part of U.S. expansionism and war in 1898 and 1917), the teaching of Modernism, and the inclusion of living authors on reading lists. Such developments were all seen as inimical to true learning by the traditionalists of that time—until the newcomers themselves won out, only to become orthodoxy and be challenged in turn by the following generation.[15]

What is perhaps different about the multicultural moment is its having come at a time when U.S. wealth and power are in slow decline, and when the golden age of sustained, overall growth for the American university seems definitively over. The gains made by the various multicultural constituencies are hence precarious and subject to possible shrinkage and loss, due either to political force or to economic considerations.

In the meantime, major contributions and advances, resulting in part from the multiculturalist drift, can be singled out on the literary-artistic front. The rediscovery of Zora Neale Hurston would have been less than likely without both the civil rights surge and the subsequent rise of a critical mass of minority and female scholars in the 1970s and 1980s. (For an analogy, one might think of the rehabilitation of Melville and of John Donne at the time of the Modernist revolution.) Similarly, works of fiction by Sandra Cisneros, Cristina García, and Oscar Hijuelos have widened and further enriched the range of American narrative, while the opening of a jazz department at Lincoln Center in New York City is a major step in bestowing official recognition on a musical tradition long neglected in the country of its origin.

Of course there are multiculturalist abuses, plenty of instances of dogmatism, poor judgment, and just plain silliness in identity politics thinking—just as was the case, *mutatis mutandi,* during the heyday of aestheticist and formalist hegemony in the academy. Reductive formulas about "phallocentrism" probably crop up in numbers no greater than at one time obtained with erstwhile buzzwords on the order of "tone" and "archetype." That mediocre writers, past and present, who happen to be women or non-European are studied and sometimes hailed solely on account of their gender or their Third World backgrounds is an inevitable side effect of this new wave of pedagogy and scholarship, though no more objectionable, perhaps, than are such honored and reputable activities as teaching minor Jacobean playwrights, or specializing in lesser male Victorian lyrists, or, in another era, praising every Russian writer whose chief authorial virtue was the courage to criticize the Soviet regime.

Meanwhile, since the mid-1970s, terms such as "representation," "articulation," and "signification" have become the preferred technical parlance in literary criticism, at the expense of the more old-fashioned words "depiction," "portrayal," "expression," and others, now thought of as ingenuous. (There is even a fine academic journal called *Representations.*) The focus, while highly technical and impersonal, still nonetheless tends to fall squarely on medium and signifiers rather than on message and signifieds, on the "how" rather than on the "what" or (perish the thought) the "who," on the windowpane rather than on the garden outside, to cite Ortega y Gasset once again.

It is hardly surprising that this theoretical emphasis on the process of representation should come at a time when the very means of representation—the media—are being developed and marketed at a dizzying rate. The familiar list since 1945 comprises, for example, 33-and 45-rpm recordings, high fidelity, stereophony, quadrophony, compact disks; wire recording, audiotape (reel-to-reel, eight-track, and cassettes); Muzak, the Walkman, electric instruments, synthesizers; black-and-white, color, cable, and high-definition TV; widescreen, three-dimensional, and multiplex cinemas; videotape, videocassettes, home video players and recorders, camcorders, videodiscs, and video games; multiple-capability and portable telephones; electric and electronic typewriters; CD-ROM; covered shopping malls; the vast and ever growing worlds of communication via satellite, of electronic storage and retrieval of information, of computer software; hypertext; virtual reality; and much, much more.

The information revolution, as some experts call it; or "the society of mass consumption" that is global utopia in the eyes of Walt Rostow and the Pyramid Malls corporation; or, my own preference, Fredric Jameson's phrase "the media society": however we designate the phenomenon, it amounts to a new phase in the history of industrial capitalism. Surrounded as we are by a myriad of mass-produced, readily available representations, we tend to forget how few were such means throughout most of the nineteenth century: industrialized print (books, the daily press), the telegraph, and still photography. That really was about all, for the bulk of large-scale technical advances during that time continued to be in the areas of manufacturing and transport. To produce and reproduce acceptable, lasting images required long, hard labors before the full development of the modern camera, and the use of photographs in journalism did not become commonplace until the 1920s. Mass distribution of a recorded voice or symphony was still in the future, and quality sound even further away — the 1950s, to be exact.

The first half of the twentieth century saw the growth and spread of those media — the telephone, moving pictures, phonographs, and radio — that served as the experiential bases for much of what followed. The changes since 1945 have been exponential and dramatic, and today words, sounds, and images beyond counting, most of them technically well reproduced, can be conjured up by the flick of a switch or a button. The cultural habitat in our opulent, "developed" north is a manmade, artificial jungle of simulacra, a force expanding as fast as the natural, biological jungles of vegetation in the south are shrinking. And with satellite transmission the sky's the limit, literally.

In all, it is a qualitative leap from the classic, productivist, nineteenth-century capitalism of coal and iron, steel and textiles, so powerfully and famously anatomized by Karl Marx. It is a total market in which potentially every inch of space we gaze at, the very air's invisible waves, and the human sensorium itself are up for grabs, and what is sold is not so much palpable goods as assorted pleasures, or dreams and promises thereof. George Orwell in *1984* raised the specter of universal surveillance by Big Brother, watching each one of us over the telescreen. History, however, has played the trick of reversing Orwell's prophecy: throughout much of our world, people of all socioeconomic levels are subtly urged, coaxed, persuaded, pressured, and otherwise conditioned to watch, listen, and tune in to the media's infinite verbal, aural, and visual panoply—the inescapable Muzak and the ubiquitous TV that Americans watch on the average of six hours per day at home or at the bar (and leave switched on for even longer).

It is a transformation, moreover, whose political consequences are only partly understood, though we do know that whoever controls a society's representational media also has substantial control over the direction and operation of those media and, by extension, of the larger society itself. To cite a concrete instance: in Western European countries, until recently, TV was run entirely by the state, which permitted only a fixed number of channels, disallowed broadcasting in the mornings, and to this day limits advertising to the time slots between programs. In direct contrast, in a free market society like that of the United States, the only limits on TV scheduling, channels, and commercials have been the available technology and "what the market will bear."

Living as we do in a wilderness of replicas, there have been theorists, from media guru Marshall McLuhan (a onetime Agrarian literary disciple and Modernist literary critic) on down to poststructuralist philosophers like Jean Baudrillard, who claim in so many words that there is no reality out there, that reality per se does not exist, that the only reality *is* representations.[16] To such thinkers and their many followers, reality qualifies as something fictional—"virtual," as it were. This confusion between simulacra and source can be found at all levels of our baroque society. Prior to his career in politics, the entire professional history of Ronald Reagan had been in media—first as a radio sports announcer, then as grade B actor for the California studios, finally as TV publicist for General Electric. Having gone on to become the first full-fledged Media President of any nation, during his press conferences and other public appearances Reagan, as is well known, was given to alluding in great earnest to powerful world events that in fact were no more than episodes from Hollywood movies.[17]

Much the same tendency, though with a more sophisticated software, cropped up in the world of literary criticism, where buzz-phrases such as "History is a fiction," "Truths are fictions," and "There is no foundation" gained maturity, prestige, and the status of conventional wisdom in the 1970s and 1980s. Even some years before the Americanization of deconstruction, when Northrop Frye witnessed in person the violent People's Park clashes in Berkeley, California, he saw in them not tear gas or broken heads, but such mythic archetypes as the expulsion from Eden and the murder of Abel.[18]

To other theorists on the campuses or in broadcasting, a riot can appear to be just another "story." And while relativism long preceded the rise of the media society (as we saw in Pater and Wilde, chapter 3), today's infinity of available representations and "perspectives" further encourages this sort of thinking. (During the 1992 riots in Los Angeles, mothers reportedly had to inform their children that the images on TV were not a movie but reality, live.) Meanwhile the old notion that certain narrative representations (denials of the Holocaust, say) are simply wrong, and hence that falsehood and misrepresentation exist, is politely ignored or not taken seriously. In all probability it will take some generalized crisis on U.S. soil, some terrible, cataclysmic reminder of reality, to bring the whole array of relativistic and antifoundationalist ideas into question. As Argentine critic Ana María Barrenechea once observed in a riposte to her compatriot Jaime Alazraki: for the victims of police torture, history is not a fiction.[19]

The sense that we stand at the end of a process and are in the throes of beginning another is suggested in the divers "post-" locutions burgeoning in our day—"postindustrial," "post-Modern," and "post–cold war" being the most familiar instances. In postindustrial society, we are told, "information" replaces "production" as the main thrust of the economy—hence the primacy of computer chips and data processing, rather than sheet metal or auto manufacture.[20] The reality, it goes without saying, is much more complex. Many key U.S. "smokestack industries" have either moved their production plants abroad or have rested on past laurels and lost out to foreign competition. At the same time the U.S. "communications revolution" has moved to fill the vacuum, becoming the latest bulk production industry, the one segment of the world civilian economy (along with aerospace) that remains dominated by American business: the notorious mass culture of technorock music, Hollywood and TV entertainments, and pulp paperbacks, but also such higher-level sectors as news production services, computers and software development, translated textbooks, graduate schools in science and engineering and management, and the like.

Information is no doubt being produced, and by the megaton, though much of it in its rawest, most fragmented and undigested form. On the tube and in the glossies there is *information* aplenty about weather, stocks, wrestling, sailing, bridal wear, golf, stereos, cutlery, soap operas, physical fitness, duck hunting, handguns, home furnishings, shopping opportunities, personal computers, and every special interest imaginable. This does not mean, however, that there is necessarily a great deal more *knowledge* (other than of a strictly cumulative or purely technical kind); nor is there all that much more *understanding* of the world we live in, let alone a legitimate *wisdom*. The years of the Reagan presidency in fact made know-nothingism respectable, glamorous, even cute, and there were reporters who found Reagan's ignorance an endearing trait.

For certain post-Modern aesthetes, of course, "knowledge," "understanding," and the rest are themselves illusions; and the lack of concrete information in their own highly speculative texts aptly emblematizes their turn of mind. Still, if a society is first of all stupid or demented or idiot savant in its dominant drift, then its communications media, from the giant networks to the tiniest quarterlies, will mostly tend to reflect, reinforce, romanticize, and otherwise "represent" the reigning stupidities or dementia or idiot savantry. To a certain extent, people get the media they deserve, and our society gets some truly sophisticated stupidity. Garbage in, garbage out (GIGO), as computer hackers like to say. Or, in the wise words of Bruce Springsteen, "Fifty-seven channels and nothin' on." [21] The nothingness will further expand when the channels grow to five hundred.

As we saw in chapter 5, literary life in the United States had already begun its inexorable move to the university by the 1920s. Along with postwar social developments and the growth of the media society, the ensconcement of literature in a safe haven on the campuses is now so common as to constitute a norm. In the larger nation beyond the ivied walls, accordingly, print culture has become little more than an "arts and leisure" adjunct to the information economy, the software section of the entertainment industries.[22] And even as the media churn out infinite supplies of "just entertainment," much of the academy presents poetry and fiction, old and new, as "just art" or "just texts." (Entertainment for Entertainment's Sake and Art for Art's Sake may indeed represent differing aspects of the same phenomenon.)

The drift is reflected even in our taxation categories. Schedule C, the federal form for filing profit (or loss) on a small business, has on its reverse side a long list of economic activities, each with a numerical code, from which the taxpayer chooses one and places it in the appropriate box. While there are separate categories for "Motion picture & video production" (no. 9597) and for "Theatrical performers, musicians, . . . & related services" (no. 9811), there is none for "Writer" or "Artist." The only code that remotely describes these professions is no. 9837, "Other amusement and recreational services."

This broad set of tendencies can also be seen currently even in a mass medium such as film. Since the late 1980s, the majority of the movie houses in the Boston area have passed into the hands of only two conglomerates. The result is that, as of this writing, the theater marquees list mostly the same, safe, Hollywood fare, with only slight variations. In compensation, premier screenings of foreign or of offbeat American films are regularly picked up by the art museums or the universities (notably Harvard). Given capital concentration and urban gentrification, coupled with a lack of major public funding for the arts in the United States, the academicizing trend is inevitable.

Meanwhile it is quite possible that, for reasons already cited, the glory days both of novelistic preeminence and of freewheeling literary Bohemia are temporarily over, and equally possible that quality prose fiction will assume a marginality comparable in kind if not in degree to that of verse during the nineteenth century. Of course, the advent of some future upheaval, such as large-scale economic dislocation or protracted war, would generate a demand for newer sorts of literary chroniclers, lyrists, and thinkers (as happened in Germany and Latin America in the 1950s and 1960s). At this point, however, an eerie stagnation and slow deterioration, equally sustained and confounded by a relentlessly triumphalist ideology ("We are the greatest country in the world!"), seems more the order of the day. Within this ongoing scenario, somewhat analogous to that of a later Imperial Spain and perhaps not the worst of human situations, many literary-critical minds have celebrated the very marginality of literature and insisted on its self-contained role as text, sign, and discourse—the most recent installment, we have seen, in the history of the ideology of Art for Art's Sake. We could not be more distant from what was intended by Kant and Schiller, for whom art and the aesthetic were but one, though essential, aspect in our growth as human beings.

When I originally took up this project in 1974, my aim was to write a book on the question of literature and society. Having come intellectually of age in the decade of the 1960s, I was at the time profoundly weary of the assorted formalisms that, to my view, kept verse and fiction cut off and at a lofty remove from the rest of human experience. For my initial working plan I envisioned a chapter or so dealing with aestheticism as the historically recent, locally based (that is, Western) conception of literature it happens to be. As the chapters expanded and multiplied, I came to realize that a full-length volume, focused exclusively on the changing issues surrounding Art for Art's Sake and aesthetic separatism, would be necessary. In the meantime a whole new generation of imported and domestic formalisms had been moving into the academy, dislodging the old, and some comment would hence be required on the matter of their place within aestheticism's longer history.

The final result, some nineteen years, two scholarly books, and one published novel later, is this incomplete and far from perfect volume. Every book has its gaps, and I cannot lay claim to any exception here. Time and constraints of background have not allowed for sections, say, on Russia and Central Europe, or Argentina and Brazil. And for some important Anglophone authors like Poe, Pater, and Wilde, I rely mostly on the established secondary sources, even if at the expense of more recent and venturesome investigations such as Jonathan Dollimore's *Sexual Dissidence.*

After a certain point, however, one must simply draw the line on reading and get on with the writing, if only to avoid the trap of imitating Casaubon in *Middlemarch,* whose interminable researches for his grandiose *Key to All Mythologies* yielded not a single line of prose from his pen. Moreover, the narrative profile sketched in the foregoing pages is, I trust, sufficiently accurate and fruitful to provide leads for the further study of *l'art pour l'art* within the context of other national literatures or the work of other writers. Indeed, for all its limits, this book is, to my knowledge, the first consciously *comparative* overview of aestheticist doctrine as it has reshaped itself in differing countries and times throughout its gradual process of diffusion. Like neoclassicism in previous eras, Art for Art's Sake has been international in its range of influence.

I have learned many things in the process of preparing this book, not the least of them being a new respect for the poets and novelists who faced a constant struggle simply to be the kind of writers they felt best suited to be. For many of those authors, the doctrine of Art for Art's Sake, whatever they chose to call it, provided a kind of metaphor serving obliquely to define and sum up their struggle.

What has perhaps proved most rewarding about researching aestheticism, however, has been the opportunity to go back to the roots of the ideology and locate its intellectual origins in the Enlightenment, particularly in Kant and Schiller. Though generally associated with nineteenth-century literary cultures from Romanticism on through the English 1890s, Art for Art's Sake, as it turns out, has its ultimate foundations in the eighteenth-century critical ferment that led up to the two great liberal revolutions, the consequences of which we are still living today. After having once followed custom and defined aestheticism exclusively in its separatist version, I found it enormously refreshing to discover that the doctrine actually came about as a misreading of Kant and Schiller, those humanistic and dissident optimists for whom the aesthetic belonged within the framework of our total growth and development as individual and social beings. It was a bit like going back to the original texts of a religion and realizing that the priesthood by and large had been misinterpreting them.

And yet, despite the richer understanding I have gained of aestheticism in its many incarnations, my original conception of the doctrine as just one idea of art among a possible many has remained central to my thinking. Flaubert's novelistic form and prose style are no doubt a human achievement deserving of admiration, but they can prove confining to our other needs as readers. Balzac's work, by contrast, with its raw vitality and profound knowledge of human society, provides attractions, satisfactions, and uses of its own, despite the author's flaws of execution and lapses in taste. A diet consisting of nothing but artistic perfection has its limits too; Art for Art's Sake, though a legitimate yardstick, is neither absolute nor universal.

Aestheticism, however much certain of its adherents have attempted to negate history, is itself a participant in history, and, as with other human endeavors and doctrines, it forms part of economic, political, and cultural developments. And while those so involved would reject the rubric, the ideology of late has spread to such an extent as to become manifest as Criticism for Criticism's Sake and Media for Media's Sake. The story of Art for Art's Sake is not concluded . . .

NOTES

1. "Literature shapes itself, and is not shaped externally." Frye, *Anatomy of Criticism*, p.97.

2. De Man, *Blindness and Insight*; White, *Metahistory*; Levinson, "Law as Literature." See also rebuttal by Graff, " 'Keep Off the Grass,' 'Drop Dead,' and Other Indeterminacies: A Response to Sanford Levinson."

3. Benjamin, "The Work of Art," p.242. For a pertinent discussion of morality and art in narrative, see Booth, *The Rhetoric of Fiction*, pp. 397–98.

4. Moore, *Confessions of a Young Man*, pp.106–7; emphasis added.

5. Nabokov, *Strong Opinions*, passim.

6. As in the case of the otherwise monumental book by Wimsatt and Brooks, *Literary Criticism*, 2:476–98.

7. Guérard, *Art for Art's Sake*, pp.xiv and 34.

8. Cassagne, *La théorie de l'art*, pp.6. Rosenblatt, *L'idée de l'art*, pp.15–43.

9. Wilcox, "The Beginnings of *l'art pour l'art*," p.361.

10. Egan, *The Genesis of the Theory of "Art for Art's Sake" in Germany and England*, passim.

11. Plekhanov, *Art and Social Life*, pp.11 and 45; excerpted in Lang and Williams, *Marxism and Art*, pp.88 and 94.

12. See Solomon, *Marxism and Art*, p.238.

1. Scott, *Francis Hutcheson*, pp.149–52.

2. Shaftesbury, *Characteristics*. All page references are made in the body of the text.

3. Abrams convincingly traces both Shaftesbury's ideas and vocabulary to neo-Platonist thought and to early Christian theology, notably to that of St. Augustine. See Abrams, "Art-as-Such," in *Doing Things with Texts*, pp.154–55. These ancient origins of course do not negate what is new and distinctive in Shaftesbury's ethics.

4. Hutcheson, *An Inquiry into the Original of Our Ideas of Beauty and Virtue*. Page references are made in the body of the text.

5. Cited in Burke, *A Philosophical Enquiry*, p.xxvii.

6. Cassirer, *Philosophy of the Enlightenment*, p.347.

7. Abrams argues that, in spite of its logical baggage and Latin expository prose, Baumgarten's theory of poetry makes him "a Continental Formal-

ist, and . . . a New Critic, *avant la lettre*—by some two hundred years." See his "From Addison to Kant: Modern Aesthetics and the Exemplary Art," in *Doing Things with Texts*, p.175.

8. Cassirer, *Philosophy of the Enlightenment*, p.275.
9. Wimsatt and Brooks, *Literary Criticism*, 2:381.
10. Kant, *Critique of Pure Reason*. All page references are made in the body of the text.
11. Cited in Cassirer, *Kant's Life and Thought*, pp.235–36.
12. Cited in Cassirer, *Kant's Life and Thought*, p.52; emphasis in the original.
13. Kant, *Critique of Practical Reason*. All page references are made in the body of the text.
14. Kant, *Critique of Judgment*. All page references are made in the body of the text.
15. Engell, *The Creative Imagination*, pp.129–39.
16. Schiller, *On the Aesthetic Education of Man* (Ungar edition). The number of the letter quoted, followed by page reference, is indicated in the body of the text.
17. Marcuse, *Eros and Civilization*, p.174.
18. Ewing, *Short Commentary on Kant's* Critique of Pure Reason, p.10.
19. Mill, *Autobiography*. Page references are made in the body of the text.
20. Koch, *Wishes, Lies, and Dreams*, p.53.
21. Koch, *Rose, Where Did You Get That Red?*, pp.28–29; emphasis added.

CHAPTER 2

1. For a pioneering account of this historical process, see Wilcox, "The Beginnings of *l'art pour l'art*," an essay to which I am much indebted.
2. Constant, *Journal intime*, p.8; my translation.
3. Staël, *Germany*. Page references to this work are included within the body of the text.
4. Simon, *Victor Cousin*, pp.14–15.
5. Janet, *Victor Cousin et son oeuvre*, pp.28–35.
6. Simon, *Victor Cousin*, pp.17–22.
7. Simon, *Victor Cousin*, p.80.
8. Janet, *Victor Cousin et son oeuvre*, p.181.
9. Hugo, *Les Orientales*, 1:5, 8, 10.
10. Hugo, *Cromwell*, pp.444, 451; my translation.
11. Hugo, *Hernani*, p.1147; my translation.
12. Graña, *Modernity and Its Discontents*, p.46.
13. Cited in Allen, *Popular French Romanticism*, p.89.
14. Graña, *Modernity and Its Discontents*, p.37.

15. Grolier, *Histoire du livre*, p.93.
16. Grolier, *Histoire du livre*, p.114. George, *The Development of French Romanticism*, pp.19–22. Clair, *A History of Printing in Britain*, p.208. Allen, *Popular French Romanticism*, p.112.
17. Allen, *Popular French Romanticism*, pp.127–28.
18. Polanyi, *The Great Transformation*, p.41.
19. Cassagne, *La théorie de l'art*, pp.19–20.
20. Graña, *Modernity and Its Discontents*, p.34.
21. Cited in Allen, *Popular French Romanticism*, p.96.
22. Graña, *Modernity and Its Discontents*, p.34.
23. Cassagne, *La théorie de l'art*, p.21.
24. Jakobson, "Linguistics and Poetics," pp.85–122.
25. Horace, "On the Art of Poetry," pp.80, 89.
26. Boileau, *L'art poétique*, Chant premier, lines 163–74, p.74.
27. Braverman, *Labor and Monopoly Capital*, passim.
28. *Baudelaire as a Literary Critic*, pp.315–17.
29. Gautier, *Mademoiselle de Maupin*, French version, p.253; my translation.
30. Allen, *Popular French Romanticism*, p.131.
31. Page 12.
32. Seigel, *Bohemian Paris*, pp.130, 215–41.
33. Seigel, *Bohemian Paris*, p.132.
34. Baudelaire, *The Flowers of Evil*, p.240; translation of the quote is my own.
35. Balzac, *Lost Illusions*, pp.214, 367.
36. Sartre, *The Family Idiot*, 3:368.
37. In a creative writing course at Stanford University, Nabokov "exhorted his students to defy the American tyranny of the marketplace." He saw little difference between "the Soviet literature of social command" and "the American best-sellers designed to satisfy the desires of the mass market." Boyd, *Vladimir Nabokov: The American Years*, pp.32, 96.
38. Cited in Marx and Engels, *Literature and Art*, p.28.
39. Carrel, "D'un commencement." See also the discussion of key passages from Carrel in Wilcox, pp.373–74.
40. Saint-Cheron, "De la direction," p.269.
41. Charléty, *Histoire du Saint-Simonisme*, p.357.
42. Saint-Simon, *The Doctrine: An Exposition*, pp.18, 240.
43. Fortoul, "De l'art actuel," pp.108–10.
44. Rousseau, review of *Chants de la Révolution de 1830*, p.436.
45. Carrel, "D'un commencement," p.4.
46. Gautier, preface to *Mademoiselle de Maupin*, English version. Page references are made in the body of the text.

47. Mallarmé, "Quant au livre," pp.179, 185, 188. I have slightly altered Hartley's translations.

48. Page 196.

CHAPTER 3

1. De Tocqueville, *The Old Régime*, pp.5, 6, 149, 156–57.

2. Cobban, *History of Modern France*, 2:81, 82, 86.

3. Thompson, *The Making of the English Working Class*, p.175.

4. Thompson, *The Making of the English Working Class*, pp.174–78. See also Trevelyan, *History of England*, pp.662–68, 684, 738; and Chew, "The Nineteenth Century," pp.1114–19.

5. Thompson, *The Making of the English Working Class*, pp.377, 379, 381, 388–89.

6. Rubinstein, *The Great Tradition*, pp.411–55.

7. Cited in McNiece, *Shelley and the Revolutionary Idea*, pp.135–36. See also Rubinstein, *The Great Tradition*, pp.518–50.

8. Gittings, *John Keats*, p.52.

9. Gittings, *John Keats*, pp.355–56. *The Letters of John Keats*, 2:176, 178–80.

10. Rosenblatt, *L'idée de l'art*, pp.15–36, 42–43.

11. Gaunt, *The Aesthetic Adventure*, pp.16, 17.

12. Coleridge, *Biographia Literaria*, pp.88, 173.

13. See chapter 2.

14. Shelley, *A Defence of Poetry*. Page references are cited in the body of the text.

15. Bell, *Ruskin*, p.142.

16. Ellmann, *Oscar Wilde*, p.48.

17. Cited in Bell, *Ruskin*, pp.22, 41.

18. Hough, *The Last Romantics*, pp.11–12.

19. Cited in Buckley, *The Victorian Temper*, p.149; Hough, *The Last Romantics*, p.13.

20. Cited in Ruskin, *The Seven Lamps of Architecture*, p.122.

21. Ruskin, *The Seven Lamps of Architecture*, p.124.

22. Ruskin, "Modern Manufacture and Design," pp.223–24.

23. Ruskin, "The Squirrel Cage," in *Fors Clavigera*, p.399.

24. Ruskin, *The Stones of Venice*, p.180.

25. Gaunt, *The Aesthetic Adventure*, p.87.

26. For a fuller account of this episode, see Buckley, *The Victorian Temper*, pp.157–59.

27. Pater, "Style," p.110.

28. Introduction to *Selected Writings of Walter Pater*, pp.xv–xvi.

29. Gaunt, *The Aesthetic Adventure*, p.64.

30. Gaunt, *The Aesthetic Adventure*, pp.54–55. Wright, *The Life of Walter Pater*, 1:21, 33, 51–53, 64, 99, 110. Benson, *Walter Pater*, pp.2–5.

31. Wright, *The Life of Walter Pater*, 1:136–206.

32. Introduction to *Selected Writings of Walter Pater*, p.xxiv.

33. Pater, *Marius the Epicurean*. Page references appear in the body of the text.

34. Pater, "Coleridge," pp.143–44.

35. Pater, *The Renaissance*. Page references appear in the body of the text.

36. Cited in Benson, *Walter Pater*, p.48–49. The phrase was used in a review Pater wrote for *The Guardian*.

37. Cited in *Selected Writings of Walter Pater*, p.xxi.

38. Benson, *Walter Pater*, p.47.

39. Rosenblatt, *L'idée de l'art*, p.179.

40. Bloom, ed., *Selected Writings of Walter Pater*, pp.62–63, nn. 10, 13, 19; emphasis added.

41. Swinburne, "Dolores," cited in Buckley, *The Victorian Temper*, pp.172–73.

42. Swinburne, *Notes on Poems and Ballads*, pp.8, 9, and 10.

43. Swinburne, *William Blake*, pp.5, 6, and 4.

44. Page 10.

45. Hough, *The Last Romantics*, p.188.

46. Buckley, *The Victorian Temper*, p.222.

47. Gagnier, in *Idylls of the Marketplace*, p.8, notes that one of the goals of Wilde's comedies was "to be commercially competitive."

48. Cited in Ellmann, *Oscar Wilde*, pp.30–32, 19, 34, 93–94, 138–39, 583–84.

49. Cited in Ellmann, *Oscar Wilde*, p.50.

50. Wilde, "De Profundis," p.158.

51. Cited in Ellmann, *Oscar Wilde*, pp.83–85.

52. Wilde, "The Critic as Artist." Page references to this work are included in the text.

53. Wilde, "The Decay of Lying." Page references to this work are included within the text.

54. Freedman, *Professions of Taste*, p.31.

55. Freedman, *Professions of Taste*, p.72.

56. Cited in Ellmann, *Oscar Wilde*, p.372.

57. W. S. Gilbert, *Patience*, act 1, in Small, *The Aesthetes*, pp.178–79.

58. Neruda, "Oda a la crítica," in *Odas elementales*, pp.50–53.

CHAPTER 4

1. Thompson, "Edgar Allan Poe," pp.264–68.

2. Cited in Thompson, "Edgar Allan Poe," p.276.

3. Poe, *Literary Criticism of Edgar Allan Poe.* Page references from this volume appear within the body of the text.

4. Cited in Thompson, "Edgar Allan Poe," p.275.

5. Johnson, "Dreams of E. A. Poe," p.7.

6. Krutch, *Edgar Allan Poe.*

7. Parrington, *Main Currents,* 2:57–59.

8. Cited in Charvat, *The Profession of Authorship in America,* p.95.

9. Anderson-Imbert, *Historia,* 1:356.

10. Schulman, *Génesis del modernismo,* p.115. Henríquez Ureña, *Las corrientes literarias,* p.175.

11. Darío, *Obras completas;* translations mine. Page numbers from these volumes are provided within the body of the text.

12. Verlaine, *Oeuvres poétiques,* p.326.

13. Silva, *Obra Completa,* pp.35–37.

14. For a fine, lucid summation of *modernismo,* see Jean Franco, *An Introduction to Spanish-American Literature,* chap. 5.

15. Cited in Schulman, *Génesis del modernismo,* p.18.

16. Franco, *An Introduction to Spanish-American Literature,* pp.142, 124.

17. Quotations, including that in previous paragraph, are from Silva, *De sobremesa,* pp.134, 133, 138, 173, 286; translation mine.

18. Cited in Rama, *Rubén Darío,* p.63; translation mine.

19. For a summary of positivism on the Continent, see Davis, *Latin American Thought,* pp.97–134.

20. For a discussion of *científico* ideology during the Porfiriato regime, see Womack, *Zapata and the Mexican Revolution.*

21. Paz, *El laberinto de la soledad,* p.120.

22. Pérus, *Literatura y sociedad,* p.135.

23. Rama, *Rubén Darío y el modernismo,* pp.43, 86, 88.

24. Lévi-Strauss, *Tristes Tropiques,* pp.105–07.

25. Rama, *Los poetas modernistas,* p.8.

26. Pérus, *Literatura y sociedad,* pp.102, 118, 120, 129.

27. Rama, *Rubén Darío y el modernismo,* p.69.

28. Cited in Rama, *Rubén Darío y el modernismo,* p.70.

29. Cited in Rama, *Rubén Darío y el modernismo,* pp.51 and 55.

30. Cited in Rama, *Rubén Darío y el modernismo,* p.73.

31. Rama, *Rubén Darío y el modernismo,* pp.63, 73–74.

32. Cited in Rama, *Rubén Darío y el modernismo,* pp.76–77.

33. Rodó, *Ariel.* Page numbers of quotations from this book are included parenthetically within the text; translations mine.

34. Cited in Schulman, "Modernismo/modernidad," p.5.

CHAPTER 5

1. Ortega y Gasset, *The Dehumanization of Art*, p.10.
2. Frank, "Spatial Form," pp.15, 16, 59.
3. In their videotape *Text/Tiles, Jujol/Gaudí*, Christ and Dollens demonstrate that Jujol anticipated the cubists by a good number of years in his ceramic work at Park Güell. Picasso would most probably have been familiar with these artifacts.
4. Stravinsky, *Poetics of Music*, p.34.
5. Williams, *Keywords*, pp.208–9.
6. Baudelaire, *Baudelaire as a Literary Critic*, p.82.
7. Trans. J. M. Cohen. Cited in Ellmann and Feidelson, *The Modern Tradition*, p.132.
8. Zola, "The Novel as Social Science," pp.271, 273.
9. Hughes, *The Shock of the New*, p.114.
10. Woolf, "Mr. Bennett and Mrs. Brown," p.72.
11. Woolf, "The Novel of Consciousness," pp.124–25.
12. Cited in Budgen, *James Joyce and the Making of Ulysses*, p.21.
13. Ellmann, *The Consciousness of Joyce*, p.76.
14. In Cather, *On Writing*. Page references to this volume are made in the body of the text.
15. See essay by Bernice Slote, "The Kingdom of Art," *passim*, in Cather, *The Kingdom of Art*, pp.31–112.
16. See discussion of Flaubert in chap. 6.
17. Mayer, *The Persistence of the Old Regime*, p.192.
18. Baudelaire, *Baudelaire as a Literary Critic*, pp.43–44.
19. Baudelaire, *Baudelaire as a Literary Critic*, p.45.
20. Bradbury, "The Cities of Modernism," pp.99–100.
21. Berman, *All That Is Solid Melts to Air*, pp.151, 158.
22. Clark, *The Painting of Modern Life*, pp.49, 63.
23. Clark, *The Painting of Modern Life*, p.56.
24. Bradbury, "The Cities of Modernism," p.100. Howe, "The Culture of Modernism," pp.4–5.
25. See Benjamin, *Charles Baudelaire*, passim.
26. Cited in Richardson, *Verlaine*, p.22.
27. Shattuck, *The Banquet Years*, p.24.
28. Cahm, "Revolt, Conservatism, and Reaction," pp.166–67.
29. Woolf, "The Novel of Consciousness," p.124.
30. Bradbury and McFarlane, "The Name and Nature of Modernism," p.29.
31. Eliot, "Tradition and the Individual Talent," in *Selected Poems*, pp.37–44.

32. In this connection, Stravinsky says of himself, "[I]t was wrong to have considered me a revolutionary. . . . [R]evolution is one thing, innovation another." *Poetics of Music,* p.13.

33. White and White, *Canvases and Careers.* Page references for this book are cited parenthetically within the text.

34. Sheppard, "The Crisis of Language," pp.327, 328, 330.

35. Calinescu, in *Five Faces of Modernity,* p.101, says that "the first important modern literary critic to make use of the term avant-garde in a figurative sense seems to have been Sainte-Beuve" in December 1856.

36. Bradbury and McFarlane, "Movements, Magazines, and Manifestos," pp. 202–4.

37. Shattuck, *The Banquet Years,* p.272.

38. See Willis, *Leonard and Virginia Woolf as Publishers,* passim.

39. The glorification of the inventor that characterizes Ayn Rand's *Atlas Shrugged* and her cultists is mostly an aggressive and ignorant pop romanticism.

40. Stravinsky, *The Poetics of Music,* p.53.

41. Poggioli, *The Theory of the Avant-Garde,* p.106.

42. Cohen, *Bukharin and the Bolshevik Revolution,* p.272.

CHAPTER 6

1. Cited in Berger, *The Success and Failure of Picasso,* p.34.

2. Eliot, introduction to *The Sacred Wood,* p.xiii.

3. Eliot, preface to *The Sacred Wood,* pp.viii, x.

4. Eliot, "Religion and Literature," pp.97–98.

5. Eliot, *On Poetry and Poets,* p.129.

6. Bürger, *Theory of the Avant-Garde,* pp.49–50; second emphasis is added. I have slightly altered Shaw's translation in the interests of contextual clarity.

7. Baudelaire, *Baudelaire as a Literary Critic.* All page references to the essays in this volume are made within the body of the text.

8. Flaubert, *The Selected Letters,* Steegmuller edition. Unless otherwise indicated, parenthetical page numbers within the text refer to this volume.

9. Trans. J. M. Cohen. In Ellmann and Feidelson, *The Modern Tradition,* p.72.

10. Cited in Ellmann and Feidelson, *The Modern Tradition,* p.195.

11. Cited in Ellmann and Feidelson, *The Modern Tradition,* p.197; emphasis in original.

12. Sartre, *The Family Idiot,* 3:487, 499; emphasis in original.

13. Cited in Ellmann and Feidelson, *The Modern Tradition,* p.72.

14. Flaubert, *Letters,* Rumbold edition, pp.151–52.

15. Vargas Llosa, *La orgía perpetua,* pp.245–57.

16. Flaubert, *Letters,* Rumbold edition, p.85.

17. Flaubert, *Letters,* Rumbold edition, p.234.

18. Joyce, *My Brother's Keeper,* pp.107–8.

19. Cited in Ellmann, *James Joyce,* p.710.

20. Cited in Budgen, *James Joyce and the Making of Ulysses,* p.176.

21. Joyce, *The Critical Writings.* All page references to this volume are made in the body of the text.

22. Joyce, *A Portrait of the Artist.* All page references to this volume are made in the body of the text.

23. Blades, *James Joyce,* p.42.

24. Blades, *James Joyce,* p.116.

25. Cited in Cowan, *The Fugitive Group,* p.44. Much of my account of the Fugitives is based on this book.

26. Ransom, *God without Thunder,* pp.177, 185.

27. Tate, *On the Limits of Poetry,* p.4.

28. Tate, *On the Limits of Poetry,* p.266.

29. Ransom, *The World's Body,* p.329.

30. Blackmur, "A Critic's Job of Work," p.339.

31. For my account of Nabokov's life I rely on Field, *Nabokov,* and Boyd, *Vladimir Nabokov,* both volumes.

32. "A work of art has no importance whatever to society. . . . I don't give a damn for the group, the community, the masses. . . . Although I do not care for the slogan 'art for art's sake'—because . . . such promoters of it as . . . Oscar Wilde . . . were in reality rank moralists and didacticists—there can be no question that what makes a work of fiction safe from larvae and rust is not its social importance but its art and only its art." Nabokov, *Strong Opinions,* interview with Alvin Toffler, p.33.

33. Pifer, in *Nabokov and the Novel,* tries to make the case for the Russian novelist's "abiding interest in human beings, not only as artists and dreamers but as ethical beings subject to moral law and sanction" (iii–iv). Though she makes a worthy effort at showing Nabokov's "commitment to certain moral . . . principles" (170), her argument amounts ultimately to a denial of everything Nabokov stood for. (See note 31.) Nabokov had his own ideas about morality and justice (see chap. 7), but his entire approach to literature, as shown in his lectures, interviews, and fiction, is staunchly aesthetical and solidly against *any* extraliterary considerations.

34. Nabokov, *Lectures on Literature,* pp.68, 65.

35. Nabokov, *Strong Opinions,* interview with Hughes, p.55.

36. Nabokov, *Lectures on Literature*, p.126.

37. Nabokov, *Strong Opinions*, interview with Nicholas Garnham, p.116. See also Field, *Nabokov*, p.199.

38. Nabokov, *Look at the Harlequins!*, pp.124–25.

39. Boyd sees *Bend Sinister* as one of Nabokov's "less successful" works. "The plot has its poignancy, but it remains too meager in proportion to the self-consciousness and obscurity that surround it." *The American Years*, p.105.

40. For an exploration of this issue, see chap. 2, "The Myth of the Postmodern Breakthrough" in Graff, *Literature against Itself*.

41. Johnson, as cited in Bernstein, "The de Man Affair."

42. De Man, *Blindness and Insight*; emphasis in the original.

43. Graff, *Literature against Itself*, p.179.

44. Miller, "The Fiction of Realism," pp.116, 121.

45. Krauss, "Poststructuralism and the 'Paraliterary,'" pp.36–40.

46. Hartman, *Criticism in the Wilderness*, passim. Fish, "Demonstration vs. Persuasion," in *Is There a Text*, p.368.

47. Hughes, *The Shock of the New*, p.111.

CHAPTER 7

1. All citations are from Gautier, *Mademoiselle de Maupin*, English version; page references are cited parenthetically in the text.

2. Mayer, *Why Did the Heavens Not Darken?*, p.96.

3. Citations, including that in the preceding paragraph, from Gooch, *Germany and the French Revolution*, pp.281, 269.

4. John Kemp, *The Philosophy of Kant*, p.87.

5. Kant, *On History*, pp.4, 9.

6. Cassirer, *Kant's Life and Thought*, p.376.

7. Kant, "The End of All Things," in *On History*, pp.83, 84.

8. Citation, as in the preceding paragraph, from Cassirer, *Kant's Life and Thought*, pp.376, 380–81, 392–94.

9. Introduction, by J. F. Lamport, to Schiller, *The Robbers* and *Wallenstein*, p.7.

10. Cited in *Schiller: An Anthology*, p.31.

11. *Schiller: An Anthology*, p.285.

12. Schiller, *The Robbers*, p.12.

13. Schiller, *Wilhelm Tell*, pp.115, 140.

14. Schiller, *Don Carlos*, pp.109, 113.

15. Gooch, *Germany and the French Revolution*, p.210.

16. Herold, *Mistress to an Age*, pp.449–50.

17. Ruskin, "Charitas," in *Fors Clavigera*, p.374.
18. Bell, *Ruskin*, pp.69–74.
19. Wilde, in *De Profundis*. Page references to this work are cited parenthetically within the text.
20. On Luddites, see Thompson, *The Making of the English Working Class*, pp.192–98, 547–602.
21. Marx, *The 18th Brumaire of Louis Bonaparte*, p.75.
22. Seigel, *Bohemian Paris*, p.63.
23. Arendt, *The Origins of Totalitarianism*, p.317.
24. Flaubert, *Letters*, Rumbold edition, p.162.
25. Flaubert, *Letters*, Rumbold edition, p.74.
26. Cited in Harrison, *The Reactionaries*, p.47.
27. Yeats, *The Collected Poems*, p.302; emphasis added.
28. Yeats, *The Collected Poems*, pp.148–49.
29. Yeats, *The Collected Poems*, pp.191–92 and 243–44.
30. Yeats, *A Vision*, pp.277–80; emphasis in original.
31. Ellmann, *Yeats*, p.177.
32. Ellmann, *Yeats*, p.277.
33. Eliot, *The Waste Land*, in *The Complete Poems and Plays*. References to this poem are to specific line numbers. Other poems are cited by page number in this collection.
34. For a superb analysis of the *passéiste* vision in this poem, see Craig, "The Defeatism of *The Waste Land*."
35. Matthews, *Great Tom*, p.163.
36. Cited in Ricks, *T. S. Eliot and Prejudice*, p.38.
37. Cited in Sharpe, *T. S. Eliot*, p.171.
38. Cited in Ackroyd, *T. S. Eliot*, p.18.
39. Gordon, *Eliot's Early Years*, p.55.
40. Gordon, *Eliot's Early Years*, p.126.
41. Cited in Margolis, *T. S. Eliot's Intellectual Development*, p.18. Lyndall Gordon, *Eliot's New Life*, p.271.
42. Cited in Matthews, *Great Tom*, p.100.
43. Cited in Gordon, *Eliot's Early Years*, p.18.
44. Ackroyd, *T. S. Eliot*, p.39.
45. Ackroyd, *T. S. Eliot*, p.44.
46. Simpson, *Three on the Tower*, p.133.
47. Ortega y Gasset, *La rebelión de la masas*, p.72.
48. Kojecky, *T. S. Eliot's Social Criticism*, pp.58–69.
49. Cited in Kojecky, *T. S. Eliot's Social Criticism*, p.59.
50. Ackroyd, *T. S. Eliot*, p.41.

51. Pope Pius XI, cited in Kojecky, *T. S. Eliot's Social Criticism*, pp.64–65.

52. Cited in Kojecky, *T. S. Eliot's Social Criticism*, pp.63, 68.

53. Cited in Simpson, *Three on the Tower*, p.162.

54. Eliot, *After Strange Gods*. Page references are cited parenthetically within the text.

55. Citation in Ricks, *T. S. Eliot and Prejudice*, pp.44–47. Ackroyd, *T. S. Eliot*, pp.201, 304.

56. Cited in Simpson, *Three on the Tower*, pp.162, 163.

57. Margolis, *T. S. Eliot's Intellectual Development*, pp.193, 200.

58. On this score see Bell-Villada, "No More Munichs!" and Gannon, *The British Press and Germany, 1936–39*, passim.

59. Praising Hitler's anti-Marxism and his war against the Soviet Union is a view that has never faded away and that was even passionately revived by prominent German conservative intellectuals in the 1980s. See *Forever in the Shadow of Hitler?* passim.

60. Gordon, *Eliot's New Life*, pp.128, 144.

61. Gordon, *Eliot's New Life*, p.270.

62. Cowan, *The Fugitive Group*, p.239.

63. Bradbury, *The Fugitives*, p.93.

64. Cited in Sutton, *Modern American Criticism*, p.102.

65. Ransom and others, *I'll Take My Stand*. Page references from this volume are cited parenthetically within the text.

66. Cited in Meiners, *The Last Alternative*, p.29.

67. Cited in Bradbury, *The Fugitives*, p.90.

68. Cited in Meiners, *The Last Alternative*, p.25.

69. Cited in Bradbury, *The Fugitives*, p.92.

70. Cited in Ransom and others, *I'll Take My Stand*, p.xxvii. See also the biographical essay on Warren, p.403.

71. Tate, *On the Limits of Poetry*, p.268.

72. Tate, *On the Limits of Poetry*, p.266.

73. Tate, *On the Limits of Poetry*, pp.275–76.

74. On the matter of Martí's social and literary ideas, and his profound differences with the other *modernistas*, see Pérus, *Literatura y sociedad*, pp.94–99.

75. Ellmann, *The Consciousness of Joyce*, p.75.

76. Ellmann, *The Consciousness of Joyce*, pp.78, 82.

77. Cited in Ellmann, *The Consciousness of Joyce*, p.85.

78. Cited in Manganiello, *Joyce's Politics*, p.113.

79. Joyce, *The Critical Writings*. Page references to the Joyce collection appear parenthetically in the text.

80. Ellmann, *James Joyce,* p.312.

81. Cited in Ellmann, *James Joyce,* p.225.

82. Joyce, *Ulysses.* Page references to this volume are cited parenthetically within the text.

83. Cited in Ellmann, *James Joyce,* p.175.

84. Joyce, *My Brother's Keeper,* p.107.

85. Cited in Joyce, *My Brother's Keeper,* p.130.

86. Cited in Ellmann, *James Joyce,* p.199.

87. Arno Mayer, *The Persistence of the Old Regime.*

88. See Schrecker, *No Ivory Tower,* especially pp.86–92, 267–70.

89. Cited in Cohen, "Toontown's Reds," p.190. I am grateful to Steven Kovács for this item.

90. Tate, *On the Limits of Poetry,* p.266.

91. Tate, *Essays of Four Decades,* p.26.

92. Tate, *Essays of Four Decades,* p.15.

93. Boyd, in *Vladimir Nabokov: The Russian Years,* p.72, quotes the novelist's stated indifference "to organized mysticism, to religion, to the church— any church." On Nabokov's antireligiosity, see also pp.295, 354.

94. Nabokov, *Strong Opinions,* pp.34–35.

95. Boyd observes that "the Nabokovs believed that many of [McCarthy's] charges were correct, that there was serious Communist infiltration of high places in American officialdom." *Vladimir Nabokov: The American Years,* p.186.

96. Nabokov, *The Real Life of Sebastian Knight,* p.166.

97. Nabokov, *Transparent Things,* p.66.

98. Nabokov, *Look at the Harlequins!,* pp.139, 163.

99. See Pipes, *Russia under the Old Regime,* especially chap. 8, "The Missing Bourgeoisie," pp.191–220.

100. See Moore, *Social Origins of Dictatorship and Democracy,* pp.3–108, as well as concluding chapters.

101. Jameson, *The Political Unconscious,* p.54, footnote.

102. For a fuller examination of this issue, see Bell-Villada, "Is the American Mind Getting Dumber?" and "Critical Appraisals of American Education." For a fictional treatment of the debate, see Bell-Villada, *The Carlos Chadwick Mystery,* especially part 3, "Perspectives Industries Ltd.," pp.197–249.

103. Eagleton, *The Function of Criticism,* p.98.

104. Johnson, cited in Bernstein, "The de Man Affair."

105. Graff, *Literature against Itself,* p.213.

106. For a full account, see Lehman, *Signs of the Times*. Material on de Man's personal conduct is added in the afterword to the paperback edition of this volume.
107. De Man, *Blindness and Insight*, p.11.
108. De Man, *Blindness and Insight*, p.17.
109. De Man, *Blindness and Insight*, pp.34, 35.

CONCLUSION

1. Bloom, *The Closing of the American Mind*, pp.73–81.
2. Paz, *El arco y la lira*, p.258; translation mine.
3. García Márquez and Mendoza, *The Fragrance of Guava*, p.59.
4. Salusinszky, *Criticism in Society*, interview with Bloom, p.65.
5. Burke, "Literature as Equipment for Living," p.300.
6. Graff, *Literature against Itself*, p.13.
7. MacAdam, *Latin American Narratives*, p.89.
8. Young, Letter to the editor, PMLA, p.998–99.
9. Weber, *The Protestant Ethic*, p.182.
10. "In many ways we *are* Alexandrian; and we do not grow less so with the years." Jarrell, "The Age of Criticism," p.77.
11. In this regard see Jacoby, *The Last Intellectuals*, passim.
12. Brooks, "Aesthetics and Ideology," p.512.
13. Greenblatt, *Shakespearean Negotiations*, pp.1–2.
14. Will, "Literary Politics," *Newsweek*, 22 April 1991, p.72; cited in Graff, *Beyond the Culture Wars*, p.158.
15. See Graff, *Professing Literature*, passim, and *Beyond the Culture Wars*, chap. 8.
16. McLuhan, *Understanding Media*. Baudrillard, *America*.
17. Rogin, *Ronald Reagan, the Movie*, pp.7–8.
18. Frye, *The Critical Path*, p.146.
19. The exchange took place at a conference on Julio Cortázar held at Barnard College, April 1980.
20. This is the general thrust of Daniel Bell's *The Coming of Post-Industrial Society*.
21. I am grateful to Kerry Batchelder and to Sandi Clark Watson for this item.
22. Whiteside, *The Blockbuster Complex*, p.65. This is a first-rate look at the effects of conglomerate publishing.

BIBLIOGRAPHY

Almost twenty years have gone into the making of this study. In the process I have had occasion to read large amounts of material, some of it on an ad hoc basis, some for general ideas, and some for other ongoing projects or for ordinary keeping-up purposes, all of which nonetheless ended up contributing to my narrative. Some reading goes back to my student days (standard critical references by M. H. Abrams and by René Wellek and Austin Warren, for instance).

All of those many works have helped me — and, in some cases, inspired me — to put this volume together. The following bibliography, then, is intended to be as inclusive as possible; I have chosen to list every publication that played a part in my long-range researching, thinking, and crafting of the present book. Most of the items found here are alluded to specifically either in my notes or in the body of the text. Some, however, are not so cited; yet they too are spiritually, subliminally present in these pages. My thanks to all who have provided conceptual design, bricks-and-mortar, essential furnishings, and hidden corners for this house of print.

Abrams, M. H. *Doing Things with Texts: Essays in Criticism and Critical Theory.* Edited, with a foreword, by Michael Fischer. New York: W. W. Norton, 1989.

———. *The Mirror and the Lamp: Romantic Theory and the Critical Tradition.* New York: Oxford University Press, 1953.

———. *Natural Supernaturalism: Tradition and Revolution in Romantic Literature.* New York: W. W. Norton, 1971.

Ackroyd, Peter. *T. S. Eliot: A Life.* Simon & Schuster, 1984.

Adorno, Theodor W. "On Lyric Poetry and Society." In *Notes to Literature,* edited by Rolf Tiedemann, translated by Shierry Weber Nicholsen, pp. 37–54. New York: Columbia University Press, 1991.

A.G. "Académie Française: reception de M. Charles Nodier." *Le Temps* (Paris), 29 December 1893.

Allen, James Smith. *Popular French Romanticism: Authors, Readers and Books in the Nineteenth Century.* Syracuse: Syracuse University Press, 1981.

Alterton, Margaret. *Origins of Poe's Critical Theory.* Iowa City: University of Iowa Press, 1920. Reprint, New York: Russell & Russell, 1965.

Althusser, Louis. *For Marx.* Translated by Ben Brewster. London: New Left Books, 1977.

Bibliography

Altick, Richard. *The English Common Reader: A Social History of the Mass Reading Public, 1800–1900.* Chicago: University of Chicago Press, 1957.

Anderson, Benedict. *Imagined Communities: Reflections on the Origin and Spread of Nationalism.* New York: Verso, 1983. Revised and extended edition, 1991.

Anderson-Imbert, Enrique. *Historia de la literatura hispanoamericana.* 2 vols. Mexico: Fondo de Cultura Económica, 1954.

Arendt, Hannah. *The Origins of Totalitarianism.* New edition with added prefaces. New York: Harcourt Brace Jovanovich, 1973.

Ashton, Dore. *A Fable of Modern Art.* Los Angeles: University of California Press, 1991.

Balzac, Honoré de. *Lost Illusions.* Translated by Kathleen Raine, with an introduction by Raymond Mortimer. London: John Lehmann, 1951.

Baudelaire, Charles. *Baudelaire as a Literary Critic: Selected Essays.* Introduced and translated by Lois Boe Hyslop and Francis E. Hyslop Jr. University Park: Pennsylvania State University Press, 1964.

———. *The Flowers of Evil.* Selected and edited by Martiel and Jackson Mathews. Bilingual edition. New York: New Directions, 1955.

———. *My Heart Laid Bare and Other Prose Writings.* Edited with an introduction by Peter Quennell. Translated by Norman Cameron. London: George Weidenfeld & Nicolson, 1950.

Baudrillard, Jean. *America.* Translated by Chris Turner. New York: Verso, 1988.

Baugh, Albert C., editor. *A Literary History of England.* New York: Appleton-Century-Crofts, 1948.

Bell, Daniel. *The Coming of Post-Industrial Society: A Venture in Social Forecasting.* New York: Basic Books, 1973.

Bell, Quentin. *Ruskin.* New York: George Braziller, 1978.

Bell-Villada, Gene H. *The Carlos Chadwick Mystery: A Novel of College Life and Political Terror.* Albuquerque NM: Amador Publishers, 1990.

———. "Critical Appraisals of American Education: Dilemmas and Contradictions in the Work of Hirsch and Bloom." *International Journal of Politics, Culture, and Society* 3, no.4 (fall 1990): 485–512.

———. "Criticism and the State (Political and Otherwise) of the Americas." In *Criticism in the University,* edited by Gerald Graff and Reginald Gibbons, pp.124–44.

———. "Is the American Mind Getting Dumber?" *Monthly Review* 43, no.1 (May 1991): 41–55.

———. "No More Munichs! What the Media Won't Tell." *Monthly Review* 39, no.11 (April 1988): 9–21.

Benjamin, Walter. *Charles Baudelaire: A Lyric Poet in the Era of High Capitalism.* Translated by Harry Zohn. London: New Left Books, 1973.

———. "The Work of Art in the Age of Mechanical Reproduction." In *Illuminations,* edited with an introduction by Hannah Arendt, translated by Harry Zohn, pp.217–51. New York: Schocken Books, 1969.

Benson, A. C. *Walter Pater.* New York: Macmillan, 1906.

Berger, John. *The Success and Failure of Picasso.* New York: Pantheon Books, 1980.

Berman, Marshall. *"All That Is Solid Melts to Air": The Experience of Modernity.* New York: Simon & Schuster, 1982.

Bernstein, Richard. "The de Man Affair." *New York Times,* Week in Review, 17 July 1988, p.6.

Blackmur, R. P. "A Critic's Job of Work." In *Form and Value in Modern Poetry,* pp.339–67. New York: Doubleday, 1957.

Blades, John. *James Joyce: A Portrait of the Artist as a Young Man.* New York: Penguin Books (Penguin Critical Studies), 1991.

Bloom, Allan. *The Closing of the American Mind.* New York: Simon and Schuster, 1987.

Bloom, Harold, ed. *Selected Writings of Walter Pater* (q.v.).

Boileaux, Nicholas. *L'art poétique.* Edited by Guy Riegert. Paris: Librairie Larousse, 1972.

Booth, Wayne. *The Rhetoric of Fiction.* Chicago: University of Chicago Press, 1961.

Boyd, Brian. *Vladimir Nabokov: The Russian Years.* Princeton: Princeton University Press, 1990.

———. *Vladimir Nabokov: The American Years.* Princeton: Princeton University Press, 1991.

Bradbury, John. *The Fugitives: A Critical Account.* Chapel Hill: University of North Carolina Press, 1958.

Bradbury, Malcolm. "The Cities of Modernism." In Bradbury and McFarlane, eds., *Modernism: A Guide to European Literature, 1890–1930* (q.v.), pp.96–104.

———. "London 1890–1920." In Bradbury and McFarlane, eds., *Modernism: A Guide to European Literature, 1890–1930* (q.v.), pp.172–91.

——— and James McFarlane, eds. *Modernism: A Guide to European Literature, 1890–1930.* New York: Penguin Books, 1976.

——— and James McFarlane, "Movements, Magazines, and Manifestos: The Succession from Naturalism." In Bradbury and McFarlane, eds., *Modernism: A Guide to European Literature, 1890–1930* (q.v.), pp.192–205.

——— and James McFarlane. "The Name and Nature of Modernism." In

Bradbury and McFarlane, eds., *Modernism: A Guide to European Literature, 1890–1930* (q.v.), pp.19–55.

Braverman, Harry. *Labor and Monopoly Capital: The Degradation of Work in the Twentieth Century.* New York: Monthly Review Press, 1974.

Brereton, Geoffrey. *An Introduction to the French Poets: Villon to the Present Day.* London: Methuen and Co., 1973.

Brett, R. L. *The Third Earl of Shaftesbury: A Study in Eighteenth Century Literary Theory.* London: Hutchinson's University Library, 1951.

Brooks, Peter. "Aesthetics and Ideology: What Happened to Poetics?" *Critical Inquiry* 26, no.3 (spring 1994): 509–23.

Bruford, W. H. *Germany in the Eighteenth Century: The Social Background of the Literary Revival.* New York: Cambridge University Press, 1965.

Buchez, P. J. B. "De l'art théatral considéré dans ses moyens d'utilité sociale." *L'Européen: Journal de sciences morales et économiques* 1, no.19 (7 April 1832): 291–94.

Buckley, Jerome H. *The Victorian Temper.* Cambridge: Harvard University Press, 1951.

Budgen, Frank. *James Joyce and the Making of Ulysses.* Bloomington: Indiana University Press, 1960.

Bürger, Peter. *Theory of the Avant-Garde.* Translated by Michael Shaw. Foreword by Jochen Schulte. Minneapolis: University of Minnesota Press, 1984.

Burke, Edmund. *A Philosophical Enquiry into the Origins of Our Ideas of the Sublime and the Beautiful.* Edited with an introduction by James T. Boulton. Notre Dame: University of Notre Dame Press, 1968.

————. *Reflections on the Revolution in France.* Edited with an introduction by Conor Cruise O'Brien. New York: Penguin Books, 1969.

Burke, Kenneth. "Literature as Equipment for Living." In *The Philosophy of Literary Form,* pp.293–304. Los Angeles: University of California Press, 1973.

Cahm, Eric. "Revolt, Conservatism and Reaction in Paris, 1915–25." In Bradbury and McFarlane, *Modernism: A Guide to European Literature, 1890–1930* (q.v.), pp.162–71.

Calinescu, Matei. *Five Faces of Modernity: Modernism, Avant-Garde, Decadence, Kitsch, Postmodernism.* Durham NC: Duke University Press, 1987.

Carrel, Armand. "D'un commencement de réaction contre la littérature." *Le National,* 2 and 3 January 1834, p.4.

Cassagne, Albert. *La théorie de l'art pour l'art en France des les derniers romantiques et les premier réalistes.* Paris: Hachette, 1906.

Cassirer, Ernst. *Kant's Life and Thought.* Translated by James Haden, with an introduction by Stephen Körner. New Haven: Yale University Press, 1981.

————. *The Philosophy of the Enlightenment.* Translated by Fritz C. A. Haden and James P. Pettegrove. Princeton: Princeton University Press, 1951.

Cather, Willa. *The Kingdom of Art: Willa Cather's First Principles and Critical Statements, 1893-1896.* Edited, with two essays, by Bernice Slote. Lincoln: University of Nebraska Press, 1966.

————. *On Writing: Critical Studies on Writing as an Art.* Foreword by Stephen Tennant. New York: Alfred A. Knopf, 1953.

Chai, Leon. *Aestheticism: The Religion of Art in Post-Romantic Literature.* New York: Columbia University Press, 1990.

Chace, William M. *The Political Identities of Ezra Pound and T. S. Eliot.* Stanford: Stanford University Press, 1973.

Chamberlin, J. F. *Ripe Was the Drowsy Hour: The Age of Oscar Wilde.* New York: Seabury Press, 1977.

Charléty, Sebastien. *Histoire du Saint-Simonisme.* Paris: P. Hartmann, 1931.

Charvat, William. *The Profession of Authorship in America, 1800-1870 (The Papers of William Charvat).* Edited by Matthew Bruccoli. Foreword by Howard Mumford Jones. Columbus: Ohio State University Press, 1968.

Chew, Samuel C. "The Nineteenth Century and After (1789-1939)." In Baugh, ed., *A Literary History of England* (q.v.), pp.1111-1605.

Christ, Ronald, and Dennis Dollens. *Text/Tiles, Jujol/Gaudí, Bench/Park Güell.* New York: Lumen, 1985. Videotape.

Clair, Colin. *A History of Printing in Britain.* London: Cassell, 1965.

Clark, T. J. *The Painting of Modern Life.* Princeton: Princeton University Press, 1984.

Cobban, Alfred. *A History of Modern France.* Vol.2, *1799-1945.* New York: Penguin Books, 1962.

Cohen, Karl. "Toontown's Reds: HUAC's Investigation of Alleged Communists in the Animation Industry." *Film History* 5 (June 1993): 199-203.

Cohen, Stephen. *Bukharin and the Bolshevik Revolution.* New York: Alfred A. Knopf, 1973.

Cohen, Ted, and Paul Guyer, eds. *Essays in Kant's Aesthetics.* Chicago: University of Chicago Press, 1982.

Coleridge, Samuel Taylor. *Biographia Literaria.* London: J. M. Dent & Sons, 1965.

Constant, Benjamin. *Journal intime.* Edited by D. Melegari. Paris: Albin Michel, 1925.

Cousin, Victor. *Cours de philosophie professé à la faculté des lettres pendant l'année 1818 sur le fondement des idées du vrai, du beau et du bien.* Paris: Hachette, 1836.

————. "Du beau et de l'art." *Revue des Deux Mondes* 10 (1 September 1845): 773–81.

Cowan, Louise. *The Fugitive Group.* Baton Rouge: Louisiana State University Press, 1959.

Craig, David. "The Defeatism of *The Waste Land.*" In *The Real Foundations: Literature and Social Change,* pp.195–212. New York: Oxford University Press, 1974.

Culler, Jonathan. *On Deconstruction: Theory and Criticism after Structuralism.* Ithaca: Cornell University Press, 1982.

C.V. "De la moralisation de la societé par les beaux-arts." *L'Artiste* 11 (1836): 245–47.

Darío, Rubén. *Obras completas.* 5 vols. Edited by M. Sanmiguel Raimúndez. Madrid: Afrodisio Aguado, 1953.

Davidson, Edward H. *Poe: A Critical Study.* Cambridge: Harvard University Press, 1957.

Davis, Harold Eugene. *Latin American Thought: A Historical Introduction.* New York: Free Press (Macmillan), 1974.

Debord, Guy. *The Society of Spectacle.* (Translator anonymous.) Detroit: Black and Red, 1983.

de Man, Paul. *Blindness and Insight: Essays in the Rhetoric of Contemporary Criticism.* 2d ed. Introduction by Wlad Godzich. Minneapolis: University of Minnesota Press, 1983.

Derrida, Jacques. *Of Grammatology.* Translated with a preface by Gayatri Chakravorti Spivak. Baltimore: Johns Hopkins University Press, 1976.

————. "Structure, Sign, and Play in the Discourse of the Human Sciences." In Richard Macksey and Eugenio Donato, eds., *The Structuralist Controversy,* pp.247–65. Baltimore: Johns Hopkins University Press, 1970.

————. *Writing and Difference.* Translated, with an introduction and additional notes, by Alan Bass. Chicago: University of Chicago Press, 1978.

Diggins, John P. *Mussolini and Fascism: The View from America.* Princeton: Princeton University Press, 1972.

Dollimore, Jonathan. *Sexual Dissidence: Augustine to Wilde, Freud to Foucault.* New York: Oxford University Press, 1991.

du Camp, Maxime. *Théophile Gautier.* Port Washington NY: Kennikat Press, 1973.

Eagleton, Terry. *The Function of Criticism: From "The Spectator" to Post-Structuralism.* New York: Verso, 1984.

————. *The Ideology of the Aesthetic.* Cambridge MA: Basil Blackwell, 1990.

Egan, Rose Frances. *The Genesis of the Theory of "Art for Art's Sake" in Germany and England.* Part 1: Smith College Studies in Modern Languages 2, no.4

(July 1921); part 2: same series, 5, no.3 (April 1924). Northampton: Smith College.

Eggli, Edmond. *Schiller et le romantisme français.* Geneva: Slatkine Reprints, 1970.

Eliade, Mircea. *The Sacred and the Profane: The Nature of Religion.* Translated by Willard R. Trask. New York: Harcourt Brace, 1959.

Eliot, T. S. *After Strange Gods: A Primer of Modern Heresy.* London: Faber and Faber, 1934.

———. *The Complete Poetry and Plays, 1909–1950.* New York: Harcourt, Brace & World, 1962.

———. *The Sacred Wood: Essays on Poetry and Criticism.* London: Methuen, 1920. 2d ed., 1928.

———. "The Frontiers of Criticism." In *On Poetry and Poets,* pp.113–31. New York: Farrar, Straus & Cudahy, 1957.

———. "Religion and Literature." In *Selected Prose,* edited by Frank Kermode, pp.97–106. New York: Harcourt Brace Jovanovich, 1975.

Ellmann, Richard. *The Consciousness of Joyce.* New York: Oxford University Press, 1977.

———. *James Joyce.* New York: Oxford University Press, 1959.

———. *Oscar Wilde.* New York: Alfred A. Knopf, 1984.

———. *Yeats: The Man and the Masks.* New York: E. P. Dutton, 1948.

——— and Charles Feidelson Jr., eds. *The Modern Tradition: Backgrounds of Modern Literature.* New York: Oxford University Press, 1965.

Engell, James. *The Creative Imagination: Enlightenment to Romanticism.* Cambridge: Harvard University Press, 1981.

Escarpit, Robert. *The Book Revolution.* London: George G. Harrap, 1966.

———. *Sociologie de la littérature.* Paris: Presses Universitaires de France, 1958.

Evans, David Owen. *Social Romanticism in France, 1830–1848.* New York: Oxford University Press, 1951.

Ewing, A. C. *A Short Commentary on Kant's* Critique of Pure Reason. Chicago: University of Chicago Press, 1974.

Eysteinsson, Astradur. *The Concept of Modernism.* Ithaca: Cornell University Press, 1990.

Field, Andrew. *Nabokov: His Life in Part.* New York: Viking, 1977.

Fish, Stanley. *Is There a Text in This Class? The Authority of Intepretive Communities.* Cambridge: Harvard University Press, 1980.

Flaubert, Gustave. *Letters.* Edited, with an introduction, by Richard Rumbold. Translated by J. M. Cohen. London: Weidenfeld & Nicholson, 1950.

————. *The Selected Letters.* Translated and edited, with an introduction, by Francis Steegmuller. New York: Farrar, Straus & Cudahy, 1953.

Fletch, John, and Malcolm Bradbury. "The Introverted Novel." In Bradbury and McFarlane, eds., *Modernism: A Guide to European Literature, 1890-1930* (q.v.), 394-415.

Forever in the Shadow of Hitler? Original Documents of the Historikerstreit, the Controversy concerning the Singularity of the Holocaust. Editor anonymous. Translated by James Knowlton and Truett Cates. Atlantic Highlands NJ: Humanities Press, 1993.

Forster, E. M. "Art for Art's Sake." In *Two Cheers for Democracy,* pp.98-104. London: Edward Arnold, 1951.

Fortoul, Hippolyte. "De l'art." *L'Artiste* 17 (December 1838): 29-32.

————. "De l'art actuel." *Revue Encyclopédique* 59 (1833): 107-53.

————. "Souvenirs Romantiques." *Revue Encyclopédique* 60 (1833): 264-98.

Foster, David William. Reply to James E. Young. PMLA 9, no.5 (October 1984): 999.

Franco, Jean. *An Introduction to Spanish-American Literature.* New York: Cambridge University Press, 1969.

Frank, Joseph. "Spatial Form in Modern Literature." In *The Widening Gyre: Crisis and Mastery in Modern Literature,* pp.3-62. New Brunswick: Rutgers University Press, 1963.

Freedman, Jonathan. *Professions of Taste: Henry James, British Aestheticism, and Commodity Culture.* Stanford: Stanford University Press, 1990.

Friedman, Melvin J. "The Symbolist Novel: Huysmans to Malraux." In Bradbury and McFarlane, eds., *Modernism: A Guide to European Literature, 1890-1930* (q.v.), pp.453-66.

Frye, Northrop. *Anatomy of Criticism: Four Essays.* New York: Atheneum, 1968.

————. *The Critical Path.* Bloomington: Indiana University Press, 1970.

Gagnier, Regenia. *Idylls of the Marketplace: Oscar Wilde and the Victorian Public.* Stanford: Stanford University Press, 1986.

Gannon, Franklin Reed. *The British Press and Germany 1936-39.* New York: Oxford University Press, 1971.

García Márquez, Gabriel, and Plinio Apuleyo Mendoza. *The Fragrance of Guava.* Translated by Ann Wright. London: Verso, 1982.

Gaunt, William. *The Aesthetic Adventure.* New York: Harcourt, Brace, 1945.

Gautier, Théophile. *Histoire du romantisme, suivie de notices romantiques et d'une étude sur la poésie française, 1830-1868.* Paris: Charpentier, 1874.

————. *Les Jeunes-Frances: Romans goguenards.* Paris: Charpentier, 1873.

————. *Mademoiselle de Maupin.* Paris: Garnier, 1966.

―――. *Mademoiselle de Maupin*. Translated, with an introduction, by Joanna Richardson. New York: Penguin, 1981.

―――. *Poésies complètes*. Paris: Nizet, 1970.

―――. *Works*. Translated and edited by F. C. de Sumichrast. New York: G. D. Sproul, 1903.

Genovese, Eugene. *The World the Slaveholders Made*. New York: Random House, 1971.

George, Albert Joseph. *The Development of French Romanticism: The Impact of the Industrial Revolution on Literature*. Syracuse: Syracuse University Press, 1955.

Gilbert, Sandra M., and Susan Gubar. *The Madwoman in the Attic: The Woman Writer and the Nineteenth-Century Literary Imagination*. New Haven: Yale University Press, 1979.

Gilbert, W. S. *Plays and Poems by W. S. Gilbert*. Preface by Deems Taylor. New York: Random House, 1932.

Gissing, George. *New Grub Street*. Troy NY: 1904.

Gittings, Robert. *John Keats*. Boston: Little, Brown, 1965.

Gooch, G. P. *Germany and the French Revolution*. New York: Russell and Russell, 1966.

Gordon, Lyndall. *Eliot's Early Years*. New York: Oxford University Press, 1977.

―――. *Eliot's New Life*. New York: Farrar, Straus & Giroux, 1988.

Graff, Gerald. *Beyond the Culture Wars: How Teaching the Conflicts Can Revitalize American Education*. New York: W. W. Norton, 1992.

―――. " 'Keep Off the Grass,' 'Drop Dead,' and Other Indeterminacies: A Response to Sanford Levinson." *Texas Law Review* 60, no.3 (March 1982): 405–13.

―――. *Literature against Itself: Literary Ideas in Modern Society*. Chicago: University of Chicago Press, 1978.

―――. *Professing Literature: An Institutional History*. Chicago: University of Chicago Press, 1987.

Graña, César. *Modernity and Its Discontents: French Society and the French Man of Letters in the Nineteenth Century*. New York: Harper & Row, 1967.

Gray, Alexander. *The Socialist Tradition: Moses to Lenin*. New York: Longmans, Green, 1946.

Greenblatt, Stephen. *Learning to Curse: Essays in Early Modern Culture*. New York: Routledge, 1990.

―――. *Shakespearean Negotiations: The Circulation of Social Energy in Renaissance England*. Berkeley: University of California Press, 1988.

Grolier, Eric de. *Histoire du livre*. Paris: Presses Universitaires de France, 1954.

Bibliography

Gross, John. *The Rise and Fall of the Man of Letters: English Literary Life since 1800.* London: Penguin Books, 1973.

Guérard, Albert. *Art for Art's Sake.* New York: Shocken, 1963.

Guilbaut, Serge. *How New York Stole the Idea of Modern Art: Abstract Expressionism, Freedom, and the Cold War.* Translated by Arthur Goldhammer. Chicago: University of Chicago Press, 1983.

Habermas, Jürgen. *The Structural Transformation of the Public Sphere: An Inquiry into a Category of Bourgeois Society.* Translated by Thomas Burger, with the assistance of Frederick Lawrence. Cambridge: Massachusetts Institute of Technology Press, 1991.

Harrison, John. *The Reactionaries: A Study of the Anti-Democratic Intelligentsia.* Preface by William Empson. New York: Shocken Books, 1967.

Hartman, Geoffrey. *Criticism in the Wilderness: The Study of Literature Today.* New Haven: Yale University Press, 1980.

Hartz, Louis. *The Liberal Tradition in America: An Interpretation of American Political Thought since the Revolution.* New York: Harcourt, Brace, 1955.

Heller, Tamar. *Dead Secrets: Wilkie Collins and the Female Gothic.* New Haven: Yale University Press, 1992.

Henríquez Ureña, Max. *Breve historia del modernismo.* Mexico: Fondo de Cultura Económica, 1954.

Henríquez Ureña, Pedro. *Las corrientes literarias en la América Hispánica.* Mexico City: Fondo de Cultura Económica, 1949.

Herold, J. Christopher. *Mistress to an Age: A Life of Madame de Staël.* New York: Crown Publishers, 1979.

Hoffman, *Poe Poe Poe Poe Poe Poe Poe.* New York: Doubleday, 1972.

Homberger, Eric. "Chicago and New York: Two Versions of American Modernism." In Bradbury and McFarlane, eds., *Modernism: A Guide to European Literature, 1890–1930* (q.v.), pp.151–61.

Horace. "On the Art of Poetry." In *Classical Literary Criticism,* edited and translated, with an introduction, by T. S. Dorsch. Baltimore: Penguin Books, 1965.

Horkheimer, Max, and Theodor W. Adorno. *Dialectic of Enlightenment.* Translated by John Cumming. New York: Continuum, 1991.

Hough, Graham. *The Last Romantics.* London: Gerald Duckworth, 1949.

———. "The Modernist Lyric." In Bradbury and McFarlane, eds., *Modernism: A Guide to European Literature, 1890–1930* (q.v.), pp.312–22.

Houston, John Porter. *Victor Hugo.* New York: Twayne Publishers, 1974.

Howe, Irving. "The Culture of Modernism." In *Decline of the New,* pp.3–33. New York: Harcourt, Brace 1963.

Hughes, Robert. *The Shock of the New.* New York: Alfred A. Knopf, 1980.

Hugo, Victor. *Oeuvres complètes.* Vol.38, *Littérature et philosophie melées.* Edited by Jeanlouis Cornuz. Lausanne: Editions Rencontre, 1968.

———. *Notre-Dame of Paris.* Translated by John Sturrock. New York: Penguin Books, 1978.

———. *Les Orientales.* Edited by Elisabeth Barineau. 2 vols. Paris: Librairie Marcel Didier, 1952.

———. Preface to *Cromwell.* In *Théatre complet* (q.v.), 1:409–54.

———. Preface to *Hernani.* In *Théatre complet* (q.v.), 1:1147–51.

———. *Les rayons et les ombres.* Paris: Hachette, 1869.

———. *Théatre complet.* Edited and annotated by J.-J. Thierry and Josette Mélèze. Preface by Roland Purnal. Paris: Gallimard, Pléiade, 1964.

———. *William Shakespeare.* Translated by A. Baillot. London: Hurst and Blackett, 1864.

Hunt, John Dixon. *The Wider Sea: A Life of John Ruskin.* New York: Viking, 1982.

Hutcheson, Francis. *An Inquiry into the Original of Our Ideas of Beauty and Virtue.* London: J. Darby, 1726.

Huysmans, J. K. *Against Nature.* Translated by Robert Baldick. Baltimore: Penguin Books, 1959.

Hyde, G. M. "The Poetry of the City." In Bradbury and McFarlane, *Modernism: A Guide to European Literature, 1890–1930* (q.v.), pp.337–48.

Jacoby, Russell. *The Last Intellectuals: American Culture in the Age of Academe.* New York: Basic Books, 1987.

Jakobson, Roman. "Linguistics and Poetics." In Richard DeGeorge and Fernande DeGeorge, eds., *The Structuralists,* pp.85–122. New York: Doubleday, 1972.

Jameson, Fredric. *Marxism and Form: Twentieth Century Dialectical Theories of Literature.* Princeton: Princeton University Press, 1972.

———. *The Political Unconscious: Narrative as a Socially Symbolic Act.* Ithaca: Cornell University Press, 1981.

Janet, Paul. *Victor Cousin et son oeuvre.* Paris: Calmann Lévy, 1885.

Jarrell, Randall. "The Age of Criticism." In *Poetry and the Age,* pp.70–95. New York: Farrar, Straus and Giroux, 1972.

Jasinski, René. *Les années romantiques de Théophile Gautier.* Paris: Vuibert, 1929.

Johnson, Diane. "Dreams of E. A. Poe." *New York Review of Books* 3, no.13 (18 July 1991): 7–10.

Joyce, James. *The Critical Writings.* Edited by Ellsworth Mason and Richard Ellmann. Foreword by Guy Davenport. Ithaca: Cornell University Press, 1989.

———. *Dubliners.* In *The Portable James Joyce,* edited, with an introduction and notes, by Harry Levin, pp.19–242. New York: Viking, 1947.

———. *A Portrait of the Artist as a Young Man.* New York: Penguin Books, 1976.

———. *Ulysses.* New York: Random House, 1961.

Joyce, Stanislaus. *My Brother's Keeper: James Joyce's Early Years.* Edited, with an introduction and notes, by Richard Ellmann. Preface by T. S. Eliot. New York: Viking, 1958.

Kant, Immanuel. *Critique of Judgment.* Translated, with an introduction, by J. H. Bernard. New York: Hafner, 1972.

———. *Critique of Practical Reason.* Translated, with an introduction, by Lewis White Beck. New York: Bobbs Merrill, 1956.

———. *Critique of Pure Reason.* Translated by F. Max Müller. New York: Doubleday, 1966.

———. *On History.* Edited, with an introduction, by Lewis White Beck. Translated by Lewis White Beck, Robert E. Anchor, and Emil L. Fackenheim. New York: Bobbs Merrill, 1963.

Keats, John. *The Letters of John Keats, 1814–1821.* Edited by Hyder Edward Rollins. 2 vols. Cambridge: Harvard University Press, 1958.

Kemp, John. *The Philosophy of Kant.* New York: Oxford University Press, 1965.

Kermode, Frank. *Romantic Image.* London: Routledge and Kegan Paul, 1957.

Kernan, Alvin. *The Death of Literature.* New Haven: Yale University Press, 1990.

Kirkpatrick, Gwen. *The Dissonant Legacy of Modernismo: Lugones, Herrera y Reissig, and the Voices of Spanish American Poetry.* Los Angeles: University of California Press, 1989.

Koch, Kenneth. *Rose, Where Did You Get That Red? Teaching Great Poetry to Children.* New York: Random House, 1973.

———. *Wishes, Lies, and Dreams: Teaching Children to Write Poetry.* New York: Random House, 1971.

Kojecky, Roger. *T. S. Eliot's Social Criticism.* New York: Farrar, Straus and Giroux, 1972.

Krauss, Rosalind. "Poststructuralism and the 'Paraliterary.'" *October,* no.13 (1980): 36–40.

Kristeva, Julia. *Revolution in Poetic Language.* Translated by Margaret Walker, with an introduction by Leon S. Roudiez. New York: Columbia University Press, 1984.

Krutch, Joseph Wood. *Edgar Allan Poe: A Study in Genius.* New York: Alfred A. Knopf, 1926.

Lamennais, F. *De l'art et du beau.* Paris: Garnier, 1865.

Lang, Berel, and Forrest Williams, eds. *Marxism and Art: Writings in Aesthetics and Criticism.* New York: David McKay, 1972.

Lanson, Gustave. Review of Albert Cassagne's *La théorie de l'art pour l'art en France. Revue d'histoire littéraire de la France* 14 (1907):163–67.

Laprade, Victor de. "La question littéraire." *Revue indépendante* 10 (10 October 1843): 351–97.

Larsen, Neil. *Modernism and Hegemony: A Materialist Critique of Aesthetic Agencies.* Foreword by Jaime Concha. Minneapolis: University of Minnesota Press, 1990.

Leavis, Q. D. *Fiction and the Reading Public.* London: Chatto and Windus, 1932.

Lehman, David. *Signs of the Times: Deconstruction and the Fall of Paul de Man.* New York: Poseidon Press, 1991.

Levin, Harry. "What Was Modernism?" In *Refractions: Essays in Comparative Literature,* pp.271–95. New York: Oxford University Press, 1966.

Levinson, Sanford. "Law as Literature." *Texas Law Review* 60, no.3 (March 1982): 373–403.

Lévi-Strauss, Claude. *Tristes Tropiques.* Translated by John Russell. New York: Atheneum, 1967.

Lord, Albert B. *The Singer of Tales.* New York: Atheneum, 1978.

Lough, John. *Writer and Public in France: From the Middle Ages to the Present Day.* New York: Oxford University Press, 1978.

Lunn, Eugene. *Marxism and Modernism: An Historical Study of Lukács, Brecht, Benjamin and Adorno.* Los Angeles: University of California Press, 1982.

Mallarmé, Stephane. Untitled selection. Edited, with an introduction and prose translations, by Anthony Hartley. Baltimore: Penguin Books, 1965.

MacAdam, Alfred. *Latin American Narratives: The Dreams of Reason.* Chicago: University of Chicago Press, 1977.

Manganiello, Dominic. *Joyce's Politics.* London: Routledge & Kegan Paul, 1980.

Marcuse, Herbert. *Eros and Civilization.* New York: Viking, 1962.

Margolis, John T. *T. S. Eliot's Intellectual Development 1922–1939.* Chicago: University of Chicago Press, 1972.

Marx, Karl. *The Eighteenth Brumaire of Louis Bonaparte.* New York: International Publishers, 1963.

——— and Frederick Engels. *Literature and Art.* (Translator anonymous.) New York: International Publishers, 1947.

Masiello, Francine. *Between Civilization and Barbarism: Women, Nation, and Literary Culture in Modern Argentina.* Lincoln: University of Nebraska Press, 1992.

Matthews, T. S. *Great Tom: Notes towards the Definition of T. S. Eliot.* New York: Harper & Row, 1974.

Mayer, Arno. *The Persistence of the Old Regime: Europe to the Great War.* New York: Pantheon Books, 1981.

——. *Why Did the Heavens Not Darken? The "Final Solution" in History.* New York: Pantheon Books, 1990.

McLuhan, Marshall. *Understanding Media: The Extensions of Man.* New York: McGraw-Hill, 1964.

McNiece, Gerald. *Shelley and the Revolutionary Idea.* Cambridge: Harvard University Press, 1969.

Meiners, R. K. *The Last Alternative: A Study of the Works of Allen Tate.* Denver: Alan Swallow, 1963.

Michaut, Gustave. *Pages de critique et d'histoire littéraire.* Paris: Fontemoing, 1910.

Mill, John Stuart. *Autobiography.* Preface by Harold Laski. New York: Oxford University Press, 1924.

——. "On Poetry." In *John Stuart Mill: A Selection of His Works,* edited by John M. Robson, pp.422–26. New York: St. Martin's Press, 1966.

Miller, J. Hillis. "The Fiction of Realism." In *Dickens Centennial Essays,* edited by Ada Nisbet and Blake Nevius, pp.85–153. Berkeley: University of California Press, 1971.

Moore, Barrington, Jr. *Social Origins of Dictatorship and Democracy: Lord and Peasant in the Making of the Modern World.* Boston: Beacon Press, 1966.

Moore, George. *Confessions of a Young Man.* New York: Brentano's, 1906.

Mumby, Frank Arthur. *Publishing and Bookselling: A History from the Earliest Times to the Present Day.* 4th ed. London: Jonathan Cape, 1956.

Nabokov, Vladimir. *Ada, or Ardor: A Family Chronicle.* New York: McGraw-Hill, 1969.

——. *Bend Sinister.* London: Penguin Books, 1974.

——. *The Gift.* Translated by Michael Scammell in collaboration with the author. New York: Putnam, 1963.

——. *Glory.* Translated by Dmitri Nabokov in collaboration with the author. New York: McGraw-Hill, 1971.

——. *Laughter in the Dark.* (*Kamera Obskura* in the Russian original.) Translated by the author. London: Penguin Books, 1963.

——. *Lectures on Literature.* Edited by Fredson Bowers. Introduction by John Updike. New York: Harcourt Brace Jovanovich, 1980.

——. *Look at the Harlequins!* New York: McGraw-Hill, 1974.

——. *Lolita.* New York: Fawcett World Library, 1959.

——. *Pale Fire.* New York: Putnam, 1972.

————. *Pnin.* Garden City NY: Doubleday, 1957.

————. *The Real Life of Sebastian Knight.* London: Penguin Books, 1964.

————. *Speak, Memory.* New York: Putnam, 1966.

————. *Strong Opinions.* New York: McGraw-Hill, 1973.

————. *Transparent Things.* New York: McGraw-Hill, 1972.

Neruda, Pablo. *Odas elementales.* Buenos Aires: Losada, 1958.

Nisard. "D'un commencement de réaction contre la littérature facile." *Revue de Paris* 57 (1833): 211–28, 261–87.

Nolte, Ernst. *Three Faces of Fascism.* Translated by Leila Vennewitz. New York: Holt, Rinehart & Winston, 1966.

Ohmann, Richard. *English in America: A Radical View of the Profession.* New York: Oxford University Press, 1976.

Ortega y Gasset, José. *The Dehumanization of Art and Notes on the Novel.* Translated by Helene Weyl. Princeton: Princeton University Press, 1948.

————. *La rebelión de las masas.* Buenos Aires: Espasa-Calpe, 1937.

Parrington, Vernon Louis. *Main Currents in American Thought.* Vol.2, *The Romantic Revolution in America, 1800–1860.* New York: Harcourt, Brace, 1927.

Pater, Walter. "The Child in the House." In *Selected Writings of Walter Pater* (q.v.), pp.1–16.

————. "Coleridge." In *Selected Writings of Walter Pater* (q.v.), pp.143–70.

————. Conclusion to *The Renaissance.* In *Selected Writings of Walter Pater* (q.v.), pp.58–63.

————. *Marius the Epicurean: His Sensations and Ideas.* New York: Random House, Modern Library, n.d.

————. *The Renaissance: Studies in Art and Poetry.* New York: New American Library, 1959.

————. *Selected Writings of Walter Pater.* Edited, with an introduction and notes, by Harold Bloom. New York: New American Library, 1974.

————. "Style." In *Selected Writings of Walter Pater* (q.v.), pp.103–25.

Paz, Octavio. *El arco y la lira: El poema. La revelación poética. Poesía e historia.* Mexico City: Fondo de Cultura Económica, 1967.

————. *El laberinto de la soledad.* Mexico City: Fondo de Cultura Económica, 1959.

Peacock, Thomas Love. *Four Ages of Poetry.* Edited by H. F. B. Brett-Smith. Oxford: Basil Blackwell, 1929.

Pearson, Hesketh. *Oscar Wilde.* London: Methuen, 1946.

Pérus, Françoise. *Literatura y sociedad en América Latina: El modernismo.* Mexico City: Siglo Veintiuno, 1976.

Pifer, Ellen. *Nabokov and the Novel*. Cambridge: Harvard University Press, 1980.

Pipes, Richard. *Russia under the Old Regime*. New York: Scribner's, 1974.

Planche, Gustave. "Moralité de la poésie." *Revue des deux mondes*, 4th series, 1 (1 February 1933): 241–63.

Plekhanov, Gyorgy. *Art and Social Life*. Translated by A. Fineberg. Moscow: Progress Publishers, 1957. Also excerpted in Lang and Williams, eds., *Marxism and Art: Writings in Aesthetics and Criticism* (q.v.), pp.88–99.

Poe, Edgar Allan. *Literary Criticism of Edgar Allan Poe*. Edited by Robert L. Hough. Lincoln: University of Nebraska Press, 1965.

Poggioli, Renato. *The Theory of the Avant-Garde*. Translated by Gerald Fitzgerald. Cambridge: Harvard University Press, 1960.

Polanyi, Karl. *The Great Transformation: The Political and Economic Origins of Our Time*. Boston: Beacon Press, 1957.

Quennell, Peter. *John Ruskin: The Portrait of a Prophet*. New York: Viking, 1949.

Rama, Angel. *Los poetas modernistas en el mercado económico*. Montevideo: Universidad de la República, Facultad de Humanidades y Ciencias, 1967. (This short work is also a chapter in the following book.)

———. *Rubén Darío y el modernismo*. Caracas/Barcelona: Alfadil Ediciones, 1985.

Rand, Ayn. *The Fountainhead*. New York: Bobbs-Merrill, 1943.

Ransom, John Crowe, and others. *I'll Take My Stand: The South and the Agrarian Tradition, by Twelve Southerners*. Introduction by Louis D. Rubin Jr. Biographical essays by Virginia Rock. Baton Rouge: Louisiana State University Press, ca.1962.

———. *God without Thunder*. Hamden CT: Archon Books, 1965.

———. *The New Criticism*. Norfolk CT: New Directions, 1941.

———. *The World's Body*. Baton Rouge: Louisiana State University Press, 1968.

Richards, Thomas. *The Commodity Culture of Victorian England: Advertising and Spectacle, 1851–1914*. Stanford: Stanford University Press, 1990.

Richardson, Joanna. *Théophile Gautier: His Life and Times*. London: Max Reinhardt, 1958.

———. *Verlaine*. New York: Viking, 1971.

Ricks, Christopher. *T. S. Eliot and Prejudice*. Boston: Faber & Faber, 1988.

Robbins, Bruce. "Modernism in History, Modernism in Power." In *Modernism Reconsidered*, edited by Robert Kiely, pp.229–45. Harvard English Studies no.11. Cambridge: Harvard University Press, 1983.

Read, Herbert. *Education through Art*. New York: Pantheon Books, 1945.

Bibliography

Rodó, José Enrique. *Ariel.* Translated by Margaret Sayers Peden. Foreword by James W. Symington. Prologue by Carlos Fuentes. Austin: University of Texas Press, 1988.

Rogin, Michael. *Ronald Reagan, the Movie, and Other Exercises in American Political Demonology.* Los Angeles: University of California Press, 1987.

Rosenblatt, Louise. *L'idée de l'art pour l'art dans la littérature anglaise pendant la période victorienne.* Paris: Librairie Ancienne Honoré Champion, 1931.

Rousseau, A. Review of Adolphe Dumas's *Chants de la Révolution de 1830. Le Globe,* 18 April 1832, p.436.

Rubinstein, Annette. *The Great Tradition in English Literature: From Shakespeare to Shaw.* New York: Citadel Press, 1953.

Ruskin, John. *Fors Clavigera.* Excerpted in *The Genius of John Ruskin* (q.v.), pp.362–433.

—————. *The Genius of John Ruskin: Selections from His Writings.* Edited, with an introduction, by John D. Rosenberg. Boston: Houghton Mifflin, 1965.

—————. *The Seven Lamps of Architecture.* Excerpted in *The Genius of John Ruskin* (q.v.), pp.124–30.

—————. *The Stones of Venice.* Excerpted in *The Genius of John Ruskin* (q.v.), pp.139–217.

—————. "Modern Manufacture and Design." In *The Genius of John Ruskin* (q.v.), pp.223–28.

Said, Edward. *Culture and Imperialism.* New York: Alfred A. Knopf, 1993.

—————. *Orientalism.* New York: Pantheon Books, 1978.

Saint-Chéron, Alexis de. "De la direction actuelle des beaux-arts et de leur avenir." *L'Artiste* 10 (1835): 269–73.

—————. "Philosophie de l'art. La vie poétique et la vie privée." *L'Artiste* 4 (1832): 269–71.

Sainte-Beuve, Charles Augustin. Review of André Chenier's *Poésies inédits. Le National,* 18 January 1834, pp.3–4.

Saint-Simon, Henri de. *The Doctrine: An Exposition.* Translated by Georg Iggers. Boston: Beacon Press, 1958.

Salusinszky, Imre, ed. *Criticism in Society: Interviews with Jacques Derrida, Northrop Frye, Harold Bloom, Geoffrey Hartman, Frank Kermode, Edward Said, Barbara Johnson, Frank Lentricchia, and J. Hillis Miller.* New York: Methuen, 1987.

Sartre, Jean-Paul. *Baudelaire.* Translated by Martin Turnell. New York: New Directions, 1967.

—————. *The Family Idiot: Gustave Flaubert, 1821–1857.* Vol.3. Translated by Carol Cosman. Chicago: University of Chicago Press, 1989.

——. *Mallarmé, or the Poet of Nothingness.* Translated and introduced by Ernest Sturm. University Park: Pennsylvania State University Press, 1988.

Saussure, Ferdinand de. *Course in General Linguistics.* Edited by Charles Bally and Albert Sechehaye in collaboration with Albert Riedlinger. Translated, with an introduction and notes, by Wade Baskin. New York: McGraw-Hill, 1966.

Schiller, Friedrich. *Schiller: An Anthology for Our Time.* Edited, with an introduction, by Frederick Ungar. New York: Ungar Publishing, 1959.

——. *Don Carlos.* In *Historical Dramas.* Translator anonymous. London: Bell, 1910.

——. *Naive and Sentimental Poetry* and *On the Sublime.* Translated, with an introduction, by Julius Elias. New York: Ungar Publishing, 1966.

——. *On the Aesthetic Education of Man.* Translated, with an introduction, by Reginald Snell. New York: Ungar Publishing, 1965.

——. *On the Aesthetic Education of Man: In a Series of Letters.* Edited and translated, with an introduction, by Elizabeth M. Wilkinson and L. A. Willoughby. New York: Oxford University Press, 1967.

——. *The Robbers* and *Wallenstein.* Translated, with an introduction, by F. J. Lamport. New York: Penguin Books, 1979.

——. *Wilhelm Tell.* Translated by William F. Mainland. Chicago: University of Chicago Press, 1972.

Schlesinger, Arthur M., Jr. *The Vital Center: The Politics of Freedom.* Boston: Houghton Mifflin, 1949.

Schrecker, Ellen W. *No Ivory Tower: McCarthyism in the Universities.* New York: Oxford University Press, 1987.

Schücking, Levin. *The Sociology of Literary Taste.* Translated by Brian Battershaw. Chicago: University of Chicago Press, 1966.

Schulman, Ivan. *Génesis del modernismo.* Mexico City: El Colegio de México, and St. Louis: Washington University Press, 1966.

——, ed. *Nuevos asedios al modernismo.* Madrid: Taurus, 1987.

——. "Modernismo/modernidad: Metamorfosis de un concepto." In Schulman, ed., *Nuevos asedios al modernismo* (q.v.), pp.11–38.

Scott, William Robert. *Francis Hutcheson: His Life, Teaching and Position in the History of Philosophy.* New York: Augustus M. Kelley, 1966.

Seigel, Jerrold. *Bohemian Paris: Culture, Politics, and the Boundaries of Bourgeois Life, 1830–1930.* New York: Penguin Books, 1986.

Shaftesbury, Anthony, Earl of. *Characteristics of Men, Manners, Opinions, Times, etc.* 2 vols. Edited by John M. Robertson. Gloucester MA: Peter Smith, 1963. Also in a single volume, with an introduction by Stanley Green. New York: Bobbs-Merrill, 1964.

Bibliography

Sharpe, Tony. *T. S. Eliot: A Literary Life.* London: Macmillan, 1991.

Shattuck, Roger. *The Banquet Years: The Origins of the Avant-Garde in France, 1885 to World War I.* New York: Doubleday, 1961.

Shelley, Percy Bysshe. *A Defence of Poetry.* (With *The Three Ages of Poetry,* by Thomas Love Peacock.) Edited by H.F.B. Brett-Smith. Oxford: Basil Blackwell, 1929.

Sheppard, Richard. "The Crisis of Language." In Bradbury and McFarlane, eds., *Modernism: A Guide to European Literature, 1890–1930* (q.v.), pp.19–55.

Shumway, Nicholas. *The Invention of Argentina.* Berkeley: University of California Press, 1991.

Sigg, Eric. *The American T. S. Eliot: A Study of the Early Writings.* New York: Cambridge University Press, 1989.

Silva, José Asunción. *De sobremesa.* In *Obra completa,* pp.127–310. Medellín: Editorial Bedout, 1970.

Silverman, Kenneth. *Edgar A. Poe: Mournful and Never-Ending Remembrance.* New York: HarperCollins, 1991.

Simon, Jules. *Victor Cousin.* Translated by Melville B. Anderson and Edmund Playfair Anderson. Chicago: A. C. McClurg, 1888.

Simpson, Louis. *Three on the Tower: The Lives and Works of Ezra Pound, T. S. Eliot, and William Carlos Williams.* New York: William Morrow, 1975.

Small, Ian, ed. *The Aesthetes: A Sourcebook.* With an introduction by the editor. Boston: Routledge & Kegan Paul, 1979.

Snow, C. P. *The Two Cultures and a Second Look.* Cambridge: Cambridge University Press, 1959.

Solomon, Maynard, ed. *Marxism and Art: Essays Classic and Contemporary.* With historical and critical commentary by the editor. New York: Random House, 1974.

Spender, Stephen. *The Struggle of the Modern.* London: Hamish Hamilton, 1963.

Staël, Madame Anne Louise Germaine de. *Germany.* 2 vols. Edited and translated by O. W. Wight. New York: Hurd & Houghton, 1875.

Stapfer, P. *Questions esthétiques et religieuses.* Paris: Alcan, 1906.

Starkie, Enid. *Baudelaire.* Norfolk CT: New Directions, ca.1958.

———. *From Gautier to Eliot.* London: Hutchinson, 1960.

Steinberg, S. H. *Five Hundred Years of Printing.* Foreword by Beatrice Warde. Baltimore: Penguin Books, 1955.

Stravinsky, Igor. *Poetics of Music in the Form of Six Lessons.* Translated by Arthur Knodel and Ingolf Dahl. Cambridge: Harvard University Press, 1947.

Sutton, Walter. *Modern American Criticism.* Englewood Cliffs NJ: Prentice-Hall, 1963.

Swanberg, W. A. *Luce and His Empire.* New York: Scribner's, 1972.

Swinburne, Algernon Charles. *Notes on Poems and Reviews* (excerpts). In Small, ed., *The Aesthetes: A Sourcebook* (q.v.), pp.7-10.

————. *William Blake* (excerpts). In Small, ed., *The Aesthetes: A Sourcebook* (q.v.), pp.5-7.

Sychrava, Juliet. *Schiller to Derrida: Idealism in Aesthetics.* New York: Cambridge University Press, 1989.

Symons, Arthur. *The Symbolist Movement in Literature.* Rev. ed. New York: E. P. Dutton, 1919.

Tate, Allen. *Essays of Four Decades.* Chicago: Swallow Press, 1968.

————. *On the Limits of Poetry: Selected Essays, 1928-48.* New York: William Morrow, 1948.

Temple, Ruth Zabriskie. *The Critic's Alchemy: A Study of the Introduction of French Symbolism into England.* New Haven: College and University Press, 1953.

Thompson, E. P. *The Making of the English Working Class.* New York: Pantheon Books, 1963.

————. *William Morris: Romantic to Revolutionary.* New York: Pantheon Books, 1977.

Thompson, G. R. "Edgar Allan Poe and the Writers of the Old South." In *Columbia Literary History of the United States,* edited by Emory Elliott, pp.262-77. New York: Columbia University Press, 1988.

Tocqueville, Alexis de. *The Old Regime and the French Revolution.* Translated by Stuart Gilbert. Garden City NY: Doubleday, 1955.

Torre, Guillermo de. *Historia de las literaturas de vanguardia.* Madrid: Ediciones Guadarrama, 1965.

Trevelyan, E. M. *History of England.* New illustrated edition. London: Longman Group Ltd., 1973.

Trilling, Lionel. "On the Teaching of Modern Literature." In *Beyond Culture,* pp.3-30. New York: Viking, 1965.

Trollope, Anthony. *An Autobiography.* London: Williams & Norgate, 1946.

Vargas Llosa, Mario. *La orgía perpetua: Flaubert y Madame Bovary.* Madrid: Taurus, 1975.

Verlaine, Paul. *Oeuvres poétiques complètes.* Edited by Y.-G. LeDantec. Revised by Jacques Borel. Paris: Gallimard, 1962.

Vigny, Alfred de. *Chatterton.* In *Oeuvres complètes,* edited by M. Fernand Baldensperger. Vol.6, *Théatre II,* pp.231-346. Paris: Louis Conard, 1927.

Webb, R. K. "The Victorian Reading Public." In *The Pelican Guide to English*

Literature, edited by Boris Ford. Vol.6, *From Dickens to Hardy*, pp.205–06. London: Penguin Books, 1958.

Weber, Max. *The Protestant Ethic and the Spirit of Capitalism.* Translated by Talcott Parsons. New York: HarperCollins, 1990.

Wellek, René, and Austin Warren. *Theory of Literature.* New York: Harcourt, Brace, 1949.

White, Harrison C., and Cynthia A. White, *Canvases and Careers: Institutional Change in the French Painting World.* New York: John Wiley and Sons, 1965.

White, Hayden. *Metahistory: The Historical Imagination in Nineteenth Century Europe.* Baltimore: Johns Hopkins University Press, 1973.

Whiteside, Thomas. *The Blockbuster Complex: Conglomerates, Show Business, and Book Publishing.* Middletown CT: Wesleyan University Press, 1981.

Wilcox, John. "The Beginnings of *l'art pour l'art.*" *Journal of Aesthetics and Art Criticism* 11 (June 1953): 360–77.

Wilde, Oscar. *De Profundis and Other Writings.* Edited by Hesketh Pearson. Baltimore: Penguin Books, 1973.

———. *The Picture of Dorian Gray.* New York: Penguin Books, 1985.

———. "The Critic as Artist." In Small, ed., *The Aesthetes* (q.v.), pp.46–100.

———. "The Decay of Lying." In *De Profundis* (q.v.), pp.57–87.

———. "De Profundis." In *De Profundis* (q.v.), pp.91–211.

———. "The Soul of Man under Socialism." In *De Profundis* (q.v.), pp.19–53.

Will, Frederic. *Flumen Historicum: Victor Cousin's Aesthetic and Its Sources.* Studies in Comparative Literature, no.36. Chapel Hill: University of North Carolina Press, 1965.

Williams, Raymond. *The Long Revolution.* London: Penguin, 1965.

———. *Keywords: A Vocabulary of Culture and Society.* Rev. ed. New York: Oxford University Press, 1983.

Williams, Rosalind. *Notes on the Underground: An Essay on Technology, Society, and the Imagination.* Cambridge: Massachusetts Institute of Technology Press, 1990.

Willis, J. H., Jr. *Leonard and Virginia Woolf as Publishers: The Hogarth Press, 1917–41.* Charlottesville: University Press of Virginia, 1992.

Wilson, Edmund. *Axel's Castle: A Study in the Imaginative Literature of 1870–1930.* New York: Scribner's, 1930.

Wimsatt, William K., Jr., and Cleanth Brooks. *Literary Criticism: A Short History.* 2 vols. Chicago: University of Chicago Press, 1978.

Womack, John. *Zapata and the Mexican Revolution.* New York: Random House, 1969.

Woolf, Virginia. "Mr. Bennett and Mrs. Brown." In *Criticism: The Foundations of Modern Literary Judgment,* edited by Mark Schorer, Josephine Miles, and Gordon McKenzie, pp.66–75. New York: Harcourt Brace, 1958.

———. "The Novel of Consciousness." In Ellman and Feidelson, eds., *The Modern Tradition: Backgrounds of Modern Literature* (q.v.), pp.121–26.

Wright, Thomas. *The Life of Walter Pater.* 2 vols. New York: G. P. Putnam's Sons, 1907.

Yeats, William Butler. *The Collected Poems of W. B. Yeats.* New York: Macmillan, 1959.

———. *A Vision.* London: Macmillan, 1937.

Young, James E. Letter to the editor, PMLA 9, no.5 (October 1984): 998–99.

Zamora, Margarita. *Reading Columbus.* Berkeley: University of California Press, 1993.

Zola, Émile. "The Novel as Social Science," from *The Experimental Novel,* translated by Belle M. Sherman. In Ellmann and Feidelson, eds., *The Modern Tradition: Backgrounds of Modern Literature* (q.v.), pp.270–89.

INDEX

Abrams, M. H., 293, 294
abstract art, 127, 128, 158
Académie de Peinture et Sculpture, 149
Académie Julien, 149
Académie Suisse, 149
Action Française, 207, 232
Aeschylus, 225
aestheticism (British movement), 2, 57, 68–96, 132, 214–18, 290
Africa, 95, 246
African Americans, 98, 241, 270, 281
After Strange Gods (Eliot), 234–36
Agrarians. *See* Fugitive Agrarians
Alazraki, Jaime, 286
Albee, Edward, 158
Althusser, Louis, 11
Amis, Kingsley, 194
anarchism, 247
Anderson, Benedict, 278
Antheil, George, 131
anticommunism, 191, 195, 207, 227, 252, 253, 263, 265
anti-Semitism, 206, 226–27, 231, 232, 236, 258, 262, 269
Apollinaire, Guillaume, 131, 143, 146, 154, 155, 156
Aquinas, St. Thomas, 180
Arendt, Hannah, 220
Argentina, 116, 118, 280, 289
Ariel (Rodó), 120–23
Arnold, Matthew, 57, 71, 112, 145, 161
Artaud, Antonin, 147
Art for Art's Sake: as an issue, 1–12; and literary markets, 41–56; overview of, 267–91; politics of, 203–65. *See also* under deconstruction; England; Enlightenment; France; Poe; Latin America; Modernism; New Criticism
L'Artiste (journal), 47
Asia, 95, 105
Asian Americans, 281
atonality, 126, 129, 199, 200
Au Bon Marché, 140
Auden, W. H., 28

Augustine, Saint, 4
Austen, Jane, 273
avant-garde, 126, 140, 143, 153–54, 157, 162

Babbitt, Irving, 233, 239
Bach, J. S., 45, 52
Bailey, Benjamin, 62
Bakhtin, Nikolai, 67
Bakunin, Mikhail, 247
Baldwin, James, 185
Balzac, Honoré de, 7, 9, 41–42, 43, 46, 49, 89, 146, 166, 172, 193, 257, 291
Barnard College, 306
Barrenechea, Ana María, 286
Barthes, Roland, 198
Bartók, Bela, 126, 147, 153
Barton, Bruce, 6
Baudelaire, Charles, 1, 46, 49, 55, 84, 100, 104, 106, 131, 136, 139, 141, 142, 143, 144, 162, 163–65, 166, 168, 171, 172, 182, 218
Baudrillard, Jean, 285
Bauhaus, 156
Baumgarten, Alexander, 18, 19
Beaumont, Sir George, 61
Beckett, Samuel, 195
Bécquer, Gustavo Adolfo, 106
Beethoven, Ludwig van, 129, 147, 213, 238
Belgium, 248, 262
Belinsky, V. I., 191
Bello, Andrés, 105
Bellow, Saul, 282
Bend Sinister (Nabokov), 257, 302
Benedict, Ruth, 261
Benjamin, Walter, 6
Bennett, Arnold, 135
Bennington College, 184
Bentley, Eric, 183
Berg, Alban, 129, 147
Bergson, Henri, 232
Berkeley, Bishop George, 89, 181
Berlin, 141, 190, 191, 256
Berlitz, 174
Berman, Marshall, 140

Bernard, Claude, 134
Bernstein, Henri, 232
Berry, duc de, 39
Bible, 4, 70, 107
Biely, Andrey, 141
Biographia Literaria (Coleridge), 48, 64–65, 101
Birth of a Nation (film), 241
Bismarck, Otto von, 95
Blackmur, R. P., 190
Blake, William, 33, 83
Bloom, Allan, 260, 268
Bloom, Harold, 73, 76, 81, 270–71
Blue Rider group, 126
Boas, George, 236
Boer War, 217
Bohemianism, 35, 48, 51, 126, 141, 146, 169, 184, 185, 288
Boileau, Nicolas, 41, 45
Bolshevism, 190, 234, 237, 239
Bonaparte, Napoleon, 36, 58, 59, 61, 214
Borges, Jorge Luis, 158, 195, 258, 277
Boston, 229, 230, 288
Bounderby, Mr. (character), 206
Bourbons, 36, 39, 40, 42, 200, 207
Boyd, Brian, 302, 305
Bradbury, Malcolm, 142, 146
Brancusi, Constantin, 129
Brandeis University, 254
Braque, Georges, 128, 151
Braverman, Harry, 45
Brazil, 116, 274, 289
Brecht, Bertold, 126, 144
Breton, André, 154
Bridgewater, Earl of, 242
Brooks, Cleanth, 2, 188
Brooks, Peter, 278
Broom, 156
Broughton, Rhoda, 93
Brown, Charles, 63
Brown, Clifford, 273
Brown, John, 241
Browning, Robert, 103
Bruno, Giordano, 172, 173
Buck, Pearl, 253
Budgen, Frank, 136, 170
Buenos Aires, 117, 119
"Burbank with a Baedeker. . . (Eliot)," 226

Bürger, Peter, 162
Burke, Edmund, 18, 206
Burke, Kenneth, 183, 253, 271
Burnand, F. C., 93
Butor, Michel, 57
Byron, Lord, 180, 216
Byzantium, 223–24, 231

Calvin, John, 4
Cambridge University, 61, 190
Camus, Albert, 7, 9
Caribbean, 244, 274
Carlyle, Thomas, 119
Carpentier, Alejo, 277
Carrel, Armand, 51, 53
Casal, Julián del, 113, 118, 119
Cassagne, Albert, 9
Cassirer, Ernst, 9
categorical imperative, 23
Cather, Willa, 137–38, 148
Catholic Church, 13, 34, 35, 51, 58, 59, 86, 87, 110, 114, 125, 169, 170, 172, 174, 175, 176, 177, 178, 180, 205–6, 207, 214, 221, 229, 233, 245, 246, 247, 249, 250, 264
Céline, Louis-Ferdinand, 193
Central Intelligence Agency (CIA), 256
centrism, 251–52, 255, 256, 261
Cervantes, Miguel de, 193
Cézanne, Paul, 126, 128, 144, 147
Chamberlain, Neville, 237
Champfleury, 44
Chaplin, Charles, 253
Charles X, 59, 209
Chaucer, Geoffrey, 225
Chernyshevsky, N. G., 192
Chevreul, Eugène, 135
Chile, 4, 117, 118
Chippewa Indians, 199
Chomsky, Noam, 263
Christian Democracy, 252
Christianity, 4, 13, 55, 60, 62, 63, 68, 71, 74, 75, 76, 81, 109–10, 132, 144, 155, 186, 209–10, 216, 252, 264
Church of England, 61, 81, 161, 229
Cisneros, Sandra, 282
Civil War (U.S.), 229, 235, 243, 256, 268, 270, 272
Clark, Kenneth, 69

Clark, T. J., 140
Coghill, Neville, 230
Cohen, Stephen, 158
cold war, 183, 254, 259, 270
Coleridge, Samuel Taylor, 48, 60, 61, 63,
    64–65, 72, 77, 101, 102, 107, 121
Colet, Louise, 165, 166, 167, 168, 221
Collier's, 185
Colombia, 112, 245
Columbia University, 254
Comédie Française, 40
Commager, Henry Steele, 97
Communist parties (Europe), 252–53
Communist Party U.S.A., 253
Comte, Auguste, 80, 115
Condillac, 38
Congo, 248
Congress for Cultural Freedom, 256
Congress of Vienna, 61
Conrad, Joseph, 193
conservatism, 113, 205–7, 208, 227, 231,
    251, 252, 253, 254, 256, 264, 265
Conservative Party (U.K.), 237
Constable, John, 128
Constant, Benjamin, 36, 214
Le Constitutionnel, (newspaper), 44
Coover, Robert, 272
Corneille, Pierre, 41
Cornell University, 191, 192
Corot, Camille, 89
Cortázar, Julio, 158, 277, 306
Courbet, Gustave, 128, 149
Cousin, Victor, 1, 37–40, 41, 64, 82, 101,
    214
Cowley, Malcolm, 253
Crane, Hart, 187
The Criterion, 156, 224, 234, 236, 237
"The Critic as Artist" (Wilde), 88, 90–92
Criticism, New. *See* New Criticism
The Critique of Judgment (Kant), 12,
    20–24, 28, 36, 208
The Critique of Practical Reason (Kant),
    22, 208
The Critique of Pure Reason (Kant), 21, 22,
    23, 36, 208
Cromwell, Preface to (Hugo); 41
Cromwell, Oliver, 5, 238, 264
Crystal Palace, 280

Cuauhtémoc, 245
Cuba, 104, 245, 246
cubism, 126, 128, 143, 147, 151
Czechoslovakia, 207, 237

dadaism, 126
Daily Chronicle, 87
D'Annunzio, Gabriele, 174
Dante, 84, 177, 233
Darío, Rubén, 106, 107–11, 113, 115,
    116–20, 205, 244, 245
Darwin, Charles, 13, 71, 74
Davis, Miles, 273, 274
Day Lewis, C., 236
Debussy, Claude, 126, 129, 200
"The Decay of Lying" (Wilde), 89–90, 91
deconstruction, 2, 4, 79, 89, 260–63, 270,
    278, 286; and Art for Art's Sake,
    196–98
A Defence of Poetry (Shelly), 65–66
Defoe, Daniel, 43
de Kock, Paul, 43, 166
Delaney, Father William, 173
de Maistre, Joseph, 206
de Man, Paul, 4, 197, 262–63
department stores, 140
De Profundis (Wilde), 87, 92
Derrida, Jacques, 198, 260, 271
Descartes, René, 39, 221
Diaghilev, Sergei, 155
The Dial, 156, 239
Díaz, Gen. Porfirio, 114
Dickens, Charles, 9, 192, 197–98, 206, 218
Diderot, Denis, 11, 19
Dilke, C. W., 63
Doctorow, E. L., 272
Dollimore, Jonathan, 290
Don Carlos (Schiller), 212
Donne, John, 282
Dorfman, Ariel, 195
Dos Passos, John, 128, 132, 272
Dostoyevski, Fyodor, 14
Dowson, Ernest, 84
Doyle, Clyde, 254
Dreiser, Theodore, 272
Dreyfus case, 232
Drumont, Edouard, 206
Dryden, John, 239

Dublin, 125, 138, 248
Dubliners(Joyce), 136, 174, 178, 182, 248
Dubois, P. F., 53
Dubos, Abbé, 19
Duchamp, Marcel, 155
Dumas, Alexandre, 43, 46
du Maurier, George, 93
Durand-Ruel, 150, 151
Durkheim, Emile, 133

Eagleton, Terry, 261
École des Beaux-Arts, 149
Edison, Thomas A., 117, 156
Egan, Rose Francis, 10
The Egoist, 156
Egypt, 204
Eiffel Tower, 131, 140-41
Einstein, Albert, 133, 193
Eliot, Charles W., 228
Eliot, Henry Ware, 228
Eliot, T. S., 138, 141, 144, 147, 154, 156, 161-62, 183, 205, 217, 224-39, 240, 243, 246, 250, 252, 255, 256, 258, 263, 273
Eliot, William Greenleaf, 228
Ellington, Duke, 199, 274
Ellis, Havelock, 133
Ellman, Richard, 86, 136
Encyclopédie, 11, 13, 19, 58
Engell, James, 23
Engels, Friedrich, 177, 215
England, 7, 9, 57, 59-68, 97, 101, 109, 114, 126, 154, 177, 178, 179, 183, 185, 206, 247-49, 250, 260; Art for Art's Sake in, 68-96
Enlightenment, 2, 7, 52, 53, 56, 71, 90, 97, 171, 181, 183, 208, 210, 213, 251, 256, 290; and origins of Art for Art's Sake, 13-29
epiphanies, 178, 182
La Epoca (newspaper), 116
Erdrich, Louise, 199
Erikson, Erik, 30
Estrada, Angel de, 116
Euripides, 86,
Europe, 71, 114, 115, 125, 126, 179, 200, 229, 231, 233, 251, 260, 279, 285
Evans, Bill, 199
evolution, theory of, 14, 71

existentialism, 14, 71
expressionism, 126, 144

Falwell, Jerry, 6
fascism (general movement), 5, 207, 217, 220, 224, 227, 234, 236, 252, 254, 264, 267-68
Fascist party, 158, 207, 217
Fast, Howard, 253
Faulkner, William, 128, 137, 193, 270, 272
Fauvism, 126, 128, 199
Federal Bureau of Investigation (FBI), 253
feminism, 278
feuilletons, 44
Feydeau, Ernest, 167
Fischer, Bobby, 193
Fish, Stanley, 91, 198, 261
Fitzgerald, F. Scott, 272
Fitzhugh, George, 243
flaneurs, 142
Flaubert, Gustave, 50, 76, 85, 128, 134, 136, 137, 138, 146, 154, 162, 165-69, 171, 172, 174, 182, 191, 192, 193, 204-5, 218, 220-22, 271, 291
Fletcher, John Gould, 239
Forster, E. M., 280
Fortoul, Hyppolite, 53
Foster, David William, 272
Foucault, Michel, 278
Four Quartets (Eliot), 237-39, 252, 273
Fragonard, Jean-Honoré, 204
Frame-Breaking Bill, 59
France, 7, 57-59, 63-64, 81, 93, 95, 100, 101, 104, 106, 107-9, 114, 115, 118, 126, 154, 183, 185, 196, 206, 214, 252, 253, 260, 280; Art for Art's Sake in, 35-56
Franco, Gen. Francisco, 207
Frank, Joseph, 127-28, 133
Frankfurt School, 278
Franklin, Benjamin, 165
Frederick the Great, 209
Freedman, Jonathan, 89, 92
French Revolution, 13, 25, 58, 59, 60, 61, 62, 64, 146, 201, 206, 209, 212, 213, 242, 252, 264, 290
Freud, Sigmund, 36, 133, 193, 273
Friedman, Milton, 4, 206

Friedrich Wilhelm II, 210
Frye, Northrop, 2, 89, 270, 286
Fuentes, Carlos, 272, 277
The Fugitive (journal), 186
Fugitive Agrarians, 4, 50, 144, 186–87,
    205, 235, 239–44, 254–56, 258
futurism, 126, 131

Gagnier, Regena, 297
Galeano, Eduardo, 277
García, Cristina, 282
García Márquez, Gabriel, 113, 268, 271,
    272, 277
Gauguin, Paul, 128, 149, 151
Gaunt, William, 64
Gautier, Théophile, 1, 4, 40, 41, 45–46,
    49, 53–54, 55, 62, 84, 86, 88, 100, 103,
    117, 121, 152, 162, 187, 198, 203–4, 214,
    218, 222, 244, 258, 267
General Electric, 130–31, 285
George III, 209
Gerard, Alexander, 18
Géricault, Théodore, 128
German philology, 188, 282
Germany, 18, 19–28, 35–38, 39–40, 53,
    69–70, 95, 157, 190, 212, 213, 248, 280,
    289
Giacometti, Alberto, 129
Gibbon, Edward, 13
G.I. Bill, 184
Gilbert, Sandra, 281
Gilbert, W. S., 93
Gillespie, Dizzy, 274
Gingrich, Newt, 207
Gippius, Zenaida, 258
Girardin, Emile de, 43
Girondins, 60, 65, 213
Gissing, George, 152
Le Globe, 53
Goethe, Johann Wolfgang von, 38, 174
Goldwater, Sen. Barry, 257
Gone with the Wind (film), 243
Gordon, Lyndall, 239
Gothic art, 5, 69
Göttingen, University of, 236
Gradgrind (character), 206
Graff, Gerald, 197, 261, 271, 282
Gramsci, Antonio, 278

Greece, ancient, 121
Greenblatt, Stephen, 279
Greenwich Village, 185
Gregory, Lady, 222
Griffiths, D. W., 241
Gris, Juan, 155
Grosvenor Gallery, 72, 87
Grotowski, Jerzy, 158
Gubar, Susan, 281
Guérard, Albert, 9
Guillén, Nicolás, 277
Gulf & Western Corporation, 185

Haigh-Wood, Vivian, 234
Hamlet (Shakespeare), 91
Hammett, Dashiell, 253
Hanslick, Eduard, 8
Hardy, Thomas (activist), 59
Hardy, Thomas (novelist), 152
Hartman, Geoffrey, 91, 198
Harvard University, 191, 228, 270, 288
Haussmann, Baron de, 139, 140
Hawthorne, Nathaniel, 98
Hegel, G. F. W., 38, 76, 80
Heidegger, Martin, 260
Heiden, K., 220
Heller, Tamar, 281
Hernani (Hugo), 40, 41, 143
Herrera y Reissig, Julio, 113
Hijuelos, Oscar, 282
Hindemith, Paul, 126
historicism, 188, 189, 254
Hitler, Adolf, 208, 220, 236, 237, 256, 304
Hogarth, William, 19
Hogarth Press, 156
Hollywood, 4, 90, 148, 285, 287, 288
Holocaust, 236, 282, 286
Homer, 192, 232
Hopkins, Gerard Manley, 235
Horace, 45
Hotten, John Camden, 83
Hough, Graham, 84
House Un-American Activities
    Committee (HUAC), 253, 254
Howe, Elias, 157
Howe, Irving, 142, 183
Hubbard, Freddie, 273
Hubley, John, 254

Hughes, Robert, 200
Hugo, Victor, 9, 40–41, 46, 55, 65, 78, 84,
    108, 110, 115, 140, 164, 180, 214, 217
Hume, David, 13, 18, 181
Hunt, Leigh, 62
Hurston, Zora Neale, 282
Hutcheson, Francis, 17–18
Huysmans, J. K., 93

Ibsen, Henrik, 126, 134, 173
identity politics, 281–83
Ignatius Loyola, Saint, 177
income tax, and entertainment, 288
information economy, 284–87
The Iliad (Homer), 102; Pope's
    translation of, 42
I'll Take My Stand, 240–43
imagism, 126
imperialism, 279
The Importance of Being Earnest (Wilde),
    93, 267
Impressionism, 126, 128, 131, 134, 141, 148,
    150–51, 199
Inkas, 244, 245
Inquisition, Spanish, 4
Intrigue and Love (Schiller), 212
inventions, 42, 130, 148
Ireland, 86, 92, 154, 169–70, 173, 178–79,
    216, 224, 229, 230, 247–50
Italy, 126, 213, 229, 234, 252, 253
International Telephone & Telegraph
    (ITT), 185
"ivory tower," 118, 275

Jacobins, 60, 61, 209, 213
Jakobson, Roman, 44, 66
James, Henry, 128, 168, 185, 229
James, William, 261
Jameson, Fredric, 29, 200, 278, 284
Japan, 270
Jarrell, Randall, 194, 275
Jarry, Alfred, 147, 154, 199
jazz, 273–74, 282
Jesuits, 250
Jesus Christ, 107
Jewish Americans, 282
Jews, 206, 236, 249
John Paul II, Pope, 4

Johns Hopkins University, 236
Johnson, Barbara, 196, 261
Johnson, Lionel, 84
Johnson, Dr. Samuel, 72, 201
Jowett, Benjamin, 79
Joyce, James, 5, 50, 125, 127, 128, 131, 133,
    135, 136, 137, 138, 141, 147, 152, 153, 154,
    155, 156, 158, 162, 169–82, 192, 193, 199,
    246–51, 156, 280
Joyce, Stanislaus, 169, 170, 250
July Monarchy, 36, 47, 51, 198

Kafka, Franz, 125, 128, 146–47, 154
Kahnweiler, Daniel-Henri, 151
Kandinsky, Wassily, 128
Kant, Immanuel, 1, 4, 10, 12, 14, 15, 16,
    19–24, 26, 28, 29, 30, 35, 36, 37, 38, 54,
    56, 57, 64, 69, 78, 91, 101, 110, 120, 121,
    164, 168, 171, 181, 208–10, 267, 289, 290
Karlschule, 211
Keats, John, 61, 62–63, 67–68
Kennedy, Pres. John F., 281
Kenyon College, 189
Kingsley, Charles, 74
King's School, 74
Kiwanis, 53
Koch, Kenneth, 32–33
Königsberg, 19, 21, 30, 209
Kosciuszko, Count Tadeusz, 62, 212
Krafft-Ebbing, Richard, 133
Krakow, 158
Krauss, Rosalind, 198
Kristallnacht, 227
Kropotkin, Pyotr, 247
Krutch, Joseph Wood, 99

Lamartine, Alphonse de, 103
Last Year at Marienbad (film), 158
Latin America, 3, 7, 244–46, 270, 272,
    277, 280, 281, 289; Art for Art's Sake
    in, 104–23
Latinos, 281
Lawrence, D. H., 137, 199, 235
Leavis, F. R., 57
Leavis, Q. D., 57
Leconte de Lisle, 108, 205, 218
Leibniz, G. W., 22
Le Poittevin, Alfred, 167

334

Leroyer de Chantepie, Mlle., 134, 167
Lessing, Gotthold, 19
Letters on Aesthetic Education (Schiller), 12, 24-30, 32, 121, 210, 213
Lévi-Strauss, Claude, 116
Lewis, Wyndham, 144
liberalism (economic), 4, 113, 114, 115
liberalism (general ethos), 234-35, 255, 256
Liberation Theology, 4
libertarianism, 4, 169, 205, 207, 254, 281
Lincoln Center for the Arts, 282
Liszt, Franz, 112
The Little Review, 156, 192
Locke, John, 4, 14, 15, 97, 209, 261
London, 52-53, 88, 89, 141
Lord, Albert, 35
Lorilleux, Pierre, 42
Los Angeles riots (1992), 286
Lost Illusions (Balzac), 49
Louis XIV, 41
Louis XVI, 60, 209, 212
Louis XVIII, 58, 214
Louis Napoleon, 139, 149, 164, 219
Louis Philippe, King, 41, 54, 214
Lowell, Robert, 189
Loyola, Saint Ignatius, 177
Luce, Henry, 207
Luddites, 59, 219
Lugones, Leopoldo, 113
Lukacs, György, 183
lumpenproletariat, 219-20
Luther, Martin, 4

MacAdam, Alfred J., 271
MacLeish, Archibald, 255
Mademoiselle de Maupin (Gautier), 46, 54-55, 88, 152, 198, 203-4, 244
Madrid, 114, 117, 199
Maeterlinck, Maurice, 152
Magritte, René, 199
Mahler, Gustav, 129, 153
Malamud, Bernard, 194, 282
Malevich, Kazimir, 128
Mallarmé, Stephane, 55, 84, 86, 104, 108, 153, 154, 217
Managua, 117
Manchester, 59, 60, 166

Manchester Guardian, 237
Manet, Edouard, 150-51
Mann, Thomas, 142, 147
Mao Zedong, 5
Marcuse, Herbert, 29
markets: for art, 148-52; general, 145-46, 147, 153, 155-56; for art, 148-52; for literature, 41-44, 55, 100, 103, 118-19, 123, 147, 148, 152, 187, 214, 217, 218, 264, 268-69, 276. *See also* Art for Art's Sake: and literary markets
Marr, J. E., 69
Marshall Plan, 253
Martí, José, 104, 105, 106, 107, 115, 117, 246
Marx, Karl, 30, 36, 50, 215, 216, 219, 284
Marxism, 10-11, 95, 96, 188, 189, 196, 225, 234, 252, 253, 265, 268, 278
Masiello, Francine, 280
Mathew, George Felton, 62
Matisse, Henri, 128
Maupassant, Guy de, 168
Maurras, Charles, 232-34, 236
Mayer, Arno, 138, 252
Mazzini, Giuseppe, 217
McCarthyism, 189, 253-54, 257, 272, 305
McFarlane, James, 146
McLuhan, Marshall, 285
McWilliams, Carey, 253
media, 200, 283-84, 287
Melville, Herman, 98, 282
Mencken, H. L., 240
Mendès, Catulle, 108
El Mercurio, 118
Methodism, 60
Mexico, 119
Middlemarch (G. Eliot), 290
Mill, James, 31
Mill, John Stuart, 4, 31-32, 261, 273
Miller, Henry, 137, 199
Miller, J. Hillis, 197-98
Millin, Justice, 226
Millin, Sarah, 226
Milton, John, 73, 235, 242
Milton Academy, 228
Miró, Joan, 199
Moctezuma, 244, 245
Modernism, 7, 8, 29, 125-59, 189, 193-94,

Index

198–201, 267, 277, 282, 285; and Art for Art's Sake, 161–83

Modernism (religious), 125

modernismo, 32, 50, 104–23, 187, 244–46, 267

Molière, 46

Mona Lisa, 143

monarchism, 206, 207, 264

Mondrian, Piet, 128

Monet, Claude, 144, 151

Monk, Thelonious, 199

Montebello, Duke of, 39

Moore, Barrington, 259

Moore, George, 6, 173

Morison, Samuel Eliot, 228

Morris, William, 246

Moussorgsky, Modeste, 130

Mowrer, Edgar Ansel, 229

Moxon, Edward, 83

Mozart, Wolfgang A., 147

multiculturalism, 281–83

Munich, 237

music. *See* atonality; jazz; Muzak; rock music; *and names of composers and musicians*

Mussolini, Benito, 6, 205, 207, 217

Muzak, 200, 283, 285

Nabokov, V. D., 256, 259

Nabokov, Vladimir, 4, 7, 50, 79, 80, 182, 190–95, 256–60, 295, 301, 305

Nashville, 239

Le National (newspaper), 51

Native Americans, 281

naturalism, 126, 134, 167

Nazi Germany, 6, 156, 158, 207, 220, 227, 236, 237, 252, 256, 258, 271

neoclassicism, 14, 34, 35, 37, 38, 41, 51, 55, 146, 200–201, 210, 212, 290

Neruda, Pablo, 95–96, 144, 273, 277

Netzahualcóyotl, 245

New Criticism, 2, 4, 79, 198, 205, 254–56, 263, 278, 280; and Art for Art's Sake, 183, 186, 187–88, 190

New Deal, 253, 281

New England, 98, 99, 242

New Historicism, 278, 279

Newman, Cardinal John Henry, 86

New York City, 54, 235

Nicaragua, 117, 244

Nicolovius, 209

Nicolson, William, 42

Nietzsche, Friedrich, 6, 10–11, 14, 260

Nordau, Max, 11

nouveau roman, 57

Nouvelle Revue Française, 233

Novalis, 76

Nozick, Robert, 4, 206–7

O'Duffy, General, 224

The Odyssey (Homer), 251

Olmedo, José Joaquín, 105

Ortega y Gasset, José, 127, 231, 283

Orwell, George, 285

Oslo, 125

Oxford University, 1, 62, 71, 72, 73, 74, 83, 87, 88, 93, 236, 249

Paine, Thomas, 212

Palais d'Industrie, 149

Palenke, 244

Pall Mall Budget, 93

Panama, 245

Paris, 107–8, 114, 117, 139–42, 204, 232

Paris Commune, 218, 221

Paris Review, 276

Parnassians, 50, 108, 119

Parrington, Vernon, 99

Parsifal (Wagner), 5

passéisme, 204–5, 220, 244, 245, 246, 258, 263

Pater, Walter, 1, 4, 67, 73–82, 83, 84, 87, 88, 90, 91, 92, 101, 102, 109, 110, 177, 216, 286, 289

Patience (Gilbert and Sullivan), 93–94

Paul, Saint, 4

Paz, Octavio, 115, 116, 268, 277

Peacock, Thomas Love, 65

Pétain, Marshal Henri, 233

Peterloo Massacre, 60, 62, 63

Philippe, Charles-Louis, 232

"Philosophy of Composition" (Poe), 101

Piaget, Jean, 30

Picasso, Pablo R., 7, 128, 143, 151, 161, 193, 199

336

The Picture of Dorian Gray (Wilde), 1, 88, 89, 93, 169
Pifer, Ellen, 301
Pinochet, Gen. Augusto, 4
Pipes, Richard, 259
Pissarro, Camille, 151
Planck, Max, 133
Plato, 39
Plekhanov, Georgy, 10–11
PM (newspaper), 253
Poe, Edgar Allan, 1, 4, 46, 50, 105, 118, 119, 121, 164, 267, 289; Art for Art's Sake in, 98–104
"The Poetic Principle" (Poe), 100, 101, 102
Poetry (journal), 156
Poggioli, Renato, 157
pointillism, 128, 134
Poland, 158, 207
Polanyi, Karl, 43
Pompidou Center for the Arts, 139
Poole's Index, 63
Pope, Alexander, 42, 201, 239
Popular Front, 258
A Portrait of the Artist as a Young Man (Joyce), 152, 174–82, 249–50
positivism, 115, 119
postcolonial studies, 278
postmodernism, 195–96, 199
Poujadism, 219
Pound, Ezra, 2, 138, 144, 145, 154, 155, 205, 217, 255
Pre-Raphaelites, 8, 86
Proudhon, Pierre Joseph, 247
Proust, Marcel, 125, 131, 141, 152, 154, 193
Prussia, 209, 210
Puccini, Giacomo, 35
Puig, Manuel, 277
Punch, 83, 93
Puritanism, 97, 229, 260
Pyramid Malls Corp., 284

Queensberry, Marquess of, 85
Queen's College (England), 74
Queneau, Raymond, 182
Quinn, John, 227

Racine, Jean, 41, 201
railroads, 47, 48

Rama, Angel, 118, 119
Rambo (film), 90
Rand, Ayn, 4, 6, 192, 205, 257, 300
Ransom, John Crowe, 186, 187–88, 189, 239, 240, 241, 242
rationalism, 19, 22
Ravel, Maurice, 129, 130, 153, 200
Ravenna, 231
RCA, 185
Read, Sir Herbert, 29, 187, 229
Reagan, Pres. Ronald, 285–86, 287
Reed, Ishmael, 272
Reformation, 228–29
Reform Bills, 58
relativism, 77, 78, 80, 90, 132, 144, 228, 260–62, 286
Republican Party (U.S.), 253
The Renaissance (Pater), 81, 82, 87, 90, 91, 92
Resnais, Alain, 158
Restoration (French), 39–41, 42, 51, 58, 61, 214
Revolution of 1848, 58, 143, 146
Revue des Deux Mondes, 116
Reynolds, J. H., 67
Ricardo, David, 31, 114
Richards, Thomas, 280
Riefenstahl, Leni, 5
Rimbaud, Arthur, 84, 154
Rivera, Diego, 131
Robbe-Grillet, Alain, 57, 168
Robert, Nicolas-Louis, 42
Robeson, Paul, 253
Robinson, Henry Crabb, 36
rock music, 268, 287
Rodó, José Enrique, 120–23
Romanticism (English), 60–63, 64–68, 102, 103, 105, 146, 201, 290
Romanticism (French), 10, 40–41, 68, 105, 146, 201, 290
Romanticism (Latin American), 105
Rome, 13, 125, 155, 205, 207, 221
Roosevelt, Theodore, 245
Rosenbergs case, 272
Rosenblatt, Louise, 9
Rostow, W. W., 284
Rotarians, 53
Roth, Philip, 282

Index

Rousseau, A., 53
Rousseau, Henri, 155
Rousseau, Jean-Jacques, 21, 30
Rulfo, Juan, 277
Ruskin, John, 1, 9, 68–73, 83, 87, 92, 110, 121, 177, 214–15, 264
Russia, 95, 126, 154, 157, 190, 256, 259, 289.
   See also Soviet Union

Said, Edward, 279
Saint-Charon, Alexis de, 51–52
Sainte-Beuve, Charles, 44, 300
Saint-Simon movement, 51, 52–53
salons (painting), 149–50
Samaritaine, La, 140
Sand, George, 167, 221
Sarah Lawrence College, 254
Sarmiento, Domingo, 114–15
Sartre, Jean-Paul, 50, 90, 167
Saturday Review, 276
Saulnier, Paul, 48
Saussure, Ferdinand de, 133, 196
Schedule C (tax form), 288
Schelling, Friedrich, 36
Schiller, Friedrich, 4, 12, 14, 24–30, 32, 35, 36, 37, 56, 65, 66, 69, 76, 91, 101, 120, 121–22, 123, 163, 164, 168, 183, 210–13, 216, 267, 289, 290
Schlegel, August, 37, 38
Schlesinger, Arthur M., 251
Schleswig-Holstein, Prince Friedrich, 25
Schoenberg, Arnold, 129, 147, 153, 199
Schumann, Robert, 153
Schumpeter, Joseph, 145
sciences, 132–34, 240
Scopes trial, 240
Second Empire (French), 139
Seigel, Jerrold, 220
Senate Internal Security Sub-committee, 253
Seurat, Georges, 128, 134
Shaftesbury, Earl of, 1, 4, 14, 15–17, 28, 69, 91, 181
Shakespeare, William, 66, 91, 120, 162, 170, 225, 273, 279
Shattuck, Roger, 143
Shelley, Percy, 61, 62, 65–67, 84, 162, 163, 180, 216

Sheppard, Richard, 152
Sholes, Christopher, 156–57
Shumway, Nicolas, 280
Silva, José Asunción, 109, 110, 118
Sinn Fein, 247, 248
Singer, Isaac, 157
slavery (U.S.), 98, 241–42, 270, 271, 273
Slonim, Véra, 258, 305
Smith, Adam, 4, 17
Snow, C. P., 277
socialism, 154, 207, 214, 215–16, 201, 247, 264
Le Soir (Belgium), 262
Solomon, Maynard, 11
Sorbonne, 38
"The Soul of Man under Socialism" (Wilde), 215–16, 247
South Africa, 226
Southey, Robert, 60
Soviet Union, 5, 63, 131, 158, 170, 171, 191, 252, 254, 255, 256, 257, 258, 283, 304
Spain, 104, 105, 106, 107, 108, 119, 120, 177, 207, 234, 237, 244, 245
Spenser, Edmund, 225
Springsteen, Bruce, 287
Staël, Madame Germaine de, 37, 38, 64, 214
Stanislavsky, Konstantin, 82
St. Louis, 228
St. Petersburg, 125
Stein, Gertrude, 151
Stein, Leo, 151
Steinbeck, John, 272
Stravinsky, Igor, 5, 8, 126, 129, 130, 143, 147, 153, 155, 157, 199, 200, 300
Strindberg, August, 126, 128, 152
structuralism, 265, 270
Sue, Eugène, 44
surrealism, 126, 144, 199
"Sweeney among the Nightingales" (Eliot), 225–26
Swinburne, Algernon, 67, 68–69, 83–84, 86, 216–17
symbolism, 1, 50, 119, 125, 126, 162

Tarde, Gabriel, 130
Tate, Allen, 186, 187, 198, 239, 241, 242–43, 255

338

Tennessee Agarians. *See* Fugitive
  Agarians
Tennyson, Alfred, 14, 63, 64, 71, 180, 249
Thackeray, William M., 73, 215
Thomas, D. M., 195
Thomas, Dylan, 45
Time-Life, 207, 237
Tocqueville, Alexis de, 58
Toffler, Alvin, 257
Tolstoy, Leo, 147
totalitarianism, theory of, 254, 263
Tree, Beerbohm, 172
Trieste, 247
Trilling, Lionel, 145
Trinity College (Dublin), 86
Triumph of the Will (film), 243
Trollope, Anthony, 9, 44
Turgenev, Ivan, 89, 167, 221
Turner, Joseph M., 69
Tzara, Tristan, 155

Ulysses (Joyce), 133, 136, 137, 138, 141, 147,
  156, 169, 175, 178, 182, 192, 247, 248-49,
  251, 280
Unitarianism, 228, 234, 236
United States, 3, 4, 7, 14, 95, 97-98, 104,
  105, 109, 117, 118, 120, 145, 151, 183, 185,
  217, 229, 244, 245, 246, 251, 252, 255,
  261, 275, 277, 282, 285
The Universal Spectator (periodical), 18
universities, 183-85, 253-54, 260, 269,
  274, 276-77, 282
University College, Dublin, 171, 174, 250
Uruguay, 120
U.S. Marines, 244
Utatlán, 244

Valéry, Paul, 104
Vallejo, César, 144, 277
Vanderbilt University, 186
Van Gogh, Vincent, 126, 128, 151, 153, 154,
  155, 199
Varèse, Edgar, 126
Vargas Llosa, Mario, 277
Vatican, 125, 200, 233, 250
Vauxcelles, Louis, 143
Vega Belgrano, Carlos, 116
Verdi, Giuseppe, 45, 213, 279

Verlaine, Paul, 84, 109, 143, 154
Verne, Jules, 109, 205, 244, 246
Versailles, 41, 109, 205, 244, 246
Vichy, 207, 233
Victoria, Queen, 280
Vienna, 157, 212
Vietnam, U.S. War in, 281
Vigny, Alfred de, 48
Viguier, Epagomène, 37
Vincent de Paul, Saint, 221
Virginia, University of, 234
Voltaire, 13, 14, 62
Vorticism, 126

Wagner, Richard, 5, 129, 152, 207
Wajda, Andrzei, 158
Wake, Kyd, 59
Walcott, Derek, 103
Walsh, Rodolfo, 271-72
Warren, Austin, 2, 89, 189, 198
Warren, Robert Penn, 2, 186, 188, 239,
  241
Washington, George, 212
Washington University, 228
The Waste Land (Eliot), 141, 225, 226-27,
  239
Watts-Dunton, Theodore, 217
Weber, Max, 133, 261, 275
Webern, Anton, 129, 147, 153
Wellek, René, 2, 89, 189, 198
Wellesley College, 191
Wells, H. G., 134, 135
Whistler, James M., 8, 72
White, Cynthia, 149, 151-52
White, Harrison, 149, 151-52
Whitman, Walt, 106, 115
W. H. Smith (stores), 47, 48
Wilcox, John, 10
Wilde, Oscar, 1, 2, 5, 40, 57, 73, 77, 79, 82,
  83, 84, 85-95, 101, 110, 121, 169, 177, 191,
  214, 215-16, 247, 267, 287, 289, 301
Will, George, 279
Williams, Rosalind, 280
Williams College, 254
Woellner, J. Christoph, 209-10
Wolff, Christian, 22
Woolf, Virginia, 128, 135-36, 145-46, 155,
  156

Index

Wordsworth, John, 79
Wordsworth, William, 32, 60, 61, 63, 65, 68, 273
The World (periodical), 18
World War I, 95, 154, 272
World War II, 185, 251, 262, 273, 276
Wright, Orville, 157
Wright, Wilbur, 157
Württemberg, Duke Karl Eugen of, 211

Yale University, 82, 189, 260, 262
Yeats, John, 224
Yeats, William Butler, 126, 128, 134, 173, 205, 217, 222–23, 235, 251, 258
Young, James, 271–72

Zamora, Margarita, 280
Zhdanov, Andrei, 11, 193
Zola, Emile, 134, 141, 167
Zürich, 141

In the STAGES series

Volume 1
The Rushdie Letters: Freedom to Speak,
Freedom to Write
Edited by Steve MacDonogh in
association with Article 19

Volume 2
Mimologics
By Gérard Genette
Edited and translated by Thaïs Morgan

Volume 3
Playtexts: Ludics in Contemporary Literature
By Warren Motte

Volume 4
New Novel, New Wave, New Politics:
Fiction and the Representation of History
in Postwar France
By Lynn A. Higgins

Volume 5
Art for Art's Sake and Literary Life:
How Politics and Markets Helped Shape the
Ideology and Culture of Aestheticism,
1790–1990
By Gene H. Bell-Villada

Volume 6
Semiotic Investigations: Towards an Effective
Semiotics
By Alec McHoul

Volume 7
Rue Ordener, Rue Labat
By Sarah Kofman
Translated by Ann Smock

Volume 8
Palimpsests: Literature in the Second Degree
By Gérard Genette
Translated by Channa Newman
and Claude Doubinsky

Volume 9
The Mirror of Ideas
By Michel Tournier
Translated by Jonathan F. Krell

Volume 10
*Fascism's Return: Scandal, Revision,
and Ideology since 1980*
Edited by Richard J. Golsan

Volume 11
*Jacob, Menahem, and Mimoun:
A Family Epic*
By Marcel Bénabou
Translated by Steven Rendall